SPACE, DIFFERENCE, EVERYDAY LIFE

Space, Diff
Henri Le
commitn
Belatedly
European
life, and
architect
spatial d
discussio
by comp
those of t
proposin
"politica
to propo
and prov
intellectι
contemp
coloniza

Kanishk
urban de
books, *TI*
Sensorium:
capitalisι

Stefan K
Environr
especiall
on comp

Richard
Departm
as an arc
with communities. His research focuses on participatory design in culturally diverse
environments.

Christian Schmid teaches urban sociology in the Department of Architecture at ETH
Zurich and is senior researcher at ETH Studio Basel, Switzerland. He is the author
of *Stadt, Raum und Gesellschaft: Henri Lefebvre und die Produktion des Raumes*, a leading work on
Henri Lefebvre, as well as numerous publications on urban development, social
movements, regulation theory, and urban social theory.

SPACE, DIFFERENCE, EVERYDAY LIFE

Reading Henri Lefebvre

Edited by
Kanishka Goonewardena
Stefan Kipfer
Richard Milgrom
Christian Schmid

Routledge
Taylor & Francis Group

NEW YORK AND LONDON

First published 2008
by Routledge
270 Madison Ave, New York, NY 10016

Simultaneously published in the UK
by Routledge
2 Park Square, Milton Park, Abingdon, Oxon OX14 4RN

Routledge is an imprint of the Taylor & Francis Group, an informa business

© 2008 Taylor & Francis

Typeset in Joanna and Scala Sans by
Keystroke, 28 High Street, Tettenhall, Wolverhampton
Printed and bound in the United States of America on acid-free paper by
Sheridan Books, Inc.

Library of Congress Cataloging in Publication Data
Lefebvre, Henri, 1901–1991.
    Space, difference, everyday life : reading Henri Lefebvre/edited by
    Kanishka Goonewardena . . . [et al.].
        p. cm.
    Includes bibliographical references.
    1. Lefebvre, Henri, 1901–1991.   2. Social sciences—Philosophy.
    3. Space and time.   4. Cities and towns.   I. Goonewardena, Kanishka.
    II. Title.
    H61.15.L44 2008
    307.7601—dc22   2007027484

ISBN10: 0–415–95459–2 (hbk)
ISBN10: 0–415–95460–6 (pbk)
ISBN10: 0–203–93321–4 (ebk)

ISBN13: 978–0–415–95459–4 (hbk)
ISBN13: 978–0–415–95460–0 (pbk)
ISBN13: 978–0–203–93321–3 (ebk)

CONTENTS

LIST OF FIGURES

CONTRIBUTORS

Neil Brenner is Professor of Sociology and Metropolitan Studies at New York University. His research on state theory, space, scale, and neoliberal urban governance has appeared in *New State Spaces: Urban Governance and the Rescaling of Statehood* (2004), *State/Space: A Reader* (2003), and *Spaces of Neoliberalism: Urban Restructuring in Western Europe and North America* (2002).

Mustafa Dikeç is Lecturer in Human Geography, Royal Holloway, University of London. His research focuses on space, politics and democracy, with particular emphasis on French urban policy, exile, and asylum-seekers in Paris. He is the author of *Badlands of the Republic* (2007).

Stuart Elden is Professor of Political Geography at Durham University and the author of *Speaking Against Number: Heidegger, Language and the Politics of Calculation* (2005), *Understanding Henri Lefebvre: Theory and the Possible* (2006), *Mapping the Present: Heidegger, Foucault and the Project of a Spatial History* (2001) as well as co-editor of Henri Lefebvre, *Key Writings* (2003). He is currently working on a history of the concept of territory.

Liette Gilbert is Associate Professor in the Faculty of Environmental Studies, York University, Toronto. Her research focuses on identity, citizenship, migration, urban movements, and regional planning in Montreal, Toronto and Southern California. She is working on a book on Ontario's "Green Belt."

Kanishka Goonewardena was trained as an architect in Sri Lanka and now teaches urban design and critical theory at the University of Toronto. He is working on two books, *The Future of Planning at the "End of History"* and *The Urban Sensorium: Space, Ideology and the Aestheticization of Politics*, exploring cities, imperialism, and ideology.

Stefan Kipfer teaches urbanization, urban politics, and planning in the Faculty of Environmental Studies, York University, Toronto. Informed by urban social theory, especially Henri Lefebvre, Frantz Fanon, and Antonio Gramsci, his research is focused on comparative politics, restructuring and colonization in metropolitan regions.

Andy Merrifield is a writer on Marxism and urbanism now living in France. His most recent books include *Guy Debord* (2006), *Henri Lefebvre: A Critical Introduction* (2006), *Metromarxism: A Marxist Tale of the City* (2002), and *Dialectical Urbanism: Social Struggles in the Capitalist City* (2002).

Kurt Meyer is a philosopher and published one of the earliest and most influential monographs on Henri Lefebvre in German, *Henri Lefebvre, ein romantischer Revolutionär* (1973). He has just published a new book on Lefebvre: *Von der Stadt zur urbanen Gesellschaft — Jacob Burckhardt und Henri Lefebvre* (2007).

Richard Milgrom teaches community design and urban planning processes in the Department of City Planning at the University of Manitoba. Based on his experiences as an architect and social justice activist, his courses encourage direct involvement with communities. His research focuses on participatory design in culturally diverse environments.

Sara Nadal-Melsió is Assistant Professor of Romance Languages at the University of Pennsylvania, specializing in contemporary Peninsular culture, literature, and philosophy, and critical theory. She is the co-author of a book on the role of the "periphery" as a social space in architecture's political imagination, *Alrededor de: periferias* (2002). She is currently at work on a book entitled *For Realism: On the Question of Ontological Transfer*.

Walter Prigge teaches philosophy, social theory, and design at the Bauhaus in Dessau. He has written and published extensively on urbanity, urbanism, and urban theory. He is author of *Urbanität und Intellektualität im 20. Jahrhundert* (1996), and editor of *Peripherie ist Überall* (1998) and *Bauhaus Brasilia Auschwitz Hiroshim. Weltkulturerbe im 20. Jahrhundert: Modernität und Barbarei* (2003).

Klaus Ronneberger is a well-known independent urban researcher in Frankfurt, Germany. Informed by decades of experience in urban social movements, he has edited and authored numerous articles and books on urban theory, regional restructuring, local politics, and law and order, including *Die Stadt als Beute* (1999).

Christian Schmid teaches urban sociology in the Department of Architecture at ETH Zurich and is Senior Researcher at ETH Studio Basel, Switzerland. He is the author of *Stadt, Raum und Gesellschaft: Henri Lefebvre und die Produktion des Raumes*, a leading work on Lefebvre, as well as numerous publications on urban development, social movements, regulation theory, and urban social theory.

Andrew Shmuely was trained as an anthropologist at Concordia University in Montreal and is currently a graduate student in the Department of Geography at the University of Toronto. His research interests include critical theory and the politics of space.

Łukasz Stanek is an architect, philosopher, and doctoral student at the Department of Architectural Theory, Technical University, Delft, Netherlands. His research interests in Henri Lefebvre straddle philosophy, planning, and architecture. He has published articles on city building, mass media, and the production of space in former state-socialist cities like Nowa Huta, Poland.

Geoffrey Waite is Associate Professor of German Studies and the Field of Comparative Literature at Cornell University. He is the author of *Nietzsche's Corps/e: Aesthetics, Politics, Prophecy, or, The Spectacular Technoculture of Everyday Life* (1996), and is currently finishing *Heidegger: The Question of Esoteric Political Ontology*.

Preface and Acknowledgments

This book has a long history. The editors have worked on, with, and beyond Henri Lefebvre's work for a considerable length of time, in some cases since the 1980s. Indeed, some contributors encountered Lefebvre as far back as the 1960s. Our readings of him have been strongly influenced by social struggles and political engagements in the various cities the editors have inhabited: youth revolt and squatter movements in the Zürich of the 1980s; anti-Olympic protests, labor-community mobilizations, housing activism, anti-globalization, anti-war and anti-racist politics in the Toronto of the 1990s and early 2000s; struggles over slums and neoliberalism in Colombo; the 1992 uprising in Los Angeles; and a number of urban struggles in Paris.

Around the mid-1990s, our different paths started to overlap. For some of us, this occurred at the annual meetings and during various publication projects of the International Network of Urban Research and Action (INURA), an international, predominantly European-based grouping of researchers and activists that breaches the walls of academic institutions. Another node for collective discussions was the Toronto editorial group of the journal *Capitalism, Nature, Socialism*.

We would like to acknowledge the many friends and comrades who helped shape the collective contexts which themselves have informed at least indirectly how we made sense of Lefebvre's relevance. They are too numerous to list individually here.

More concrete ideas for a common publication project with a Lefebvrean theme were first generated in discussions during a series of academic meetings. The first of these involved Christian Schmid, Neil Brenner, Stefan Kipfer, and Roger Keil during the annual meeting of Research Committee 21 of the International Sociological Association in Berlin, 1997. Explorations were also undertaken by Elizabeth Lebas, Julie-Anne Boudreau, Nathan Sayre, Richard Milgrom, and Stefan Kipfer during and after a panel on Lefebvre at the World Congress of Sociology in Montreal in 1998. Ideas published in some of the articles in this volume were first presented at a series of Lefebvre or Lefebvre-related sessions at the annual conferences of the American Association of Geographers in New York City (2001), Los Angeles (2002),

Philadelphia (2004), and Denver (2005), and at the Studies in Political Economy Conference on scale in Toronto in 2005. Organizers and contributors to these panels included Eleonore Kofman, Kanishka Goonewardena, Ute Lehrer, Rob Shields, Neil Brenner, Neil Smith, Stuart Elden, Nathan Sayre, Joe Painter, Roger Keil, Stefan Kipfer, Richard Milgrom, and Christian Schmid. Ideas about the relevance of Lefebvre for research on colonization and imperialism were first presented by Kipfer and Goonewardena at the Denver conference, a workshop on "urbicide" in Durham, UK in the fall of 2006, and in publications for *Canadian Dimension, New Formations* and *Theory and Event*. For support and critical comments on these writings, we are grateful to Greg Albo, David Campbell, Deborah Cowan, Priyamvada Gopal, Neil Lazarus, Stephen Graham, and Daniel Bertrand Monk.

Different versions and fragments of the chapters by Liette Gilbert and Mustafa Dikeç, Stefan Kipfer, Richard Milgrom, and Klaus Ronneberger were first published in a special issue on Lefebvre edited by Kipfer and Milgrom for the Toronto editorial group of *Capitalism, Nature, Socialism* (CNS) 13 (June 2002), for which thanks are due to Barbara Laurence at CNS and the various reviewers who offered insightful comments and precious editorial assistance. This CNS special issue was preceded by "Rhubarb Pie," a CNS public forum in the spring of 2001. Organized by Roger Keil and Harriet Friedmann and moderated by Sue Ruddick, the forum included presentations by Russ Janzen, Liette Gilbert and Mustafa Dikeç, Kanishka Goonewardena, Stefan Kipfer, and Richard Milgrom. Neil Brenner's contribution to this book is based in part on ideas first published for a special issue on Lefebvre edited by Brenner and Stuart Elden of *Antipode* 33 (2001). Walter Prigge's contribution is translated from the German original published by Campus and edited by Martin Wentz in a 1991 collection entitled *Stadt-Räume*.

We thank David McBride, Steve Rutter, and Anne Horowitz at Routledge for their support and enthusiasm for this project. Translations from the German originals were done by Bandulasena Goonewardena (for Kurt Meyer, Walter Prigge, and Christian Schmid) and Stefan Kipfer and Neil Brenner (Klaus Ronneberger). These translations were made possible with financial support from the Faculty of Environmental Studies (York University, Toronto) and the Social Sciences and Humanities Research Council of Canada. Thanks to Ahmed Allahwala, doctoral candidate, Department of Political Science, York University, for his help with the index and Amy Siciliano, doctoral candidate, Department of Geography, University of Toronto, for editorial assistance, including work on the index. Last but by no means least, we would like to thank our various partners and family members for their invaluable patience, crucial intellectual stimulus, and loving support: Leah Birnbaum, Anik and Leo Gunawardena, Chantal, Ernst and Stefi Kipfer, Yves Périllard, Karen and Felix Wirsig, and Sarah Dooling. Without all of you, this book would never have seen the light of day.

1

ON THE PRODUCTION OF HENRI LEFEBVRE

Stefan Kipfer, Kanishka Goonewardena, Christian Schmid, Richard Milgrom

SPACE, DIFFERENCE, EVERYDAY LIFE

The deepest troubles of the planet today do not lie only with geopolitical conflicts and world-economic ravages. They are also brewing in the metropolitan centers, as we saw most recently and clearly in the "French" suburban uprising of fall 2005, led by not quite so *post*-colonial subjects. Yet what happened in France in this case remains to be properly understood, especially by students of politics engaged with critical theory. After all, a few radical exponents of the latter joined the struggles against the conditions that spectacularly engulfed *les banlieues* in flames, placing them on a spatio-temporal axis aligned with the events of 1848, 1871, and 1968: Alain Badiou advocating for *sans-papiers*, Pierre Bourdieu denouncing neoliberalism, and Étienne Balibar arguing for the "right to the city" against neo-racism.[1] Even Jacques Derrida's post-9/11 book *Rogues*[2] may be extended with a little imagination to touch on the formidable forces bearing down on the predominantly North and Black Africans now living in the formerly "red" rings of French working-class suburbs, while being subjected to the worst deprivations registered in vivid detail by Bourdieu and his colleagues.[3] But an adequate account of *les banlieues* should exceed the work of any one of these critical thinkers. It demands a historical perspective capable of articulating spatial forms with social relations at various levels of our new global reality—from the quotidian, through the urban, to the global. Moving through these levels of analysis to make sense of rebellious actions, and their mediation by emerging relations between cities and world order, now requires a critique sharply focused on three key terms: *space*, *difference*, and *everyday life*.

Henri Lefebvre springs to our minds when we think of these terms with necessary reference to each other as well as the world in which we live, given how he elaborated them in a remarkably supple oeuvre of idiosyncratic marxist thought intent on the revolutionary transformation of his own times and spaces. Of course, his work will have to be considerably adapted—globalized, even—to do justice to the transnational realities of contemporary metropolitan life, in France as much as elsewhere. For Lefebvre lived the adventure of the twentieth century, not the twenty-first, to play with the title of Rémi Hess's biography.[4] He wrote over sixty books and numerous other publications, covering an astonishingly wide range of subjects, including philosophy, political theory, sociology, literature, music, linguistics, and urban studies, in formats that vary from popular tomes on marxism to difficult, meandering writings that escape conventional academic protocols. Having helped introduce Hegel and Marx's early work into French debates, he developed his original heterodox marxism through a series of critical engagements with French phenomenology, existentialism, structuralism, and the surrealist, dadaist, and situationist avant-gardes. His most striking contributions include a critique of every-day life and studies of urbanization, space, and state—alongside studies of various prominent strands of French left intellectual discourse and a series of conjunctural meditations on such vital political moments as May 1968. Lefebvre was also a lifelong proponent of left-communist politics. Following his stint as an active member of the French Communist Party (PCF) from 1928 to his expulsion in 1958, he became an important exponent of the new left, contributing seminally to debates on self-management (*autogestion*). In addition, he directed research at the Centre National de la Recherche Scientifique (CNRS) (1949–61) and enjoyed a career as a charismatic university professor in Strasbourg (1961–5), where he collaborated with situationists, and Nanterre (1965–73), the hotbed of the 1968 student rebellion.

To contextualize Lefebvre's reception, here we want to look at how certain Anglo-American academic circles have influentially "produced" Lefebvre, as it were. Although Lefebvre receives passing mention in various anthologies of Western Marxism, his influence in the field of critical theory broadly understood pales in comparison to the considerable attention still commanded by, say, Theodor Adorno and Louis Althusser. But matters are different in some fields of academic inquiry with which we have working relationships, ranging from architecture through urban studies to radical geography, where Lefebvre enjoys some celebrity status. Spirited but limited work in these fields, however, is beginning to make its mark in critical theory at large, especially with help from the recent publication of two quite different studies of Lefebvre by Stuart Elden and Andy Merrifield.[5]

Briefly, such is the backdrop against which we hope to lay here the interpretative ground for a "third" constellation of Lefebvre readings, one different from the two major interpretations of his work that have invariably dominated the last three decades of English-speaking "space" debates: the "postmodern" appropriations led by Edward Soja that followed the "urban political-economic" renderings centered on David Harvey. Hardly any contribution to the present volume can be adequately captured by these two avowedly spatial lines of interpretation. We contend that Lefebvre's own view of the terms "space," "difference," and "everyday life" was significantly different from, if not altogether incompatible with, the particular uses of these terms in those two readings. As such, the Lefebvre that has been typically available for consumption in the Anglo-American academy amounted to a significant abstraction from Lefebvre's self-understanding of his own interventions in revolutionary theory and practice, suitably packaged for the postmodern Zeitgeist. With the waning fortunes of the latter,[6] however, subjective and objective conditions are now at hand for more fruitful examinations of Lefebvre.

The "third" wave of Lefebvre readings we propose links urban-spatial debates more persistently and substantively with an open-minded appropriation of his metaphilosophical epistemology shaped by continental philosophy and Western Marxism. In so doing, it also rejects the debilitating dualism between "political economy" and "cultural studies" that in effect marked the distinction between the "first" and "second" waves of Lefebvre studies, making it impossible for us to return to a simply updated or expanded earlier school of thought on Lefebvre. Indeed, one of the legacies of the debates within and on "post" theory of the 1980s and early 1990s was an often acute bifurcation of theoretical debate that identifies marxism with studies of material social relations, class, and political economy while relegating considerations of subjectivity, identity, difference, and culture to poststructuralist versions of cultural studies.[7]

Certainly, this bifurcation of theory profoundly influenced how key intellectuals—Walter Benjamin, Antonio Gramsci, Frantz Fanon, and others—were received within contemporary academic debates. This volume joins interpretive efforts on these authors by those who attempt to overcome the divide between culturalism and economism in a substantive way. We have in mind interpreters who have reignited supposedly "postmodern" problems—difference, identity, language, body, and the like—in "outdated" if not forgotten materialist, dialectical, and marxist theoretical contexts, instead of joining theoretically disparate and politically distinct strands of cultural studies and political economy.[8] What emerges from such a reinscription in Lefebvre's case is a heterodox and open-ended historical materialism that is committed to an embodied, passionately engaged, and politically charged form of critical knowledge. Within this context, his writings about everyday life and the city are not to be understood simply as sociological extensions of his oeuvre attractive only to specialists of "space": urban sociologists, geographers, planners, and architects. For it was precisely through his concrete contributions to these fields that Lefebvre worked out his overall political and theoretical orientation. In that sense, we hope to demonstrate that Lefebvre's urban and spatial writings are of more general interest for radical social and political theory. In turn, we intend to show that his adventures in French Marxism shed much-needed light on his pioneering work on space, difference, and everyday life.

THE ECONOMIC GEOGRAPHY OF LEFEBVRE STUDIES

In 1951, an exiled Theodor Adorno noted the prevalence of the commodity form in shaping knowledge production and complained about how the disarmingly practical but hierarchically ordered procedures encouraged in intellectual work fostered a servile "departmentalization of mind" that was ready to be used for whatever practical purpose power had for it.[9] This departmentalization obtained under administered mass production in the postwar period has now been partly superseded, to be sure, but only with even more intense forms of instrumentalization and commodification. After-Fordist conditions in the academy herald less a new level of creativity than an intensified pressure to produce innovatively. The analogy between industrial practice and knowledge production indicates that university work even of the critical variety now mimics the commodity form more clearly than ever. What matters above all for those in the running for academic employment and recognition is to maximize output measured largely in quantitative terms; supplement regular university resources with external research grants that are increasingly tied to state and corporate interests; and establish hyper-specialized niches of innovation that facilitate the "branding" of one's professional identity along with what is left of critical inquiry. This pressure for "ceaseless intellectual innovation is symptomatic of academic capitalism."[10] Entrepreneurial scholarship approximates the time-space of fashion, where the commodity fetish establishes itself through the worship of the marginally new but structurally repetitive.[11] This situation invites all manner of intellectual cannibalism, involving opportunistic combinations and permutations of pre-existing knowledge fragments. Translated into postmodern culture, this yields the technique that represents the reformatting of modernist parody after the deletion of its subversive intent: *pastiche*.[12]

Publishing a new book on Lefebvre inevitably risks adding more of the same to at least some such trends. After all, references to his work have become increasingly commonplace in Anglo-American academic circles over the last fifteen years, mostly but not exclusively in the spatial disciplines, following the 1991 translation of *The Production of Space*. Since the issue of this challenging but apparently popular book, there followed a steady stream of English translations of his writings on everyday life, modernity, the city, rhythmanalysis; special issues of journals; conference papers; a reader; and three book-length studies of Lefebvre.[13] Such an array of translations and a sizeable secondary literature means that citing Lefebvre's triadic notion of social space and his insistence on the "political" nature of space is now *de rigueur* for anyone trained with even a homeopathic dose of critical theory in geography, planning, or architecture. For better or worse, an academic industry on Lefebvre has developed. His increasing popularity, especially in the New World, was undoubtedly part and parcel of the prestige enjoyed by "French theory" (liberal adaptations of Derrida, Lacan, Foucault, Lyotard, Guattari) in the English-speaking academy and its transnational outposts.[14]

Until recently, Anglo-American interest in Lefebvre has stood in contrast to his intellectual marginalization in some other contexts.[15] In France itself, Lefebvre was relegated to the margins of intellectual life after the early 1970s.[16] As Gilbert and Dikeç remind us in this volume, some of his concepts of the urban such as "centrality" and "festival" were taken up in French urban policy circles during the 1980s, but only in highly coopted forms.[17] Otherwise, Lefebvre remained unpopular for refusing to follow the fashions of structuralism, post-structuralism, and the subsequent wave of media-savvy *nouveaux philosophes* intent on expunging "totalitarianism" (read: marxism and the new left) from French thought to turn France into a bastion of (neo-)liberalism.[18] Since the mid-1990s, however, he has resurfaced from obscurity in his native country. Under the initiative of "old" Lefebvreans, including his biographer Rémi Hess, and, ironically, intellectuals close to the PCF, a broad range of Lefebvre's books have been reissued by French publishers.[19] University students familiarize themselves with his work. Conferences and symposia have been stimulated by his work. In some instances, such as *Espaces et Sociétés* (1994), this meant reimporting Lefebvre from the Anglo-American scene in a form reminiscent of the recent fate of "French theory" in France itself.[20] All this has led some to suggest, optimistically, that the intellectual pendulum in French intellectual life is swinging back towards a more favorable consideration of Lefebvre's work.[21]

In the German-speaking context, too, Lefebvre has been a rather marginal figure within critical or radical intellectual circles. As Klaus Ronneberger argues in this volume, Lefebvre's work, particularly his critique of everyday life, acquired "underground status" among the West German new left in the 1970s. At that time, he inspired debates about alienation, critical theory, and the culture of postwar capitalism. Swiss-based Kurt Meyer, whose recent article on rhythmanalysis we have the privilege of publishing here, was a leading contributor to the debates at that time with his book *Henri Lefebvre: Ein romantischer Revolutionär* published in 1973. But Lefebvre largely disappeared from the radar screen of critical theory after the mid-1970s, only resurfacing occasionally in philosophical debates in the 1990s.[22] His influence on critical urbanism in the German-speaking world remained restricted to two small critical intellectual milieus in Frankfurt[23] and Zürich.[24] This work drew extensively on Lefebvre to understand the role of intellectual practice, everyday life, and social movements in the dynamics of urban conflict and restructuring. With a few exceptions, including Schmid's and Prigge's contributions here, it remains unfortunately untranslated. Epitomized in the works of Prigge and Schmid, these intellectual milieus have produced some of the most exemplary and judicious studies of Lefebvre to date.

THE MANY LIVES OF HENRI LEFEBVRE

The lay of the Lefebvre land in the English-speaking academy can be characterized as specialist, dualist, and historicist: *specialist* insofar as many Lefebvre scholars are concentrated in geography, urban studies, planning, and architecture, and associated with the spatial turn in social and cultural theory in conjunction with the linguistic turn of what the French call human sciences, suggesting in effect that "doing Lefebvre" means "doing space" and "being postmodern"; *dualist*, as noted earlier, to the extent that Lefebvre has been read especially in Anglo-America through the often mutually exclusive lenses of urban political economy and postmodern cultural studies, both essentially blind to his involvement in earlier debates concerning postwar marxism in particular and French intellectual life more generally; and *historicist*, in a related sense, because, in spite of considerable evidence to the contrary, Lefebvre exhibited the uncanny habit of appearing as a "forerunner" for various projects—an ultimately disappointing one for urban political economy[25] but a very good one, a postmodernist *avant la lettre*,[26] for a certain brand of urban-cultural studies. Taken as readings of Lefebvre, all of these dominant tendencies are inadequate, but they do provide us with some coordinates for locating the two most influential appropriations of his work in Anglo-America. Sustained and admirable attempts to read Lefebvre differently (neither as urban political economist nor as an embryonic postmodernist) have been made, but with little impact.[27]

Lefebvre first figured prominently in the pioneering marxist attempts to theorize urbanization—or, more specifically, the role of urbanization in the accumulation and reproduction of capital—especially in the invaluable body of work produced by David Harvey since the publication of his urban political economy classic *Social Justice and the City* in 1973. Lefebvre's positive influence in this context stood in stark contrast to the hostile reaction his work faced from structuralist marxists, especially Manuel Castells, who in *The Urban Question* (first published in France in 1972) saw the city as a mere product of abstractly conceived instances of the social formation rather than as a contradictory mediation between everyday life and the social order, as Lefebvre did. Castells accordingly labeled Lefebvre as a left-wing exponent of mainstream urban sociology.[28] Although he subsequently revised his position,[29] his critique contributed to Lefebvre's marginalization in France and in English-speaking urban sociology.[30] Harvey, on the other hand, has never hidden his admiration for Lefebvre, and acknowledged the Frenchman's role in politicizing and radicalizing him.[31] Harboring no sympathies for Althusserian Marxism, he was particularly taken by the utopian dimensions of Lefebvre's urban writings and accepted urbanization not as a thing in itself but as a strategic entry point to understand and revolutionize the capitalist mode of production as a whole.

Harvey probed Lefebvre for an alternative to the "counter-revolutionary" mainstream in geography, looking for a rigorous account of urbanization in relation to the crisis-ridden dynamics of capitalist accumulation. He was intrigued by Lefebvre's notion in *The Urban Revolution* (1970) that in the process of urbanization, a secondary circuit of real estate investment becomes increasingly important in advanced capitalism, producing the distinct patterns of spatial homogenization and differentiation so characteristic of postwar metropolitan areas. Yet Harvey conceived the ascendance of this secondary circuit not as a secular trend that was gradually becoming more influential than the primary industrial circuit of capital, as Lefebvre suggested, but as a cyclical process of expansion and contraction synchronized with the pattern of capitalist growth and crisis. Even as Harvey glimpsed the profound implications of Lefebvre's fundamental thesis, he found it not sufficiently rigorous in terms of economic theory.[32] In one sense Harvey was correct: Lefebvre offered no finished theory of urban political economy. Along similar lines, Neil Smith is also factually correct to announce his disappointment at Lefebvre's failure to produce a satisfactory theory of uneven development, the production of nature, and scale.[33] Both are mistaken, however, to assume that Lefebvre's life-long ambition was to produce a political-economic theory of space or scale. With his contributions to debates on the state, self-management, alienation, and everyday life, rather, Lefebvre proposed a *critique* of political economy:

> How much time is it going to take to recognize that the subtitle of *Capital* (*Critique of Political Economy*) had to be taken literally? Despite the subtitle, *Capital* was considered as a treatise of the economy for more than a half-century. After that, it was interpreted as a critique of bourgeois political economy that contained the premise for a political economy called "socialist." Yet *Capital* must be taken as a critique of all political economy: of the economic as a separate sphere, a narrow field of science that morphs into a restraining device, of the "discipline" which fixes and immobilizes momentary relations by elevating them to the rank of scientific truths. In the same way, the critique of the State does not just include a critique of the Hegelian state, the bourgeois state, but also of democracy, of the supposedly democratic and socialist State: of every State (as form of power).[34]

Notwithstanding such pleas, Harvey's engagement with Lefebvre was ultimately circumscribed by the political-economic parameters of a neoclassical marxism. He contributed immensely to the visibility of this French marxist in the Anglo-American world, aside from spawning the most powerful and prodigious current of radical urban theory.[35] But the Lefebvre that survived in this tradition was also radically reduced, barely recognizable as the prolific philosopher who theorized everyday life while drinking with Guy Debord and wrestling with continental social and political thought. This has had serious conceptual consequences. First, Harvey treats everyday life in a derivative way, as a repository of larger processes rather than a semi-autonomous and contradictory level of totality, and an ultimate yardstick of revolution, as Lefebvre did. As a result of the ensuing difficulty to deal with the "lived experiences of people in history,"[36] Harvey has exhibited impatience with Lefebvre's open-ended, three-dimensional notion of the production of space, privileging the production of material (perceived) over ideological-institutional (conceived) and lived-symbolic (experienced) space.[37] As Schmid puts it, "while Lefebvre promoted the development of a comprehensive theory of the production of space, Harvey pursued a more narrow project: a political economy of space."[38] Finally, Harvey's neoclassical marxism tends to shrink problematics of difference to an effect of political economies of spatial differentiation. In response to postmodern critics, his fundamentally political-economic conception of uneven geographical development comes to underwrite the dialectic of identity and difference, within which the autonomous and subjective aspects of everyday life remain undertheorized and devalued.[39] This is not only in contrast to Derrida's notion of *différance* mobilized by postmodern critics. It also differs from Lefebvre's primarily political understanding of the urban revolution as a dialectical transformation of minimal into maximal difference (described in *Le manifeste différentialiste, The Production of Space*, and the third volume of *The Critique of Everyday Life*).[40] This transformation can be achieved only by social struggles for political self-determination and a new spatial centrality, which help liberate difference from the alienating social constraints produced by capital, state, and patriarchy.

In the 1980s, Soja's early explorations into the role of space in critical social theory promised a broader engagement with Lefebvre. Shifting from urban political economy to wider debates, he readily acknowledged Lefebvre's continental philosophical heritage and political pedigree, noting a "flexible, open, cautionary, eclectic Marxism" influenced by Hegel, the early Marx, and the surrealists that gestured towards a holistically spatialized marxism.[41] Everyday life, lived space, and difference figured prominently in this perspective, even though these terms were ultimately deployed very differently by Soja than in Lefebvre's own work. Soja's extremely influential book *Postmodern Geographies* thus offered much hope for critical theory, and was warmly welcomed by no less an authority on marxist cultural theory than Fredric Jameson, for placing the "new spatiality implicit in the postmodern . . . on the agenda in so eloquent and timely a fashion."[42] This generous feeling, however, was not mutual. For already in *Postmodern Geographies*, Soja had provided a sweeping and generic indictment of "historicism" (of which Jameson must appear as a chief proponent) and mobilizes Lefebvre alongside Foucault for a veritable ontology of space:[43] a less than dialectical conception of the relationship between space and society, which are treated as ontologically distinct categories.[44]

Lefebvre did not privilege space at the expense of time, or vice versa.[45] While committed to rectifying the undertheorization of space in marxist traditions, he wrote a great deal on precisely the deplorable consequences of *spatializing* time into a series of measurable instants.[46] As he himself once said, "time may have been promoted to the level of ontology by the philosophers, but it has been murdered by society."[47] This pervasive tendency of modern society that also disturbed Benjamin, Debord, and E. P. Thompson[48] offers Lefebvre no cause for postmodern celebration, but rather the occasion to demonstrate his commitment to temporal and historical categories—moments, rhythms, events—within his inquiries into space, and this with a persistent reluctance to ontologize space, time, or anything else.[49] The emphasis lay for him not on space as an a priori or ontological entity, but on the processes and strategies of producing space, which are by definition historical. For *ontologizing* space and spatiality symptomatically replicates, in the realm of thought, the domination of linear time over lived time already occurring more generally in modern society, inscribing the alienation of the rhythms of everyday life in what Lefebvre called "abstract space."[50] It was not for nothing that the book that started all this was entitled *The Production of Space*.

How did Soja get so lost looking for Lefebvre in the prison-house of spatial ontology? At least a partial explanation must lie with his decision to treat Lefebvre as a forerunner of postmodernism, a strategy begun in *Postmodern Geographies* and completed, under pressure from his critics, in *ThirdSpace*.[51] One now finds Soja's Lefebvre in "third space," which lies at the end of a road named post-structuralism here and postmodernism there, after going through not only the spatial but the cultural and linguistic turns. Drawing eclectically on bell hooks's "margins," Gloria Anzaldua's "borderlands," Michel Foucault's "heterotopia," and, most importantly, Homi Bhabha's own third space, Soja's subsumes lived space under the "new cultural politics of identity and difference" located in thirdspace.[52] Within his misleadingly ontologizing "epistemological trialectics" of space,[53] thirdspace signals, in contrast to Lefebvre, an epistemological and linguistic principle of non-representability. Closely resembling Bhabha,[54] Soja's thirdspace is an anti-representational site of "radical openness," "otherness," "margins," and "hybridity," where "*everything* comes together" in a place of "all-inclusive simultaneity."[55] What is not allowed in here is any sense that, in Lefebvre, difference and everyday life are categories of dialectical critique, such that lived space entails a contradictory realm of alienation and liberation. For Lefebvre, to extricate the promising aspects from this contradictory realm of lived space required reassembling and transforming fragments of urban life, not reifying existing separations of modernity as forms of absolute simultaneity or separate spatialities.[56] Such transformative assembly is possible only with an open-ended (but not postmodern) search for totality as revolutionary possibility.

LEFEBVRE AND WESTERN MARXISM

The postmodern and neoclassical political-economic appropriations of Lefebvre—epitomized by Soja and Harvey—patently fail to do justice to his work spanning space, difference, and everyday life. While Lefebvre shared concerns with both traditions, he pursued neither an urban political economy (which includes a geographic theory of differentiation but treats everyday life as a passive site) nor an ontology of spatiality (where difference and everyday life are at one with the play of signifiers in deconstructive linguistic theory). "Sharing concerns does not mean shared analyses or conclusions," aptly note Eleanore Kofman and Elizabeth Lebas.[57]

This holds most clearly for the post-structuralist appropriation of him and its strictures against subjectivity, alienation, dialectics, and totality.[58] The latter remain central concepts in Lefebvre[59] and his insightful explorations into such issues as language, body, space, time, difference, and everyday life, which are typically assumed to be postmodern terrain. As demonstrated by David McNally, a radical approach to language such as Mikhail Bakhtin's and Benjamin's cannot abstract it, as do structuralism and post-structuralism, from the "historical bodies" theorized by Marx, Darwin, and Freud and their material practices.[60] Lefebvre, though not discussed by McNally, understood this when he refused Foucault's notion of the body as the "effect" of discursive practices and declined the invitations of Ferdinand de Saussure or Derrida into a "world of signs" followed by an "erasure of referentials." For him, the abstraction and self-referentiality of the linguistic turn in social theory represented not so much a critique as an alienated symptom of profoundly modern-capitalist phenomena: the instrumentalization of knowledge, the universalization of commodification, and the coronation of exchange-value.[61] In addition, while Lefebvre's dealings with Nietzsche are questionable,[62] they are meant to qualify and extend, not undermine Hegel and Marx.[63] Lefebvre has no use for Nietzsche's mythical identity of knowledge and the Will to Power, which one can also detect in the neo-Nietzschean formations of post-theory.[64]

How then does Lefebvre fare in studies of Western Marxism? In much of the literature surveying the latter, one finds him either missing altogether or mentioned only in passing. This should seem surprising, given the crucial import accorded to space in the prodigious theorization of postmodernism as the cultural logic of late capitalism by Jameson, the leading representative of this tradition today. Yet the fleeting references to Lefebvre in his work are more allusive than substantive.[65] Lefebvre plays no role at all in Jameson's most original contributions to marxist theory.[66] Neither does he appear in Terry Eagleton's popular and pioneering studies.[67] Martin Jay devotes a chapter to him in *Marxism and Totality*, the quality of which stands in negative contrast to the breadth and depth of his treatment of George Lukács, Jean-Paul Sartre, and the Frankfurt School thinkers in the same book.[68] Lefebvre also features only superficially in the studies and anthologies of Roger Gottlieb, Russell Jacoby, Tony Judt, Leszek Kolakowski, George Lichtheim, Bertell Ollman, and other surveyors of marxism.[69]

With some justification, one may submit that Lefebvre's enigmatic absence from literatures on Western Marxism in particular (and continental philosophy more generally)[70] can be explained by his occasional intellectual imprecision and political opportunism, evidenced in disappointing relations to the ideological vagaries of the PCF.[71] But not everyone has taken these limitations as an excuse to bypass Lefebvre. An especially noteworthy early contribution is late Frankfurt School scholar Alfred Schmidt's sketch of Lefebvre's anti-ontological marxism, a prophetic counterpoint to postmodern reifications of his thought on space.[72] Sticking close to the orbit of French communism, Michael Kelly traces Lefebvre's often subterranean contributions to debates on materialism and idealism within the Philosophies group and the PCF.[73] Lefebvre also plays a leading part in Bud Burkhard, who provides the most detailed treatment of his interwar activities, intellectual and political, and stresses his crucial role in introducing and popularizing marxism in France, especially by means of the short-lived journal Revue Marxiste (1929–30).[74] In this context, Burkhard discusses, above all, the co-authored (with Norbert Guterman) introductions to Morceaux choisis de Marx (1934), Morceaux choisis de Hegel (1938), Cahiers sur la dialectique de Hegel (1938), and Conscience mystifiée (1936), as well as Dialectical Materialism (1939) and Nietzsche (1939).

The most nuanced theoretical treatment of Lefebvre's relationship to marxism in this period can be found in Kevin Anderson's excellent study on the importance and historical journey of Lenin's 1914–15 Hegel Notebooks. In Cahiers sur la dialectique, Dialectical Materialism, Logique formelle, logique dialectique (1947), and Pour connaître la pensée de Lénine (1957) Lefebvre appears as the main and controversial defender of Lenin's Hegelianism in France.[75] Finally, Mark Poster's account of the convergence of existentialism and marxism in postwar France considers at some length Lefebvre's trajectory from early existentialism in the 1920s through Hegelian Marxism in the 1930s to his prominent role in the Arguments group (1956–62).[76] Next to Lefebvre's central role in the French new left,[77] he pays particular attention to his shifting relationship to Sartre and his comprehensive critique of structuralism.[78] Together, these interventions testify, first, to Lefebvre's crucial role in explicating a dialectical and humanist version of marxism in France critically rooted in Hegel and the early Marx and, second, his strategic place in the non-structuralist marxist side of the new left after 1956.

Despite these promising forays, only a few students of Lefebvre have seriously linked his heterodox European philosophy and Western Marxism to his writing about space, everyday life, and difference. With regard to the critique everyday life,

Lefebvre has been appearing more regularly and systematically in an expanding literature on this concept. Here, he is compared and contrasted to a range of political and cultural forces (dada, surrealism, communism, situationism) and a wide variety of individual contributors: Boris Arvatov, Bakhtin, Benjamin, Michel de Certeau, Debord, Gramsci, Martin Heidegger, Agnes Heller, Tosaka Jun, Lukács, and Dorothy Smith.[79] The most philosophically ambitious exponent in this recent literature is John Roberts, whose *Philosophizing the Everyday* offers a poignant contrast to postmodern readings of Lefebvre and traces the radical politics of the quotidian in marxism from the early Soviet debates through Lukács and Benjamin to Lefebvre and the situationists.[80] This brief but powerful study ranks among the few rewarding inquiries into Lefebvre's thought in the tradition of Western Marxism. It also offers a fine complement to Harry Harootunian's comparative account of modernity, where Lefebvre appears alongside Japanese marxist Jun,[81] and Peter Osborne's penetrating *The Politics of Time*, which includes the most theoretically advanced comparison to date between the concepts of everyday life developed by Heidegger and Lefebvre.[82]

What about the links between Lefebvre's meta-philosophy, his critique of everyday life, and his urban and spatial analyses? While Poster's aforementioned work appropriately mentions the importance of these links, they are explored and developed in an exemplary fashion in Kristin Ross's *Fast Cars, Clean Bodies*.[83] Lefebvre's anti-structuralist romantic-revolutionary claim for a new subjectivity is superbly discussed here in ways that highlight its essential connections to a critique of everyday life that is itself decisively refracted through an urban lens. In the footsteps of her earlier intriguing book on revolutionary culture leading up to the Commune,[84] Ross weaves Lefebvre's critique of everyday life (and Fanon's anti-colonial writing) into a feminist excavation of postwar culture in France. In so doing, she clearly demonstrates that Lefebvre's meta-philosophical orientation and dialectical critique of everyday life are fused organically with his urban and spatial analyses. In this regard, Ross's insight is powerfully confirmed by Andy Merrifield's monograph *Henri Lefebvre: A Critical Introduction*, where Lefebvre's overall politico-theoretical orientation is integral to both his urban and spatial writings and his fully lived critique of everyday life.[85] Ross and Merrifield leave us with a clear sense that Lefebvre's dialectical critique of everyday life reached its most explosive potential when his attention shifted to "the urban."

A THIRD CONSTELLATION OF LEFEBVRE READINGS

This collection of essays follows the lead of Ross, Merrifield, and a number of other authors[86] who have taken Lefebvre out of the confines of the so-far dominant specialist, dualist, and historicist readings in the Anglo-American spatial debate. The contributions to this volume share a number of commonalities. First, they hope to provide well-founded treatments of Lefebvre while paying careful attention to the overall orientation and historical context of his work. They are committed to an undogmatic reading of Lefebvre and are thus more precise and open than many previous attempts. Second, they consider Lefebvre as a point of departure. They make an effort to think with and beyond his texts and theories by incorporating them into contemporary contexts and making them work for reflections and analyses that reach beyond Lefebvre himself. Third, they emphasize the role of Lefebvre's conception of space, time, and the urban in his overall (meta-)philosophical approach, and vice versa. Fourth, many of the essays make Lefebvre useful for purposes of a type of empirical research that does not only cite Lefebvre's work but incorporates his theories and concepts into the very heart of the investigation itself.

It is possible to discern from our contributions the rough contours of a "third" wave of Lefebvre. This does not imply a unified approach, nor does it mean agreement on all aspects of Lefebvre's work, of course. There is no consensus among authors about the precise nature and conceptual importance of his marxism. And not everyone is on the same page as far as the centrality of the urban is concerned for Lefebvre's other preoccupations. With their contributions to the links between Lefebvre, Kostas Axelos, Gaston Bachelard, Balibar, Fernand Braudel, André Breton, Debord, Gramsci, Heidegger, Jameson, Lukács, Lucien Kroll, Maurice Merleau-Ponty, Raymond Williams, and some others, the authors in this volume substantively extend our knowledge of Lefebvre's heterodox, open-ended and broadly conceived form of marxism, however. We also think it is possible to identify with this volume a loose constellation of Lefebvre scholarship that is rooted in attempts to expand on the explosive political implications that follow from the links between Lefebvre's peculiar meta-philosophical orientation and his observations on space, time, and the urban.

With respect to space, Christian Schmid and Łukasz Stanek explicate the philosophical sources informing Lefebvre's theory of the production of space. Stanek demonstrates that Lefebvre's notion of space as concrete abstraction can be traced to Hegel's concept of the concrete universal and Marx's elaboration of it in *Grundrisse* and *Capital*. Schmid points out that Lefebvre's three-dimensional dialectical theory of the production of space is best understood with reference to, first, the trinity of Hegel, Marx, and Nietzsche; second, his three-pronged treatment of linguistic theory; and, finally, a materialist adaptation of French phenomenologists Merleau-Ponty and Bachelard. As his careful theoretical reconstruction indicates,[87] and as Walter Prigge also forcefully argues, Lefebvre's writing about space is not simply a concretization of broader theoretical (philosophical or sociological) concerns. It is definitive and productive of his overall theoretical orientation. For Prigge, this shows that urban research has epistemological implications not only for sub-disciplinary investigations but for our understanding of modernity as a whole. Therein lies the materiality of the urban.[88]

Left unresolved in these opening contributions is the role of Heidegger in Lefebvre. Both Stuart Elden and Geoff Waite affirm Heidegger's presence in words Lefebvre uses: mondialisation/mondialité, dwelling/inhabiting, and several others. They radically disagree on how to make proper sense of this presence, though. Elden extends his own elaborate study[89] with a careful review of Lefebvre's relationship to Kostas Axelos, the exiled resistance fighter and former Communist Party member from Greece who translated Heidegger and Lukács, and worked closely with Lefebvre as the editor of Arguments from 1957 to 1962. He argues that Axelos was an influential source behind Lefebvre's use of the word mondialisation, which as a philosophical category must be distinguished from analytical or instrumental ways of grasping processes of globalization. The Heideggerian currents that come together in the Axelos and Lefebvre pairing are subjected to exacting scrutiny by Waite, a pioneering critic of Nietzsche and Heidegger.[90] He insists that "left-Heideggerian" attempts to marry Marx with Heidegger are doomed to fail: they are "philologically incompetent" and "philosophically incoherent." Waite takes to task not only contemporary authors as distinct as Elden and Harvey but Lefebvre himself for failing to recognize this. Lefebvre may have avoided Heidegger's darkly disturbing "jargon of authenticity,"[91] but he read Heidegger too carelessly to understand the dangers that inhere in Heidegger's esoteric style.

Lefebvre's spatial writing emerged, of course, from a response to processes of "modernizing the city" and "urbanizing space" (Prigge), which culminated in the fully fledged crystallization of abstract space in the middle of the twentieth century (Stanek). As Ronneberger reminds us in his discussion of Lefebvre's presence in Germany, Lefebvre gave considerable weight to the materiality of the urban with his distinction between three levels of the social totality: G ("global," meaning general), M (mixed, urban), and P (private, everyday). This analytical device integrates instead of separates urban questions from other levels of totality: the macro-order of society and the micro-realities of everyday life, as is highlighted also by Kanishka Goonewardena and Stefan Kipfer. In his sharp treatment of the subject, Goonewardena takes us back all the way to Marx and Engels's German Ideology and suggests that Lefebvre's own vital contribution to the problematic of everyday life compares best with Benjamin, Gramsci, Debord, and the mature Lukács but differs clearly from Heidegger, Adorno, Horkheimer, and de Certeau. Nothing less than the benchmark of success for marxist theory, everyday life captures the contradictions of reality and possibility within the very interstices of advanced capitalism. Goonewardena's chapter resonates well with Sara Nadal-Melsió's insightful comparison between Lefebvre and the surrealists (Breton) and Merrifield's witty portrait of the multifaceted relationship between Debord and Lefebvre. While Nadal-Melsió underscores the importance of art as everyday poetic practice for Lefebvre's view of philosophy, the aesthetic, and the city, Merrifield holds that Debord

(Mephistopheles) and Lefebvre (Faust) are both necessary poles in a dialectical and militant urban marxism.

If, for Lefebvre, considerations of space are closely tied to (rather than ontologically distinct from) those of time, this is particularly clear at the level of everyday life, which can also be understood as a confluence of multiple rhythms. Meyer describes the emphasis Lefebvre placed on the interplay of linear and cyclical rhythms in Mediterrenean cities as well as in metropolitan Paris and Los Angeles. Borrowing from Brazilian philosopher Pinheiro dos Santos and Bachelard, Lefebvre's *Rhythmanalysis* rearticulates his own critique of everyday life and includes important implications for our understanding of urban nature. Meyer also detects resonances with Braudel's conception of history as an interplay of multiple rhythms as well as the artistic echoes of writers, painters, and musicians like Calvino, de Maupassant, Hodler, and Jaques-Dalcroze. As Nadal-Melsió and Merrifield note, the polyrhyth-micity of everyday life can be explosive. In their contributions, we learn that Lefebvre's notions of "moment" (in close dialogue with Debord's more spatial "situation") and "event" highlight temporalities which conflict with linear-repetitive time either within the residualized habits of daily life or in intense periods of political struggle. In Nadal-Melsió's terms, it is through such events as "1968" that the city becomes a moment-ary work of art which promises to sublate philosophy and disalienate the aesthetic from the purview of specialized activity.

Subversive moments and revolutionary events are also key to liberate fragments of modern life from their separate existence within the confines of abstract space. There is thus a particularly differential aspect to his critique of lived space and daily temporalities. Within this context, Lefebvre's distinction between minimal/induced and maximal/produced difference is particularly important, as Kipfer, Richard Milgrom, and Andrew Shmuely point out. It is key to understanding his open-ended concept of totality as well as the fate of hegemonic projects of producing space. Kipfer discusses this with respect to Lefebvre's critique and urbanized appropriation of Gramsci. In a similar vein, Shmuely offers an intriguing comparison between Lefebvre and Williams's Gramsci-inspired differentiation between dominant, residual, and emergent social formations. Complementing Stanek, Milgrom brings Lefebvre's differential insight to bear on urban design practice, notably the situationist architecture of Lucien Kroll. In clearly demonstrating the implication of Lefebvre's differential method for projects to produce differential space, he joins others who have elaborated on Lefebvre's interest in situationists like Constant Nieuwenhuys and helped us understand his dialectical critique of modernist urbanism.[92]

These insights lead us to questions of political analysis in the more specific sense of the term. Lefebvre's differential critique of everyday life is of immediate consequence for his approach to the state and his critique of statism, the epistemological implications of which took him beyond Gramsci, according to

Kipfer, but remain to be explored with respect to his relationship to Poulantzas, as Neil Brenner indicates. Building on his path-breaking research on state, scale and globalization,[93] Brenner's chapter shows how Lefebvre's analysis of the "state mode of production" ushers in a critique of both social democratic and neoliberal versions of state productivism in the France of the late 1970s. These are counterposed to *autogestion* (territorial and industrial self-management), which, in contrast to those who turned it into a business management model, Lefebvre saw not as a static institutional form but an ongoing dialectically utopian practice of transforming everyday life in all its aspects. One may add that such far-reaching democratic transformations are central to realizing difference in post-capitalist urban society. They will have to take into account the socio-spatial unevenness of everyday life in ways that go beyond Lefebvre.[94] In this spirit, Liette Gilbert and Mustafa Dikeç draw on Étienne Balibar to extend Lefebvre's late work on citizenship (with the Groupe de Navarrenx) into analyses of migrant struggles against exclusion, segregation, and criminalization in the United States and France. They trace the relevance of Lefebvre to citizenship studies to his earlier comments about the role of immigrant workers in claims to the right to the city as the right to difference in the 1960s and 1970s. We will resume this theme in our conclusion.

NOTES

1. Alain Badiou, *Ethics*, trans. P. Hallward (London: Verso, 2001 [1998]), 96–105; Pierre Bourdieu, *Acts of Resistance: Against the Tyranny of the Market*, trans. R. Nice (New York: The New Press, 1998) and *Firing Back: Against the Tyranny of the Market 2*, trans. L. Wacquant (New York: The New Press, 2003 [2001]); Étienne Balibar, "*Droit de cité* or Apartheid," in *We, the People of Europe: Reflections on Transnational Citizenship*, trans. J. Swenson (Princeton: Princeton University Press, 2004 [2001]), 31–50.

2. Jacques Derrida, *Rogues: Two Essays on Reason*, trans. P.-A. Brault and M. Naas (Stanford: Stanford University Press, 2005 [2003]).

3. Pierre Bourdieu et al., *The Weight of the World: Social Suffering in Contemporary Society*, trans. P. Parkhurst Ferguson et al. (Stanford: Stanford University Press, 1999 [1993]).

4. Rémi Hess, *Henri Lefebvre et l'aventure du siècle* (Paris: Metailie, 1988).

5. Stuart Elden, *Understanding Henri Lefebvre: Theory and the Possible* (London: Continuum, 2004), and Andy Merrifield, *Henri Lefebvre: A Critical Introduction* (New York: Routledge, 2006).

6. Terry Eagleton, *After Theory* (London: Allen Lane, 2003). An indication of this fizzling are debates looking for "new" avenues to reinvigorate post-theory. See Judith Butler, John Guillory, Kendall Thomas, eds., *What's Left of Theory? New Work on the Politics of Literary Theory* (New York: Routledge, 1998); Deborah P. Dixon and John Paul Jones III, "Guest Editorial: What Next?," *Environment and Planning A* 36 (2004): 381–90.

7. Himani Bannerji, *Thinking Through: Essays on Feminism, Marxism and Anti-Racism* (Toronto: Women's Press, 1995), 18.

8. *Ibid.*; Ato Sekyi-Otu, *Fanon's Dialectic of Experience* (Cambridge, MA: Harvard University Press 1996); Esteve Morera, "Gramsci's Critical Modernity," *Rethinking Marxism* 12,

no.1 (2000): 16–46; Rosemary Hennessy, *Profit and Pleasure: Sexual Identities in Late Capitalism* (New York: Routledge, 2000); David McNally, *Bodies of Meaning: Studies on Language, Labor, and Liberation* (Albany: State University of New York Press, 2001).

9. Theodor W. Adorno, *Minima Moralia: Reflections from Damaged Life*, trans. E. F. N. Jephcott (London: Verso, 1974 [1951]), 21.

10. Noel Castree and Thomas MacMillan, "Old News: Representation and Academic Novelty," *Environment and Planning A* 36 (2004): 470.

11. Walter Benjamin, "Convolut B," in *The Arcades Project*, trans. H. Eiland and K. McLaughlin (Cambridge: Belknap, 1999), 62–81.

12. Fredric Jameson, *The Cultural Turn: Selected Writings on the Postmodern* (London: Verso, 1998), 4–5, 7–10.

13. Since 1991, translations have been made of all three volumes of *La Critique de la vie quotidienne; Introduction à la modernity; Le Droit à la ville; Espaces et politiques; La révolution urbaine;* and *Éléments de rythmanalyse.* A cross-section of philosophical and sociological texts can be found in Stuart Elden, Elizabeth Lebas, and Eleonore Kofman eds., *Henri Lefebvre: Key Texts* (New York: Continuum, 2003). Recently translated fragments on the state include a chapter from the fourth volume of *De l'État,* a short article and a forthcoming collected volume "Space and the State," trans. A. Kowalski-Hodges, N. Brenner, A. Passell, and B. Jessop in *State/Space,* ed. N. Brenner, B. Jessop, M. Jones, and G. MacLeod (Oxford: Blackwell, 2003), 84–100; "Comments on a New State Form," trans. Neil Brenner and Stuart Elden, *Antipode* 33, no. 5 (2001): 783–808; and Neil Brenner and Stuart Elden eds., *Henri Lefebvre: State, Space, World* (Minneapolis: University of Minnesota Press, forthcoming). Special issues were edited by Brenner and Elden in *Antipode* (January 2002) and Stefan Kipfer and Richard Milgrom in *Capitalism, Nature, Socialism* (June 2002). The three English monographs on Lefebvre are Elden, *Understanding,* Merrifield, *Henri Lefebvre,* and Rob Shields, *Lefebvre, Love, and Struggle: Spatial Dialectics* (London and New York: Routledge, 1999).

14. François Cusset, *French Theory: Foucault, Derrida, Deleuze et cie. et les mutations de la vie intellectuelle aux États-Unis* (Paris: La Découverte, 2005).

15. Even though Lefebvre is well known in some circles in countries like Brazil, our comments are restricted to France and Germany. Linguistic limitations and time constraints made it inadvisable for us to pursue Lefebvre's traces in the Spanish, Portuguese, Japanese, Serbo-Croat, Italian and Arabic literatures, where multiple translations of his works are available.

16. Monique Coornaert and Jean-Pierre Garnier, "Présentation: actualités de Henri Lefebvre," *Espaces et Sociétés* 76 (1994): 5–11.

17. Roland Castro, *Civilisation urbaine ou barbarie* (Paris: Plon, 1994); Jean-Pierre Garnier, "La Vision urbaine de Henri Lefebvre: des prévisions aux révisions," *Espaces et Sociétés* 76 (1994): 123–45; Eleonore Kofman and Elizabeth Lebas, "Lost in Transposition— Time, Space, and the City," in Henri Lefebvre, *Writings on Cities,* ed., trans. and introduction by E. Kofman and E. Lebas (Oxford: Blackwell, 1996), 35–6.

18. Peter Dews, "The 'New Philosophers' and the End of Leftism," in *Radical Philosophy Reader,* ed. R. Edgley and P. Osborne (London: Verso, 1985), 361–84, and "The *Nouvelle Philosophie* and Foucault," *Economy and Society* 8, no. 2 (1979): 127–71; Perry Anderson, *In the Tracks of Historical Materialism* (Chicago: University of Chicago Press, 1984), 27–31 as well as "Dégringolade" and "Union Sucrée," *London Review of Books* 26, no. 17 (2 September 2004), and 26, no.18 (23 September 2004). Available at: <http://www.lrb.co.uk>.

19. Among them are *Métaphilosophie; Nietzsche; L'irruption; La conscience mystifiée; Le nationalisme contre les nations; Rabelais; La production de l'espace; Espace et Politique; La survie du capitalisme; Contribution à l'esthétique; L'existentialisme; La fin d'histoire;* and *Méthodologie des sciences.*

20. Cusset, *French Theory,* 353–7.

21. Georges Labica, "Marxisme et poésie," preface to Henri Lefebvre, *Métaphilosophie* (Paris: Syllepse, 1997), 6.

22. Hajo Schmidt, *Sozialphilosophie des Krieges: Staat- und Subjekttheoretische Unter-suchungen zu Henri Lefebvre und Georges Bataille* (Essen: Klartext, 1990); Ulrich Müller-Scholl, *Das System und der Rest. Kritische Theorie in der Perspektive Henri Lefebvres* (Mössingen-Talheim: Talheimer, 1999).

23. Walter Prigge, *Die Materialität des Städtischen* (Basel: Birkhäuser, 1987) and *Urbanität und Intellektualität im 20. Jahrhundert. Wien 1900, Frankfurt, 1930, Paris, 1960* (Frankfurt and New York: Campus, 1996).

24. Rudolf M. Lüscher, *Einbruch in den Gewöhnlichen Ablauf der Ereignisse* (Zürich: Limmat, 1984); Roger Hartmann *et al., Theorien zur Stadtentwicklung* (Oldenburg: Geographische Hochschulmanuskripte, 1986); Hansruedi Hitz *et al.* eds., *Capitales Fatales: Urbanisierung und Politik in den Finanzmetropolen Frankfurt und Zürich* (Zürich: Rotpunkt, 1995); Christian Schmid, "The Dialectics of Urbanisation in Zurich: Global-City Formation and Urban Social Movements," in *Possible Urban Worlds: Urban Strategies at the End of the 20th Century,* ed. INURA (Basel: Birkhäuser, 1998), 216–25; "Raum und Regulation: Henri Lefebvre und der Regulationsansatz," in *Fit für den Postfordismus? Theoretisch-politischePerspektiven des Regulationsansatzes,* ed. U. Brand and W. Raza (Münster: Westfälisches Dampfboot, 2003), 217–42; and *Stadt, Raum und Gesellschaft: Henri Lefebvre und die Theorie der Produktion des Raumes* (München: Franz Steiner, 2005); Christian Schmid, "Theory," in *Switzerland – an Urban Portrait,* ed. R. Diener *et al.* (Basel: Birkhäuser, 2005), 163–222.

25. David Harvey, *Social Justice and the City* (Oxford: Basil Blackwell, 1988).

26. Michael Dear, *The Postmodern Urban Condition* (Oxford: Blackwell, 2000), 51, and "Les Aspects Postmodernes de Henri Lefebvre," *Espaces et Sociétés* 76 (1994): 34; Pierre Hamel and Claire Poitras, "Henri Lefebvre, penseur de la postmodernite," *Espaces et Sociétés* 76 (1994): 41–55; Michael Keith and Steve Pile, "Introduction Part 1" and "Introduction Part 2," in *Place and the Politics of Identity,* ed. M. Keith and S. Pile (London: Routledge, 1993), 24–5; Edward Soja and Barbara Hooper, "The Spaces that Difference Makes: Some Notes on the Geographical Margins of the New Cultural Politics," in *Place and the Politics of Identity,* 183–205; Barbara Hooper, "The Poem of Male Desires: Female Bodies, Modernity, and 'Paris Capital of the Nineteenth Century,'" in *Making the Invisible Visible,* ed. L. Sandercock (Berkeley: University of California Press, 1998), 230–1; Edward Soja, *Thirdspace: Journeys to Los Angeles and Other Real-and-Imagined Places* (Oxford: Basil Blackwell, 1996).

27. Mark Gottdiener, "A Marx for Our Time: Henri Lefebvre and the Production of Space," *Sociological Theory* 11, no. 1 (1993): 129–34; and *The Social Production of Urban Space* (Austin: University of Texas Press, 1985).

28. *The Urban Question: A Marxist Approach* (London: Edward Arnold, 1977), 86–94. Castells's early objections are one-sidedly echoed in Ira Katznelson's more recent *Marxism and the City* (Oxford: Clarendon, 1993), 101, 290, 306.

29. In the afterword to the 1975 edition of *The Urban Question* (438–65), and his after-marxist *City and the Grassroots* (Berkeley: UCLA Press, 1983), 15–6, 296.

30. Chris Pickvance, *Urban Sociology: Critical Essays* (London: Methuen, 1976); Michael Harloe ed., *Captive Cities* (London: Wiley, 1977).

31. For a fascinating interview with Perry Anderson on Harvey's contributions to marxism and geography, see David Harvey, "Reinventing Geography," *New Left Review* 4 (2000): 75–97.

32. Harvey, *Social Justice*, 73, 149–52, 303–12; *The Urbanization of Capital* (Oxford: Basil Blackwell, 1985), 62, 64, 82, 88; *The Urban Experience* (Oxford: Basil Blackwell,1989), 53–4, 177–8, 230.

33. Neil Smith, *Uneven Development: Nature, Capital and the Production of Space* (London: Basil Blackwell, 1984), 90–3, 100; Foreword in Henri Lefebvre, *The Urban Revolution*, trans. R. Bononno (Minneapolis: University of Minnesota Press, 2003), xix; "Space and Substance in Geography," in *Envisioning Human Geographies*, ed. P. Cloke, P. Crang, and M. Goodwin (New York: Edward Arnold, 2004), 11–29.

34. Henri Lefebvre, *La pensée marxiste et la ville* (Paris: Casterman, 1972), 70 (translated by Stefan Kipfer).

35. This is evident in influential debates on such crucial matters as uneven development, suburbanization, gentrification, public space, urban political ecology, scale, state, and imperialism. Within these debates, Lefebvre is occasionally deployed in a stimulating fashion. See Erik Swyngedouw, "The City as a Hybrid: On Nature, Society, and Cyborg Urbanization," *Capitalism, Nature, Socialism* 7, no. 2 (1996): 65–81; Neil Brenner, "Global, Fragmented, Hierarchical: Henri Lefebvre's Geographies of Globalization," *Public Culture* 10, no. 1 (1997): 137–69; and "The Urban Question as Scale Question: Reflections on Henri Lefebvre, Urban Theory and the Politics of Scale," *International Journal of Urban and Regional Research* 24, no. 2. (2000): 361–78; Don Mitchell, *The Right to the City: Social Justice and the Fight for Public Space* (New York: Guildford, 2003).

36. Noel Castree "On Theory's Subject and Subject's Theory: Harvey, Capital, and the Limits to Classical Marxism," *Environment and Planning D: Society and Space* 27 (1995): 269–97.

37. Harvey, *The Urban Experience*, 263. Lived space never becomes a central category in his work, despite later qualifications to his earlier determinist reading of Lefebvre's triad of the production of space. See for example *Justice, Nature, and the Geography of Difference* (Oxford: Basil Blackwell, 1996), 322; "Space as a Keyword," in *David Harvey: A Critical Reader*, ed. N. Castree and D. Gregory (New York: Routledge, 2006), 279.

38. Schmid, *Stadt*, 41.

39. Some of the harshest criticisms to which Harvey's *The Condition of Postmodernity* (Oxford: Basil Blackwell, 1989) was subjected during the heyday of postmodernism owe something to this derivative status of everyday life and difference in his work, although some of these critics overshot their target, following the temptations of the day, to attack marxism *in toto*; see Doreen Massey, "Flexible Sexism," *Environment and Planning D: Society and Space* 9, no. 1(1991): 31–57; Rosalyn Deutsche, *Eviction: Art and Spatial Politics* (Cambridge, MA: The MIT Press, 1996); Meaghan Morris, "The Man in the Mirror," *Theory, Culture, and Society* 9 (1992): 253–79. Harvey's response to these critics, which can be found in *Justice, Nature*, are not fully satisfactory. His limitations, most notoriously expressed in his recurrent tendency to reduce non-class movements to postmodern commodity culture, are noted clearly even by those feminists open to marxist projects: see Melissa Wright, "Differences that Matter," and Nancy Hartsock, "Globalization and Primitive Accumulation," in *David Harvey: A Critical Reader*, 80–101, 167–90.

40. Lefebvre, *Le manifeste différentialiste* (Paris: Gallimard, 1970); *The Production of Space*, trans. D. Nicholson-Smith (Oxford: Basil Blackwell, 1991); *Critique of Everyday Life, Volume III: From Modernity to Modernism (Towards a Metaphilosophy of Daily Life)*, trans. G. Elliott (London: Verso, 2005 [1981]).

41. Edward W. Soja, *Postmodern Geographies: The Reassertion of Space in Critical Social Theory* (London/New York: Verso, 1989), 47–50, 90–2.

42. Fredric Jameson, *Postmodernism, or, The Cultural Logic of Late Capitalism* (Durham, N.C.: Duke University Press, 1991), 418.

43. Soja, *Postmodern Geographies*, 3, 119, 127.

44. *Ibid.*, 69–71, 76–8, 81.

45. Kofman and Lebas, "Lost in Transposition."

46. Henri Lefebvre, *Rhythmanalysis: Space, Time, and Everyday Life*, trans. S. Elden and G. Moore (London: Continuum, 2004). A close accord with Lefebvre is evident in Guy Debord's forceful formulations on the spatialization of time in *The Society of the Spectacle*, trans. K. Knabb (Berkeley: Bureau of Public Secrets, 2002 [1967]). See <http://www.bopsecrets.org/SI/debord/>.

47. Henri Lefebvre, *Production of Space*, 96.

48. Benjamin, *Arcades Project*; E. P. Thompson, "Time, Work-Discipline and Industrial Capitalism," *Past and Present* 38 (1967): 56–97.

49. Alfred Schmidt, "Henri Lefebvre and Contemporary Interpretations of Marx," trans. J. Heckmann, in *The Unknown Dimension: European Marxism since Lenin*, ed. D. Howard and K. E. Klare (New York: Basic Books, 1972), 322–41.

50. Lefebvre, *Production of Space*, 83–5, 98, 278, 281.

51. Massey, "Flexible Sexism"; Deutsche, *Eviction*; Dear, *Postmodern Urban Condition*, ch. 3; Derek Gregory, *Geographical Imaginations* (Oxford and Cambridge: Basil Blackwell, 1994), 289; Soja, *Thirdspace*, 38.

52. *Ibid.*, 52.

53. Noting the recurrent use of conceptual triads in Lefebvre, Soja reifies them into "trialectics" (*sic*) of ontology (spatiality, historicity, sociality) and epistemology (first, second, third space) (*ibid.*, 70–3, 78–81). In Soja, Lefebvre's triad of the production of space is transformed into an "epistemological trialectics" of objectivist (first), subjectivist (second), and lived (third) space. This overlooks that, for Lefebvre, the third term in a triad is not an expression of trialectics but a product of three-dimensional dialectical transformation (Lefebvre, "Twelve Theses on Logic and Dialectic," *Key Writings*, 58; Schmid, this volume).

54. Homi Bhabha, *The Location of Culture* (London: Routledge, 1994), 36–7, 50.

55. *Ibid.*, 12–14, 56, 57. This simultaneity Soja found in the "bubbly, postmodern complexity" of Southern California's Orange County (*Thirdspace*, 247).

56. Henri Lefebvre, *Writings on Cities*, 222; see also Nadal-Melsió, this volume.

57. Kofman and Lebas, "Lost in Transposition," 44.

58. See Martin Jay, *Marxism and Totality: The Adventures of a Concept from Lukács to Habermas* (Berkeley: University of California Press, 1984); Robert Albritton, *Dialectics and Deconstruction in Political Economy* (New York: St. Martin's Press, 1999); Perry Anderson, *Tracks*.

59. See, above all, Norbert Guterman and Henri Lefebvre, *La conscience mystifiée* (Paris: Syllepse, 1999); Henri Lefebvre, *Dialectical Materialism*, trans. J. Sturrock (London: Jonathan Cape, 1968); *La somme et le reste* (Paris: Bélibaste, 1973), and *Métaphilosophie* (Paris: Syllepse, 1997).

60. McNally, *Bodies of Meaning*; see also Fredric Jameson, *The Prison-House of Language* (Princeton: Princeton University Press, 1972).

61. For his multifaceted foray into linguistic theory and his critique of structuralism, see Henri Lefebvre, *Le langage et la société* (Paris: Gallimard, 1966); *L'idéologie structuraliste* (Paris: Anthropos, 1971); *Au-delà du structuralisme* (Paris: Anthropos, 1971); *Introduction to Modernity*, trans. J. Moore (London: Verso, 1995); and *Everyday Life in the Modern World*, trans. S. Rabinovitch (Harmondsworth: Penguin, 1971). As a consequence, attempts to integrate Lefebvre with Lacan's linguistically inflected psychoanalysis are recognized to lead to failure: Schmid, *Stadt*, 241–3; see also Derek Gregory, "Lefebvre, Lacan, and the Production of Space," in *Geography, History, and Social Sciences*, ed. G. Benko and U. Strohmayer (New York: Kluwer, 1995), 15–44; Virginia Blum and Heidi Nast, "Where's the Difference? The Heterosexualization of Alterity in Henri Lefebvre and Jacques Lacan," *Environment and Planning D: Society and Space* 14 (1996): 559–80; Steve Pile, *The Body and the City* (London: Routledge, 1996).

62. Henri Lefebvre, *Nietzsche* (Paris: Syllepse, 2003); *La somme et la reste; Métaphilosophie, Hegel, Marx, Nietzsche ou le royaume des ombres* (Paris: Castermann, 1975). Lefebvre does not properly understand the seductive and dangerous character of Nietzsche's style: see in this regard Geoff Waite, *Nietzsche's Corps/e: Aesthetics, Politics, Prophecy, or, The Spectacular Technoculture of Everyday Life* (Durham, N.C.: Duke University Press, 1996).

63. Michel Trebitsch, "Préface: Henri Lefebvre et le Don Juan de la Connaissance," in Lefebvre, *Nietzsche*, 5–21.

64. Lefebvre, *Critique*, III, 122; *Production of Space*, 10; see also Lynn Stewart, "Bodies, Visions, and Spatial Politics: A Review Essay on Henri Lefebvre's *The Production of Space*," *Environment and Planning D: Society and Space* 13 (1995): 609–18

65. Perry Anderson credits Lefebvre as one of the key resources for Jameson in the formulation of *his* concept of postmodernism, especially with respect to "urban space," while noting perceptively that in general he and Gramsci are conspicuous by their absence in the latter's formidable appropriation and extension of Western Marxism: see *The Origins of Postmodernity* (London: Verso, 1998), 69–71. Lefebvre does not fare better in Anderson's own original survey, however: see *Considerations of Western Marxism* (London: Verso, 1976), 27, 37, 63.

66. Fredric Jameson, *Marxism and Form: Twentieth Century Dialectical Theories of Literature* (Princeton: Princeton University Press, 1971); and *The Political Unconscious: Narrative as a Socially Symbolic Act* (Ithaca: Cornell University Press, 1981). In the former, Lefebvre finds a cameo role for his musings on Pascal and Rabelais.

67. Terry Eagleton, *The Ideology of the Aesthetic* (Oxford: Blackwell, 1990); *Marxism and Literary Criticism* (London: Routledge, 1976); and *Ideology: An Introduction* (London: Verso, 1991).

68. Martin Jay, *Marxism and Totality*, 276–99. A brief comment on Lefebvre's and Guy Debord's shared critiques of the *spectacle* appears in his *Downcast Eyes: The Denigration of Vision in Twentieth-Century French Thought* (Berkeley: University of California Press, 1993), 418–20.

69. George Lichtheim, *Marxism in Modern France* (New York and London: Columbia Unversity Press, 1967); Leszek Kolakowski, *Main Currents of Marxism: Its Origin, Growth and Dissolution, Volume III: The Breakdown* (Oxford: Clarendon, 1978), 176–7, 481–2; Russell Jacoby, *Dialectic of Defeat: Contours of Western Marxism* (Cambridge: Cambridge University Press, 1981), 109; Roger Gottlieb, "Introduction," in *An Anthology of Western Marxism: From Lukàcs to Gramcsi to Socialist-Feminism* (Oxford: Oxford University

Press, 1989); Bertell Ollman, "Review of Henri Lefebvre's Sociology of Marx," in *Social and Sexual Revolution: Essays on Marx and Reich* (Montreal: Black Rose, 1978); Alastair Davidson, "Henri Lefebvre" (Obituary), *Thesis Eleven* 31 (1992); Tony Judt, *Marxism and the French Left* (Oxford: Clarendon, 1982), 179–80, 188–9; Keith Reader, *Intellectuals and the Left in France since 1968* (Basingstoke: Macmillan, 1987), 53–6.

70. Lefebvre is not mentioned in Vincent Descombes's *Modern French Philosophy*, trans. L. Scott-Fox and J. M. Harding (Cambridge: Cambridge University Press, 1991), nor in Eric Matthews, *Twentieth Century French Philosophy* (Oxford: Oxford University Press, 1996).

71. Kolakowski, *Main Currents*, 176; Kevin Anderson, *Lenin, Hegel and Western Marxism: A Critical Study* (Chicago: University of Illinois Press, 1995), 190; for deplorable examples, see Henri Lefebvre, *L'Existentialisme*, 2nd edn (Paris: Anthropos, 1946) and "Auto-critique: contribution à l'effort d'éclaircissement idéologique," *La Nouvelle Critique* 1, no. 4 (March 1949): 51.

72. Alfred Schmidt, "Henri Lefebvre."

73. Michael Kelly, *Modern French Marxism* (Baltimore: Johns Hopkins University Press, 1982).

74. Bud Burkhard, *French Marxism between the Wars: Henri Lefebvre and the "Philosophies"* (New York: Humanity, 2000).

75. *Ibid.*, especially 186–97, 211–16.

76. Mark Poster, *Existential Marxism in Postwar France: From Sartre to Althusser* (Princeton: Princeton University Press, 1975), 238–60. Some similar ground is covered in Shields, *Lefebvre*, ch. 7.

77. This is also a key theme in the Lefebvre chapter in Arthur Hirsh's *The French Left* (Montreal: Black Rose, 1982).

78. Lefebvre's critique is also taken up in Steven B. Smith, *Reading Althusser: An Essay on Structural Marxism* (Ithaca: Cornell University Press, 1984); Edith Kurzweil, *The Age of Structuralism: Lévy-Strauss to Foucault* (New York: Columbia University Press, 1980); and William Lewis, *Louis Althusser and the Tradition of French Marxism* (Lanham: Lexington Books, 2005).

79. For sociologically inspired examples, see Michael E. Gardiner, *Critiques of Everyday Life* (New York: Routledge, 2000) and Ben Highmore, *Everyday Life and Cultural Theory* (London: Routledge, 2002). From this, Highmore has proposed a very suggestive urban application of Lefebvre's rhythmanalysis in *Cityscapes: Cultural Readings in the Material and Symbolic City* (New York: Palgrave, 2005).

80. John Roberts, *Philosophizing the Everyday: Revolutionary Praxis and the Fate of Cultural Theory* (London: Pluto, 2006).

81. Harry Harootunian, *History's Disquiet: Modernity, Cultural Practice and the Question of Everyday Life* (New York: Columbia University Press, 2000).

82. Peter Osborne, *The Politics of Time: Modernity and Avant-Garde* (London: Verso, 1995).

83. Kristin Ross, *Fast Cars, Clean Bodies: Decolonization and the Reordering of French Culture* (Cambridge, MA: The MIT Press, 1995), 157–96; see also "French Quotidian," in *The Art of the Everyday: The Quotidian in Postwar French Culture*, ed. L. Gumpert (New York: New York University Press, 1997), 19–29.

84. Kirstin Ross, *The Emergence of Social Space: Rimbaud and the Paris Commune*, foreword by Terry Eagleton (Minneapolis: University of Minnesota, Press, 1988).

85. Merrifield, *Henri Lefebvre*; see also his *Metromarxism: A Marxist Tale of the City* (London: Routledge, 2002).

86. We would like to mention in particular the works by Neil Brenner, Stuart Elden, Mark Gottdiener, Harry Harootunian, Eleonore Kofman, Elizabeth Lebas, Eugene McCann, Don Mitchell, Peter Osborne, Mark Poster, Walter Prigge, John Roberts, Hajo Schmidt, Lynn Stewart, and Erik Swyngedouw.

87. See also the monograph Schmid, *Stadt*.

88. See Prigge, *Die Materialität*.

89. Elden, *Understanding*.

90. Waite, *Nietzsche's Corps/e*.

91. Theodor Adorno, *The Jargon of Authenticity*, trans. T. Schroyer (Chicago: Northwestern University Press, 1973). See: <http://links.jstor.org/sici?sici=0010-4124(199222)44%3A3%3C327%3ATEOSSR%3E2.0.CO%3B2-1>.

92. Anatole Kopp, *Town and Revolution: Soviet Architecture and City Planning 1917–1935*, trans. T. E. Burton (New York: George Braziller, 1970); Mary McCleod, "Henri Lefebvre's Critique of Everyday Life," in *Architecture of the Everyday*, ed. S. Harris and D. Berke (New York: Princeton Architectural Press, 1997), 9–29; Simon Sadler, *The Situationist City* (Cambridge, MA: The MIT Press, 1999); Eleonore Kofman and Elizabeth Lebas, "Recovery and Reappropriation," in *Non-Plan: Essays on Freedom, Participation and Change in Modern Architecture and Urbanism*, ed. J. Hughes and S. Sadler (Oxford: Architectural Press, 2000), 80–9.

93. Neil Brenner, *New State Spaces: Urban Governance and the Rescaling of Statehood* (Oxford: Oxford University Press, 2004).

94. Lefebvre's critique of everyday life was refracted through an analysis of multiple lines segregating workers, students, women, and immigrant workers. It remained seriously undertheorized with respect to particular social relations (not only gender, race, and sexuality but class), however. See Eugene McCann, "Race, Protest, and Public Space: Contextualizing Lefebvre in the US City," *Antipode* 31, no. 2 (1999): 163–84; Blum and Nast, "Where's the Difference?"

PART I

DIALECTICS OF SPACE AND TIME

2

HENRI LEFEBVRE'S THEORY OF THE PRODUCTION OF SPACE

Towards a three-dimensional dialectic

Christian Schmid
(translated by Bandulasena Goonewardena)

THE PRODUCTION OF SPACE

Lefebvre's theory of the production of space has undergone a remarkable renaissance during recent years. This is all the more surprising as it had hardly elicited any response when published in the early 1970s. Although Lefebvre's texts on Marxism, on everyday life, and on the city were widely read at the time, his reflections on space aroused little interest. The problematic of space did not as yet figure on the theoretical agenda. But today, Lefebvre's book *The Production of Space* is routinely quoted. The "spatial turn" has taken hold of the social sciences and questions of space are accorded a great deal of attention, extending beyond geography. In essence, this is linked with the combined processes of urbanization and globalization: at every scale new geographies have developed. These new space–time configurations determining our world call for new concepts of space corresponding to contemporary social conditions.

Lefebvre's theory of the production of space seems highly attractive in this context. Its significance lies especially in the fact that it systematically integrates the categories of *city* and *space* in a single, comprehensive social theory, enabling the understanding and analysis of spatial processes at different levels. Yet, the extensive reception accorded to Lefebvre's theory has by no means made full use of these categories. Above all, its postmodern reformulation and monopolization has contributed to a great deal of confusion. This necessitates a reconstruction of the theory of the production of space that in particular would also include context. What follows intends to clarify the formative elements of its basic structure and to lay bare the fundamentals of Lefebvre's epistemology, based on a comprehensive analysis and reconstruction of his theory of the production of space.[1]

The analysis shows that, above all, three hitherto neglected aspects are crucial to an understanding of Lefebvre's theory. First, a specific concept of dialectics that can be considered as his original contribution. In the course of his extensive oeuvre Lefebvre developed a version of dialectics that was in every respect original and independent. It is not binary but triadic, based on the trio of Hegel, Marx, and Nietzsche. This has not been properly grasped as yet and has led to considerable misunderstanding. The second determining factor is language theory. The fact that Lefebvre developed a theory of language of his own[2] while leaning on Nietzsche was hardly ever considered in the reception and interpretation of his works, the linguistic turn notwithstanding. It was here that he also for the first time realized and applied his triadic dialectic concretely. The third crucial element is French phenomenology. While Heidegger's influence on Lefebvre's work has already been discussed in detail (see Elden and Waite in this volume), the contribution of the French phenomenologists Maurice Merleau-Ponty and Gaston Bachelard has, for the most part, not received due consideration. These three neglected aspects could contribute decisively to a better understanding of Lefebvre's work and to a fuller appreciation of his important and path-breaking theory of the production of space.

A RELATIONAL CONCEPTION OF SPACE AND TIME

The concept of producing space was still unusual at the time when Lefebvre developed his theory. Today this proposition almost seems an empty formula. It has been quoted so often that its meaning has been eroded beyond recognition. Yet this formulation and its implications should be taken seriously since they signal a paradigmatic change in the sociological conception of space and time.

(Social) space is a (social) product; in order to understand this fundamental thesis it is necessary, first of all, to break with the widespread understanding of space imagined as an independent material reality existing "in itself." Against such a view, Lefebvre, using the concept of the *production of space*, posits a theory that understands *space* as fundamentally bound up with social reality. It follows that space "in itself" can never serve as an epistemological starting position. Space does not exist "in itself"; it is produced.

But how is one to grasp this social space? As in most contemporary theories of space,[3] Lefebvre proceeds from a relational concept of space and time. *Space* stands for simultaneity, the synchronic order of social reality; *time*, on the other hand, denotes the diachronic order and thus the historic process of social production. *Society* here signifies neither a spatial-temporal totality of "bodies" or "matter" nor a sum total of actions and practices. Central to Lefebvre's materialist theory are human beings in their corporeality and sensuousness, with their sensitivity and imagination, their thinking and their ideologies; human beings who enter into relationships with each other through their activity and practice.

Lefebvre constructs his theory of the production of social space and social time on these assumptions. According to this understanding, space and time are not purely material factors. Neither can they be reduced to the status of pure, a priori concepts. They are understood as being integral aspects of social practice. Lefebvre sees them as social products; consequently, they are both result and precondition of the production of society.

Accordingly, space and time do not exist universally. As they are socially produced, they can only be understood in the context of a specific society. In this sense, space and time are not only relational but fundamentally historical. This calls for an analysis that would include the social constellations, power relations, and conflicts relevant in each situation.

How is (social) space produced? Key to Lefebvre's theory is the view that the production of space can be divided into three dialectically interconnected dimensions or processes. Lefebvre also calls them formants or moments of the production of space. They are doubly determined and correspondingly doubly designated. On the one hand, they refer to the triad of "spatial practice," "representations of space," and "spaces of representation." On the other, they refer to "perceived," "conceived," and "lived" space. This parallel series points to a twofold approach to space: one phenomenological and the other linguistic or semiotic.

In Lefebvre's work, however, these three dimensions exist in a state of uncertainty. Faithful to his epistemological premises, Lefebvre introduces them first as approximations. He explores their range of validity and modifies them in the course of his theoretical excursions. There followed then in the reception of the theory a near-total confusion of opinion about these three dimensions. The discussion ranged over all aspects of the three dimensions: their status, their inner construction, and their interconnections. Mere references to passages in the texts to define these dimensions, however, are insufficient. The meaning of the three dimensions becomes clear only in the overall context of the theory, and can be reconstructed only out of Lefebvre's entire work. In order to understand them, one has to begin with the dialectic.

DIALECTICAL THINKING

What does dialectical thinking mean? First of all, it means the recognition that social reality is marked by contradictions and can be understood only through the comprehension of these contradictions.

At the core of the dialectic lies a concept whose deeper meaning emerges only in German: *das Aufheben des Widerspruchs* (sublation of the contradiction). *Aufheben* signifies, on the one hand, negation and overcoming; on the other hand, preservation and placing on a higher level. This ambiguity is completely lost in most translations: for example, in the French (*dépasser*) or English ("transcend" or "sublate").

On the concept of *Aufheben*, Lefebvre writes: "It is obvious that this concept does not have that simplicity, that clarity and refinement which Cartesian thinking leads one to look for in concepts. What do we find at the origin of this essential concept? A word play, an untranslatable pun, nothing formal and perhaps also nothing that could be formalized in a perfectly coherent discourse."[4]

Hegel used the concept *Aufheben* precisely on account of its dazzling polysemy:

> "*To sublate*" has a twofold meaning in the language: on the one hand it means to preserve, to maintain, and equally it also means to cause to cease, to put an end to. Even "to preserve" includes a negative element, namely, that something is removed from its immediacy and so from an existence which is open to external influences, in order to preserve it. Thus what is sublated is at the same time preserved; it has only lost its immediacy but is not on that account annihilated. The two definitions of "to sublate" which we have given can be quoted as two dictionary *meanings* of this word. But it is certainly remarkable to find that a language has come to use one and the same word for two opposite meanings. It is a delight to speculative thought to find in the language words which have in themselves a speculative meaning; the German language has a number of such . . . Something is sublated only in so far as it has entered into unity with its opposite; in this more particular signification as something reflected, it may fittingly be called a *moment*.[5]

As opposed to bivalent or formal logic, in dialectics no construction of unequivocal relationships and rules of logical association of the truth and falsehood of propositions is possible. Where formal logic says: "No proposition can simultaneously both be true and false," the dialectician Lefebvre maintains: "If we consider the content, if there is a content, an isolated proposition is neither true nor false; every isolated proposition must be transcended; every proposition with a real content is both true and false, true if it is transcended, false if it is asserted as absolute."[6] This quotation is the key to Lefebvre's famous rhetorical figure of speech in which he answers a self-addressed question with "yes" *and* "no."

In Lefebvre's opinion a contradiction when sublated does not reach its true final state or destination but its transformation—it is overcome, but at the same time also preserved and further developed in keeping with this twofold determination.[7] Thus, sublation in this radical sense does not mean at all finding a higher, so to speak, ultimate truth. The contradiction tends towards its resolution, yet since the resolution does not simply negate the old contradiction, it also simultaneously preserves it and brings it to a higher level. Therefore, the resolution bears in it the germ of the new contradiction. This understanding of the dialectic is characterized by a deep historical and dynamic interpretation of development and history. Lefebvre remarks: "Movement is thus a transcending."[8] This could just as well be read in reverse: transcending (sublation) means (historical) movement.

But Lefebvre does not stop there. Read materialistically, the concept of sublation denotes an act(ion), a creative activity, not so much a *real* but much more a *realization*: a becoming. Between the two determinations, the negation and the conservation, lies, according to Lefebvre, the indefinite, the opening: the possibility of realizing, through an action, the project. Logical and analytical reason, coherent, strictly formal discourse, cannot capture the becoming, the movement of the sublation in the creative act. "We would like to say that the 'concept' of sublation points to that which, in living (productive, creative) activity, cannot be grasped through the concept itself. Why not? Because this creative force just cannot be fully defined, cannot be exhaustively determined." In the sublation there is always a risk, a possible failure, and at the same time a possibility—a promise.[9]

These passages demonstrate clearly that Lefebvre's dialectic has extremely different sources. These lines voice the thinking not only of Hegel and Marx but—above all—of Nietzsche.

THE GERMAN DIALECTIC: HEGEL, MARX, AND NIETZSCHE

In the course of his lengthy creative endeavor Lefebvre worked out a highly original version of the dialectic based on his sustained critical engagement with Hegel, Marx, and Nietzsche, three German thinkers who have been by far the most influential in shaping his theory.

Here it is not possible to present even a partly "valid" exposition of Lefebvre's dialectic, all the more so since he has modified his position time and again, enriching it with new facets. His acquaintance with the dialectic dates back to his days as a young philosophy student. The essential elements of Lefebvre's early dialectics are already spelt out in *La conscience mystifiée*. *Dialectical Marxism* presents a broader discussion of Hegel's dialectic and its critique by Marx. Finally, a detailed and extremely sophisticated formulation is found in *Logique formelle, logique dialectique*, planned as the first volume and introduction of a highly ambitious eight-volume series on dialectical materialism. The next important stage is *Métaphilosophie*. There Lefebvre works out a radical critique of philosophy oriented to Nietzsche, articulating at the same time a new triadic dialectic. The most important realization and application of this new dialectic finds its expression in *The Production of Space*. However, it is fully worked out only in later studies, particularly in *Le petour de la dialectique*.[10]

Following the Hegelian dialectic, Lefebvre's dialectic begins at the level of the *concept*: the identity of a term can be grasped only in relation to other terms and thus to its own negation. Positing an object, therefore, means also always positing its opposite: that is, the term acquires its identity only from its dialectical relationship to its opposite. A third term emerges thereby that both negates and embodies the other two. The positing of a term thus initiates a self-movement of the term that can be summarized in the well-known figure: affirmation, negation, negation-of-the-negation. The first posited term, the affirmation, also contains in itself its negation that negates and at the same time completes it. Based on their inner connection, the two terms exert a reciprocal influence on each other and produce a third term in which the first term reappears more closely defined and enriched, and also the second whose definition joins the first. The third term turns against the first by negating the second and thus redeems the content of the first term by overcoming what was incomplete and limited in it—destined to be negated.[11]

Lefebvre criticizes this Hegelian dialectic on two grounds. First, he rejects its idealistic conception. For Hegel, dialectical movement takes place in the concept and thus only in thought. Lefebvre's critique points out that this dialectic cannot be applied to reality. Yet the contradictory nature of life is not imagined but real. Consequently, it is most important to grasp real life in all its contradictions. Hence Lefebvre follows Marx who had "stood" Hegel's dialectic "on its feet" and gave precedence not to the idea but to the material process of social production.

Lefebvre's second critique relates to the dialectical "system" constructed by Hegel: in systematizing philosophy Hegel arrests the flow of time, declares the process of "becoming" closed, thus shattering his own most valuable approach. This line of thought hinders the liberation of man because it tends to dominate practice and thereby allies itself with power, even becoming power itself. This critique of practical power and the force of abstraction—of thinking, of writing, and of language—is a *leitmotiv* that runs through the whole of Lefebvre's work. It also forms the basis of his biting, often furious attacks on contemporary philosophy and science, and, in his later works, on planning and architecture.

Against the deadly power of the sign Lefebvre, following Nietzsche, posits the metamorphosis of the sign: *poesy*. In Lefebvre's view, the work of art alone is the unity of the finite and the infinite, endlessly determined and living.[12] In the course of a struggle that overcomes the contradiction between work and play the poet rescues the word from death—a struggle that is just as dreadful as the shaky terrain on which it is fought out. Here Lefebvre's concern is not highbrow art but everyday art, the poetry of daily life, the art of life: "In this way, Marxist rationality joins with Nietzschean thought in the justification of becoming."[13]

Through his adoption of the "German dialectic" Lefebvre attains a renewed, three-dimensional dialectic that has no parallel in philosophy and the history of knowledge. Lefebvre himself describes his dialectic as a radical critique of Hegel based on Marx's social practice and Nietzsche's art.[14] At a general level, the fundamental dialectical figure in Lefebvre's work can be understood as the contradiction between social thought and social action, supplemented by the third factor of the creative, poetic act.

A THREE-DIMENSIONAL DIALECTIC

Thus Lefebvre develops a three-dimensional figure of social reality. Material social practice taken as the starting point of life and of analysis constitutes the first moment. It stands in contradiction to the second moment: knowledge, language, and the written word, understood by Lefebvre as abstraction and as concrete power, and as compulsion or constraint. The third moment involves poesy and desire as forms of transcendence that help becoming prevail over death. Lefebvre, however, does not stop at this sublation in transcendence and poesy. He does not drift into metaphysics but returns again to practice and activity. In this way a three-dimensional dialectical figure emerges, wherein the three moments are dialectically interconnected: material social practice (Marx); language and thought (Hegel); and the creative, poetic act (Nietzsche).

It is of decisive importance that with this three-dimensional figure the nature of the dialectic has fundamentally altered. Whereas the Hegelian (and also the Marxian) dialectic rests on two terms in contradiction with each other that are sublated through a third term, Lefebvre's triadic dialectic posits three terms. Each of these can be understood as a thesis and each one refers to the other two and would remain a mere abstraction without the others. This triadic figure does not end in a synthesis as in the Hegelian system. It links three moments that are left distinct from each other, without reconciling them in a synthesis—three moments that exist in interaction, in conflict or in alliance with each other.[15] Thus the three terms or moments assume equal importance, and each takes up a similar position in relation to the others. In this way a new, three-dimensional or triadic version of the dialectic emerges.

It was only in his late works that Lefebvre explicitly defined this three-dimensional dialectic.[16] According to him, its development was to some extent subterranean for a long time and emerged fully only later.[17] He considers this basic three-dimensional figure a further development of the dialectic that he compares with its famous predecessors, the Hegelian dialectic and the Marxian dialectic. According to Lefebvre, the Hegelian triad of "thesis–antithesis–synthesis," purported to construe the process of becoming, is an illusion since it constructed only a representation. In contrast to this, the Marxian triad of "affirmation–negation–negation-of-the-negation" claimed to produce the process of becoming but has not redeemed this ambitious claim. It would seem that in historical time there have not been so many deep chasms, surprises, and unbridgeable gaps as there have been bifurcations, about-turns, and detours that this dialectic could not comprehend. In contrast Lefebvre advances his own version of the dialectic, the "triadic" or the "ternary," that is three-valued analysis. It posits three moments of equal value that relate to each other in varying relationships and complex movements wherein now one, now the other prevails against the negation of one or the other. Lefebvre's claim is no longer the construal of becoming, not even the production of becoming, but the analysis of becoming. His analytical method enables the discovery or recognition of a meaning; a horizon of becoming— of possibilities, uncertainties, chances. And it permits the formulation of a strategy— without the certainty of achieving the aim.[18]

The idea that this could be a "spatial dialectic"[19] is nevertheless misleading. It is rather a general principle applied by Lefebvre to very different fields. Thus the triad form–structure–function, for example, appears repeatedly in various passages of his work. In his theory of language, he follows this triadic principle and differentiates carefully between a paradigmatic, a syntactic, and a symbolic dimension of language (see below). In *Rhythmanalysis* the triad reads: melody–harmony–rhythm.[20] In *La présence et l'absence* he questions: "Is there ever a relationship between two terms, except in representation? They are always three. There is always the other."[21] And then he adds a list of triads that relate to the most varied aspects of reality. Finally mention should be made of Lefebvre's fundamental triadic unity of the space–time conception: space–time–energy.[22]

THEORY OF LANGUAGE

The first detailed application of this three-dimensional principle occurs in *Le langage et la société*, published in 1966. Here Lefebvre develops his own Nietzsche-oriented theory of language, which in many respects breaks with the basic premises of contemporary semiotics. With its three-dimensional construction, this forms a kind of preliminary stage in the theory of the production of space, even if Lefebvre does not explicitly refer to it.

The point of departure of Lefebvre's theory of language is Nietzsche's poetics, especially his text "On Truth and Lie in an Extra-Moral Sense," published in 1873.[23] Lefebvre holds that Nietzsche alone posed the problem of language correctly in proceeding from the actually spoken word and not from a model, and by linking, from the very beginning, meaning with values and knowledge with power. Lefebvre refers especially to the classical concept of metonymy and metaphor that took on a radical meaning in Nietzsche's work. Words here go beyond the immediate, the sensuous, the chaos of impressions and feelings. They replace this chaos with an image or a spoken representation, a word, and thereby a metamorphosis. The words of a language thus give us possession only of metaphors of things, and concepts grow out of an identification of the non-identical, and therewith, of a metonymy.[24] Nietzsche wrote: "We think we know something of the things themselves, when we speak of trees, colors, snow and flowers, and yet possess nothing but metaphors of things, which do not by any means corresond to their original essence."[25] For Nietzsche, "every word immediately becomes a concept, not in having to serve as a reminder of the unique and fully individualized original experience to which it owes its birth, but in having simultaneously to fit innumerable more or less similar cases, that is, strictly speaking never equal, thus altogether unequal ones. Every concept comes into being by equalizing the unequal."[26] What, then, is language? Lefebvre answers with Nietzsche's definition of truth: "What, then, is truth? A mobile army of metaphors, metonyms, anthropomorphisms, in short, a sum of human relations that have been poetically and rhetorically heightened, transposed, and embellished, and which seem to a people, after a long usage, fixed, canonical and binding."[27] Lefebvre, then, views metaphor and metonymy in the original sense as acts that become rhetorical figures only through use. Accordingly, he understands society as a space and an architecture of concepts, forms, and rules whose abstract truth prevails over the reality of the senses, of the body, of wishes, and of desires.[28]

Starting from such considerations Lefebvre develops a theory of the three-dimensionality of language in his *Le langage et la société*. The first, the *syntactic or syntagmatic dimension*, is here, so to speak, the classic dimension of linguistics and grammar. It deals with the formal rules of combination that determine the relationship between the signs, their possible combinations, sentence structure, and syntax.[29]

Lefebvre differentiates in addition a paradigmatic dimension. This concept refers to Roman Jakobson, who developed a two-dimensional theory of language, distinguishing between two kinds of classification of a linguistic sign.[30] The first is the combination or the context; every sign consists of a combination of signs or appears in combination with other signs. Every linguistic unit therefore serves as a context for simpler units or occurs in the context of more complex units. This first classification of the sign that corresponds to a metonymic process can be assigned to the syntagmatic dimension. Jakobson then differentiated a second linguistic operation: selection or substitution. This operation implies the possibility of substituting one term for another that is equivalent to the first from one point of view and different from it when viewed from another angle. This second classification of the sign corresponds to a metaphorical process and relates to a code, a system of meanings: paradigms. Lefebvre terms this dimension, accordingly, the *paradigmatic dimension*.

Finally, Lefebvre adds a third dimension to these two: the *symbolic dimension*. As he himself admits, the concept of the symbol is confusing here, since various meanings can be attributed to it. On the one hand, it denotes the formalized sign of mathematics; on the other, it is also charged with images, emotions, affectivity, and connotations. Lefebvre is aiming at precisely this second meaning of the symbol: that is, its substantiality, its ambiguities, and its complexity that are integral to the lived and living language. Even philosophy has not succeeded, in his view, in dispensing with images and symbols and, therefore, with poesy, although it has committed itself to discursive rigor. Thus, even within philosophy there are ambiguities and misunderstandings, "a happy ambiguity, the chance of a misunderstanding. That discourse proceeds from the master to the pupil happens not in *spite of* but *on the basis of* these ambiguities and misunderstandings: on the basis of spoken words which underpin discourse, and of images or symbols which lend force to the concepts."[31]

Hence, Lefebvre does not by any means intend lapsing into irrationality and mysticism. On the contrary, he wants to investigate the instinctive, the emotional, and the "irrational" as social facts. It is only in this sense that he intends taking up the symbol again: in its significance for human beings in a given society. The symbol thus enters into social structures and ideologies and serves as a pillar for allegory and fetish. It constitutes the basis of the social imaginary that is different from the individual imaginary. Consequently, there is also a clear distinction between the philosophical function of the imaginary and the social function of the symbol. That symbols are inexhaustible is for Lefebvre of decisive significance here. Accordingly, their formalization is not possible.[32]

LANGUAGE AND SPACE

The application of this schema to *space* would now seem literally obvious. Thus, Lefebvre postulates repeatedly that activity in space establishes a system that corresponds to the system of words up to a certain point.[33] From this perspective the three-dimensional analysis of spatial production appears as follows:

- *Spatial practice*: this concept designates the material dimension of social activity and interaction. The classification *spatial* means focusing on the aspect of simultaneity of activities. Spatial practice, in analogy to the syntagmatic dimension of language, denotes the system resulting from articulation and connection of elements or activities. In concrete terms, one could think of networks of inter-action and communication as they arise in everyday life (e.g., daily connection of residence and workplace) or in the production process (production and exchange relations).

- *The representation of space*: representations of space give an image and thus also define a space. Analogous to the paradigmatic dimension of language, one spatial representation can be substituted by another that shows similarities in some respects but differences in others. Representations of space emerge at the level of discourse, of speech as such, and therefore comprise verbalized forms such as descriptions, definitions, and especially (scientific) theories of space. Furthermore, Lefebvre counts maps and plans, information in pictures, and signs among representations of space. The specialized disciplines dealing with the production of these representations are architecture and planning, but also the social sciences (and here of special importance is geography).

- *Spaces of representation*: the third dimension of the production of space is defined by Lefebvre as the (terminological) inversion of "representations of space."[34] This concerns the symbolic dimension of space. According to this, spaces of representation do not refer to the spaces themselves but to something else: a divine power, the logos, the state, masculine or feminine principle, and so on. This dimension of the production of space refers to the process of signification that links itself to a (material) symbol. The symbols of space could be taken from nature, such as trees or prominent topographical formations; or they could be artifacts, buildings, and monuments; they could also develop out of a combination of both, for example as "landscapes."

According to this schema, (social) space can be analyzed in relation to these three dimensions. In the first, social space appears in the dimension of spatial practice as an interlinking chain or network of activities or interactions which on their part rest upon a determinate material basis (morphology, built environment). In the second, this spatial practice can be linguistically defined and demarcated as space and then constitutes a representation of space. This representation serves as an organizing schema or a frame of reference for communication, which permits a (spatial) orientation and thus co-determines activity at the same time. In the third, the material "order" that emerges on the ground can itself become the vehicle conveying meaning. In this way a (spatial) symbolism develops that expresses and evokes social norms, values, and experiences.

PHENOMENOLOGY

If Lefebvre's theory of language is seen as one source of the theory of the production of space, the other source can be located in phenomenology. The phenomenological reference points also become clear in the basic terms: the perceived, the conceived, and the lived.

Perception is a central concept of phenomenology. How does a subject perceive an image, a landscape, a monument? Evidently perception depends upon the subject: a peasant does not see "his" landscape in the same way as a city-dweller enjoying a walk there.[35] Nevertheless, Lefebvre's attitude towards the phenomenological version of perception is quite skeptical. Therefore, he combines it with the concept of spatial practice in order to show that perception not only takes place in the mind but is based on a concrete, produced materiality.[36]

The concept of the lived (le vécu) too reveals a phenomenological point of reference. Lefebvre thinks that the lived cannot be understood historically without the conceived. According to his understanding, the separation of the conceived from the lived occurred first in Western philosophy. This is how the basic contradiction between living and thinking arose, between "vécu" and "conçu." Rob Shields asserts, without any reference, that Lefebvre adopted the "central dualism" between lived and conceived from Nietzsche and Spinoza.[37] However, Lefebvre himself relates the concept of the lived to phenomenology and existentialism, especially to Jean-Paul Sartre. In Métaphilosophie he regards the lived as the philosophical term for everydayness (la quotidienneté).[38]

Even the interlinking of the lived with space, and so the concept of lived space, was not created by Lefebvre. The problem of lived space was taken up at the beginning of the 1930s, not least on account of observations of anomalies of spatial experience in psychiatry, under hypnosis and the consumption of psychedelic substances.[39]

Descriptive phenomenology was of greater importance for Lefebvre, however. In Phenomenology of Perception, published 1945,[40] Maurice Merleau-Ponty had developed a theory grounded on the basic concepts: "space," "time," and "lived world" (monde vécu). Already explicit here is the difference between a lived world and a perceived world; as well as the thought that, on the one hand, science refers to an experience of the world (and so the lived world) without which the symbols of science would have no meaning and that, on the other hand, science is a determination and an explication of the perceived world. Correspondingly, Merleau-Ponty distinguishes a physical space constructed by perception, a geometrical space conceptually comprehended, and, finally, a lived space (espace vécu): the mythical space, the space of dreams, of schizophrenia, and of art. This space is based on the relationship of the subject to his or her world and is embodied in the corporeality of this subject.[41]

Nevertheless, Lefebvre's theory is grounded much more in Heidegger and Bachelard, whose thoughts especially on living and dwelling he emphasizes. Of particular significance in this context is Gaston Bachelard's The Poetics of Space, the classic phenomenological analysis of lived space, published in 1957. In this work Bachelard pursues the demanding project of drafting a phenomenology of the imagination based on poetic images of "felicitous space" in literature.[42] Over long stretches in this work there are reflections that already mark out Lefebvre's three-dimensional concept of space. These images of felicitous space seek to define the human value of "possessed space" (espaces de possession). Bachelard means here spaces defended against hostile forces, beloved spaces, or extolled spaces. "Attached to its protective value, which can be a positive one, are also imagined values, which soon become dominant. Space that has been seized upon by the imagination cannot remain indifferent space subject to the measures and estimates of the surveyor. It has been lived in, not in its positivity, but with all the partiality of the imagination."[43] Thus, there appears here the first distinction between a "real" (or material) aspect of space and a lived aspect whereby it is clear that both aspects could refer to one and the same "space." Felicitous space is not merely imagined or lived but has an original, real protective value. Thus, it also corresponds to spatial practice.

The third aspect of space, conceived space, also appears in Bachelard's work, and indeed is explicitly demarcated from imagined space. In the context of the aesthetic of the hidden, that deals with chests, wardrobes, and drawers, Bachelard writes: "an empty drawer is *unimaginable. It can only be* thought of. And for us, who must describe what we imagine before what we know, what we dream before what we verify, all wardrobes are full."[44] Lefebvre's following passage, intended as critique, reads like a continuation: "Empty space in the sense of a mental and social void which facilitates the socialization of a not-yet-social realm is actually merely a *representation of space.*"[45]

Thus, a second central reference point of the theory of the production of space is revealed in this way: (French) phenomenology. Nevertheless Lefebvre regards this approach quite critically; in his opinion, it is an approach that is as yet very strongly influenced by Descartes's separation of subject and object. Accordingly, he criticizes Husserl, the founder of phenomenology, as much as his pupil Merleau-Ponty, above all because they still make the subjectivity of the ego the central point of their theory and so cannot overcome their idealism.[46] Lefebvre's aim is, so to speak, a materialist version of phenomenology—a project Merleau-Ponty pursued too but could not complete.

THE DIALECTICAL TRINITY OF MAN

Lefebvre marks the phenomenological access to the three dimensions of the production of space with the concepts of the perceived (*perçu*), the conceived (*conçu*), and the lived (*vécu*). This trinity is at once individual and social; it is not only constitutive for the self-production of man but for the self-production of society. All three concepts denote active and at once individual and social processes.

- *Perceived space*: space has a perceivable aspect that can be grasped by the senses. This perception constitutes an integral component of every social practice. It comprises everything that presents itself to the senses; not only seeing but hearing, smelling, touching, tasting. This sensuously perceptible aspect of space directly relates to the materiality of the "elements" that constitute "space."
- *Conceived space*: space cannot be perceived as such without having been conceived in thought previously. Bringing together the elements to form a "whole" that is

then considered or denoted as space presumes an act of thought that is linked to the production of knowledge.

- Lived space: the third dimension of the production of space is the lived experience of space. This dimension denotes the world as it is experienced by human beings in the practice of their everyday life. On this point Lefebvre is unequivocal: the lived, practical experience does not let itself be exhausted through theoretical analysis. There always remains a surplus, a remainder, an inexpressible and unanalysable but most valuable residue that can be expressed only through artistic means.

Viewed from a phenomenological perspective, the production of space is thus grounded in a three-dimensionality that is identifiable in every social process. Lefebvre demonstrates this by using the example of exchange. Exchange as the historical origin of the commodity society is not limited to the (physical) exchange of objects. It also requires communication, confrontation, comparison, and, therefore, language and discourse, signs and the exchange of signs, thus a mental exchange, so that a material exchange takes place at all. The exchange relationship also contains an affective aspect, an exchange of feeling and passions that, at one and the same time, both unleashes and chains the encounter.[47]

SPATIO-TEMPORAL DIMENSIONS OF SOCIAL REALITY

The fundamental principles of Lefebvre's theory of the production of space are now clear. What is space? Lefebvre understands it as a production process that takes place in terms of three dialectically interlinked dimensions. He defines these dimensions in two ways: on the one hand, he uses the three concepts "spatial practice", "representation of space," and "spaces of representation" that are grounded in his own three-dimensional language theory. The special feature of his language theory consists, on the one hand, in its three-dimensional basic dialectical construction, and, on the other, in his "symbolic" dimension oriented to Nietzsche. However, the theory of the production of space goes one decisive step further than the three-dimensional language theory. It seeks to encompass the entirety of social practice and not merely a partial aspect of this practice. It is thus directed towards the crucial point of every theory of space: the materiality of social practice and the central role of the human body.

Lefebvre now comes to a second set of concepts: "the perceived," "the conceived," and "the lived." As shown already, these concepts are derived from French phenomenology, especially from Bachelard and Merleau-Ponty. Compared to these approaches, however, Lefebvre attempts consistently to maintain his dialectical-materialist standpoint. In this way the epistemological perspective shifts from the subject that thinks, acts, and experiences to the process of social production of thought, action, and experience.

When applied to the production of space this phenomenological approach leads to the following conclusion: a social space includes not only a concrete materiality but a thought concept and a feeling—an "experience." The materiality in itself or the material practice per se has no existence when viewed from a social perspective without the thought that directs and represents them, and without the lived-experienced element, the feelings that are invested in this materiality. The pure thought is pure fiction; it comes from the world, from Being, from material as well as from lived-experienced Being. And pure "experience" is in the last analysis pure mysticism: it has no real—that is, social—existence without the materiality of the body on which it is based and without the thought that structures and expresses it. These three dimensions of the production of space constitute a contradictory dialectical unity. It is a threefold determination: space emerges only in the interplay of all three.

The core of the theory of the production of space identifies three moments of production: first, material production; second, the production of knowledge; and, third, the production of meaning. This makes it clear that the subject of Lefebvre's theory is not "space in itself," not even the ordering of (material) objects and artifacts "in space." Space is to be understood in an active sense as an intricate web of relationships that is continuously produced and reproduced. The object of the analysis is, consequently, the active processes of production that take place in time.

DIALECTICAL CONFUSIONS

This contextual reconstruction of the theory of the production of space shows clearly how some of today's most influential interpretations of it have considerable shortcomings and contribute more to confusion than to clarification.

Even David Harvey, who had creatively appropriated so many of Lefebvre's concepts, had problems with the three-dimensionality of Lefebvre's theory. He concludes his one short excursus on this question with the following argument: "But to argue that the relations between the experienced, the perceived, and the imagined are dialectically rather than causally determined leaves things much too vague."[48] This skepticism of the three-dimensionality of Lefebvre's theory is particularly noteworthy, despite Harvey's later revisions (see Chapter 1, this volume). However, this dialectical theory was precisely what helped Lefebvre advance beyond a narrow Marxism and the limitations of the classical critique of political economy. To follow this would have compelled Harvey to scrutinize closely the basic premises of his own theoretical edifice. According to Lefebvre's own analysis, this question forms the dividing line between the theory of the production of space and a "political economy of space" as it was subsequently further developed by Harvey.[49]

Major problems are posed particularly by Edward Soja's interpretation, which has been extremely influential both within and without the field of geography.[50] The basic problem with this postmodern appropriation of Lefebvre's theory lies in the fact that it constructs, so to speak, independent spaces out of the three dimensions or moments of the production of space. Soja postulates the autonomous existence of three spaces: a first physical space, a second mental space, and a third social space. He sees a strategic importance in the social space and coins it "thirdspace." He understands it to mean a comprehensive space, a lived space of representation, and sees it as a place from where all spaces can be grasped, understood, and transformed at one and the same time.[51] Corresponding to his schema of three spaces, Soja also distinguishes specific spatial "epistemologies" that are meant to investigate, respectively, the first, the second, or even the third space. In *Postmetropolis* he uses this differentiation in order to divide the different approaches of urban research into three basic categories. Although such a conception may seem interesting, it does not have much in common with Lefebvre's theory. According to Lefebvre, there cannot be a "third space," nor a first or second space. As demonstrated conclusively here, Lefebvre never proceeds from three independent spaces but from three dialectically interconnected processes of production. Although Soja repeatedly cites Lefebvre, his spatial theory is, in the last analysis, fundamentally different from Lefebvre's theory of the production of space.

Yet, Soja is not alone in having difficulties with understanding Lefebvre's dialectic. Rob Shields, who brought out the first comprehensible exposition of Lefebvre's work in English, also experiences considerable problems with this dialectic. In his interpretation, partly inspired by Soja, he asserts that Lefebvre has not fully exhausted the meaning of his "spatial dialectic."[52] He asserts without any evidence that the "usual interpretation" of Lefebvre's dialectic is a thesis with two antitheses: the thesis is "everyday practice and perception"; the first antithesis is "analytical theory and institutions"; and the second antithesis comprises the "fully lived moments." However, Shields himself considers such an exposition confusing, and then attempts to retranslate Lefebvre's dialectic back to the classical Hegelian schema of affirmation, negation, and negation of negation. To complete this schema, Shields then finds a fourth, transcendental concept that he terms "the spatialisation." Grappling with Lefebvre's dialectic finally ends—in Shields's case—in total confusion.

Even Stuart Elden has considerable difficulty in coming to terms with Lefebvre's dialectic.[53] In his critique of Soja and Shields he correctly states that Lefebvre's conception neither replaces dialectical thinking nor signifies the introduction of space into the dialectic. He locates "Lefebvre's problems with dialectical materialism in its tendency towards a linear, teleological picture of historical change." Therefore, he argues, Lefebvre posits that "the third term is not a result of the dialectic . . . it is there but it is no longer a culmination."[54] The dialectic is thus not simply the resolution of two conflicting terms but a three-way process, where the synthesis is able to react upon the first two terms. Yet, it is questionable if such a construction could still be termed dialectical, because dialectical thinking is fundamentally based on the dynamic of contradictions and is not restricted to the mutual interaction of elements. Correspondingly, Elden asserts that Lefebvre's *dépassement* (the French term for sublation) is more a translation of Nietzsche's *Überwinden* (overcoming) than the Hegelian or Marxist *Aufhebung* (abolition and preservation).[55] However, as I have tried to show, this interpretation cannot be supported by Lefebvre's work. Thus, even Elden's exposition fails to reduce the confusion concerning Lefebvre's dialectic.

FUTURE PERSPECTIVES

The decisive conclusion to be drawn from the analysis and reconstruction of Lefebvre's theory of the production of space is the following: the three dimensions of the production of space have to be understood as being fundamentally of equal value. Space is at once perceived, conceived, and lived. None of these dimensions can be posited as the absolute origin, as "thesis," and none is privileged. Space is unfinished, since it is continuously produced, and it is always bound up with time.

I hope that with the present "third wave" of Lefebvre interpretation his theoretical project will be better understood. To this end, three tasks will be vital. First, it is important to grasp the basic construction of Lefebvre's epistemology in order to achieve a sound theoretical basis for empirical analyses. Second, fruitful applications of Lefebvre's theory have to be found. Manifold possibilities have arisen for this purpose, which remain to be fully explored. Some promising analyses do exist, however.[56] Third, the crucial point of Lefebvre's approach should be taken into consideration: to go beyond philosophy and theory, and to arrive at practice and action.

NOTES

1. Christian Schmid, *Stadt, Raum und Gesellschaft: Henri Lefebvre und die Theorie der Produktion des Raumes* (Stuttgart: Steiner, 2005).
2. Henri Lefebvre, *Le langage et la société* (Paris: Gallimard, 1966).
3. See, among others: David Harvey, *Justice, Nature and the Geography of Difference* (Oxford: Blackwell, 1996); Benno Werlen, *Society, Action and Space—An Alternative Human Geography* (London: Routledge, 1993).
4. Henri Lefebvre, *Métaphilosophie* (Paris: Édition Syllepse, 2000), 40.
5. G. W. F. Hegel, *Science of Logic*, trans. A. V. Miller (London: George Allen & Unwin, 1969), 107.
6. Henri Lefebvre, *Dialectical Materialism*, trans. J. Sturrock (London: Jonathan Cape, 1968), 42.
7. Lefebvre, *Métaphilosophie*, 40.
8. Lefebvre, *Dialectical Materialism*, 36.
9. *Ibid.*

10. Henri Lefebvre and Norbert Guterman, *La conscience mystifiée* (Paris: Gallimard, 1936); Henri Lefebvre, *Logique formelle, logique dialectique* (Paris: Éditions Sociales, 1947); Henri Lefebvre, *Le retour de la dialectique* (Paris: Messidor/Éditions Sociales, 1986).

11. Lefebvre, *Dialectical Materialism*, 34.

12. *Ibid.*, 49.

13. Lefebvre, *Métaphilosophie*, 129.

14. Henri Lefebvre, *The Production of Space*, trans. D. Nicholson-Smith (Oxford: Basil Blackwell, 1991), 406.

15. Henri Lefebvre, *Rhythmanalysis: Space, Time and Everyday Life*, trans. S. Elden and G. Moore (New York: Continuum, 2004), 12.

16. Lefebvre, *Le retour;* Henri Lefebvre, *La présence et l'absence—contribution à la théorie des représentations* (Paris: Casterman, 1980).

17. Compare in the following: Lefebvre, *Le retour*, 41–2.

18. *Ibid.*

19. Rob Shields, *Lefebvre, Love and Struggle: Spatial Dialectics* (London: Routledge, 1999).

20. Lefebvre, *Rhythmanalysis*, 12.

21. Lefebvre, *La présence*, 143.

22. Lefebvre, *La retour de la dialectique*, 42.

23. Friedrich Nietzsche, "On Truth and Lie in an Extra-Moral Sense," in *The Portable Nietzsche*, ed. and trans. W. Kaufmann (New York: Viking, 1968 [1873], 42–7). See also Lefebvre, *Production of Space*, 138.

24. *Ibid.*

25. Friedrich Nietzsche, "Truth and Lie in an Extra-Moral Sense" (translated by B. Goonewardena).

26. *Ibid.*, (translated by B. Goonewardena).

27. *Ibid.*, (translated by B. Goonewardena); see also Lefebvre, *Production of Space*, 138.

28. *Ibid.*, 139.

29. Lefebvre, *Le langage*, 242.

30. Roman Jakobson, "Two Aspects of Language and Two Types of Aphasic Disturbances," in *Selected Writings II* (The Hague: Mouton, 1971), 239–59.

31. Lefebvre, *Le langage*, 247–8.

32. *Ibid.*, 258, 269.

33. See, e.g., Lefebvre, *Production of Space*, 117; Henri Lefebvre, *De l'État, tome IV: les contradictions de L'État moderne* (Paris: Union Générale d'Éditions, 1978), 282.

34. I use here the term "spaces of representation" instead of "representational spaces," which is used in the translation of *The Production of Space*. The reason for this is not only linguistic precision (Lefebvre's French term is *"espaces de représentation"*) but to stress the term "representation" that is directly linked to Lefebvre's (unfinished) theory of representation (see Lefebvre, *La présence*).

35. Lefebvre, *Production of Space*, 113.

36. *Ibid.*, 183.

37. Shields, *Lefebvre*, 9.

38. Lefebvre, *Métaphilosophie*, 79.

39. See also Alexander Gosztonyi, *Der Raum—Geschichte seiner Probleme in Philosophie und Wissenschaft* (Freiburg/München: Karl Alber, 1976).

40. Maurice Merleau-Ponty, *Phenomenology of Perception*, trans. C. Smith (New York: Humanities Press, 1962).

41. *Ibid.*, 243–4, 291.

42. Gaston Bachelard, *The Poetics of Space*, trans. M. Jolas (Boston, MA: Beacon Press, 1969), xxxi.

43. *Ibid.*, xxxi–xxxii.

44. *Ibid.*, xxxiii–xxxiv.

45. Lefebvre, *Production of Space*, 190.

46. *Ibid.*, 4, 22.

47. Henri Lefebvre, *De l'État, tome III: Le mode de production étatique* (Paris: Union Générale d'Éditions, 1977), 20–2.

48. David Harvey, *The Condition of Postmodernity* (Oxford: Blackwell, 1989), 219.

49. Lefebvre, *Production of Space*, 350.

50. Edward W. Soja, *Postmodern Geographies: The Reassertion of Space in Critical Social Theory* (London/New York: Verso, 1989); *Thirdspace: Journeys to Los Angeles and Other Real-and-Imagined Places* (Oxford: Blackwell, 1996); *Postmetropolis: Critical Studies of Cities and Regions* (Oxford: Blackwell, 2000).

51. Soja, *Thirdspace*, 68–9.

52. Shields, *Lefebvre*, 120.

53. Stuart Elden, *Understanding Henri Lefebvre* (London/New York: Continuum, 2004), 37.

54. *Ibid.*

55. *Ibid.*

56. See Richard Milgrom, this volume; Roger Diener, Jacques Herzog, Marcel Meili, Pierre de Meuron, and Christian Schmid, *Switzerland—An Urban Portrait*, (Basel: Birkhäuser, 2005); Łukasz Stanek, "The Instrumental Use of Representations of Space in the Practices of Production of Space in a Postcommunist City," in *De-/signing the Urban: Technogenesis and the Urban Image*, ed. P. Healy and G. Bruyns (Rotterdam: 010 Publishers, 2006), 284–301.

3

READING *THE URBAN REVOLUTION*
Space and representation
Walter Prigge
(translated by Bandulasena Goonewardena)

The present age may be the age of space . . . We are in the era of the simultaneous, of juxtaposition, of the near and the far, of the side-by-side, of the scattered.

Michel Foucault, 1967[1]

We have often been told . . . that we now inhabit the synchronic rather than the diachronic, and I think it is at least empirically arguable that our daily life, our psychic experience, our cultural languages, are today dominated by categories of space rather than by categories of time, as in the preceding period of high modernism.

Fredric Jameson, 1984[2]

Appropriated space is one of the sites where power is consolidated and realized, and indeed in its surely most subtle form: the unperceived force of symbolic power. Architectonic spaces whose silent dictates are directly addressed to the body are undoubtedly among the most important components of the symbolism of power, precisely because of their invisibility . . . Social space is thus inscribed in the objective nature of spatial structures and in the subjective structures that partly emerge from the incorporation of these objectified structures. This applies all the more in so far as social space is predestined, so to speak, to be visualized in the form of spatial schemata, and the language usually used for this purpose is loaded with metaphors derived from the field of physical space.

Pierre Bourdieu, 1991[3]

1

The debate about the social and historical power of the *spatial* is now more than twenty years old, but progress in its development has encountered an obstacle. Undoubtedly this obstacle consists of the *significant* capacity of spatial structures to symbolize, in a seemingly natural way, something that cannot be visualized and, therefore, cannot be perceived: social relations and the distribution of social positions and roles. Social and cultural scientists have become concerned with this naturalizing effect:

> They have attempted to grasp everything that—through the subconscious submission to the naturalizing effect that results from the transformation of social space into appropriated physical space—is often attributed to the effects of physical or geographical space, but can and also must, in fact, be derived from the spatial distribution of public and private resources. In turn, the latter only represents the crystallization of the local basic unit in question (region, department, etc.) at a definite time in its history, and of its position within national space and so on. Once the totality of the phenomena that are apparently bound up with physical space, but in reality reflect economic and social differences, have been identified and evaluated, an attempt would have to be made to isolate the irreducible remainder that must be attributed to the genuine effect of proximity and distance in purely physical space.[4]

During this critical reduction of physical or geographical to social relations, one arrives at that irreducible remainder of proximity, distance, or density. But this often leads to the analytical destruction of space: why still grapple with the problem of the spatiality of social relations if it can be isolated as a physical and geographical problem and handed over to the corresponding social disciplines, and if the trap of the geographical naturalization of the social can thus be avoided?

With this reduction, epistemologically critical social scientists have returned to the social. They grapple with the objective, economic, political, and cultural practices that explain social processes, and ultimately also the spatiality of these processes. They cannot avoid perceiving the everyday power of that naturalization, the practical "dominance" of categories of space in everyday speech acts. They proceed to banish the practices of appropriating space that undergird the naturalization to the imaginary realm of ideologies of space and consider even these ideological and symbolic discourses as explicable with reference to the objective context of social relations.

However, it should be noted, with the help of the authors quoted at the beginning of this chapter, that the power of spatial structures to represent something is an irreducible feature of the symbolic and imaginary which itself produces social meaning that is not explained by an understanding of social processes. The empirically demonstrable everyday transformation of social space into physical or geographical space produces the symbolic meaning of a spatial representation of social reality. This link of social power and representation in the spatialization of social relations has been the subject of debate among authors who speak of the epochal dominance of the spatial and of the everyday domination of space in culture and social relations.

If social power is symbolized in the appropriation of space, the significance of such spatialization is revealed only through an analysis of these relations as relations of meaning. In contrast, avoiding the geographical often leads to a sociological naturalization that defines symbolic reality as more or less embedded in social context: "the naturalization of social processes conceals from us the process by which social reality is discursively constituted."[5] How the imaginary and the symbolic character of the spatial is historically inscribed in social contexts remains concealed, therefore, if it is not theoretically reconstructed as a real object of discursive and symbolic practice and therewith recognized as a specific form of constituting the social. Such an analysis must clarify the daily dominance of spatial concepts as the discursive hegemony of spatial modes of speech.

2

Lefebvre was aware of the complexity of imaginary and symbolic processes in the realm of space. His urban theory reconstructs the increasing spatialization of social relations through philosophy of history and structural analysis. It occupies a central position in the social-theoretical reflection on space, time, and modernity in European social theory. In sociology and urban research in the Federal Republic of Germany, this position was considered as an epistemological hindrance. Dominated by history and the philosophy of time, vehement discussions about the relationship between history and structure have prevented reflection about the historical and structural significance of the spatial in contemporary social formations and thus also kept intellectuals from recognizing the epochal importance of historical transformations of space and time.

> It is amazing how long it has taken for the problem of space to appear as a historical and political problem. Space was ascribed to "nature," to the given, to immediate circumstances, to mere geography, to a part of pre-history, so to speak. Otherwise, space was conceived as living space and the space for expansion of a people, a culture, a language, a state. One analyzed space as land, as surface or as expanse: only space as such and its boundaries were important. At the same moment when (towards the end of the eighteenth century) there developed gradually an explicit politics of space, the new

insights of theoretical and experimental physics deprived philosophy of its ancient right to speak of the world, of the cosmos, of finite and infinite space. The problem of space was now tackled in a twofold fashion: on the one hand by political technology, on the other by scientific practice. Philosophy, however, was relegated to the problematic of time. After Kant, time is the subject that remains for the philosophers, Hegel, Bergson, Heidegger.[6]

The analytics of space between knowledge and power as an apparatus (*dispositif*) of political technologies and scientific discourses has earned Foucault the title "new cartographer of modern topology," who "no longer designates a privileged location as the source of power and no longer accepts any localization of power at one single point."[7]

In contrast to Foucault, Lefebvre sets out to identify this modern topology in the *urban*. Foucault analyzes the connection of political technologies and their associated knowledge strategies as spatio-temporal matrices of power (Poulantzas) in the transition from the absolutist form of power to disciplinary society (and thus discovers the industrial "disciplines" as epistemological units of knowledge). Lefebvre, however, connects the thesis of the dominance of the spatial to the present stage of capitalist societalization that is characterized, according to him, by the totalizing tendency of urbanization, and that, therefore, must cause an epistemological shift. It is no longer the *industrial* and its disciplines focusing on capital and labor, classes and reproduction that constitute the episteme (the possibility of knowing the social formation), but the *urban* and its forms focused on everydayness and consumption, planning and spectacle, that expose the tendencies of social development in the second half of the twentieth century.

The urban is, therefore, pure form; a place of encounter, assembly, simultaneity. This form has no specific content, but is a center of attraction and life. It is an abstraction, but unlike a metaphysical entity, the urban is a concrete abstraction, associated with practice[8] . . . What does the city create? Nothing. It centralizes creation. Any yet it creates everything. Nothing exists without exchange, without union, without proximity, that is, without relationships. The city creates a situation, where *different* things occur one after another and do not exist separately but according to their differences. The urban, which is indifferent to each difference it contains, . . . itself unites them. In this sense, the city constructs, identifies, and sets free the essence of social relationships[9] . . . We can say that the urban (as opposed to urbanism, whose ambiguity is gradually revealed) rises above the horizon, slowly occupies an epistemological field, and becomes the episteme of an epoch. History and the historic grow further apart.[10]

Compared to homogeneous industrial space, urban space is differentially constituted. This heterogeneous structure predestines urban space to clarify contemporary social forms.

3

The epochal shift from the temporal to the spatial manifests itself in the radical transformation of the modern social formation. The "postmodern" stands for the loss of the critical and modern historicity, and a new "spatial" logic of the cultural representation of the world that reacts to the transformed relationships of image, language, sound, and reality (Jameson). "Post-Fordism" implies flexible and qualitative modes of regulating social and political-economic relations that are restructured in the capitalist apparatus (dispositif) of space—cities, regions, and nations—and evoke a "revenge of the urban" (Lipietz) at an international scale. "Information society" denotes the daily technology-intensive transformation of production and reproduction which infuses modern relations of money, time, and urban space with information (Castells). And "culture society" (Kulturgesellschaft) refers to the tendency of social space to differentiate between a plurality of lifestyles that are symbolized as "fine distinctions" in differential representations of urban lifeworlds (Bourdieu). What are the consequences of this transformed geography and topology of social relations for the epistemology of the urban?

Urban research sets out to analyze the epochal shift from the temporal to the spatial in concrete historical and geographical forms by reconstructing the theoretical and cultural shift in modernity from the "industrial" to the "urban." It thus secures the possibility of positioning the urban as the current apparatus (dispositif) of capitalist space in the process of urban development. Even if one considers the theses about postindustrial, postmodern, information, or culture society, and especially Lefebvre's claim that they are "ideological," one can still produce a varied body of knowledge about the relationship of industry and city and their representations in modernity, particularly the manifold ideological and real shifts in contemporary urban structure. In the process, one learns, however, that the modern, Fordist relationship between industry and city no longer represents the current social structure in toto, in Althusser's sense that the modern industrial, urban-determined ideologies represent knowledge about the imaginary relations of the subjects to their real living conditions in postmodern culture:

> The cognitive map is called to . . . enable a situational representation on the part of the individual subject to that vaster and properly unrepresentable totality which is the ensemble of the city's structure as a whole . . . What is affirmed is not that we cannot know the world and its totality . . . It has never been said here that a global world system is unknowable, but merely that it

was unrepresentable, which is a very different matter. The Althusserian formula in other words designates a gap, a rift, between existential experience and scientific knowledge: ideology has then the function of somehow inventing a way of articulating those two distinct dimensions with each other. What a historicist view of this "definition" would want to add is that such coordination, the production of functioning and living ideologies, is distinct in different historical situations, but above all, that there may be historical situations in which it is not possible at all—and this would seem to be our situation in the current crisis.[11]

In this crisis of representation, the thread has snapped between the real and the symbolic, between the existential experiences of everyday space and their representations in ideology, science, and culture.

4

The irreducible symbolic quality of spatial representations of daily social reality (the ideological hegemony of the spatial), the urban as the decisive episteme of the contemporary social structure (urbanity as the central apparatus [*dispositif*] of space) and the gulf between the spaces of subjective experience and objective perception (crisis of representation): how can this tangle of problems concerning an epistemology of space be unraveled? Lefebvre's answer was a differentiated schema of the social production of space.

a. *Spatial practice*: the spatial practice of a society secretes that society's space; it propounds and presupposes it, in a dialectical interaction; it produces it slowly and surely as it masters and appropriates it. From the analytic standpoint, the spatial practice of a society is revealed through the deciphering of its space. What is spatial practice under neo-capitalism? It embodies a close association within perceived space between daily reality (daily routine) and urban reality (the routes and networks which link up the places set aside for work, "private" life, and leisure). This association is a paradoxical one, because it includes the most extreme separation between the places it links together. The specific spatial competence and performance of every member of society can only be evaluated empirically. "Modern" spatial practice might thus be defined—to take an extreme but significant case—by the daily life of a tenant in a government-subsidized high-rise housing project. Which should not be taken to mean that motorways or the politics of air transport can be left out of the picture. A spatial practice must have a certain cohesiveness, but this does not imply that it is coherent (in the sense of intellectually worked out or logically conceived).

b. *Representations of space*: conceptualized space, the space of scientists, planners, urbanists, technocratic subdividers and social engineers, as of a certain type of artist with a scientific bent—all of whom identify what is lived and what is perceived with what is conceived (Arcane speculation about Numbers, with its talk of the golden number, moduli, and "canons," tends to perpetuate this view of matters). This is the dominant space in any society (or mode of production). Conceptions of space tend, with certain exceptions to which I shall return, towards a system of verbal (and therefore intellectually worked out) signs.

c. *Representational spaces*: space as directly *lived* through its associated images and symbols, and hence the space of the "inhabitants," and "users," but also of some artists and perhaps of those, such as a few writers and philosophers, who *describe* and aspire to do no more than describe. This is the dominated—and hence passively experienced—space which the imagination seeks to change and appropriate. It overlays physical space, making symbolic use of its objects. Thus representational spaces may be said, though again with certain exceptions, to tend towards more or less coherent systems of non-verbal symbols and signs.

The (relative) autonomy achieved by space *qua* "reality" during a long process which has occurred especially under capitalism or neo-capitalism has brought new contradictions into play. The contradictions within space itself will be explored later. For the moment, I merely wish to point out the dialectical relationship which exists within the triad of the perceived, the conceived, and the lived. A triad, that is, three elements, and not two.[12]

The reality of everyday life is, not surprisingly, the entry point for urban research. Today this should hardly be questioned any longer, for it has become the object of thorough theoretical work in European social theory. As the place where structure and agency are connected and localized in time and space, the category of everyday life also discloses the link between urban sociology and social theory. Lefebvre himself prepares the ground for this. In the opposition between "spatial practice" and "space" appears the opportunity for subjective action and the objective, functional spatial structure, which are linked to each other in the perceptions of temporally determined actions. The competent use of space and, hence, successful everyday acts depend on trained perception and ways of connecting difference that are made routine. The modern separation of sites of producing and reproducing life is taken for granted as the structuring principle of everyday lived space and enters successful spatial practices as accepted standardization. From the standpoint of the theory of ideology and reproduction (the theoretical perspective on everyday life), spatial practice is, on the one hand, subjectivization. Individuals appropriate space and constitute themselves as subjects of their space(s) through spatial practice. On the other hand, spatial practice is at the same time the process by which individual spaces of action become objectified in spatial structures. Functionalist ideology, for example, establishes the connection between daily lived space and the structure of separations that is perceived as urban. These separations are reproduced and objectfied in everyday modes of speech or in work, living, or leisure spaces, which become objects of spontaneous knowledge of space. From the standpoint of reproduction, the "satellite town" is an ideological apparatus where the lived ideology of spatial separation becomes materialized through everyday practice. Spatial practices thus acquire their cohesion through the dominant ideologies of lived space. They lead a material existence insofar as Ford's Model T becomes a model of lived space.

Modern "functionalism" in architecture and urban planning, for example, is the representation of this ideology of urban space as it is lived in the material acts of individuals. It symbolizes the imaginary, "naturally" and normatively separated, relations of individuals to their real, interdependent living conditions. As ideologies of urban space, such urban concepts are produced by specialists of space—architects, urban planners, geographers, urban sociologists—and represented in spatial constructs: in the disciplines and political technologies of city building, modern space, its forms and possibilities of use become part of discursive formations. In this "disciplining" process, specific fields of knowledge are established by way of observation, maps, surveys, analysis, and representation. These determine the legitimate objects of knowledge and, at the same time, become practical factors in shaping space. The spatial disciplines define how space can be talked about and lend scientific coherence to the spontaneous ideologies of appropriated lived space (thereby ensuring the cohesion of spatial practice). Through their mechanisms of exclusion (who has the right to speak about space?), they formulate the dominant ways of representing and exercising power over space. In these disciplines, political technologies and means of spatial control, apparatuses (*dispositifs*) of spatial policy are formed in which "the formation of knowledge and the increase of power regularly reinforce one another in a circular process."[13]

The "subjective," lived and perceived spaces of action and the "objective," scientifically and technologically conceived spatial structures are coordinated through ideologies of space. In such ideologies, a society does not generate ideas about the real conditions of existence of individuals but conceptions about the relation of individuals to their real conditions of existence:

> It is this relation that contains the "cause" which has to explain the imaginary distortion of the ideological representation of the real world. Or rather, to leave aside the language of causality it is necessary to advance the thesis that it is the *imaginary nature of this relation* which underlies all the imaginary distortion that we can observe (if we do not live in its truth) in all ideology.[14]

Both the real conditions of existence of individuals and their "imaginary" ideas thereof can be scientifically established. However, one is not therefore in the realm of truth and outside ideology, for there are no true and non-ideological forms of knowledge. There are only dominant and dominated ideologies that can never be divided into two worlds (of "truth" and "ideology").[15] Ideological confrontations in everyday life seek to increase the(ir) respective room to maneuver and the(ir) articulation of interests by shifting the frontiers between dominant and dominated spaces. One possibility for increasing this room to maneuver lies in aesthetic spatial practices, where the power of images can reach beyond set frontiers towards utopias free of dominance. This allows people to imagine possibilities banished from the realm of ideology. An example is the modern *imaginaire urbain*, where the collective unconscious of functionalized metropolitan daily life can be made accessible to the inhabitants by means of shock experiences in language, images, and cinema. This is to allow inhabitants to set their own ideas of their real conditions of existence that may contradict the dominant ideological representations of these conditions.

Spatial practice as lived and taken-for-granted space of everyday production and reproduction denote "the real"; representations of space as conceptual ideologies of disciplinary and political-technical dominance over space refer to "the symbolic"; and spaces of representation as experienced and describable imagined spaces of existential experience of domination deal with "the imaginary." One can interpret in this manner Lefebvre's schema, point to possible links between synchronically co-present levels of society (with the help of theories of ideology), and analyze spaces. Such a commentary would have to be carried out and demonstrate its heuristic quality in competition with other interpretations. The logical sophistication of this schema is, however, unquestionable. Rival approaches in urban sociology tend to restrict their analysis to the first two levels (if they do not actually confine themselves to the first). Hence they remain trapped in the sociological naturalization of the social by neglecting the discursive constitution of the social: "triad: three terms and not only two."

It appears necessary to historicize this synchronic schema and thus connect it with the problematics of time and space, history and geography, industry and urbanity. In doing so, one can take up Lefebvre's own point: space is becoming a (relatively) independent "reality" as a result of the long process of modernizing society. The initial question for this sketch is the following: can the epochal shift from the temporal to the spatial, like the epistemological change from the "industrial" to the "urban," be located in the discourses and political technologies of the modern production of urban space?

THE MODERNIZATION OF THE CITY

In the process of modernization, the industrial principles of organizing time and space in the workplace spread beyond the industrial triangle of factory/villa/

workers' tenement that determines the city. They tend to take hold of the entire society and level the class structure of the bourgeois city that is divided into urban and proletarian spheres. The industrial "disciplines" break out of the "closed institutions" of "disciplinary society," penetrate the social body, and homogenize and standardize the social through separation and individualization:

> The direct producer, the worker, is now totally separated from the means of labour—a situation which is at the root of the social division of labour in machine production and large-scale industry. The latter involves as its precondition an entirely different spatial matrix: *the serial, fractured, parcelled, cellular and irreversible* space which is peculiar to the Taylorist division of labour on the factory assembly line . . . The space matrix . . . is composed of gaps, breaks, successive fracturings, closures and frontiers; but it has no end: the capitalist labour process tends towards world-wide application . . . The whole process is inscribed in fresh space . . . In this modern space, people change position *ad infinitum* by traversing separations in which each place is defined by its distance from others; they spread out in this space by assimilating and homogenizing new segments in the act of shifting their frontiers . . . Within this very space are inscribed the movements and expanded reproduction of capital, the generalization of exchange, and monetary fluctuations.[16]

The new order of social spatiality can be experienced in the modernization of metropolitan ways of life, which are already imbued with social homogenization, individualization, rationalization, the industrial division of labor, the culture of money, and the "fast" temporality of simultaneity. It is above all the urban intellectuals who digest these experiences of transition to a new social formation: Occidental rationalization and bureaucracy (Weber), love, luxury and capitalism (Sombart), individuality and the unconscious (Freud), heightened nervous stimulation and money culture (Simmel), historico-philosophical passages and modernity (Benjamin, Krakauer), political economy and culture of industrialization (Frankfurt School). These critical treatments of social development constitute the background for the concurrent practical experiments of the technological and aesthetic avant-gardes of the early twentieth century to overcome the separations and specializations of knowledge that result from the social division of labor: science and technology, art and daily life, and also theory and practice, hand and head. In this manner, urban specialists attempt to break through the epistemological barriers of the industrial disciplines of the nineteenth century by means of interdisciplinary work and cooperative efforts to bring together specialized scientific, technical, and aesthetic forms of intelligence.

The disciplines of city building are being recomposed. Translated from the sphere of production, cooperation in the division of labor is the principle for the new,

Fordist relationship of social knowledge and power, which is redeployed to shape metropolitan everyday life by means of rationalization, standardization, typification, and Taylorization. As exemplified by the New Frankfurt of the 1920s, the city is represented as an enterprise: "What is the city for? It should enable every single citizen to realize their vocation by allowing them to maximize performance with minimal effort. This principle must be the guiding star directing all future measures undertaken by the city builder."[17] This performative idea of the "city as enterprise" regulates the trend towards a new type of social rationalization, for which the New Frankfurt is paradigmatic. The new methods of planning in architecture, urban planning, and administration combine organically with the modes of life of the metropolitan masses, for whom these methods have already become a steady habit in their working lives. In these processes of modernization, the perceptions of daily lived spaces are undergoing a fundamental transformation. With this notion of the city as enterprise, the hegemony of the Fordist model makes itself felt already. "Enterprise" becomes the regulative idea of the urban that finds its appropriate symbol in the industrial machine, the engine and the automobile (Fordism). Mobility, synchronicity, speed, and traffic thus become the predominant themes in the planning and control of an economy of time that determines the functioning of metropolitan everyday life. In contrast to the backward-looking science of history of the nineteenth century, "progress" now constitutes history as an expectation of future development—and this especially through practices of metropolitan reform, which relate to the social history of the urban masses and intend to integrate the latter into society by means of "social efficiency" and "equality."

THE URBANIZATION OF SPACE

Mass media and automobiles transport modern metropolitan culture to all places that assume urban qualities through zoning and functional separation.

> The problematic of city building intensifies . . . the problems of rural areas are slowly losing significance . . . This kind of planning leads to the creation of a formal uniformity . . . But the homogeneity of space does not prevent its sprawling disarticulation . . . The state authorities and the economy are responsible for homogeneity while disarticulated sprawl can be attributed to the market and private initiative. Disarticulated, sprawling space has a strongly hierarchical structure: there are residential districts, centers for this and that, more or less refined ghettos, developments subject to various statutes etc. . . . It can be shown that this space (which was first tested in spatial planning) has been applied to other fields such as science. The results were an ever more pronounced homogeneity (identical norms, rules and restrictions following a uniform logic), differentiation (specialization), and

hierarchical gradation . . . The schema becomes a model, it shifts from reality to the sphere of culture, produces ideologies to justify itself (for example, structuralism). Yet, once turned into a model, it can also explain the collapse of ideologies.[18]

"City without limits" reads the motto of the Fordist postwar period. This becomes evident in the extension of inner-city principles of the production of space to the peripheries (homogenization and hierarchization) and, in turn, the peripheral-ization of the center that earlier symbolized the history of city and society. The center "implodes" in the banality of a modern tertiary architecture. It becomes an empty foyer that no longer symbolizes the relations of residents to their city but reveals these in their merely symbolic spatialization: "The urban is, therefore, pure form; a place of encounter, assembly, simultaneity. This form has no specific content, but is a center of attraction and life."[19]

This empty inhospitability of abstract space results in urban flight and the suburbanization of the countryside; population dispersion becomes universal. Any place can become a subcentre, space is hierarchized and dissected into differential components that are defined in terms of distance (transportation). The institutional practices of Fordist urban planning overlay the industrial and, through urbanism, become the dominant ideology of urban everyday life. However, this ideology of the urban leads to differential thinking that diagnoses a loss of the urban by analyzing abstract space (fragments, distances, grids). This loss of the urban resulted from separations in urban culture and became codified in urban consciousness as a set of oppositions (private/public, work/residence, individuality/anonymity, monotony/variety). These are in fact calculated as losses of the urban. The modern metropolis fails to redeem its "progressive" promise of urbanity. In the urban realm, the utopia of progress is shattered by the functionalized architecture of the city.

The crisis of the city is of consequence for the representation of space:

> The rediscovery of urban space took the place occupied by social utopias during the times of *Neues Bauen* . . . In the early sixties, after the essential foundations for a new concept of architecture were laid in the works of Saverio Muratoris, Carlo Aymoninos, Aldo Rossi, Oswald Mathias Ungers, the problematic of architecture undergoes radical change. The significance of space and its elements come to the fore; the construction of housing is relegated to second place behind city building.[20]

The Fordist transformations announce at the same time the end of perspectival space and of the centre, the end of the power of the enterprise and factory form over urban space, and of the social as the dominant ideology of city building. In "late capital-ism," the principle underlying structures of power and corresponding social topologies is no longer penetration but dispersion. In postmodern culture and urban protest movements, the loss of modern historicity (industry, the labor movement, intellectuals) and of relatively autonomous cultures (high and low) are being problematized as the crisis of representation. They dominate current and intellectual-historical debates between the universal intellectuals representing "the social" and specialist intellectuals. Of the latter, the architects, designers and urbanists, rather than the planners, technicians and engineers, have taken over the ideological leadership in the production of space. The modern culture of the social is being pushed to the edge of urban discourse. In contrast, "urbanity" becomes the regulative idea of the urban, hence a spatial form that replaces the historical-temporal (continuity, living standard) with a structural-spatial way of thinking difference and understanding modes of life. In addition, the crisis of Marxism casts doubt on the economy being the deciding factor in the last instance and foregrounds superstructures and representations. Historical sciences (especially the French, with the *Annales*), Anglo-American geography and urban sociology, American cultural science (Jameson, Berman, Sennett, as well as Foucault, Virilio, De Certeau, and others in Paris), and European sociology (Giddens, Bourdieu, Frisby, the regulation school) theorize representations of space and thereby discover the transformed urban forms, which allow one to concretize the general cultural and political crisis of representation. We can say that the urban (as opposed to urbanism, whose ambiguity is gradually revealed) rises above the horizon, slowly occupies an epistemological field, and becomes the episteme of an epoch.

THE MATERIALITY OF THE IMMATERIAL

Such an analytical strategy of deciphering social forms with reference to representations of space, especially spatial images of the urban, can certainly fall back on epistemological traditions of modernity:

> Just as Benjamin argues that "the *flâneur* is the priest of the genius loci," so too is Simmel's account of *modernité* located in specific spatial configurations. Simmel was the first sociologist to reveal explicitly the social significance of spatial contexts for human interaction. Spatial images of society were later to be crucial to Kracauer's own "topography of social space" as well as Benjamin's analysis of the relation between the *flâneur* and the arcades, the bourgeois *intérieur* and the spatial location of commodities. But no other social theorist was so preoccupied with social distance, with detachement from reality, with "the intersection of social circles" as was Simmel. In the analysis of modern society, all are located primarily within an urban context.[21]

Simmel analyzed the "separation from reality" as the dominance of the "objective" (objectified) culture of the rationalist money economy over "subjective" urban human relations which are forced into blasé self-preservation and nervous distantiation: "atrophy of the individual through the hypertrophy of objective culture."[22] The crystallization of objective culture, created by individuals themselves, is so far advanced that they no longer have a relationship to the individual practices of perception in quotidian urban life-worlds. Much the same applies to the diagnosis of space today. There is no coherent representation of space (the symbolic) that mediates between the existential experiences in the spatial practice of urban life-worlds (the real) and the spaces of imagining the world and nature (the imaginary). Image, concept, and reality are dissociated to the point of provoking a crisis of meaning and representation.

> What such a reality almost devoid of any reference to reality lacks is, above all, the dimension which used to be captured by manifold and differentiated metaphors of "depth." The play of signifiers divorced from meaning and reference takes the place of semantic depth. In this way, and akin to the screens of the electronic media, the dimension which was earlier defined by bodily imagination implodes. The screen is in several respects an appropriate metaphor for the new form of experiencing reality . . . Spatial and temporal "orders of things" have dissolved into a movement of freely appearing occurrences from which one can expect little . . . Locating a place where the body can register itself is as difficult as finding "spatial depth" in meaning and signification . . . In a flat world, meaning is produced and distributed in any location. The body, which emerges from this meaning, rests nowhere. Mobility is its primary characteristic.[23]

Technological spaces of robotization and computerization get superimposed onto working and living conditions; genetic engineering conquers biological corporeality; semiological image spaces replace the hermeneutic cultures of the written world; apparatuses of artificial intelligence produce hyperspaces of experience (Erlebnis), cyberspace. Such phenomena produce an immaterial spatiality of networked information, free-floating signs and codifications, which can no longer be symbolized with conventional representations of space, time, and world. In the "symptomatology of the present" (Gumbrecht) there is, next to de-temporalization (loss of historicity), de-totalization (heterogeneity of life-worlds) and de-naturalization (fusion of man, machine, nature), an uncorporeal process of spatialization whose material consequences for the relationship of individuals to their real conditions of existence can be represented at the most virtually, as transformations of a "process by which space becomes an autonomous 'reality'" mediated by images.[24]

Such a loss of "sensible" reference points also characterizes the contemporary funfair of urban ideologies. In the rapid succession of "re-construction," "de-construction," and "neo-construction," the merry-go-round of prefixes of the architecture of the city spins out of control. Even the fanciful magic of postmodern architecture (buildings with computers between the pillars) cannot put a stop to the swindle of ideological representations.

Other spaces or urban revolution? The universal intellectual Lefebvre never stopped insisting on the implications of theories of revolution, and thus the utopia of a non-alienated urban society that for him was virtually present and so could be theorized. With his happily positivist, purely descriptive grasp of power-knowledge complexes as the absent causes of social relations, Foucault, the specific intellectual, intervenes subversively in dominant discursive practices in order to restore practical power to subjected knowledges in heterogeneous sites. There does not appear to be another alternative at present. In their reflections on spatiality, both aimed at another kind of historicity and showed that the relationships between spatial practice, representations of space and the spaces of representation cannot be reduced through either ideology or cultural critique without running the risk of ignoring the critical epistemology of time and space, history and geography, industry and city of the past twenty years. Insofar as they formulated their theses of the materiality of the immaterial two decades ago, one should begin re-reading Lefebvre and Foucault.

NOTES

1. Michel Foucault, "Different Spaces," in *Aesthetics, Method, and Epistemology: Essential Works of Foucault, 1954–1984, Volume II*, ed. J. D. Faubion, trans. R. Hurley *et al.* (New York: The New Press, 1999 [1967]), 175.
2. Fredric Jameson, "Postmodernism, or, The Cultural Logic of Late Capitalism," *New Left Review* I/146 (1984): 64.
3. Pierre Bourdieu, "Physischer, sozialer and angeeigneter physischer Raum," in *Stadt-Räume*, ed. M. Wentz (Frankfurt: Campus, 1991) (translation by Bandulasena Goonewardena), 113.
4. *Ibid.*
5. Ernesto Laclau, "Diskurs, Hegemonie und Politik," *Neue Soziale Bewegungen und Marxismus*, ed. W. F. Haug and W. Elfferding, *Argument* Special issue/Sonderband (1982): 17.
6. Michel Foucault, quoted in Silviano Custoza and Pasquale Alferi, "Intercity—elf historische Stationen des Abenteuers Stadt," *Freibeuter* 3 (1980): 74 (translation by Bandulasena Goonewardena).
7. Gilles Deleuze, "Kein Schriftsteller: Ein neuer Kartograph," in *Der Faden ist gerissen*, ed. G. Deleuze and M. Foucault (Berlin: Merve Verlag, 1977), 105.
8. Henri Lefebvre, *The Urban Revolution*, trans. R. Bononno (Minneapolis: University of Minnesota Press, 2003), 118–19.
9. *Ibid.*, 117–18.

10. *Ibid.*, 191, n. 3.

11. Jameson, "Postmodernism," 90–1.

12. Henri Lefebvre, *The Production of Space*, trans. D. Nicholson-Smith (Oxford: Blackwell, 1991).

13. Michel Foucault, *Discipline & Punish: The Birth of the Prison*, trans. A. Sheridan (New York: Vintage Books 1995).

14. Louis Althusser, "Ideology and Ideological State Apparatuses (Notes towards an Investigation)," in *Lenin and Philosophy and Other Essays*, trans. B. Brewster (New York: Monthly Review Press, 1971), 164.

15. Michel Pêcheux, "Zu Rebellieren und zu Denken Wagen! Ideologien, Widerstände, Klassenkampf," *kultuRRevolution* 5–6 (1984), 17.

16. Nicos Poulantzas, *State, Power, Socialism*, trans. P. Camiller (London: Verso, 2000), 102–4.

17. Ernst May, quoted in Ruth Diehl, *Die Tätigkeit Ernst Mays in Frankfurt am Main in den Jahren 1925–30 unter besonderer Berücksichtigung des Siedlungsbaus*, Ph.d. dissertation, University of Frankfurt (1976), 75 (translated by B. Goonewardena).

18. Henri Lefebvre, "Zwischen zwei Daten," in *Paris–Paris 1937–1957*, ed. G. Viatte (Paris/Munich: Centre Georges Pompidou, 1981), 398.

19. Lefebvre, *The Urban Revolution*, 118.

20. Nikolaus Kuhnert and Peter Neitzke, "Befriedete Tradition," *Bauwelt* 19/20 (1981): 765 (translated by Bandulasena Goonewardena).

21. David Frisby, *Fragments of Modernity: Theories of Modernity in the Work of Simmel, Kracauer and Benjamin* (Cambridge, MA: The MIT Press, 1986), 71.

22. *Ibid.*

23. Hans-Ulrich Gumbrecht, "Flache Diskurse," in *Materialität der Kommunikation*, ed. H.-U. Gumbrecht and K. L. Pfeiffer (Frankfurt am Main: Suhrkamp, 1988), 918 (translated by B. Goonewardena).

24. *Ibid.*

4

SPACE AS CONCRETE ABSTRACTION

Hegel, Marx, and modern urbanism in Henri Lefebvre

Łukasz Stanek

INTRODUCTION

With the current success and proliferation of Henri Lefebvre's phrase "the production of space," it becomes increasingly necessary to oppose its banalization by revealing the philosophical sources of this concept and preventing the isolation of the thesis that space is socially produced from other dimensions of his theory. Of paramount import in this regard is Lefebvre's argument that space is a *concrete abstraction*.[1] In this chapter I would like to assert that the concept of concrete abstraction brings together the most vital elements of Lefebvre's theory of production of space, relating it to his rethinking of the philosophies of Hegel and Marx as well as studies of postwar French architecture and urbanism. In so doing, I wish to show in particular how Lefebvre's approach to space as a product of historically specific material, conceptual, and quotidian practices was facilitated by his use of the concept of concrete abstraction. This requires a brief discussion of its Hegelian origins, before examining three appropriations of concrete abstraction by Marx to highlight their mobilization in Lefebvre's theory.

I will first argue that Marx's definition of concrete abstraction as an "abstraction which became true in practice" was developed by Lefebvre into the claim that the space of capitalism is an abstraction that "became true" in social, economic, political, and cultural practice. Next, I will show that Marx's understanding of concrete abstraction as a "sensual-suprasensual thing" inspired Lefebvre to theorize the paradoxical character of contemporary space as simultaneously homogeneous and fragmented. Finally, I will claim that Marx's analysis of concrete abstraction as "form" allows us to grasp Lefebvre's thesis on the dialectical "form" of space. Significantly, Marx proposed these three ways of defining concrete abstraction in order to analyze labor and commodity in the conditions of the nineteenth-century capitalist economy. Here I will show that Lefebvre's argument about space as concrete abstraction, formulated during his Nanterre professorship (1965–73), was contextualized likewise by his empirical studies of urbanization in the trente glorieuses, his critiques of postwar functionalist urbanism, and the revision of Modernist architecture in France in the late 1960s and early 1970s.

HEGEL'S *CONCRETE UNIVERSAL* AND LEFEBVRE'S *PRODUCTION OF SPACE*

In the first chapter of The Production of Space (1974), Lefebvre writes that his aim is to develop a theory that would grasp the unity between three "fields" of space: physical, mental, and social.[2] They are distinguished not only by disciplines such as philosophy, mathematics, and linguistics, but by functionalist urbanism, which assigns specialized zones to everyday activities such as work, housing, leisure, and transportation. Critically reacting to the post-structuralist rethinking of the tradition of Western philosophy, and writing in the wake of the urban crisis in the 1960s and 1970s, Lefebvre considers this fragmentation of space as a theoretical fallacy with practical ramifications and also a symptom of the economic, social, political, technological, and cultural reality of twentieth-century capitalism. With the envisaged "unitary theory" of space, he sought to theorize space as the shared aspect and outcome of all social practices, investigating what remains common to spaces differentiated by historically specific conditions of their production. Lefebvre suggests that these demands can be addressed by a theory based on Hegel's category of concrete universal: "Does what Hegel called the concrete universal still have any meaning? I hope to show that it does. What can be said without further ado is that the concepts of production and of the act of producing do have a certain concrete universality."[3]

The category of concrete universal stems from Hegel's distinction between the abstract and the concrete. In the instructive article "Wer denkt abstract [Who Thinks Abstractly]?"[4] (1807) Hegel addresses this distinction in a way that announces the intuitions developed in his subsequent philosophical work. He writes that those who think abstractly are the "common people": the saleswomen in the market thinks abstractly by considering the convicted criminal just as a murderer—that is, by one isolated feature of the individual in question; by contrast, the "knower of men" thinks concretely, by considering the crime as a product of the conditions of the criminal's life—that is, his poor education, family, injustice he suffered, and so on. This initial distinction between the concrete, as embedded in a variety of relations, and the abstract, as impoverished, one-sided and isolated, can be applied to describe features of things, phenomena, thoughts, and experiences. It clearly influenced Lefebvre, who writes that spaces considered in isolation are "mere abstractions," while they "attain 'real' existence by virtue of networks and pathways, by virtue of bunches or clusters of relationships."[5]

In Hegel's philosophical writings there is an important line of development leading from this preliminary distinction between the concrete and the abstract to the theory of concrete and abstract universals. An *abstract universal* is an isolated feature shared by a collection of objects, while a concrete universal (*das konkrete Allgemeine*) refers to an essence of a thing considered as embedded into and constitutive of the world of related and interacting things: that is, dialectical totality.[6] This distinction was underscored by Hegel in his lectures on aesthetics where he describes a *concept* (*der Begriff*) as a concrete universal: "Now, as regards the nature of the Concept as such, it is not in itself an abstract unity at all over against the differences of reality; as Concept it is already the unity of specific differences and therefore a concrete totality."[7]

Michael Inwood explains the difference between those two types of universal by contrasting *redness* and *life*. Redness is a feature shared by all things red; this feature does not significantly influence the nature of a red thing and its relationships with other red things; thus it is an abstract universal. By contrast, life, as a concrete universal, "constitutes, in part, an essence of living things, directing their internal articulations, and living things are essentially related to each other in virtue of their life: different species feed off, and occasionally support, each other, and species reproduce themselves."[8] This understanding of the concrete universal—as the internal principle of development, or a driving force of an examined thing—will be crucial for Marx's unfolding of this concept.

Following Hegel, in *The Production of Space* Lefebvre wrote that a concrete universal is constituted by three "moments"—those of universality (or generality), particularity, and singularity.[9] They are called "moments" by Hegel in order to underscore that universality, particularity, and singularity cannot be sharply distinguished and to stress their logical, ontological, and epistemological interrelationships.[10] According to Hegel, the universal moment is the general principle of development of things of a certain type. The particular moment is determined by the universal moment, but at the same time it is a differentiation of the universal moment and thus, in Hegel's words, its negation. The singular moment is an individual thing that is concrete in the previously explained sense—it exists in a determinate embeddedness in the world. The singular is thus the final step in the differentiation of the universal moment and, simultaneously, its realization. That is why Hegel writes that "the concrete is the universal in all of its determinations, and thus contains its other in itself":[11] the concrete is the differentiated, or *negated*, universal.

Lefebvre experiments with this understanding of the moments of universality (generality), particularity, and singularity in his theory of production of space.[12] Accordingly, he distinguishes the "level of singularities" on which space is experienced sensually by endowing places with opposing qualities, such as masculine and feminine, or favorable and unfavorable. Furthermore, the "level of generalities" relates to the control and distribution of bodies in space by dominant powers, often by mobilizing symbolic attributes. Finally, the "level of particularities" is linked to smaller social groups, such as families and to spaces "which are defined as permitted or forbidden."[13] In another attempt, Lefebvre divides space into "logical and mathematical generalities" (thus, representations elaborated by scientific disciplines), particular "descriptions" of space, and singular places "in their merely physical and sensory reality."[14] It is not easy to relate these two rather scarcely explained claims to each other, and their fluidity was noticed by Lefebvre himself, who argues that a literal application of Hegelian terms to the theory of space would lead to a "new fragmentation."[15] Thus, when Lefebvre uses the Hegelian term *moment* in his theory of production of space and invokes the perceived, conceived, and lived moments of space, he intends to stress their tight bond rather than their correspondence to the three moments of the concrete universal.

Lefebvre was especially influenced by Hegel's theorizing of the internal dynamics of the concrete universal, described as a development from the universal to the singular via the particular. This dynamic shaped Lefebvre's concept of production, and, specifically, of the production of space. Lefebvre explains this by referring to Hegel: "In Hegelianism, 'production' has a cardinal role: first, the (absolute) Idea produces the world; next, nature produces the human being; and the human being in turn, by dint of struggle and labour, produces at once history, knowledge and self-consciousness."[16] Thus, Hegel's concept of production refers to the development of the concrete universal from the universal moment through the particular to the singular moment. In Lefebvre's view, it is this broad scope of the concept of production, which is not restricted to manufacturing, that makes it most inspiring. He regrets that this breadth, openness, contingency, and lack of sharp borders between the three moments of the concrete universal were lost in some strands of Marxism.

It is this internal dynamic of the concrete universal that above all influenced Lefebvre's theorizing of space. It characterizes the description of the production of space in his short preface to Philippe Boudon's *Lived-in Architecture: Le Corbusier's Pessac Revisited* (1979 [1969]). Boudon's book is an empirical study about the Quartiers Modernes Frugès in Pessac, France, designed by Le Corbusier and opened to residents in 1926. Making a common cause with the critical rethinking and reevaluation of Modernist architecture after the death of Le Corbusier (1965), Boudon investigated the changes introduced to the neighborhood's houses by their inhabitants, focusing on the relationship between the alterations of particular houses, their designs, and their positions in the district.[17] Accepting Boudon's results, Lefebvre stresses three levels on which space is produced in Pessac: in his view, the original Modernist project of the architect was initially transformed because of the site conditions and the requirements of the client, and then, after construction, appropriated by the inhabitants to their own purposes. The practice of appropriation, Lefebvre writes, manifests "a higher, more complex concrete rationality than the abstract rationality" of Modernism.[18] Significantly, as in Hegel's category of concrete universal, these steps from the abstract to the concrete are seen as a sequence of differentiations: Lefebvre writes explicitly that the inhabitants "produce differences in an undifferentiated space."[19]

The Production of Space credits Marx with discovering the "immanent rationality" of the Hegelian concept of production.[20] This "immanent rationality" allows the theorization of production neither as determined by a preexisting cause nor as teleologically guided, but as organizing "a sequence of actions with a certain 'objective' (i.e. the object to be produced) in view."[21] Lefebvre writes that even the most technologically developed system "cannot produce a space with a perfectly clear understanding of cause and effect, motive and implication."[22] These formulations may well have been inspired by Lefebvre's acquaintance with Boudon's research on Pessac: in the preface he underscores that the "concrete rationality" of production of space cannot be identified with the rationality of any one particular subject—the architect, the occupant, or the critic.

MARX'S *GRUNDRISSE* AND SPACE AS AN "ABSTRACTION TRUE IN PRACTICE"

Even though he tried to retrieve some of the initial features of Hegel's concrete universal that were lost in Marxism, Lefebvre shared Marx's critique of Hegel's stress on the intellectual characteristics of production.[23] Thus, following Hegel and Marx, Lefebvre develops a materialist interpretation of this concept that could be applied to space.[24] The need for a reconceptualization of space emerges from Lefebvre's empirical study on the new town of Lacq-Mourenx in the Pyrénées Atlantiques, which initiated his research about urban space.[25] The paper "Les nouveaux ensembles urbains," published in La Revue Française de Sociologie (1960), is based on interviews with the inhabitants carried out in 1959, two years after the construction of this city of 4,500 inhabitants. Pierre Merlin, in his 1969 book Les villes nouvelles, characterized the problems of Mourenx by noting the insufficiency of facilities, monotony of architecture, and separation of functions.[26] Lefebvre's text, however, goes beyond a critique of functionalist urbanism as it was emerging at that time in France in the publications of Pierre Francastel or the group around Paul-Henry Chombart de Lauwe.[27] He grappled with a statement of one of the interviewees—

"*ce n'est pas une ville, c'est une cité*"²⁸—and speculated that the negative connotation of the term *cité* might resonate with the concept of the "workers' city" (*cité ouvrière*). Even if the specific meaning attributed to this opposition is ambiguous, the message given by the inhabitant was clear: Mourenx was not what a city was supposed to be. Lefebvre attributes this dissatisfaction to the meaninglessness of spaces in the city and the boredom of everyday lives deprived of any unexpected and ludic situations. These interviews demonstrate that it is not enough to distribute amenities in the city: the production of urban space also involves practices of representation of space as well as the appropriation of what Lefebvre later called "spaces of representation." Thus, his research about Mourenx can be read as an anticipation of the triad of spatial practice, representations of space, and spaces of representation that Lefebvre formulated during his Nanterre professorship.

While the study of Mourenx inspired Lefebvre's subsequent theorizing of space as a product of heterogeneous, historically specific social practices, it was his reading of Marx's analysis of labor from the *Grundrisse* as an "abstraction which became true in practice" that provided him with a model for such a new concept of space.²⁹ Lefebvre's description of the emergence of the concept of space is analogous to Marx's theorization of labor, which considered every theoretical concept as a symptom of a larger social whole and related the emergence of the concept to the social, economic, political, and cultural contexts of its appearance. Although humankind has always been working, the emergence of the concept of labor is a historical fact: Marx writes that labor could have been conceptualized only when the general features conveyed by this concept became decisive in social practices, most importantly in economic reality. Thus, he claims, it is no accident that the concept of labor as a wealth-creating activity regardless of its specificity was "discovered" by Adam Smith in eighteenth-century Britain, where industry required labor to be reduced to its bare features and stripped of the personality of the worker. This type of labor—malleable, quantifiable, divisible, and measurable by time—was compatible with newly introduced machines and thus most efficient in the economic conditions of early industrialization. Marx writes that under such conditions "the abstraction of the category 'labour,' 'labour as such,' labour pure and simple, becomes true in practice [*praktisch wahr*]."³⁰ Thus, labor is seen as consisting of two aspects: the specific labor of a particular worker (in *Capital* it is called "concrete labour"—a "productive activity of a definite kind and exercised with a definite aim"³¹) and the non-specific "abstract labour," defined as "the expenditure of human labour in general."³² Labor becoming "true in practice" *is* concrete abstraction: an abstraction "made every day in the social process of production," as Marx writes in the *Contribution to the Critique of Political Economy* (1859):

> The conversion of all commodities into labour-time is no greater an
> abstraction, and is no less real, than the resolution of all organic bodies into

air. Labour, thus measured by time, does not seem, indeed, to be the labour of different persons, but on the contrary the different working individuals seem to be mere organs of this labour.[33]

This definition was borrowed by Lefebvre, who in De l'État (1977) defined concrete abstraction as an abstraction that "concretizes and realizes itself socially, in the social practice."[34] He adds that concrete abstraction is a "social abstraction," which "has a real existence, that is to say practical and not conventional, in the social relationships linked to practices."[35]

Analogous to Marx, Lefebvre looks for the "moment of emergence of an awareness of space and its production."[36] He sees this moment at the Bauhaus:

> For the Bauhaus did more than locate space in its real context or supply a new perspective on it: it developed a new conception, a global concept, of space. At that time, around 1920, just after the First World War, a link was discovered in the advanced countries (France, Germany, Russia, the United States), a link which had already been dealt with on the practical plane but which had not yet been rationally articulated: that between industrialization and urbanization, between workplaces and dwelling-places. No sooner had this link been incorporated into theoretical thought than it turned into a project, even into a programme.[37]

This discovery of a "global concept of space" was a recognition of the spatial interconnections between locations of work, habitation, and consumption in advanced capitalism. While Adam Smith demonstrated that different professions are facets of work in general, the architects, artists, and theorists gathered at the Bauhaus (particularly during the phase under Hannes Meyer's directorship) showed that different places are interrelated and are thus parts of one space.[38]

This project of designing space as a whole comprised of interdependent processes and locations was shared by progressive architects between the world wars. Ludwig Hilberseimer in his Grossstadt Architektur (1927) argued that every urban structure must be developed in relation to the whole city: "The architecture of the large city depends essentially on the solution given to two factors: the elementary cell of space and the urban organism as a whole."[39] Hilberseimer writes that the space of a single house should become a design determinant for the whole city, while the general plan of the city should influence the space of the house.[40] This continuity between all scales of a city was sought by the film Architecture d'aujourd'hui (1930), directed by Pierre Chenal with a script by Chenal and Le Corbusier. It developed a polemical narrative against the nineteenth-century city, suggesting the necessity of an organic link between the private house, represented by Le Corbusier's villas, the neighborhood, epitomized by the Quartiers Modernes Frugès in Pessac, and the urban plan, exemplified by the Plan Voisin (1925).

K. Michael Hays, in his *Modernism and the Posthumanist Subject* (1992), argues that Hannes Meyer's aim was to design space as a whole that not only encompasses interrelated economic, social, and cultural processes but strives to make those relationships visible. Meyer's projects—such as the Palace of the League of Nations in Geneva (1927), the Petersschule in Basel (1927), and the school in Bernau (1928–30)—were designed as indexes that reflected the processes of their production and thus as machines of a new, performative perception, in which the functional diagrams of the building, the transformation of raw materials and their assembling in the processes of construction are visually reestablished. For Hays, Meyer's projects seek to move their viewers "to critically produce or (re)invent relationships among the architectural fact and the social, historical, and ideological subtexts from which it was never really separate to begin with."[41]

The emergence of space and labor as general concepts in the conditions of capitalism shows the intrinsic connections between them. Whereas Adam Smith "discovered" abstract work—the aspect of work that is conditioned by the capitalist mode of production and that facilitates the capitalist development—the intellectuals at the Bauhaus "discovered" abstract space—the space of developed capitalism. In *La pensée marxiste et la ville* (1972), a response to and unfolding of Marx's and Engels's theorizing of the city, Lefebvre described urban space and urban life as the place, tool, milieu, negotiator, and scene of the transition from feudalism to capitalism.[42] Elsewhere he developed a similar argument about the relationship between twentieth-century capitalism and abstract space. In his view, the new planning procedures and new systems of representing space invented at the Bauhaus were essential for the emergence of abstract space, the space of contemporary capitalism:

> If there is such a thing as the history of space, . . . then there is such a thing as a space characteristic of capitalism—that is, characteristic of that society which is run and dominated by the bourgeoisie. It is certainly arguable that the writings and works of the Bauhaus, of Mies van der Rohe among others, outlined, formulated and helped realize that particular space—the fact that the Bauhaus sought to be and proclaimed itself to be revolutionary notwithstanding.[43]

This argument was strengthened by the architectural theorist Manfredo Tafuri, whom Lefebvre met in person in the late 1960s during the activities of the Unité Pedagogique d'Architecture n°8 in Paris.[44] Tafuri linked the new understanding of space held by the most progressive Modernist architects to the capitalist reorganization of Europe. In *Toward a Critique of Architectural Ideology* (1969) he underscores Hilberseimer's understanding that "once the true unity of the production cycle has been identified in the city, the only task the architect can have is to *organize* that cycle."[45] Both Lefebvre and Tafuri recognize that this supposedly revolutionary way of producing space served the economic and political system.[46] This new unity of space was in fact accompanying and facilitating the unity of the processes of production, distribution, and consumption.

Abstract space and abstract labor are thus both the result of a series of economic, social, political, technological, and cultural developments. Marx and Lefebvre show that these developments were followed by a shift on an emotional and personal level: they are not only perceived and conceived but lived in the everyday. Marx describes the worker's feeling of "indifference" toward a specific type of work, which cannot provide him or her with personal identity any more.[47] A hundred years later, Lefebvre wrote that abstract space is not just a perceived product of capitalist spatial practices and a projection of the representations of space conceived by planners, but that the lived practices of those inhabiting this space are themselves abstract: his examples include the one-sided perception of space by a driver or the reductive use of space in functionalist urbanism.[48]

MARX'S *CAPITAL* AND SPACE AS A "SENSUAL–SUPRASENSUAL THING"

The emergence of abstract space meant not only the mobilization of space in the chain of production, distribution, and consumption, but a transformation of space itself into a commodity: produced, distributed, and consumed. The consequence of this is the twofold character of abstract space that Lefebvre examined as being at the same time homogeneous and fragmented—a description applied to Mourenx in his *Introduction to Modernity* (1995 [1962]).[49] This investigation of abstract space is based on Marx's analysis of another concrete abstraction—the commodity.

As with every commodity, space reflects the duality of the abstract and concrete aspects of labor by which it is produced. In *Capital* (1867), Marx theorizes this dual character of a commodity as a concrete abstraction—a "sensual–suprasensual thing" (*sinnlich–übersinnliches Ding*).[50] The concrete ("useful") labor produces the use value of a commodity, while its exchange value is determined by the amount of abstract labor socially necessary for its production.

In *Capital*, Marx writes: "As use values, commodities are, above all, of different qualities, but as exchange values they are merely different quantities, and consequently do not contain an atom of use value."[51] Thus, the development of the commodity economy was conditioned by the development of universally accepted, practically applicable, and quantitative systems of representation and procedures which, applied to the goods, would allow for comparison between them.

Accordingly, in order to become a commodity, space must have been subjected to systems of representation and procedures that allow it to be divided, measured, and compared.[52] Thus—as in Marx's example of abstract labor measured by time—the historical process of the commodification of space was paralleled by an implementation of a system of representation, which would depict different "pieces of space" as distinct and endowed with comparable features. Represented by this system, a "piece of space" must radically differ from the "place" traditionally understood as characterized by blurred borders, and qualitatively defined by identity, natural peculiarities, topography, authority, religion, tradition, and history. An early symptom of this transition "from nature to abstraction" is the evolution of systems of measurements, which proceeded from measuring space with parts of the body to universal, quantitative, and homogeneous systems.[53] These requirements were fulfilled by the system within which a point in space can be determined by three coordinates, as developed over the centuries by philosophers and mathematicians, most famously by Descartes. Lefebvre writes that the space of developed capitalism "has analogical affinity with the space of the philosophical, and more specifically the Cartesian tradition."[54]

The reductionism of the Cartesian system of representation (the very cause of its practical success), which became "practically true" in the social practice of capitalism, endowed space with a simultaneous tendency towards homogenization and fragmentation. In his diagnosis of abstract space, Lefebvre writes:

> Formal boundaries are gone between town and country, between centre and periphery, between suburbs and city centres, between the domain of automobiles and the domain of people . . . And yet everything ("public facilities," blocks of flats, "environments of living") is separated, assigned in isolated fashion to unconnected "sites" and "tracts"; the spaces themselves are specialized just as operations are in the social and technical division of labour.[55]

Lefebvre argues that these two tendencies are interdependent: "It is impossible to overemphasize either the mutual inherence or the contradictoriness of these two aspects of space . . . For space 'is' whole and broken, global and fractured, at one and the same time."[56] Abstract space, writes Lefebvre, "takes account of the connections and links between those elements that it keeps, paradoxically, united yet disunited, joined yet detached from one another, at once torn apart and squeezed together."[57]

This simultaneity of homogeneity and fragmentation is determined by features intrinsic to the Cartesian model itself: homogeneity results in fragmentation, and fragmentation determines homogeneity. As a system of representation, it is unable to give an account of any other features of "pieces of space" than their location expressed with three coordinates of the analytic geometry; areas or volumes differing in location differ in "everything," have "nothing in common" besides being part of the "entirety of space." Thus, space appears as fragmented: it is an aggregate of independent, distinct areas or volumes. At the same time this system of representation offers no intrinsic criteria for delineating areas or volumes of space; by eliminating "existing differences and peculiarities"[58] this system does not suggest any intrinsic differentiation. Thus, it lends itself to *any* parceling required by land speculation, functionalist zoning, or segregation by the state. Deprived of intrinsic differentiations, the "entirety of space" is endowed with a "geometric homogeneity,"[59] which means both a representation and a practical attitude to the management of space. These descriptions of space as simultaneously homogeneous and fragmented are clearly inspired by other concrete abstractions discussed by Lefebvre: money, capital, and the market.[60]

The process of erasing differences—of homogenizing space—may be executed only by force.[61] That is why Lefebvre claims that "*there is a violence intrinsic to abstraction, and to abstraction's practical (social) use.*"[62] For Lefebvre, abstraction supported by science and technology is a tool to develop oppressive, *classificatory*, and phallic space.[63] At the same time, in *De l'État*, Lefebvre adds one more characteristic of postwar space: this space is characterized not only by a homogeneity of interchangeable places and by a fragmentation of allotments caused by real-estate speculation but by hierarchization: sensitized by the recent gentrification of the Marais and Quartier Les Halles in Paris, Lefebvre writes that the distinction between center and periphery becomes translated into social hierarchy.[64]

MARX'S *FORM OF VALUE* AND LEFEBVRE'S *FORM OF SPACE*

The historically specific analysis of abstract space—the space of capitalism—is developed in *The Production of Space* into a wider project of addressing the shared characteristics of all spaces, produced in various historical conditions by various social practices. This argument is facilitated by Lefebvre's concept of space as a concrete abstraction and by his application of the method Marx developed in *Capital* in order to describe the universal characteristics of all commodities.

According to Marx, the feature shared by every commodity is its twofold character consisting of use and exchange value. In *Capital* he writes:

> A commodity is a use value or object of utility, and a value. It manifests itself as this twofold thing, that it is, as soon as its value assumes an independent form—viz., the form of exchange value. It never assumes this form when isolated, but only when placed in a value or exchange relation with another commodity of a different kind.[65]

Marx arrives at the definition of the "general form of value" (*allgemeine Wertform*) and explains it with the example of linen: its general form of value "expresses the values of the whole world of commodities in terms of a single commodity set apart for the purpose, namely, the linen, and thus represents to us their values by means of their equality with linen."[66] Thus, the exchange value of a commodity is established in relation not to some specific commodities but precisely to all of them, and it becomes manifest only in the context of all other commodities.

According to Marx, the principle of development of capitalism is the contradiction between use value and exchange value, which characterizes every commodity and every act of exchange. In the act of exchange, the owner of one of the exchanged objects considers his or her object as deprived of use value (otherwise the owner would not exchange it) but endowed only with exchange value, while considering the object of the other owner as having only use value but no exchange value; an analogous view is held by the owner of the second exchanged object. There is a contradiction between the empirical fact of substituting the exchange and use values and the theoretical impossibility of combining both value forms in one commodity. For Marx, this contradiction points to the real impossibility of a precise measurement of value in bartering.[67]

Marx's method is to investigate how this contradiction is dealt with in social practice. He concludes that the introduction of money should be interpreted as an attempt to mediate between use and exchange values. Money is the "means by which use value begins to transform itself into exchange value, and vice versa."[68] However, the initial contradiction is not solved by money, but dialectically preserved and internalized in commodities (and generating more mediating links, like labor power, a unique commodity whose use value consists precisely in the fact that in the course of its consumption it is transformed into its counterpart—exchange value); in Marx's view this contradiction can be resolved only by the socialist revolution.[69]

Just like a commodity characterized by the general form of value, space for Lefebvre is defined by its form. Whereas the form of the commodity characterizes all commodities regardless of their specific features, the form of space is the most general relationship between locations that can be attributed to every location independently of the differences between them. Lefebvre describes the form of the commodity as the possibility of exchange conceived independently of what is exchanged, while the form of space is defined as the possibility of encounter, assembly, and simultaneous gathering regardless of what—or who—is gathered. Lefebvre writes that socially produced space "implies actual or potential assembly at a single point, or around that point."[70] This fundamental feature of such space is called *centrality*.

Drawing an analogy to the form of the commodity, which is characterized by a dialectical contradiction between use and exchange value, Lefebvre describes centrality as dialectical: there is a dialectic of centrality "because there is a connection between space and the dialectic."[71] The "dialectical movement of centrality" consists of gathering "everything" in space and of the simultaneity of "everything."[72] Lefebvre's work on space and the urban society from the late 1960s and early 1970s can be read as unfolding, developing, and differentiating this claim. In *The Urban*

Revolution (1970) he writes that in a city characterized by centrality, things, objects, people, and situations "are mutually exclusive because they are diverse, but inclusive because they are brought together and imply their mutual presence."[73] He adds that conflicts in urban space arise from differences, which recognize and test each other.[74] Thus, centrality consists of a collection of contradictory and mutually conditioned elements.

In *The Production of Space* yet another aspect of the dialectic of centrality is addressed. The process of centralization is described as conditioned by the process of dispersion: "the centre gathers things together only to the extent that it pushes them away and disperses them."[75] On the same page Lefebvre uses different wording to describe this interdependence: centrality "is based on simultaneous inclusion and exclusion precipitated by a specific spatial factor."[76] Thus, the "dialectic of centrality" consists not only of the contradictory interdependence between the objects gathered but of the opposition between center and periphery, gathering and dispersion, inclusion (to center) and exclusion (to periphery).

The descriptions of centrality from *The Production of Space* and *The Urban Revolution* resemble Lefebvre's depiction of Paris from his text "The Other Parises," published originally in *Espaces et Sociétés* (1974/5), the journal he co-founded with Anatole Kopp in 1970.[77] In this text, the various centers of Paris are addressed as gathering and dispersing living beings, things, ideas, signs, symbols, representations, projects, and ways of life.[78] The social practices of gathering and dispersion can be seen as practices of producing space—transforming the physical environment, representing space, and appropriating it in everyday life. Material practices may include or exclude not only by building bridges or walls but by making strategic investments in the built environment that render particular areas in the city central while excluding others. Representational practices develop new theories of space and set some of them in the center of public attention, damning others to library back shelves. Practices of everyday life appropriate places and ideas—giving meaning to some, while rendering others obsolete.

Lefebvre's discovery of the form of urban space as dialectical parallels the transition in his thinking from an early review "Utopie expérimentale: pour un nouvel urbanisme" (1961) to his writings in the late 1960s. Published in *La Revue Française de Sociologie*, it sympathetically discusses an urbanistic project for a new city in the Furttal valley near Zürich.[79] The authors of the project, presented in the book *Die neue Stadt* (1961), express the ambition to develop a paradigmatic solution for the problems of congestion, traffic, and housing and to tackle the aesthetic challenge of inscribing modern architecture into the Swiss landscape. The main principle of the design is the concept of a balance that regulates the social, economic, emotional, political, and aesthetic aspects of the new city.[80] In his review Lefebvre embraces this principle, praising the project for proposing "an equilibrium, at the same time stable and vivid, a sort of self-regulation."[81] This support for the project, which exposed

Lefebvre to the accusation of reformism by the *Internationale Situationniste*,[82] was soon withdrawn. In "Humanisme et urbanisme: quelques propositions" (1968), he notes that it is deceptive to envisage a perfect equilibrium between architectural concepts,[83] and in *The Urban Revolution* he claims that the concept of a "programmed" and "structured" equilibrium, as proposed by the planners, is an even greater risk for a city than chaos.[84] This revision in Lefebvre's thinking might have been influenced not only by his reevaluation of the postwar urbanism in France and an examination of the urban crisis of the 1960s but by the development of his theoretical interests: his critique of the functionalist concept of needs, his adherence to the ludic and the unforeseen as necessary aspects of urban space, his research on the Paris Commune,[85] and his rethinking of the concept of concrete abstraction.

The analysis of the form of urban space as dialectical allows Lefebvre to sharpen his claims about the role of space in the processes of capitalist production, distribution, and consumption. Whereas the contradiction between use and exchange values was shown by Marx to be the engine of the development of capitalism, Lefebvre enriches this picture by describing the contradictions inherent to space also as contributing to this development.[86] The method of both Marx and Lefebvre is based on the rather counterintuitive assumption that the principle of capitalism is preserved throughout its whole development, becoming manifest in its most advanced and complex stage. The Soviet philosopher Evald Ilyenkov demonstrated that this method is made possible by the structural features of the concept of concrete abstraction. By assuming the commodity as a concrete abstraction, Marx was able to consider it as the universal expression of the specific nature of capital, and, at the same time, as an empirical fact: a commodity exchanged in a particular act. In "Dialectics of the Abstract and the Concrete in Marx's *Capital*" (1960), Ilyenkov writes that the historically necessary conditions of emergence of every concrete abstraction are "preserved in its structure throughout its development"; thus, the development of capitalism is conceived as a reproduction of its original principle.[87] Similarly, centrality as a form of space is considered by Lefebvre as a feature of a particular location, and, at the same time, as a facilitator of economic, social, political, and cultural development.

CONCLUSION: LEFEBVRE'S THEORETICO-EMPIRICAL METHOD

This chapter has argued that Lefebvre's theory of production of space is structurally based on the concept of concrete abstraction developed by Hegel in his theorization of the concrete universal and further developed by Marx. Lefebvre refers to Hegel's dynamic and open-ended concrete universal in order to theorize space as a dynamic entity produced by historically contingent social practices. Following Marx's theorization of labor as a concrete abstraction, Lefebvre demonstrates that space is an "abstraction which became true in practice"—produced by material, political, theoretical, cultural, and quotidian practices. In analogy with Marx's analysis of abstract labor as conditioned by capitalist development and facilitating its further success, Lefebvre sees abstract space as enabling the capitalist processes of production, distribution, and consumption. In the course of the development of capitalism, space itself was turned into a commodity—a concrete abstraction described by Marx as a "sensual–suprasensual thing"—becoming at the same time homogeneous and fragmented. Like the commodity that in its most developed and differentiated stage reveals its most universal characteristics, the space of the capitalist city manifests a fundamental dialectic between the processes of centralization and dispersion, inclusion, and exclusion. This concept of space as a concrete abstraction —socially produced and thus historically contingent and yet characterized by a universal feature called centrality—is the basis of the "unitary theory of space" envisaged by Lefebvre at the beginning of The Production of Space.

Significantly, this argument that Lefebvre developed in the late 1960s and early 1970s was prepared and informed by his earlier empirical studies as well as critiques of urbanistic and architectural projects. Ilyenkov demonstrated that Marx's method in Capital mobilized both theoretical and empirical research and the procedures of induction and deduction.[88] In Lefebvre's writings one can find a similar approach, albeit not as rigorous as that of Ilyenkov. His theorization of space as concrete abstraction—developed by a close reading and appropriation of the philosophical sources in Hegel and Marx—was not merely accompanied, informed, and inspired by his texts on Mourenx, Furttal, Pessac, and Paris but questioned by them.

NOTES

All internet references for this chapter were accessed and checked on May 12, 2007.

1. Henri Lefebvre's thesis of space as a concrete abstraction is stated several times in The Production of Space, trans. D. Nicholson-Smith (Oxford: Blackwell, 1991 [1974]), 15, 86, 100, 341. This thesis is underresearched by Lefebvre's interpreters, even if it has been noticed by most of them (Gottdiener, Shields, Elden); in particular Harvey and Schmid have paid attention to its complexity. See Mark Gottdiener, The Social Production of Urban Space (Austin: University of Texas Press, 1985); "A Marx for Our Time: Henri Lefèbvre [sic] and The Production of Space," AnArchitektur, <http://www.anarchitektur. com/aa01-lefebvre/gottdiener.html>; Rob Shields, Lefebvre, Love and Struggle: Spatial Dialectics (London: Routledge, 1999); Stuart Elden, Understanding Henri Lefebvre: Theory and the Possible (London: Continuum, 2004); David Harvey, The Urban Experience (Oxford: Blackwell, 1989); Christian Schmid, Stadt, Raum und Gesellschaft: Henri Lefebvre und die Theorie der Produktion des Raumes (Stuttgart: Steiner, 2005).
2. Lefebvre, Production of Space, 11.
3. Henri Lefebvre, La production de l'espace (Paris: Anthropos, 1986), 23. Note that the English translation of this passage in Lefebvre, Production of Space (15)—where "l'universalité concrète" is rendered as "abstract universality"—is utterly misleading.

4. Georg Wilhelm Friedrich Hegel, "Wer denkt Abstrakt?," in *Gesammelte Schriften*, ed. M. Baum, K. R. Meist (Hamburg: Felix Meiner, 1998 [1807]), 5: 381–7. For an English translation see: <www.Marxists.org/reference/archive/hegel/works/se/abstract.htm>.

5. Lefebvre, *Production of Space*, 86.

6. See John W. Burbidge, *Historical Dictionary of Hegelian Philosophy* (Lanham, MD: Scarecrow, 2001); Michael James Inwood, *A Hegel Dictionary* (Cambridge, MA: Blackwell, 1992).

7. G. W. F. Hegel, *Aesthetics: Lectures on Fine Art*, trans. T. M. Knox (Oxford: Clarendon Press, 1988), 1: 108.

8. Inwood, *Hegel Dictionary*, 31.

9. Lefebvre, *Production of Space*, 15–16.

10. Inwood, *Hegel Dictionary*, 304.

11. See Dieter Wandschneider, "Zur Struktur dialektischer Begriffsentwicklung," *Philosophisches Institut der RWTH Aachen*, <http://www.phil-inst.rwth-aachen.de/lehrenden/ texte/wandschneider/wandschneider%20-%201997%20b%20-%20zur%20struktur% 20dialektischer%20begriffsentwicklung.pdf>. Moreover, Hegel applies the triad of universality, particularity, and singularity to types of judgment: a universal judgment refers to all entities of a given type, for example "all men are wise"; a particular judgment concerns some of those entities, for example "some men are wise"; while a singular judgment refers to one entity, for example "Socrates is wise." Inwood notices that both the universal and the singular judgment refer to the whole of a subject and not to a part of it (as is the case with a particular judgment); this contributed to Hegel's view that singularity is a restoration of universality on a higher level (Inwood, *Hegel Dictionary*, 303).

12. Lefebvre, *Production of Space*, 15–16 and 226–7. For a discussion, see Edward Dimendberg, "Henri Lefebvre on Abstract Space," in *The Production of Public Space*, ed. A. Light and J. Smith (Lanham: Rowman & Littlefield, 1998), 17–47.

13. Lefebvre, *Production of Space*, 226–7.

14. *Ibid.*, 15–16.

15. *Ibid.*, 15.

16. *Ibid.*, 68.

17. Philippe Boudon, *Lived-in Architecture: Le Corbusier's Pessac Revisited*, trans. G. Onn (Cambridge, MA: MIT Press, 1979 [1969]).

18. Lefebvre, preface to *ibid.*: n.p.

19. *Ibid.*

20. Lefebvre, *Production of Space*, 71.

21. *Ibid.*

22. *Ibid.*, 37.

23. Shlomo Avineri writes that for Hegel "[p]roduction is a vehicle of reason's actualization of itself in the world," *Hegel's Theory of the Modern State* (London: Cambridge University Press, 1974), 90.

24. For a discussion, see Schmid, *Stadt, Raum und Gesellschaft*, 85ff.

25. Henri Lefebvre, *Le temps des méprises* (Paris: Stock, 1975), 222.

26. Pierre Merlin, *Les villes nouvelles: urbanisme régional et aménagement* (Paris: PUF, 1969), 255.

27. Pierre Francastel, *Arts and Technology in the Nineteenth and Twentieth Centuries*, trans. R. Cherry (New York: Zone Books, 2003 [1956]), and Paul-Henry Chombart de Lauwe, *Paris: essais de sociologie* (Paris: Éditions Ouvrières, 1965).

28. Henri Lefebvre, "Les nouveaux ensembles urbains," *La Revue Française de Sociologie* 1, no. 2 (1960): 197.
29. Hiroshi Uchida, *Marx's Grundrisse and Hegel's Logic* (London: Routledge, 1988) shows that the introduction to *Grundrisse* reflects Hegel's theory of the concept. In particular, Marx theorizes production by applying Hegel's category of concrete universal with its three moments of universality, particularity, and singularity.
30. Karl Marx, *Grundrisse der Kritik der politischen Ökonomie* (Berlin [GDR]: Dietz, 1953), 25; "Outlines of the Critique of Political Economy," Marxist Internet Archive, <http://www.Marxists.org/archive/marx/works/1857/grundrisse/ch01.htm>. Here "true in practice" could also be rendered as "practical-truth."
31. Karl Marx, "Das Kapital: Kritik der politischen Ökonomie," in *Ökonomische Schriften*, ed. H. J. Lieber and B. Kautsky (Stuttgart: Cotta, 1962), 1: 12; "Capital," Marxist Internet Archive, <http://www.Marxists.org/archive/marx/works/1867-c1/ch01.htm#S2>.
32. *Ibid.*, 14.
33. Karl Marx, "Zur Kritik der politischen Ökonomie," in *Ökonomische Schriften*, ed. H. J. Lieber and B. Kautsky (Stuttgart: Cotta, 1962), 3: 847; "A Contribution to the Critique of Political Economy," Marxist Internet Archive, <http://www.Marxists.org/archive/marx/works/1859/critique-pol-economy/ch01.htm>.
34. Henri Lefebvre, *De l'État tome III* (Paris: Union Générale d'Éditions, 1977), 59.
35. *Ibid.*
36. Lefebvre, *Production of Space*, 123.
37. *Ibid.*, 124.
38. *Ibid.*
39. Ludwig Hilberseimer, *Grossstadt Architektur* (Stuttgart: Hoffmann, 1927), 100.
40. *Ibid.*
41. K. Michael Hays, *Modernism and the Posthumanist Subject: The Architecture of Hannes Meyer and Ludwig Hilberseimer* (Cambridge, MA: MIT Press, 1992), 146.
42. Henri Lefebvre, *La pensée marxiste et la ville* (Paris: Casterman, 1972), 33, 71.
43. Lefebvre, *Production of Space*, 126.
44. Łukasz Stanek, Interview with Henri Raymond, Paris, December 2006.
45. Manfredo Tafuri, "Towards a Critique of Architectural Ideology," in *Architecture Theory since 1968*, ed. K. Michael Hays (Cambridge, MA: MIT Press, 1998), 22.
46. Lefebvre, *Production of Space*, 124.
47. Marx, *Grundrisse*, 25.
48. See Lefebvre, *Production of Space*, 313, 232ff. These practices became "real abstractions," as described by the Marxist philosopher Alfred Sohn-Rethel, *Geistige und körperliche Arbeit* (Weinheim: VCH, Acta Humaniora, 1989).
49. Henri Lefebvre, *Introduction to Modernity: Twelve Preludes*, trans. J. Moore (London: Verso, 1995 [1962]), 121ff.
50. Marx, "Das Kapital," 46.
51. *Ibid.*, 6.
52. See Lefebvre, *Production of Space*, 338–9.
53. *Ibid.*, 110–11.
54. *Ibid.*, 200.
55. *Ibid.*, 97–8. However, in *Production of Space* one can find claims that "abstract space *is not* homogeneous; it simply *has* homogeneity as its goal, its orientation, its 'lens.' And indeed it renders homogeneous" (ibid., 287, see also 308). Thus, homogenization and fragmentation are tendencies of development of space rather than its stable features.

This apparent contradiction can be solved by referring to the fact that Lefebvre understands space as a concrete abstraction that can be named by its principle of development even if it did not reach this level of development yet.

56. Lefebvre, *Production of Space*, 355–6.
57. *Ibid.*, 366.
58. *Ibid.*, 52.
59. *Ibid.*, 288.
60. *Ibid.*, 306–7.
61. *Ibid.*, 308.
62. *Ibid.*, 289.
63. *Ibid.*, 280–2, 285–7, 375.
64. Lefebvre, *De l'État*, III, 309.
65. Marx, "Das Kapital," 34.
66. *Ibid.*, 40.
67. Evald Ilyenkov, "Dialectics of the Abstract and the Concrete in Marx's Capital," Evald Ilyenkov Archive, <http://Marxists.org/archive/ilyenkov/works/abstract/>.
68. *Ibid.*
69. *Ibid.*
70. Lefebvre, *Production of Space*, 101.
71. *Ibid.*, 331.
72. *Ibid.*
73. Henri Lefebvre, *The Urban Revolution*, trans. R. Bononno (Minneapolis: University of Minnesota Press, 2003 [1970]), 119.
74. *Ibid.*, 96.
75. Lefebvre, *Production of Space*, 386.
76. *Ibid.*
77. Henri Lefebvre, "The Other Parises" [1974/5], in *Key Writings*, ed. S. Elden, E. Lebas, and E. Kofman (New York: Continuum, 2003), 151–9.
78. Lefebvre, *Production of Space*, 101. See also Lefebvre, *Urban Revolution*, ch. 6.
79. Henri Lefebvre, "Utopie expérimentale: pour un nouvel urbanisme," *La Revue Française de Sociologie* 2, no. 3 (1961): 191–8.
80. Ernst Egli *et al.*, *Die neue Stadt. Eine Studie für das Furttal* (Zürich: Verlag Bauen + Wohnen, 1961).
81. Lefebvre, "Utopie expérimentale," 194.
82. See "Critique of Urbanism," *Internationale Situationniste* 6, trans. J. Shepley. Available at: <http://www.cddc.vt.edu/sionline/si/critique.html> (accessed May 12, 2007). For a discussion of the relationship between Lefebvre and the Situationists, see Simon Sadler, *The Situationist City* (Cambridge, MA: MIT Press, 1998).
83. Henri Lefebvre, "Humanisme et urbanisme: quelque propositions," *Architecture, Formes, Fonctions* 14 (1968), 22–6.
84. Lefebvre, *Urban Revolution*, 97.
85. See Henri Lefebvre, *La proclamation de la Commune, 26 mars 1871* (Paris: Gallimard, 1965).
86. See David Harvey, *The Condition of Postmodernity: An Enquiry into the Origins of Cultural Change* (Cambridge, MA: Blackwell, 1990).
87. Ilyenkov, "Dialectics of the Abstract and the Concrete."
88. *Ibid.*

5

MONDIALISATION BEFORE GLOBALIZATION

Lefebvre and Axelos[1]

Stuart Elden

INTRODUCTION

One of the key themes of *De l'État* is the question of the world. The world, *le monde*, figures both in the notion of *l'échelle mondiale*—the worldwide scale—and in that of *mondialisation*, which can only imperfectly be translated as globalization. Instead, *mondialisation* is the process of becoming worldwide, the seizing and grasping of the world as a whole, comprehending it as a totality, as an event in thought. The spread of economic and political phenomena across the surface of the globe, which English-language readers have known as *globalization* since the 1980s, is a development that is made possible by this prior comprehending of the world, *mondialisation*. This chapter seeks to understand Lefebvre's notion of *mondialisation*, suggesting that it provides a philosophical *and* practical account, theoretically grounded and politically aware. In addition it seeks to account for the genesis of the term in Lefebvre's writings, opening up a perspective on the philosophy of the world more generally.

In thinking about the question of the world, as with his work more generally, Lefebvre is seeking to develop claims from within what is generally called Western Marxism. His reading of Marx is to see his works as a whole, neither privileging the earlier "humanist" writings nor the later "scientific" ones.[2] But for Lefebvre the single most important line from Marx on the question of the world is from an earlier work, his doctoral dissertation. In this dissertation, Marx declares that "the world's becoming philosophical is at the same time philosophy's becoming worldly, that its realization is at the same time its loss."[3] What this means for Marx is that in its actualization or realization, philosophy is transcended and overcome. Lefebvre regularly cites this line from Marx,[4] and his work as a whole can be understood as an attempt to understand the relation of philosophical thought to its realization, a development he calls metaphilosophy.[5] For Lefebvre, the concern is with a critical reflection on philosophy, seeing how philosophy can be transcended or overcome. This is as much a Nietzschean or Heideggerian *überwinden*—to overcome or twist free from—as a Hegelian or Marxist *aufheben*—a word Lenin glossed as "to supersede, put an end to, but simultaneously to conserve, to maintain."[6]

In understanding the world, Lefebvre thinks that Heidegger also has an important role to play, particularly in the suggestion he makes in the 1929 essay "On the Essence of Ground" that the "world never *is*, but *worlds*."[7] This phrase is often reduced to the shorthand the "world worlds," *die Welt weltet*, and is intended to understand the way in which the world operates independently of an external cause or trigger. The standard French translation is "*le monde n'est jamais, le monde se* mondifie";[8] an alternative is that "*le monde se mondialise*."[9] For Lefebvre, this is close to a tautology, but "has great sense." He takes it to mean that

> The world-wide [*le mondial*] conceives itself in and by itself and not by another thing (history, spirit, work, science, etc.). The world becomes world, becoming what virtually it was. It transforms itself by becoming worldwide. In it discovery and creation converge. It does not exist before it creates itself, and yet, it proclaimed itself, possible-impossible, through all the powers, technology, knowledge, art.[10]

But the heritage goes back much further, and it is therefore no surprise that Marx's doctoral dissertation was on pre-Socratic thought, and that Heidegger's reflections often return to such ancient sources.[11] Indeed, the spur for Lefebvre and Heidegger here is Heraclitus, and in particular his fragment that suggests that eternity, or time (*aion*), standing as a cipher for the world, is "like a child playing a game."[12] In a 1973 piece Lefebvre declares that this fragment is the first beacon or marker; the second is Heidegger.[13]

A number of themes thus arise: the distinction between globalization and *mondialisation*, and the way in which the latter may be said to provide the conditions of possibility for the former; the internal logic of the process of becoming worldwide; and the role of play or the game in understanding this. It is at this point that juxtaposition of Lefebvre's work with another thinker is useful. This thinker is Kostas Axelos, a Greek émigré who arrived in France in 1945, fleeing from the Royalist victory in the civil war, who studied at the Sorbonne before meeting and befriending both Heidegger and Lefebvre. Lefebvre and Axelos met in 1955 at the

Centre National de la Recherche Scientifique (CNRS), when the former was in charge of the sociology division and the latter was a researcher.[14] They took part in a couple of interviews together,[15] and, as will be discussed below, Lefebvre wrote a number of short pieces on Axelos's work. Lefebvre's admiration for Axelos is somewhat unusual, given how critical he was of most of his contemporaries, but Lefebvre particularly liked the way in which Axelos analyzed Marx and brought his thought into conflict with contemporary problems.[16] This respect goes deeper than a shared approach to reading Marx. Indeed, for Lefebvre, Axelos is the only thinker who has really come close to thinking the question and distinction of thought of the world and thought in the world, as initiated by Heraclitus.[17] Lefebvre regularly refers to Axelos's writings in his own works, and indeed at one point refers to him as the "new Heraclitus."[18]

KOSTAS AXELOS AND THE PLAY OF THE WORLD

Axelos, born in 1924, is a generation younger than Lefebvre, and, although still largely unknown in the English-speaking world, has been a major intellectual figure and facilitator in his adopted homeland of France. He edited the important journal *Arguments* between 1958 and its close in 1962, and still runs the book series of that name with Éditions de Minuit, in which three of Lefebvre's books—*Introduction à la modernité*, *Métaphilosophie* and *La fin de l'histoire*—appeared.[19] Many other key figures in French and European thought had volumes appear in that series, including Gilles Deleuze, Maurice Blanchot, Georg Lukács, Herbert Marcuse, and Karl Jaspers. In his own writings, notably *Le jeu du monde*, influenced by Marx, Heidegger, and Eugen Fink, Axelos discusses the process of becoming worldly, and provides some valuable insights into this question that are of interest both in their own right and because of their impact on Lefebvre's work.[20] For Axelos, reflecting in 2004 on the advent of thought of globalization, *mondialisation* has a connection to the notion of the "world" that the more recent term no longer preserves.[21] In part this is a nuance of translation, and one that can be understood through the lens of Anglo-American cultural imperialism as Derrida suggested toward the end of his life.[22] Axelos claims that *mondialisation*, which was extensively discussed in the pages of the *Arguments* journal as early as the late 1950s, is worth preserving precisely because it retains the notion of the "world":

> *Globalisation* names a process which universalises technology, economy, politics, and even civilisation and culture. But it remains somewhat empty. The world, as an *opening* is missing. The world is not the physical and historical totality, it is not the more or less empirical ensemble of theoretical and practical ensembles. It deploys itself. The thing that is called *globalisation* is a kind of *mondialisation* without the world.[23]

The world is an object of thought in its own terms, rather than understandable through other means or ciphers; and is a necessary prerequisite before thinking the extension of other phenomena over it, taking into account the material and conceptual basis of the world and the understanding of space upon which it relies.[24] Indeed, Pierre Fougeyrollas's "Thèses sur la mondialisation," published in *Arguments*, suggests that "to the *mondialisation* of problems we must respond with the *mondialisation* of thought and action."[25] For Axelos, the human is not in the world but of the world, a relation that cannot be reduced to an identification.

Axelos is concerned with overturning the vulgar materialist reading of Marx, suggesting that it was precisely this realist, objectivist, material understanding that idealism was developed to avoid.[26] For Axelos, just as Lefebvre, the key to an unorthodox, truly Hegelian Marxism is to recognize the dialectical relation between the ideal and the material. Again, like Lefebvre, Axelos recognizes that we must seek the answer to this relation through the problematic of alienation, but not through an exclusive reading of this in the early works. Axelos declares that "Marx's starting point is economic alienation, the splitting of the world into the world of the structure (real) and the world of the superstructure (ideological). His work consists in reducing the ideological, idealistic, and ideal world to its profane foundation."[27] Axelos wants to undertake this move, but also its reverse, to recognize the ideological underpinnings of the foundation. For Axelos, the key is to situate the questions of human being, economic production, and concrete society within the wider problematic of the world. Indeed, his detailed study of Marx, profoundly influenced by Heidegger, is, in the original French title, explicit: *Marx as a Thinker of Technology: From the Alienation of Man to the Conquest of the World.*[28] For Axelos, while Marx and Heidegger do not say the same things, they are both thinkers of great crisis: "one speaks of the alienation of man and the other of the darkening [*obscurcissement*] of the world."[29]

As the 1959 interview Lefebvre and Axelos undertook with Jean Beaufret and François Châtelet demonstrates, this is a relation they considered of crucial importance. Lefebvre declares that there is "no antagonism between the cosmic-historic vision of Heidegger and the historic-practical conception of Marx" in terms of conceiving of the relation of humans to technology, but merely that their work approaches it from different directions.[30] Axelos adds that in order to think about these figures historical-political issues need to be considered, including German idealism and the failure of romanticism.[31] And of course the question of National Socialism looms large. Lefebvre notes that his initial rejection of Heidegger was before the latter's support of the Nazis, and Axelos and Beaufret add some detail to the picture of that support.[32] If those details are now somewhat more complicated by newly released writings and documents, what is clear is that the encounter they staged between Heidegger and Marx was not politically naïve.[33] Instead Heidegger could be used to shed light on Marx himself, to understand Marx better, particularly in terms of Heidegger's sustained discussion of things that Marx treated only in summary fashion, such as, for Axelos and Lefebvre, technology and the world. None the less, as Axelos states in this interview, "neither Marx nor Heidegger exhausts the problem of the totality of the world."[34]

How then are we to understand the world? For Axelos the world deploys as a game (jeu). He suggests that this a central question of Western metaphysics: "Being becoming totality, the supreme game."[35] The 1969 book Le jeu du monde, Axelos's most important work, can thus be translated as "the game of the world," but also as "the play of the world," and my translations from it and other works use "game" and "play" interchangeably for jeu, depending on context. There are other related words in Axelos's conceptual armory, particularly l'enjeu, stake, and jouet, plaything. Le Jeu du monde is a profoundly challenging book, written in a fragmented, almost aphoristic style. Yet, like Nietzsche's works, these are fragments of a whole, and can only be separated from the totality with violence.[36] Other writings are presented in a more traditional and accessible way, such as Systématique ouverte, which re-presents many of the ideas from the earlier work.[37] Axelos's key claim is that the world can only be understood on its own terms, or rules, an internal logic of interplay, rather than on the basis of anything exterior to it:

> The play of the world attempts to think the game inside of which all games and all rules, all transgressions and all calculations, all significations and all interpretations (global and particular) appear, disappear, are reborn . . . which moves the pawns and figures, figurative or not, on the chessboard of the world, according to contingency or necessity. The pawns and figures are only parts of the game, just as truth is only the triumphant figure of errancy, corresponding to it. Thus a polyvalent combination of theoretical and practical games opens up, which from including the play of the world, remains contained and crushed by it.[38]

The world as a game develops claims made in brief summary form by Heidegger—"the essence of being is the game itself [das Spiel selber]"[39]—and in much more detail in works by Eugen Fink.[40] Drawing, again, on the fragment of Heraclitus, Fink wonders if "play can become the symbolic theatrical enactment of the universe, the speculative metaphor of the world."[41] Fink is perhaps best known in the English language for his work continuing the studies of Husserl and for his seminar on Heraclitus with Heidegger,[42] although he is an important phenomenological thinker in his own right, several of whose works would merit English translation. This is perhaps especially true of Spiel als Weltsymbol, a complex analysis of the notion of play in myth, ritual, and philosophy which explores the relation of the play or the game to the world.[43] If a detailed analysis of this book is beyond the scope of this chapter, it is important to note its crucial role in a mediation between ancient, French, and

German sources for thinking these issues. Its final chapter, "The Worldness of the Human Game," is particularly important.

The making worldly of phenomena through a logic implicit only to itself, without external cause or purpose, also draws upon Heidegger's echo of Angelus Silesius's line about the rose, suggesting that the child of the *play of the world* "plays, because it plays."[44] "The 'because' is subsumed [*versinkt*] in the game. The game is without 'why'."[45] For Heidegger, the *play of the world* is the "sending [*Geschick*] of being"; for Axelos, it means that the world in a much more tangible sense can be understood only through this continual process of becoming.[46] This is what he means in the idea that the world "deploys itself [*se déploie*]," the world unfolds and unfurls itself "as a *game*. That means that it refuses any sense, any rule which is exterior to itself."[47] Deployment is an important term in Axelos, forming the unifying theme of the three trilogies he saw as the architecture of his principal works. Each of these trilogies was given a title: the unfolding, unfurling, or deployment [*déploiement*] of *errance*, of the game, and of an inquiry.[48]

Within this architectonic, which Axelos calls an "open systematic,"[49] the question of the world, the play or the game, and the relation of the human to that world of which they are both part and creator is the central theme. For Deleuze, Axelos's notion of *errance*, errancy, is a substitution for the "metaphysical opposition of true and false, error and truth," just as the play of the world between fragment and whole replaces the "metaphysical relation of the relative and the absolute."[50] In this we can see the way in which the process of becoming worldwide is both in opposition to, and the foundation of, philosophical notions of totality and globality, and a challenge to the equation of universality–rationality–totality.[51] Being is in the process of becoming a fragmentary totality, precisely through this notion of *mondialisation*.[52] This is the sense of his claim that "being becoming totality" is "the supreme game."[53] Totality is an aspiration rather than an intellectual step in the process of thought.

THE WORLD SCALE AND THE PROBLEM OF THE STATE

Lefebvre's interest in Axelos's work is pronounced, something that can be found in a number of pieces he wrote on his work, and in references elsewhere in his corpus. Two of his most explicit analyses are found in reviews of Axelos's *Marx, penseur de la technique* and *Vers la pensée planétaire* for the journal *Esprit*;[54] another is found in a long 1986 essay devoted to him which first appeared after Lefebvre's death.[55] Lefebvre praises the way that Axelos is able to shed new light on well-known texts of Marx, and brings this reflection on technology to bear on the history of the world.[56] He reads technology, in part through Axelos, as not merely a cause of alienation, but also as a potential liberation, as through technology humans are in the process of "becoming worldwide and planetary [*devenu mondial et planétaire*]," and then may "finally be able to enjoy or command [*jouir*] the Earth."[57] Yet this ability to command, or truly to "enjoy," the earth comes at a profound cost. Rendering the world amenable to control and command is at the root of a number of contemporary phenomena that are injurious to communal well-being and to the health of the earth itself. There is therefore an important distinction between the earth—*le terre*—and the world—*le monde*. The earth is the foundation, "a unity [*ensemble*] of cycles, stable systems, self-regulation: waters, winds, air light, soils, sediments." The world is "the whole of the devices [*l'ensemble des dispositifs*] assembled by man beginning to cover the earth."[58] Thus, the earth, the Planet Earth, becomes the world through our intervention:

> Technology unifies the terrestrial world only while plunging the man of this earth into anguish.
>
> Tragic vision? Yes and no. Because this drama of stability, this stability in errancy, is a "game." The tragic contradiction is the contradiction (the antagonistic unity) of the play and seriousness [*gravité*]. Man is a serious being [*un être sérieux*], but nothing is more serious than the game. Man plays his destiny seriously, and the universe plays with the planet earth, man, gravities and human games. Appearance and apparition play with reality, because reality is only the play of appearances. Being? Nature? The absolute? Let us not speak of these. When we play, without speaking of them, we are there. "It" is an eternal child, collecting his dice to launch them into the infinite.[59]

Although this is not always recognized in his contemporary Anglo-American reception, Lefebvre distinguishes between the level and the scale. Level is a mode of understanding that takes into account the range from the private, the realm of habitation, to the global or total, via the mixed, meditating level of the middle.[60] When Lefebvre talks of scale, the largest is not the global, but the world. The world scale, *l'échelle mondial*, or the simple notion of *le mondial*, the "worldwide," which is neither fixed nor accomplished, needs to be introduced as a third term in the conflicting relation of the country and the city.[61] Thus the distinction: "the total, the global, is the totality of knowledge and the world as a totality."[62] Like Axelos, then, Lefebvre wants to understand totality both as an aspiration of revolutionary praxis, but as something that cannot be grasped through totalizing thought. As Lefebvre notes, "when taken *in isolation*, in other words speculatively, outside of *praxis*, the theories of alienation and totality become transformed into systems which are very remote from Marxism—into neo-Hegelianism."[63] In distinction, in practice totality comes to us in fragments, out of partial determinisms, and is an ongoing process rather than an accomplishment:[64]

> At the world scale, the system of states introduces the worldwideness [*mondialité*] against historicity; it delineates the contours of planetary space, which does not result from the historical past but from new factors (energy, techniques, strategies, productive forces).[65]

This relation between the questions of spatiality and temporality is revealing. For Lefebvre, talk of the worldwide is tied more to spatiality than to temporality,[66] yet the crucial analysis will be of their overall interrelation. In *De l'État*, which is where Lefebvre most thoroughly treats these relations, the state seeks to transcend both history and to exploit the past.[67] The notion of the state mode of production, where the state takes responsibility for the creation and development of markets, is an inherently spatial issue. Lefebvre argues that the conflict between the worldwide and historicity, the limits of the political, is resolved "in and by the production of worldwide space, the work of a historical time in which it is realized."[68]

In this understanding we can gain a number of insights. First, the world scale or the notion of the worldwide in no way implies a transcending of spatial, territorial problematics. Rather it requires a thinking of the scale to which they are applied, and a reflection on the remaking of spatial relations. Lefebvre argues that Marx sees the world as first and foremost the world market, a worldly form that pre-dates others. But this too is a "spatial configuration," of which Marx himself offered only initial indications.[69] As Lefebvre notes: "The world market world involves a territorial distribution . . . of productive forces, flow and stocks . . . The world market is not detached from space; there is no 'deterritorialised' abstraction, even if some extra-territorial forces (the heads of some so-called supra-national businesses) operate there."[70] Second, the process of *mondialisation* requires an acceleration of the homogenization of space and time,[71] a process that, ontologically, began in the sixteenth and seventeenth centuries with the advent of the scientific revolution and modern physics. For Lefebvre, following much of the analysis of Heidegger, the key figure in this story is Descartes, whose casting of material as *res extensa* paves the way for a particular way of grasping the world. To see extension as the primary characteristic of matter is to make it amenable to science through geometry and the notions of measure and calculation.[72] Nature becomes controllable as resource, stock for the disposition of technology; a Heideggerian claim that is radicalized through a twofold process—first the recognition of the role of capital and second the refusal to entertain a regressive, reactionary return. Lefebvre was always interested in transforming the mode of urban life, and of the understanding of the world, rather than a retreat to the rural or the local. Thus, for Lefebvre, the notion of the worldwide, *le mondial*, is important but it is not without both conceptual and political problems:

> Sometimes it obscures, sometimes it illuminates: global by definition, it does not just deal with the economic, nor the sociological in isolation; neither demography separately, nor traditional historicity taken as criteria of direction. It implies the criticism of separations, especially if they have had their moment and their need. Here we try to grasp it through a process of becoming worldwide, of the State, which supposes the world market, world technicality, etc. but which goes beyond these determinations.[73]

CONCLUSION

As well as illustrating the connections between Lefebvre and Axelos on a theoretical level, this chapter has sought to document their intellectual friendship through the lens of a topic of shared interest, the question of the world and its impact on the full range of spatial scales, from the global to the local and the urban. Axelos provides the intellectual and conceptual apparatus, developing from Fink and Heidegger, although, for Lefebvre, he is still prone to lapse into speculative metaphysics.[74] In distinction, Axelos's view of Lefebvre was that he was a more concrete figure, and that ultimately the differences were profound:

> With Lefebvre I had many productive discussions. Three of his books were published in the *Arguments* collection. Bonds of friendship united us. But I consider Lefebvre, if not exclusively, as above all a theorist of Marxism, of society, the city, everyday life. What I have tried to do is different. This became clear in the course of our long conversation.[75]

Undoubtedly the two approaches are necessary together, and this is why a dialogue between Axelos and Lefebvre, and further back involving Heraclitus, Marx, Heidegger, and Fink is useful. The principal insight that such analysis provides is that the phenomena that we have taken to discuss as globalization is the political and economic outcome of a prior grasping and comprehending of the world as a globe, of the world seen as a totality or a whole. Lefebvre's analyses of the notion of *mondialisation*, developing from the abstract theorizing of Axelos, provide some insights into how that came about. The process of *mondialisation* is one that requires further study, but for Lefebvre this is tied in two ways to a historical investigation. On the one hand we should think about how globalization is dependent on *mondialisation*; on the other the conditions of possibility of *mondialisation* itself, without a lapse into either linear causality or mechanistic determinism,[76] the vulgar historical idealism or materialism he had done so much to challenge throughout his career.

Such a shift to the abstract, the thought, is a necessary, and a necessarily political, move in understanding the contemporary. In this context we would do well to consider the eleventh of Axelos's "Theses on Marx," which declares that technological operations require thought; and Lefebvre's view of the eleventh thesis of Marx himself:

> Technologists only *transform* the world in different ways in universalised indifference, what matters now is to *think* it, and to interpret the transformations in depth, by grasping and *experiencing* the difference which unites being to nothingness.[77]

Philosophy makes itself world: it makes the world and the world is made through it. The world is produced to the exact measure whereby philosophy is realized, and realizing, becomes world. Philosophers have interpreted the world: now it must be changed; can this change be accomplished without philosophy?[78]

What matters now is to think the world, and the process of becoming worldwide, the notion of *mondialisation*, in order that we may better understand globalization. Perhaps then, and perhaps only then, will we understand how to change or transform it for more radical, progressive, political goals. Radical politics requires a radicalization of the political, as we need to ask how revolutionary thought is rendered possible.[79] As Lefebvre puts it, "Kostas Axelos opens the horizon, shows the way."[80]

NOTES

1. I am grateful to the editors of this volume, Neil Brenner and, above all, Kostas Axelos for their comments on and enthusiasm for this essay. Unless otherwise noted, all translations are by the author.
2. This can be particularly seen in his *Dialectical Materialism*, trans. J. Sturrock (London: Jonathan Cape, 1968). See Stuart Elden, *Understanding Henri Lefebvre: Theory and the Possible* (London: Continuum, 2004), ch. 1, for a fuller discussion of Lefebvre's position within Marxism and his reading of Marx.
3. Karl Marx, *Writings of the Young Marx on Philosophy and Society*, ed. L. D. Easton and K. H. Guddat (New York: Doubleday, 1967), 62.
4. See, for example, Henri Lefebvre, *Marx* (Paris: PUF, 1964), 55; *Métaphilosophie*, 2nd edn (Paris: Éditions Syllepse, 2001), 33; *Dialectical Materialism*, 17.
5. Lefebvre, *Métaphilosophie*; see Elden, *Understanding Henri Lefebvre*, 83–5.
6. Lenin, *Cahiers de Lénine sur la dialectique de Hegel*, ed. H. Lefebvre and N. Guterman (Paris: Gallimard, 1967), 164.
7. Martin Heidegger, *Wegmarken*, *Gesamtausgabe*, Band 9 (Frankfurt am Main: Vittorio Klostermann), 164; *Pathmarks*, ed. W. McNeill (Cambridge: Cambridge University Press, 1998), 126.
8. Martin Heidegger, "Ce qui fait l'etre-essentiel d'un fondement ou «raison»," in *Questions I et II*, trans. H. Corbin (Paris: Gallimard, 1968), 142. This is the translation Lefebvre uses in *De l'État* (Paris: UGE, four volumes, 1976–8), IV, 416; *Key Writings*, ed. S. Elden, E. Lebas and E. Kofman (London: Continuum, 2003), 200.
9. For this translation, and a general discussion, see Catherine Malabou, "History and the Process of Mourning in Hegel and Freud," *Radical Philosophy* 106, March/April (2001), 15–16.
10. Lefebvre, *De l'État*, IV, 416; *Key Writings*, 200.
11. See also Martin Heidegger, *Heraklit: 1. Der Anfang des abendländischen Denkens 2. Logik: Heraklits Lehre Vom Logos*, *Gesamtausgabe*, Band 55 (Frankfurt am Main: Vittorio Klostermann, 1979) and *Der Satz vom Grund*, *Gesamtausgabe*, Band 10 (Frankfurt am Main: Vittorio Klostermann, 1997); trans. R. Lilly as *The Principle of Reason* (Bloomington: Indiana University Press, 1991).

12. Hermann Diels, *Die Fragmente der Vorsokratiker: Griechisch und deutsch*, 6th edn, ed. W. Kranz (Berlin: Weidmann, 1952), 162, fragment 52.

13. Henri Lefebvre, "Au-delà du savoir," in *Le jeu de Kostas Axelos*, ed. H. Lefebvre and P. Fougeyrollas (Paris: Fata Morgana, 1973), 22.

14. Kostas Axelos, discussion with Stuart Elden, Paris, July 6, 2004.

15. Kostas Axelos *et al.*, "Karl Marx et Heidegger," in *Arguments d'une recherche*, ed. K. Axelos (Paris: Éditions de Minuit, 1969 [1959]), 93–105; Kostas Axelos, "Entretien avec Henri Lefebvre," in *Entretiens: «reéls», imaginaires, et avec «soi-même»* (Montpellier: Fata Morgana, 1973), 69–84.

16. Henri Lefebvre, *Le retour de la dialectique: 12 mots clefs* (Paris: Messidor/Éditions Sociales, 1986), 167–8.

17. Henri Lefebvre, *Qu'est-ce que penser?* (Paris: Publisad, 1985), 13; "Au-delà du savoir," 24–6.

18. *Ibid.*, 32. See, above all, Kostas Axelos, *Héraclite et la philosophie: la première saisie de l'être en devenir de la totalité* (Paris: Éditions de Minuit, 1962).

19. For more general accounts of Axelos, see Mark Poster, *Existential Marxism in Postwar France* (Princeton: Princeton University Press, 1975); Ronald Bruzina, translator's introduction to Konrad Axelos, *Alienation, Praxis and Techne in the Thought of Karl Marx*, trans. R. Bruzina (Austin: University of Texas Press, 1976), ix–xxxiii; Eric Haviland, *Kostas Axelos: Une vie pensée, une pensée vécue* (Paris: L'Harmattan, 1995); Jean-Philippe Milet, ed., "Kostas Axelos et la question du monde," special issue of *Rue Descartes* 18 (1997); Giuseppe Lissa *et al.*, *Pour Kostas Axelos: Quatre études* (Bruxelles: Éditions Ousia, 2004); and Stuart Elden, "Kostas Axelos and the World of the Arguments Circle," in *After the Deluge: New Perspectives on Postwar French Intellectual and Cultural History*, ed. J. Bourg (Lanham: Lexington Books, 2004), 125–48.

20. Kostas Axelos, *Le Jeu du monde* (Paris: Les Éditions de Minuit, 1969).

21. Kostas Axelos, "*Mondialisation* without the World: Interviewed by Stuart Elden," *Radical Philosophy* 130 (2005), 27; see *Ce questionnement: approche-éloignement* (Paris: Les Éditions de Minuit, 2001), 40.

22. Jacques Derrida, *Without Alibi*, ed. and trans. P. Kamuf (Stanford: Stanford University Press, 2002); and *Acts of Religion*, ed. G. Anidjar (Routledge: London, 2002).

23. Axelos, "*Mondialisation* without the World," 27.

24. See Stuart Elden, "Missing the Point: Globalisation, Deterritorialisation and the Space of the World," *Transactions of the Institute of British Geographers* 30, no. 1, March (2005): 8–19.

25. Pierre Fougeyrollas, "Thèses sur la mondialisation," *Arguments* 15 (1959): 38–9.

26. See particularly, Kostas Axelos, *Vers la pensée planétaire: Le devenir-pensée du monde et le devenir-monde de la pensée* (Paris: Éditions de Minuit, 1964), 174; "Theses on Marx," trans. N. Georgopoulous, in *Continuity and Change in Marxism*, ed. N. Fischer, N. Georgopoulous, and L. Patsouras (New Jersey: Humanities Press, 1982), 67.

27. Axelos, *Vers la pensée planétaire*, 174–5; "Theses on Marx", 68.

28. Kostas Axelos, *Marx penseur de la technique: De l'aliénation de l'homme à la conquête du monde* (Paris: Éditions de Minuit, 1961); trans. R. Bruzina as *Alienation, Praxis and Techne in the Thought of Karl Marx* (Austin: University of Texas Press, 1976).

29. Kostas Axelos, interview with Stuart Elden, Paris, Autumn 2004.

30. Axelos *et al.*, "Karl Marx et Heidegger," 92.

31. *Ibid.*, 94.

32. *Ibid.*, 96–8.
33. For a discussion in the light of those writings and documents, see Stuart Elden, *Speaking against Number: Heidegger, Language and the Politics of Calculation* (Edinburgh: Edinburgh University Press, 2006), especially ch. 2. On the relation see the conclusion of that book, and Dominique Janicaud, *Heidegger en France* (Paris: Albin Michel, two volumes, 2001).
34. Axelos *et al.*, "Karl Marx et Heidegger," 102.
35. Axelos, *Arguments d'une recherche*, 196.
36. See Gilles Deleuze, "Faille et feux locaux, Kostas Axelos," *Critique* 275, April (1970): 345; *Desert Islands and Other Texts 1953–1974*, ed. D. Lapoujade, trans. M. Taormina (Los Angeles: Semiotext(e), 2004), 157. Axelos's work has inspired poets, such as Hughes Labrusse, *Le donateur* (Thaon: Amiot-Lenganey, 1991), who notes that the work operates "*Dans l'enjeu de Kostas Axelos.*"
37. Kostas Axelos, *Systématique ouverte* (Paris: Éditions de Minuit, 1984). Chapter 2 of this book appears as "The World: Being Becoming Totality," trans. G. Moore, *Environment and Planning D: Society and Space* 24, no. 5 (2006).
38. Axelos, *Arguments d'une recherche*, 199; see *Horizons du monde*, (Paris: Éditions de Minuit, 1974) 80; "Planetary Interlude," trans. S. Hess, in *Game, Play, Literature*, ed. J. Ehrmann (Boston, MA: Beacon Press, 1971), 8 (this book originally appeared as *Yale French Studies* 41, 1968). See Lefebvre, *De l'État*, IV, 418–19; *Key Writings*, 201.
39. Martin Heidegger, *Identität und Differenz* (Pfulligen: Neske, 1957), 64. This is cited by Axelos in *Vers la pensée planétaire*, 22, and *Horizons du monde*, 75.
40. Eugen Fink, *Oase des Glücks: Gedanken zu einer Ontologie des Spiels* (Freiburg and München: Karl Alber, 1957), excerpts of which are translated by U. Saine and T. Saine as "The Oasis of Happiness: Toward an Ontology of Play," in *Game, Play, Literature*, 15–30.
41. Fink, *Oase des Glücks*, 50; "The Oasis of Happiness," 29.
42. Eugen Fink, *Sixth Cartesian Meditation: The Idea of Transcendental Theory of Method*, with textual notations by E. Husserl, trans. R. Bruzina (Bloomington: Indiana University Press, 1995); Martin Heidegger and Eugen Fink, *Heraclitus Seminar*, trans. C. H. Seibert (Evanston: Northwestern University Press, 1993). On Fink, see Ronald Bruzina, *Edmund Husserl and Eugen Fink: Beginnings and Ends in Phenomenology 1928–1938* (New Haven: Yale University Press, 2004); on the Fink/Axelos relation, see Françoise Dastur, "Monde et jeu: Axelos et Fink" in Milet, ed., "Kostas Axelos", 25–38.
43. Eugen Fink, *Spiel als Weltsymbol* (Stuttgart: Kohlhammer, 1960). Axelos had this translated for the *Arguments* series *Le jeu comme symbole du monde*, trans. H. Hildenbrand and A. Lindenberg (Paris: Éditions de Minuit, 1966), and considers this Fink's most important book (discussion with Stuart Elden, Paris, July 6, 2004). See also Lefebvre, "Au-delà du savoir," 23.
44. See *ibid.*
45. Martin Heidegger, *Der Satz vom Grund*, 169; *The Principle of Reason*, 113 (translation modified). It is cited by Axelos in "Planetary Interlude," 8; and by Lefebvre in "Au-delà du savoir," 22–3.
46. Indeed, as Lefebvre puts it, for Axelos, "the play of the world is time – becoming," in "Le Monde selon Kostas Axelos," *Lignes* 15 (1992): 134 (reprinted as "Le Monde" in Lissa *et al.*, *Pour Kostas Axelos*, 35–49). In his most recent work, *Réponses énigmatiques: failles – percée* (Paris: Les Éditions de Minuit, 2005), 88, Axelos ties this to Heidegger's notion of *Ereignis*, the event or appropriation, which he translates as *Avènement*, "advent." *Ereignis* gives being and time, and includes the *world*.

47. Axelos, "*Mondialisation* without the World," 28.
48. Axelos's principal writings can be schematized as follows:

Le déploiement de l'errance	Le déploiement du jeu	Le déploiement d'une enquête
Héraclite et la philosophie (1962)	*Contribution à la logique* (1977)	*Arguments d'une recherche* (1969)
Marx penseur de la technique (1961)	*Le jeu du monde* (1969)	*Horizons du monde* (1974)
Vers la pensée planétaire (1964)	*Pour une éthique problematique* (1972)	*Problèmes de l'enjeu* (1979)

49. Axelos, *Systématique ouverte*.
50. Deleuze, *Desert Islands and Other Texts*, 76.
51. See Lefebvre, *Le retour de la dialectique*, 135.
52. Axelos, *Le jeu du monde*, 157. The original projected subtitle of this book was "*fragments de la totalité.*"
53. Axelos, *Arguments d'une recherche*, 196. See also Axelos, "Le jeu de l'ensemble des ensembles," in *Horizons du monde*, 75–84; translated by R. E. Chumbley as "Play as the System of Systems," *Sub-Stance*, 25 (1980): 20–4.
54. Henri Lefebvre, "Marxisme et technique," *Esprit* 307 (1962): 1023–8; "Kostas Axelos: *Vers la pensée planétaire*," *Esprit* 338 (1965): 1114–17.
55. Lefebvre, "Le monde selon Kostas Axelos."
56. Lefebvre, "Marxisme et technique," 1025.
57. *Ibid.*, 1026.
58. Lefebvre, "Kostas Axelos: *Vers la pensée planétaire*," 1115.
59. *Ibid.*, 1115–16.
60. Lefebvre, *La révolution urbaine* (Paris: Gallimard, 1970), 135; *Key Writings*, 148.
61. Lefebvre, *Qu'est-ce que penser?*, 110; see *De l'État*, II, 67.
62. Henri Lefebvre, *Une pensée devenue monde: Faut-il abandonner Marx?* (Paris: Fayard, 1980), 69.
63. Lefebvre, foreword to the 2nd edn, *Dialectical Materialism*, 77.
64. Lefebvre, *Le droit à la ville* (Paris: Anthropos, 1968), 130; *De l'État*, II, 67; see Martin Jay, *Marxism and Totality: The Adventures of a Concept from Lukács to Habermas* (Berkeley: University of California Press, 1984).
65. Lefebvre, *De l'État*, IV, 95.
66. *Ibid.*, 326.
67. *Ibid.*, 94. Lefebvre links these broader arguments to those of his better-known *The Production of Space* in "Le mondial et le planétaire," *Espaces et Sociétés* 8, February (1973): 15–22.
68. Lefebvre, *De l'État*, IV, 435; *Key Writings*, 203.
69. Lefebvre, *De l'État*, IV, 418–19; *Key Writings*, 201.
70. Lefebvre, *De l'État*, IV, 29; see *ibid.*, III, 134.
71. *Ibid.*, III, 133.
72. See Elden, *Speaking against Number*, especially ch. 3.
73. Lefebvre, *De l'État*, III, 133.
74. Henri Lefebvre, "Interview – Débat sur le Marxisme: Léninisme–Stalinisme ou auto-gestion?," *Autogestion et socialisme* 33/34 (1976): 115–26, 125.

75. Axelos, interview with Stuart Elden, Paris, Autumn 2004.
76. *De l'État*, IV, 23. On this aspect of Lefebvre's work generally, see Elden, *Understanding Henri Lefebvre*, ch. 6, and, especially, Neil Brenner, "Global, Fragmented, Hierarchical: Henri Lefebvre's Geographies of Globalization," *Public Culture* 10, no. 1 (1997): 135–67.
77. Axelos, *Vers la pensée planétaire*, 177; "Theses on Marx," 69.
78. Lefebvre, *De l'État*, IV, 420; *Key Writings*, 201–2.
79. Lefebvre, *Une pensée devenue monde*, 180. For a more detailed discussion, see Elden, *Understanding Henri Lefebvre*, 241–4.
80. Lefebvre, "Le monde selon Kostas Axelos," 38.

6

LEFEBVRE WITHOUT HEIDEGGER
"Left-Heideggerianism" *qua contradictio in adiecto*

Geoffrey Waite

For Ayça Çubukçu

This is the magic and the metaphysics of shit.

Henri Lefebvre, 1946[1]

Heidegger is the most profound modern philosopher.

Henri Lefebvre, 1980[2]

I'm tired of Nietzsche and I'm scared shitless of Heidegger.

Louis Althusser, 1984[3]

EXHIBITING DEMARCATION LINES

Hijacking and detouring a technique from phenomenology, I'll *exhibit* a hegemonic tendency in contemporary Lefebvre studies: the promotion of Left-Heideggerianism.[4] (Articulators of Lefebvre with Left-Nietzscheanism appear uncommitted to their effort.)[5] My aim is to deconstruct and destroy this project insofar as my incapacity for *Gelassenheit* (letting-be or releasement) allows. Adhering to a fundamental Leninist principle, I draw *demarcation lines* between "Left" and "Heideggerianism" on the one axis, Lefebvre and Left-Heideggerianism on the other: the crosshairs of my gun sight.[6] My nominal target is the combination of anti-thinking (taking Heidegger's side) with anti-communism (taking the side of communism's impossible possibility), which is a Left-Heideggerianism guilty of anti-communist thoughtlessness. My ultimate target is traditionally communist: "the thing itself" that is State and capitalism.[7]

Lefebvre was a sometimes avid and always mediocre and careless reader of Heidegger. He did not need to be a careful reader for his productive appropriations (not least or most of Heidegger) because he adhered to that dominant line of reading in our era which dictates that one cannot, need not, or should not understand authors as they understand themselves, though such understanding must include what they leave unsaid, for whatever reason. Thus Lefebvre might have been better off without Heidegger—perhaps his "inherent dark underside"[8]—but that was impossible for him. Lefebvre studies could acknowledge his incapacity and be better off without Heidegger until it can read him. Meantime, Lefebvre should not be employed to promote Left-Heideggerianism as is being done by Left-Liberal intellectual historians and radical geographers (or antipodes) in a garden-variety academic variant of "capitalo-parliamentarianism" that Marxism must combat as being non-Marxist and non-communist.[9] Simultaneously, their logic is non-philosophical or rather non-thinking insofar as authentic questioning and thinking are opposed to philosophy and vice versa.[10] Because the promotion of Left-Heideggerianism is part of a strangulating weed system that is anti-communist and anti-thinking, the task of thinkers and communists—not necessarily the same—is to exhibit this rhizome and eradicate it. "*Hermeneutics manages its task only on the way of destruction,*"[11] and the task of us communists is to "*smash*" the "bureaucratic-military machine" of State and capitalism.[12] In order to create.

Additionally at stake are two related but separate issues: the Marxist philosopher Lefebvre's view of Heidegger *compared to* Heidegger's view of Marxism and philosophy; and the structure of Left-Heideggerianism *independent of* reference to Lefebvre, since this project substantially pre-dates and exceeds his work.

LEFT-HEIDEGGERIANS, NOW AND THEN

The first Left-Heideggerian was Kiyoshi Miki (1897–1945), before the publication in 1927 of *Being and Time*,[13] one of several Japanese philosophers, all contemporaries of Lefebvre (1901–91), who in the 1920s studied with or read Heidegger (1889–1976)—not all Marxists, and not all the Marxists Heideggerians. (Most significant in the latter group was Tosaka Jun [1900–45] with his thesis—decades before Lefebvre—that "thought has become quotidianized" and that "everydayness was a philosophic category that needed immediate attention.")[14] Then followed Marcuse in Germany (1928) and Kojève in France (1931).[15] There have been many Left-Heideggerians, though this is rarely a self-designation, with Sloterdijk (in the 1980s) an exception.[16] Right-Heideggerians include Nolte, with his refreshingly candid thesis that "insofar as Heidegger resisted the attempted communist solution he was historically correct," and that "committing himself to the National Socialist solution . . . in no way made him historically wrong at the outset."[17] The major recently anointed Left-Heideggerian is Badiou on the grounds that he shares with Heidegger a resolute post- (not anti-) foundationalist conception of thought-and-action, due to comparable views of contingency and the aleatory ("there is": *es gibt, il y a*; "world worlds": *es weltet, monde mondanise*) and "event" (*Ereignis, événement*).[18] Badiou doubtless rejects this interpellation quite rightly, but it has conceptual clout, which cannot be said for how Lefebvre's handlers are training him in the ring of Left-Heideggerianism, crucially because contingency and the aleatory are not operative problems for Lefebvre.

Heidegger tends to reduce Marx to the young (Hegelian or Feuerbachian) co-author of Thesis XI: "The philosophers have only *interpreted* the world differently; the point is to *change* it."[19] Fighting for his own anti-humanism, Heidegger ignores the mature Marx (*Notes on Wagner*) and adopts the humanist Marx represented by Marcuse, his student, whose first publication, "Contributions to a Phenomenology of Historical Materialism" (1928), affirms that *Being and Time* "marks a turning point in the history of philosophy: the point where bourgeois philosophy dissolves itself from within and clears the way for a new 'concrete' science," adding that "to every concrete-historical Dasein belongs a concrete-historical 'living-space' ['*Lebensraum*']"[20]—an ill-starred term that Marcuse means as constructive criticism. Hereby the first significant European Left-Heideggerian is instrumental in unwittingly but forcefully nudging the teacher toward political commitments the student soon sees as opposed, indeed lethal, to his own. (Revolutions produce counterrevolutions, Left-Heideggerians produce Right-Heideggerians and vice versa.) This is before Lefebvre read Heidegger for the first time in 1930, only to reject him as nihilistic and quietist.[21] That year Benjamin hatches his scheme with Brecht to "smash that Heidegger to bits," which immediately comes to naught.[22] From the start, Left-Heideggerianism is aligned with Left-Hegelianism or Left-Kantianism; to attack the one requires attacking the other(s).

But my more important contention is that *Heidegger* is responsible for Left-Heideggerianism, *more* than for Right-Heideggerianism.[23] Soon after his de-Nazification hearings and under the irrevocably setting sun of the history of Being, Heidegger's successful attempt to orient his thinking westward toward France required displacing (not replacing) Nietzsche by Marx. In the 1960s he states: "with the reversal of metaphysics that Karl Marx already accomplished the most extreme possibility of philosophy is reached. It has entered into its end."[24] High praise. His new-found interlocutors Beaufret and Char had been *résistants*; as was Axelos in Greece, additionally a communist.—One of Heidegger's several "turns" and inceptions of Left-Heideggerianism.

Lefebvre's position on Heidegger appears to have shifted abruptly, from hostile rejection in 1930 (reading *Being and Time* as an apology for nihilistic political inactivism) and 1946 (when Lefebvre was basically a highbrow Stalinist stooge)[25] until ecstatic embrace in 1959 upon encountering *Holzwege*, essays written from Heidegger's ostensible retreat from the Nazi Party in 1935/6 up to 1946, beginning with "The Origin of the Artwork." Reading *Holzwege* within the year of his quasi-voluntary and definitive expulsion from one Communist Party, Lefebvre likely drew an analogy between Heidegger's commitment to the NSDAP and his own to the Stalinist PCF. There followed the requisite synthesis of the two Lefebvrean positions, as expressed most extensively in *Métaphilosophie* (1965) and appropriated most creatively in *La production de l'espace* (1974), among other writings preceding his timely death in 1991. But this only apparent shift was dictated by his consistent inability to read Heidegger as he understood himself, supplemented by tendentious purposes.

CONTRA SYLLOGISM, OR COLLAPSING NEW BRIDGES

Calibrating my gun sight, here is the targeted Left-Heideggerian syllogism (actually an enthymeme): 1) X is crucially Y; 2) Z is crucial for X, but Z is crucially not Y; 3) ergo Y-X is crucial.

1. Lefebvre was a Marxist philosopher. Negatively stated by a leading booster in the industry, Lefebvre is too important to be left to "pick 'n' mix" postmodernism, and must be extracted from dominant "attention . . . in the field of geography, or related areas such as urban sociology or cultural studies."[26] In opposition I hold that this is *grosso modo* exactly where Lefebvre's authentic influence should remain; the absence of Lefebvre from major histories of Heidegger's influence and of Marxism and philosophy is not a market niche to be exploited, but a reasonably accurate picture of where Lefebvre's originality does *not* lie. Positively stated by the same booster, "Lefebvre described himself, not just as a Marxist, but as a Marxist *philosopher*."[27] Neither key term, "Marxist" or "philosopher," is adequately defined by such non-Marxist non-philosophers, though they appear favorably disposed to both Marxism and philosophy, which they *therefore* talk a lot *about*. This leads me to question "who is competent to judge,"[28] insofar as from a Marxist perspective liberals are of the class enemy, and from Heidegger's perspective philosophers are enemies of thinking and questioning. "Heidegger never thinks 'about' something," Arendt observed, "he thinks something,"[29] which for him entails being *gescheitert* (shattered) and *verrückt* (displaced, insane).[30] The insistence by non-philosophers on the import of (Heideggerian) philosophy is succinctly explained in sociological terms elsewhere.[31] Lefebvre is no longer important as a "Leftist philosopher" (compared to Althusser, Badiou, Deleuze, Derrida, Karatani, Negri, and several New-Spinozists) but his remarkable thick descriptions of place (*lieu*) should continue to be tested and applied creatively, particularly outside and in comparison with the so-called first world.

2. "Heidegger was the twentieth-century philosopher with whom Lefebvre most engaged."[32] (Lefebvre much preferred nineteenth-century philosophers—but no matter.) "Lefebvre can therefore profitably be read on a political and philosophical level as operating between Marx and Heidegger."[33] So it is profitable to read Heidegger when reading our Marxist philosopher, and assuming that Heidegger was a philosopher but not Marxist. Far worse, we hear that Heidegger's "philosophy" entailed a "conservative politics"[34] and "respect for Nazism."[35] Profit motive aside, these Left-Liberal claims are made despite Heidegger's loathing of what he branded "conservatism" for its incapacity to embrace "the Revolution,"[36] by which he meant, still in 1937/8, the National Socialist revolution that he did not necessarily "respect" but had aggressively tried to lead. The same claims are also made despite Heidegger's increasingly ferocious animus against philosophy on behalf of what he called simply questioning and thinking—an animus irreducible to sociological explanation.

   Lefebvre just barely engaged what is most required to read Heidegger. Against French or English, Heidegger wrote in untranslatable Greco-German; against the insistence on public, exoteric expression, he wrote in the ancient traditions of esotericism and "efficacious speaking" (κραινειν); against dialectics, he affirmed tautology; and against more potent challenges to his thinking and questioning, he aimed to produce the comparatively impotent and relatively harmless phenomenon that has always been Left-Heideggerianism.

   My last thesis crucially supplements the view that Heidegger's position on politics (le politique et la politique) was primarily passive, defensive or prophylactic. In that view, instead of attacking the Left directly, Heidegger's Being and Time "removed the possible resistance of, so to speak, regular and extreme conservatives on the Right against National Socialism," since he "explicitly criticizes the theoretical framework" that allowed Right-wing intellectuals "to keep their distance from National Socialism."[37] Concomitantly, "the decision to cancel society does not prevent the authentic Daseine [English plural of Dasein] from taking over modern technology and capitalism as an economic system."[38] But Heidegger's position was also proactive.

3. Voilà Left-Heideggerianism. Following from 1) and 2), and assuming "Marxist" and "Leftist" to be convertible terms (contestable!), our syllogism in dispute "presupposes the possibility of somehow bridging the Marxian and Heideggerian conceptions within a new kind of radical politics."[39] "Citing" this remark as best he can,[40] our spokesman responds, "in some respects this is what Lefebvre has already done: he appropriated a number of ideas from Heidegger, whilst subjecting them to a Marxist critique."[41] And since Lefebvre's place is "between Marx and Heidegger," it is from here we are to construct a bridge "toward a Left-Heideggerianism."[42] Wherewith we have reached the conclusion of our syllogism or enthymeme.

I respond with a demarcation line. "Left-Heideggerianism" is *contradictio in adiecto* from *both* sides of the term—*except* that Heidegger programmed the project, with lots of unwitting assistance from the Left. *Otherwise*, the concept is philologically, hermeneutically, philosophically, and politically without an object. As for any bridge, "when it is an authentic bridge," it "is never first a symbol and then a thing" or "first a thing and then a symbol."[43] Since "science does not think," which absolutely includes intellectual history and geography, "there is *no bridge* away from the sciences to thinking, but instead only the leap [*nur den Sprung*] . . . which brings us not only to the other side but to a totally different *Ortschaft*"[44]—a "place" ultimately different from Left-Heideggerianism or (bridges lead in two directions) Right-Marxism.

AMBUSHING LANGUAGE

Exhibiting that place requires exhibiting Marxist philosopher Lefebvre's view of Heidegger in comparison to Heidegger's view of Marxism and philosophy, but also of politico-philosophical rhetoric, which entails deceit and entrapment. Heidegger says it seldom (once would be almost excessive), but he hints that λοyος (logos) is related etymologically to λοχος (ambush).[45]

Notwithstanding his fluency in "normal" German, Lefebvre remained clueless how to read Heidegger's peculiar language. One of the Molotov cocktails the then Stalinist philosopher hurls in *L'existentialisme* (1946) at "the profascist philosopher"[46] reads: "It is not the Hitlerian politics or the racism that the analyst re-encounters in the philosophy of Heidegger: more profoundly, more seriously [*gravement*], it is the 'style' of Hitlerism, that of the SS."[47] More grave than my inability to differentiate Hitler's SS from his politics and racism is the fact that, *however* we describe it, Heidegger's style must be precisely *analyzed*. Which is *impossible* unless we recognize its untranslatable Greek-cum-German and retrofitted variation on ancient esoteric speaking, also called "the rhetoric of silence" (*Sigetik*).

As the Ruse of Reason dictates, Lefebvre publishes *L'existentialisme* the same year Heidegger has begun publicly to woo mostly Left-leaning French intellectuals with his "Letter on 'Humanism,'" but also the year he writes, apparently for his eyes only:

> I am silent in thinking not only since 1927, since the publication of *Being and Time*, but indeed *in* it itself and prior to that constantly. This silence is the preparation for the Saying of That-Which-Is-To-Be-Thought and this preparation is the Ex-perience, which is a Doing and an Action. To be sure, "existing" without necessarily having to have an [overtly political or public] engagement [any longer].[48]

Within a year, recovering from psychosomatic collapse during his de-Nazification hearings, Heidegger pens *From the Experience of Thinking* (privately published, 1949) with its dictum, "*Wer groß denkt, muß groß irren.*"[49] Understood or translated as "He who thinks greatly errs/strays greatly," this has scandalized readers because it has been read as craven justification for Heidegger's Nazism and the Holocaust.[50] Yet the real scandal lies between the lines. Heidegger uses the verb *irren* not merely in the double (modern and exoteric) sense of "error" and "errancy" but in the supplemental (ancient and esoteric) sense of "trickery," "deceit," "trap," "ambush." The *Æneid's* Trojan horse "conceals *error*" (*latet error*, viz., "Minerva's gift of death") but also incarnates *error* because this is how Virgil translates the equivalent Greek term, $\delta o\lambda o\varsigma$, in the *Iliad* and *Odyssey* for that horse.[51] (Historically, epistemology follows stratagem.) In 1949 Heidegger hinted in a newspaper that a name for *error* in this sense is *Holzweg*.[52]

Reading *Holzwege* in 1959 and comparing it to *Being and Time* (i.e., his own hostile reaction in 1930) leaves Lefebvre puzzling if there are not "*plusieurs Heidegger.*"[53] His French is unwittingly precise because, for Heidegger, in the exoteric many there is indeed esoterically One, whereas for Lefebvre, there must be basically two: so-called Heidegger I and Heidegger II, the typology Heidegger explicitly rejects in 1962, affirming that he always maintains a single "standpoint."[54] In *Métaphilosophie* (1965), his only sustained analysis (such as it is) of Heidegger, Lefebvre predictably concocts a synthesis: "In the Heideggerian meditation is concealed something of the best and something of the worst: the archaic and the visionary, the world of discourse and at the same time the poetic word."[55] The erstwhile "worst" Heidegger, the SS *stylist*, goes incognito in "the world of *discourse*" but now policed by the "best" Heidegger of "the poetic *word*," the author of *Holzwege* and other anthologies, notably the 1954 *Vorträge und Aufsätze* (including the favorite of impressionable architects, planners, and geographers, "Building Dwelling Thinking"). What the "visionary" envisioned is *Lefebvre's* peculiarly Marxist concepts of "place," "worlding," "dwelling," "everyday life," etc. But Heidegger's *language*—whether understood as "style" or "world of discourse" or "poetic word"—remains at once studiously unanalyzed and *nonetheless or therefore* incorporated into what will henceforth be Lefebvre's lifework, his corps/e.

ON THE CONCRETE

A decade later in *Hegel–Marx–Nietzsche* (1975), Lefebvre justifies excluding Heidegger from his troika or "constellation" Hegel–Marx–Nietzsche because Heidegger "draws a disquieting apology for the German language," which "prohibits him from making a radical critique of the Occidental (European) Logos, though he comes close."[56] The idiocy that Heidegger's critique is insufficiently "radical" in this regard begs the question of Lefebvre's capacity to judge and of his own radicality given his inattention to Heidegger's language ($\lambda o\gamma o\varsigma$) also as ambush ($\lambda o\chi o\varsigma$), thus leaving whatever is truly disquieting in Heidegger as effective as ever. The accompanying charge that Heidegger is insufficiently "concrete" misses the precise linguistic place where he is more concrete than his benighted readers. Lefebvre wrote, somewhere, a remark seminal for the Left-Heideggerian project:

> Heidegger, now, shows us a world ravaged by technology, that through its ravages leads us towards another dream, another (as yet unperceived) world. He warns us: a lodging built on the basis of economic or technological dictates is as far removed from dwelling as the language of machines is from poetry. He does not tell us how to construct, "here and now" buildings and cities.[57]

Dreaming aside, what is odd in Lefebvre's statement is that Heidegger never intends to "tell us how to construct" any object hic et nunc and specifically not cities and buildings. "Building Dwelling Thinking" (1951) began:

> In the following we will attempt to think about dwelling and building. This thinking about building does *not* presume to discover ideas for building *let alone* to give rules for building. This attempt to think does *not at all* represent building from out of architecture or technology, but instead traces building back into that realm toward which everything belongs that *is*.[58]

Whatever Heidegger *does* "construct" (Latin constructio is also syntax) is within what the "Letter on 'Humanism'" (1946/7) nominates as the House of Being or Language, adding crucially that "in its saying thinking brings only the unspoken word of Being into language."[59] It is insufficient listening to what Heidegger says; you must attend to what he precisely does not say. Pace Lefebvre, Heidegger is concrete and elusive where it matters most—the very language you are reading, though mainly inscribed between the lines, never in translation.

Heidegger states early on that "purely theoretical assessment" and "affective engagement with things and with others" both derive from that "equiprimordiality" of politics and language which is quintessentially "everyday."[60] Inattentive, the mantra chanted by Lefebvre scholars, meditating close as they dare to their guru, is that "because of his abstraction and mystification, Heidegger needs to be constantly stood on his feet, grounded, rooted in material reality"[61]—by means of which presti-digitation, aided by "the Marxist philosopher Lefebvre," "Left-Heideggerianism" is to be (re)produced. (Perchance this scholar could explain his vapid conclusion, "If Lefebvre's politics were Marxist, his view of the political was close to both Marx and Heidegger,"[62] after telling us what the latter's views of the political really were.) Apart from the fact that anybody stood on her or his feet remains the same body in all other respects, Heidegger is eminently concrete and rooted, unless one illicitly abstracts language from material reality.[63] The radical phenomenological exhibitions of the lecture-room chalk quickly followed (NB!) by the gun in The Question of the Thing

(1935/6)[64] rival (when they do not surpass) any description produced by Lefebvre or certainly Lefebvreans, unless bourgeois proclivity requires that un habitat pavillionnaire (summer house, bungalow, or dacha)[65] be "more concrete" than chalk and a gun (or jug, shoes, temple), not to mention a word's trajectory from Anaxamander to the present. The concrete is where we typically don't look while walking and therefore trip—as over the writing between the lines before our eyes.

Lefebvrean Left-Heideggerians acknowledge that Heidegger's own thick descriptions are concrete when they agree with or learn from them, and their maestro's admiration is on record in La production de l'espace and elsewhere. But all wax especially befuddled when Heidegger becomes politically concrete, incapable of seeing how this dual-concreteness works. Radical geographers are duly warned that Heideggerian

> sentiments easily lend themselves to an interpretation and a politics that is both exclusionary and parochialist, communitarian if not intensely nationalist (hence Heidegger's respect for Nazism). Heidegger refuses to see mediated social relationships (via the market or any other medium) with others (things or people) as in any way expressive of any kind of authenticity.[66]

This silliness would not be worth citing were it not accompanied by the project of "finding some sort of bridge between the concerns [about place] expressed in the Marxian and Heideggerian approaches."[67] The axiomatic evidence that Heidegger did not refuse to see mediated relationships with others lies precisely in his concrete politics as noted. Read the extensive and profound exhibitions of "being-in-the-world" and "being-with-others" in Being and Time, followed by the articulation of Dasein to that quintessential "social relationship" called Volk.[68] Left-liberals may have their reasons today (though many did not in the late 1920s and early 1930s) to disapprove of Heidegger's "mediated social relationships" when they become politically radical (Nazi), but at least they should understand this for what it is— the only politico-ethical decision in his life—and not assume that Lefebvre provides an alternative on the grounds that

> the strength of the Lefebvrian [sic] construction . . . is precisely that it refuses to see materiality, representation and imagination as separate worlds and that it denies the particular privileging of any one realm over the other, while simultaneously insisting that it is only in the social practices of daily life that the ultimate significance of all forms of activity is registered.[69]

Not only is there no contrast here with Heidegger, who also refuses to see these as "separate worlds" (he did not radicalize phenomenology for nothing); the graver problem is that, if we were ever to deny "the particular privileging of any one realm over the other, while simultaneously insisting that it is *only* in the social practices of daily life that the ultimate significance of *all* forms of activity are registered," then *opposition* to the violently "particular" Nazi *and*/*or* capitalist realm reduces to historicistic and relativistic impotency.[70] This is doubtless the best Left-Heideggerianism Heidegger could have hoped for. But where is Lefebvre in this problematic?

TERRORIZING TAUTOLOGY

Heidegger's *es weltet* (it worlds) or *Welt weltet* (world worlds)—giving "middle-voiced" verbal impulsion to the substantive—emerges in the aftermath of the First World War. Another Lefebvre contemporary, Gadamer (1900–2002), pre-dates to the War Emergency Semester of 1919 the "turn" (*Kehre*) that Heidegger first mentions publicly in "Letter on 'Humanism'" (1946/7),[71] so precipitously misread by Lefebvre to demarcate "Heidegger I" from "Heidegger II." The first French translation of Heidegger's 1929 version, "Welt *ist* nie, sondern *weltet*," is in 1932; but a misleading definite article is interpolated that Lefebvre usually retained, Lefebvreans typically ape, and Heidegger never intended: "Le [*sic*] monde n'*est* point, mais *mondanise*."[72] (Add this definite article and—*presto!*—you get a "globalization" with *nothing* serious to do with Heidegger, *pace* the Lefebvre Industry.) That year Marx's Paris Manuscripts appeared, so seminal for Marcuse, Lefebvre, and yet another "origin" of Left-Heideggerianism. By the time of its reappearance in the now Nazi Heidegger's 1935/6 essay "The Origin of the Artwork," the key phrase has decidedly theologico-political valence.[73] Reading this text in 1958, in the Dionysiac rapture Bourdieu justly finds risibly elitist, Lefebvre recalled:

> I was enchanted and taken by a vision—this word is not quite accurate—all the more gripping in contrast to the triviality of the majority of the philosophical texts appearing in those years . . . There is no antagonism between the cosmic-historical vision of Heidegger and the historical-practical vision of Marx.[74]

Call him Henri (a.k.a. "Left-Heidegger") Lafièvre.

During his long life, he may have abandoned as impossible his Marxist combat against the overwhelming odds of a comparatively early stage of *mondialisation* or, more precisely, *mondialatinisation* ("this strange alliance of Christianity, as the experience of the death of God, and tele-technoscientific capitalism").[75] At age seventy-seven, he sighs:

> The Revolution was depended upon to create the "world" [*le "monde"*] and "worldliness" [*la "mondialité"*]. It was the worldwide revolution [*la révolution mondiale*]. Nowadays we must realize that the worldwide and worldliness,

with their features, hazardous and unforeseen, constitute the "revolution" itself, instead of concluding it.[76]

It is hardly fortuitous that Lefebvre had *misappropriated* this concept of "world" from Heidegger. *Voilà* again Left-Heideggerianism. In the same 1978 text we read:

When philosophy has explored worldliness, it establishes significant proposi-tions. When Heidegger says "*Die* [sic] *Welt weltet*" [*le monde se mondifie*], this statement, which is *nearly a tautology*, makes great sense. He means that the worldwide conceives itself in and by itself and not through another thing (history, spirit, work, science, etc.). The world becomes world, becoming what it was virtually. It transforms itself by becoming worldwide. In it, discovery and creation converge.[77]

Several curiosities operate Lefebvre's self-prescribed "dialectical" (or "trilectical") distinction between *le monde* and *la mondialité*, which has annihilatingly absorbed *la révolution mondiale*. The distinction appears homologous with his hackneyed version of the distinctions between *le politique* and *la politique* and between theory and practice— the exact distinction Heidegger does *worse* than disdain because it is *always already obviated in what he calls presencing*.[78] (As Althusser's Pascal remarked, "put yourself on your knees, move your lips in prayer and you'll believe.")[79]

Heidegger is *constitutively* tautological, in *explicit* opposition to dialectics—not strategically *tout court* but against the Hegelo-Marxian, no matter how fine-tuned. The asseveration that Heidegger's phrase is "*nearly* a tautology" is symptomatic of Lefebvre's absorption of Heidegger into his own dialectic, a gesture mimicked mindlessly in Lefebvre studies.

In a statement first published in French (1976), Heidegger avows:

The thinking we are asking after I call tautological thinking. That is the primordial sense of phenomenology. This manner of thinking maintains itself on this side of any possible distinction between theory and praxis. To understand that, we have to learn to distinguish between *path* and *method*. In philosophy, there are only paths; on the contrary, in the sciences there are only methods, that is, modes of procedure in the primordial sense of pheno-menology. Moreover, this kind of thinking is *prior* to any possible distinction between theory and praxis.[80]

He reiterates his position in *Being and Time* that dialectical thinking is "a genuine philosophical embarrassment,"[81] and now, nearing death, he reaffirms that "we must recognize completely that tautology is the only possibility for what dialectic can only veil."[82]

What the logical structure of the tautology veils is theologico-political (not onto-theological) violence. Tautologies are ultimately traceable to "God is God" ("I am that I am/was/will be"); and "the name of God is a veritable bomb" due to "the rapport that unites violence and monotheism."[83] From my position: *all monotheists are potential terrorists, all actual terrorists are not monotheists.*

Heidegger's style, discourse, or word is radically tautological. Its potential for terrorism obtains even (if not especially) when the late Heidegger speaks *sotto voce* of letting-be or releasement (*Gelassenheit*) and of in-dwelling (*Inständigkeit*) as the places where "something akin to power of action and decisiveness rule [*walten*]."[84] For the very early Heidegger (1919), too, "dialectic in the sense of the dissolution of contradictions that are ever newly posited" both "conceals a non-dialectical principle" (his brilliant insight) and "*is factually uncreative.*"[85] In opposition, tautologies are *factually destructive-creative*—like thinking *and/or* communism.

THE *ERROR* OF DWELLING

As for that desired bridge "between Marx and Heidegger," for Heidegger (and likely Marx) any bridge is an *Ort*, a place, site, or locale for "the production of space"—much as Lefebvre understood it.[86] In the decisive Schmittian formula of 1950,

> All subsequent regulations of a written or unwritten kind derive their power from the inner measure of an original, constitutive act of spatial ordering. This original act is *nomos*. All subsequent developments are either results of and expansions on this act or else redistributions (*anadasmoi*)—either a continuation on the same basis or a disintegration of and departure from the constitutive act of the spatial order established by land-appropriation, the founding of cities, or colonization . . . Thus, for us, *nomos* is a matter of the fundamental process of apportioning space that is essential to every historical epoch.[87]

Originary acts of founding are, as such, violent.[88] Not least the *nomos* (law or custom). "Law, the lord of all, mortals and immortals, carries everything with high hand, justifying the extreme of violence."[89] As Heidegger also knows, Ort (Germanic **uzda-*) originally signified a weapon tip, specifically the spoils of battle with which the victor stakes out the footprint for a monument, temple, or entire city—globe even.[90]

In *La révolution urbaine* (1970), Lefebvre appropriated Heideggerian *Wohnen* to remark that "the misfortune of architecture is that it wanted to construct monuments, but the idea of *habiting* them was either conceived in terms of those monuments or neglected entirely."[91] Yet Lefebvre, like the next-best Left-Heideggerian, just misses the salient Heideggerian point, so to speak, regarding Ort as site of inaugural and perduring violence.[92] This seminal misprision produces, especially in *La production de l'espace* (1974), several mistaken impressions about place that are potentially devastating—not to his own thick descriptions necessarily but certainly to the notion that one can appeal to Heidegger to produce them. (Japanese philosophers had learned this lesson before Lefebvre had heard of Heidegger.)

Lefebvre imagines that for Heidegger "dwelling stands opposed to errancy [*contrastant avec l'errance*]."[93] This makes good common or rather Hegelian sense, but is metaphysical claptrap for Heidegger. Lefebvre's *demeure* translates Heidegger's *Wohnen*, whose *Irre* or *Irrnis* becomes *l'errance*. Lefebvre makes much of what he calls the "contradiction" between "the ephemeral and the stable (between Dwelling [*la Demeure*] and Wandering [*l'Errance*], in the philosophical terminology of Heidegger)."[94] But this is *not* Heidegger's point on *Ort*. Lefebvre's relentlessly Hegelo-Marxian ideology, no matter how non-teleological it figures itself to be, is compelled to see everything in terms of contradictions somehow to be synthesized in his own work, constantly laboring to show that the tautologies in Heidegger were only *nearly* or *apparently* such, when this is what they are *precisely*.

Wherever Lefebvrean dialectics proposes, Heideggerian tautology disposes. *Wohnen* is wholly "opposed" to *habitation* inasmuch as it always already signifies *errancy*— the errancy that leads one to take, more or less violently, ownership of food, loot, bodies, or land on which to dwell. Heidegger knows that the signifier *wohnen* derives from *gewinnen* (to win, conquer) and from the Indo-European root, *uen[∂]-, "to travel in search of something," originally food and weapons to stake out any *Ort*, including linguistic ambushes. *Pace* Lefebvre, *wohnen* in no sense is "opposed" to errancy, particularly in the ancient senses of *error* as trap ($\delta o \lambda o \varsigma$) and of language ($\lambda o \gamma o \varsigma$) as ambush ($\lambda o \chi o \varsigma$). They are all of One tautological and therefore potentially violent essence.

Heidegger displaces "philosophy" by "thinking and questioning," but still adheres to one law stated in 1927: "In the end the business of philosophy is to protect the *force of the most elemental statements*, in which Dasein expresses itself, from becoming leveled off by common understanding."[95] If that is true, the task of us terrorist (not just counterterrorist) philologists thinking with clenched fist is to exhibit this "force" and use it to empower "common" people.[96]

IMPOSSIBLE POSSIBILITY VERSUS CAGED BIRDS

Nearing (non)conclusion, my salient objection to "Left-Heideggerianism" and its current boosters in Lefebvre studies specifically is that this term is *philologically incompetent* and *philosophically incoherent*. From the perspective of communism *and* thinking, "Left-Heideggerianism" is *contradictio in adiecto*. Left-Heideggerianism in skewed alliance with Right-Heideggerianism has also shown itself to be *politically and militarily destructive* since its inception in the 1920s—first in Japan, later in Germany and France, most recently in the bloodbath of ex-Yugoslavia.[97] We *cannot* say that Left-

Heideggerianism is *necessarily* destructive insofar as with eso/exoteric systems it is impossible to know apodictically their political "content." We *can* exhibit their "form," drawing this demarcation line. Accepting Heidegger's insistence that "higher than actuality stands *possibility*,"[98] Left-Heideggerianism *might* be competent, coherent, even creative, but "serious meditation" on the "reciprocal fascination–repulsion between Marxism and Heideggerianism" has indeed not begun.[99] Pace Lefebvre and Lefebvre studies.

I began with the term exhibition (*Aufweisung*) because it began the first self-conscious attempt to produce Left-Heideggerianism in the so-called Occident. Marcuse's first publication attempted to appropriate *Being and Time* to "exhibit" what he called "the fundamental situation of Marxism," viz., "its central concern with the historical possibility of the radical act—an act that should [or shall: *soll*] clear the way for a new and necessary reality, as it brings forth the realization of the whole person." Moreover, "The exhibition of this fundamental situation . . . does not intend to make the aim of this investigation that of establishing from the outset the sense of Marxism, but rather to demarcate the ground from which such an interpretation must proceed."[100] If this demarcation in 1928 continues in the twenty-first century, it is because Marcuse was right: "The question of the radical act can only sensibly be posed where the act is grasped as the decisive realization of the human essence and simultaneously precisely this realization appears as *factual impossibility*, i.e., in a *revolutionary* situation."[101] Not long after reading this text, Heidegger intervened as a Nazi leader in his own *and ever possible* revolutionary situation. Whereas on the properly communist side, our project in a precise sense *remains impossible*.

> The possibility of the impossible is the foundation of politics. This is opposed massively to everything one teaches us today, which is that politics is the management of the necessary. Politics begins with the same gesture with which Rousseau clears away the ground of inequality: by leaving to one side all the facts.
>
> It is important to leave to one side all the facts, for an event to eventuate [*pour qu'advienne l'événement*].[102]

Communism's authentic task is never the impossible construction of heaven on earth but the ever possible combat against hell; to *this* end, however, there is great heuristic value in *some* kinds of fact, if that means *philological probity*. "To read a text *as* text, without interpolating an interpretation, is the last form of 'inner experience'—perhaps one that is hardly possible."[103] (*Welt weltet* is not *LE monde SE mondifie*.)

Humankind is better off without capitalism and any State; Lefebvre's legacy is better off without Heidegger (or Nietzsche), which I say as no bad friend of Lefebvre. Philologically and philosophically careful—in *that* sense factual—readers prefer to subtract other authors from their main ones, whom they strive to understand as they understood themselves, also in the unsaid of their saying, to exhibit what the Greeks called το πραγμα αυτο (a matter of common concern), and only then begin combat if necessary. Such readers reject the multiplication of intertextual references ("X with Y" or "X and Y") at the least provocation, an occupational hazard of speed-reading producers of flashcards without philological probity in the agora.

In the Politeia Socrates informs us that, were he ever to speak "without image or symbol of my meaning" of what lies "outside the cave at the end of the dialectic," he would speak αλλ αυτο το αληθες.[104] This is commonly translated "the very truth." Schleiermacher translated αληθεια here not as Wahrheit (truth) but as die Sache selbst (the thing itself)[105]—the shibboleth of radical phenomenology. And this is how Heidegger translates το πραγμα αυτο in Plato's Seventh Letter—"the matter itself" or "the case itself" being whatever Plato says he will never render into writing.[106] Compare the root of "tautology": το αυτο + λογος. Die Sache selbst is at once "theoretical" and "practical," in that sense tautological, and in any case the last thing to be said, if ever. Destructively terrorist, it can be creative.

The prefix "Left-" affixed to Heidegger "adds nothing to that garbage-bin style [ce style de poubelle] used to spare oneself of any reflection."[107] To hijack and detour Lefebvre's own polemics, what have contemporary Left-Heideggerians done "but thrown into circulation the small change of Heidegger . . . with some counterfeit coins of their own"?[108] This was Lefebvre's own economy of reading Heidegger. But was Lefebvre therefore a Left-Heideggerian? That case I must leave open. Kafka knows: "A cage went looking for a bird."[109] With his Left-Heideggerians, Heidegger still finds easy marks, including a disproportionate number of Marxs. This case is closed henceforth.

NOTES

1. Henri Lefebvre, L'existentialisme, 2nd edn (Paris: Anthropos, 2001 [1946]), 63. Lefebvre's target is Heidegger behind Sartre.
2. Henri Lefebvre, Une pensée devenue monde: faut-il abandoner Marx? (Paris: Fayard, 1980), 40.
3. Louis Althusser, Sur la philosophie (Paris: Gallimard, 1994), 111 n.1.
4. "Exhibition" translates German Aufweisen and Greek αποδειξις (indication), whereby the implicit becomes explicit, the tacit voiced, the unconscious conscious, or the esoteric more exoteric. Aufweisen opposes Beweisen (proof), which Max Scheler argued is "monistic-metaphysical." Heidegger never proves, he exhibits.
5. Andy Merrifield's Nietzsche in "Lefebvre, Anti-Logos and Nietzsche: An Alternative Reading of The Production of Space," Antipode 27, no. 3 (1995): 294–303, nearly vanished from his MetroMarxism: A Marxist Tale of the City (New York: Routledge, 2002), and barely resurfaces in Henri Lefebvre: A Critical Introduction (New York: Routledge, 2006).
6. If one prefers a peaceful metaphor, mine is a "parallax view" opposed to the "transcendental illusion" (Kant) that "Left" and "Heideggerianism" are "mutually

translatable." See Slavoj Zizek, *The Parallax View* (Cambridge, MA: The MIT Press, 2006), 3–4.

7. *Capital*: "nihilistic in its extensive form, the market having become worldwide; nihilistic in its fetishization of the formalism of communication; and nihilistic in its extreme political poverty, that is to say, in the absence of any project other than its perpetuation—the perpetuation of hegemony for Americans and of vassalage, made as comfortable as possible, for the others"; *communism*: "the trans-temporal subjectivity of emancipation." Alain Badiou, *Infinite Thought: Truth and the Return to Philosophy*, ed. and trans. O. Feltham and J. Clemens (London: Continuum, 2003), 98, 120. *Capitalism*: "a certain force that regulates humanity beyond its intentionality, a force that divides and recombines human beings. It is a religio-generic entity"; *communism*: not "a constitutive idea, namely, 'an *ideal* to which [reality] will have to adjust itself,' but a regulative *idée*, namely, an ideal which constantly offers the ground to criticize reality." Kojin Karatani, *Transcritique: On Kant and Marx*, trans. S. Kohso (Cambridge, MA: The MIT Press, 2003), 5, 217. *State* is opposed to and by *thinking*.

8. I borrow from Bruno Bosteels, "Badiou without Zizek," *Polygraph* 17 (2005): 221–44; 221.

9. See *Quotations from Chairman Mao Tsetung* (Peking: Foreign Languages, 1966), 243, 261.

10. See Martin Heidegger, *Vorträge und Aufsätze* (Stuttgart: Neske, 1954), 125. Hereafter: *HVA*.

11. Martin Heidegger, "Phänomenologische Interpretationen zu Aristoteles," *Dilthey-Jahrbuch* 6 (1989 [1922]): 236–69; 249.

12. Karl Marx to Ludwig Kugelmann, April 12, 1871; Marx and Engels, *Writings on the Paris Commune*, ed. H. Draper (New York: Monthly Review, 1971), 221.

13. See Yasuo Yuasa, "The Encounter of Modern Japanese Philosophy with Heidegger," in *Heidegger and Asian Thought*, ed. G. Parkes (Honolulu: University of Hawaii Press, 1987), 155–74.

14. Harry Harootunian, *Overcome by Modernity: History, Culture, and Community in Interwar Japan* (Princeton: Princeton University Press, 2000), 118. Japanese writers are absent in John Roberts, "Philosophizing the Everyday: The Philosophy of Praxis and the Fate of Cultural Studies," *Radical Philosophy* 98 (November/December 1999): 16–29. The best conversation between Heidegger and Lefebvre on everydayness is in Peter Osborne, *The Politics of Time: Modernity and Avant-Garde* (London: Verso, 1995).

15. See Alexandre Kojève, *L'athéisme*, ed. with revised trans. L. Bibard (Paris: Gallimard, 1998 [1931])—the first attempt in Europe to appropriate Heidegger's concept of *Welt* (see pp. 106–10, 126–30).

16. See Peter Sloterdijk, *Critique of Cynical Reason*, trans. M. Eldred (Minneapolis: University of Minnesota Press, 1987 [1983]), 209.

17. Ernst Nolte, *Martin Heidegger: Politik und Geschichte im Leben und Denken* (Berlin: Propyläen, 1992), 296.

18. See Oliver Marchart, "Nothing but a Truth: Alain Badiou's 'Philosophy of Politics' and the Left-Heideggerians," *Polygraph* 17 (2005): 105–25. On his (bogus) definition, Left-Heideggerians constitute a group "held together by a particular 'family resemblance': the employment of the conceptual difference between *politics* and *the political*, or between 'la politique' and 'le politique'—a political descendent . . . of Heidegger's ontological difference" (105). Lefebvre's "trilectical" rehash of the same difference

(which has nothing important to do with Badiou) is expressed most concisely in *Le retour de la dialectique: 12 mots clef pour le monde moderne* (Paris: Messidor, 1986), 17. Lefebvre buys into the related distinction between "theory" and "practice" that Heidegger rejects, so this difference should not be used to explain how Lefebvre passes over what he thinks "regressive" in Heidegger for the "progressive," *pace* Stuart Elden tirelessly reiterates. See his "Between Marx and Heidegger: Politics, Philosophy and Lefebvre's *The Production of Space*," *Antipode* 36, no. 1 (2004): 86–105; 86; repeated in his *Understanding Henri Lefebvre: Theory and the Possible* (London: Continuum, 2006), 241, and in "Introduction [to Marxism and Philosophy]," Henri Lefebvre, *Key Writings*, ed. S. Elden, E. Lebas, and E. Kofman (London: Continuum, 2003), 3–5; 4. Hereafter: SEBMH, *SEUHL*, and *LKW*, respectively. Also see Stuart Elden, *Mapping the Present: Heidegger, Foucault and the Project of a Spatial History* (London: Continuum, 2001), 74–5.

19. Heidegger's criticisms of Thesis XI include a 1969 television interview. See Martin Heidegger, *Gesamtausgabe* (Frankfurt am Main: Klostermann, 2000), 16:703. This collection of "ways not works" is ongoing, with various editors. Hereafter: *HGA*.

20. Herbert Marcuse, "Beiträge zu einer Phänomenologie des Historischen Materialismus," in *Schriften* (Frankfurt am Main: Suhrkamp, 1978 [1928]), 1: 347–406, 358.

21. See Henri Lefebvre in Kostas Axelos (with Jean Beaufret, François Châtelet, and Henri Lefebvre), "Karl Marx et Heidegger," *Arguments d'une recherche* (Paris: Minuit, 1969 [1959]), 93–105; 96. Hereafter: KMH.

22. Walter Benjamin to Gershom Scholem, September 25, 1930; Walter Benjamin, *Briefwechsel 1933–1940*, ed. G. Scholem and T. W. Adorno (Frankfurt am Main: Suhrkamp, 1966), 2: 514. Brecht had "read not even two sentences of *Being and Time*," according to a mutual friend. The Frankfurt School's elaborate failure to combat Heidegger effectively may be read in Hermann Mörchen, *Adorno und Heidegger: Untersuchuung einer philosophischen Kommunikationsverweigerung* (Stuttgart: Klett-Cotta, 1981). Bataille's was then the best Leftist response.

23. According to Axelos, Heidegger "deliberately 'used'" Beaufret "to make up for his past misdeeds [literally to get past customs: *se dédouaner*] to enter into the Latin world and the world of the Left." Cited in Dominique Janicaud, *Heidegger en France* (Paris: Albin Michel, two volumes, 2001), 2: 32.

24. Martin Heidegger, *Zur Sache des Denkens* (Tübingen: Niemeyer, 1969), 63.

25. Lefebvre "did not in fact express any major political disagreements" at the time with either the Moscow show trails in the 1930s or with the Hitler–Stalin pact in 1939, and as late as 1949 he was "applauding the discussion, then taking place in Stalin's Russia, both on Stalin's concept of genetics and on socialist realism in art." Kevin Anderson, *Lenin, Hegel, and Western Marxism: A Critical Study* (Urbana: University of Illinois Press, 1995), 197, 284 n.50.

26. Stuart Elden, "Politics, Philosophy, Geography: Henri Lefebvre in Recent Anglo-American Scholarship," *Antipode* 33, no. 5 (2001): 809–25; 809. Hereafter: SEPPG.

27. Elden is fond of this formulation; see *ibid.* 809, SEBMH, 86, and Elden and Lebas, "Introduction: Coming to Terms with Lefebvre," *LKW*, xi–xiii; xii–xiii. Elden often recycles his paragraphs and elides quotation marks (though does provide references). The latter technique occasions welcome hilarity in the often lugubrious world of Heideggeriana: "Heidegger's notion of *Dasein* is criticized [by Lefebvre] for its lack of sex" (*SEUHL*, 79; also SEBMH, 90)—a lack contested by Elfride Heidegger and Hannah Arendt, most likely, without appreciating the humor.

28. Leo Strauss, "An Introduction to Heideggerian Existentialism," in *The Rebirth of Classical Political Rationalism*, ed. T. L. Pangle (Chicago: University of Chicago Press, 1989 [early 1950s]), 27–46; 28.

29. Hannah Arendt, "Heidegger at Eighty", in *Heidegger and Modern Philosophy*, ed. M. Murray (New Haven: Yale University Press, 1978 [1969]), 293–303; 296.

30. See Martin Heidegger, *Die Frage nach dem Ding* (Tübingen: Niemeyer, 1975 [1935/6]), 1–2, and HGA, 9: 343.

31. See Pierre Bourdieu, "Back to History: An Interview," in *The Heidegger Controversy: A Critical Reader*, ed. R. Wolin, 2nd edn (Cambridge, MA: The MIT Press, 1993 [1988]), 264–71; 265.

32. Eleonore Kofman and Elizabeth Lebas, "Lost in Transposition—Time, Space and the City," in Henri Lefebvre, *Writings on Cities*, ed. and trans. E. Kofman and E. Lebas (Oxford: Blackwell, 1996), 3–60; 8. Elden: "As Kofman and Lebas note, Heidegger was the twentieth-century philosopher with whom Lefebvre engaged most" (*SEUHL*, 77; also SEBMH, 88). But then "This is the West, sir. When the legend becomes fact, print the legend." *The Man Who Shot Liberty Valance* (John Ford, USA, 1962).

33. SEBMH, 101; emphases added to show the connection.

34. *SEUHL*, 77; also SEBMH, 87.

35. David Harvey, "From Space to Place and Back Again: Reflections on the Condition of Postmodernity," in *Mapping the Futures: Local Cultures, Global Change*, ed. J. Bird *et al.* (London: Routledge, 1993), 3–29; 14. Hereafter: FSP.

36. HGA, 45:41.

37. Johannes Fritsche, *Historical Destiny and National Socialism in Heidegger's* Being and Time (Berkeley: University of California Press, 1999), 140.

38. *Ibid.*, 289 n.64.

39. FSP, 16.

40. Elden: "David Harvey has recently suggested that the combination of Marx and Heidegger is an area of useful future work, when he talks of 'the possibility of somehow bridging the Marxian and Heideggerian conception [*sic*] within a new kind of radical politic [*sic*]'" (*SEUHL*, 77; also SEBMH, 88). One wonders what the radical political necessity might be for a bridge "between" a single conception.

41. *SEUHL*, 77.

42. SEBMH, 100–1. Elden does not repeat this proposal in his simultaneously published book on Lefebvre, exactly as we saw happening to Merrifield's vanishing mediator Nietzsche, and as happens to Lefebvre in Elden's *Speaking against Number: Heidegger, Language and the Politics of Calculation* (Edinburgh: Edinburgh University Press, 2006). Hereafter: SESAN. As Badiou notes, fidelity to a cause is far from any postmodern ethic.

43. HVA, 148.

44. *Ibid.*, 127, 128; emphasis added. *Sprung* also signifies "fissure" and "explosion."

45. *Ibid.*, 200.

46. Lefebvre, *L'existentialisme*, 175.

47. *Ibid.*, 180.

48. HGA, 16: 421–2.

49. HGA, 13: 81.

50. For a creative but not atypical Left-Heideggerian mistranslation, see Kostas Axelos, *Einführung in ein künftiges Denken: Über Marx und Heidegger* (Tübingen: Niemeyer, 1966), 55; or, far worse, SESAN, 179.

51. See Virgil, *Æneid* 2: 48, 31 (also *dolos* at 2: 62); see also *Iliad* 6: 187, *Odyssey* 8: 494.
52. See *HGA*, 13: 91, 66: 259, 9: 196–8.
53. Lefebvre in KMH, 96.
54. See Heidegger to William J. Richardson, S.J., April 1962; Richardson, *Heidegger: Through Phenomenology to Thought* (The Hague: Nijhoff, 1963), xxiii.
55. Henri Lefebvre, *Métaphilosophie: prolégomènes* (Paris: Minuit, 1965), 133.
56. Henri Lefebvre, *Hegel–Marx–Nietzsche ou le royaume des ombres* (Tournai: Casterman, 1975), 52.
57. In SEBMH, Elden proffers as reference "Lefebvre 1971a:161" (not in his bibliography), and in *SEUHL* he cites "*Au-delà du structuralisme*, p.161" (where the passage is not found).
58. *HVA*, 139; emphases added except on *is*. Here he uses *über* ironically.
59. *HGA*, 9: 361; emphasis added.
60. *HGA*, 18: 122–3, also 130–1, 146–7; see further Martin Heidegger, *Sein und Zeit* (Tübingen: Niemeyer, 1972 [1927]), 95–197. Hereafter: *HSZ*.
61. SEBMH, 100.
62. *SEUHL*, 242.
63. That it *cannot* be abstracted is shown by Jean-Jacques Lecercle, most recently in *A Marxist Philosophy of Language*, trans. G. Elliott (Leiden: Brill, 2006 [2004]).
64. See Heidegger, *Die Frage nach dem Ding*, 8–51.
65. See Henri Lefebvre, preface to Henri Raymond *et al.*, *L'habitat pavillonnaire* (Paris: CRU, 1966), 3–23.
66. Harvey, FSP, 14; emphases added.
67. *Ibid.*, 17.
68. Here the work of Fritsche remains groundbreaking.
69. Harvey, FSP, 23.
70. The most cogent argument that historicism and relativism *are* potent is Benito Mussolini, "Relativismo e fascismo," *Opera Omnia* (Florence: La Fenice, 1955 [1921]), 17: 267–9.
71. See Hans-Georg Gadamer, *Gesammelte Werke* (Tübingen: Mohr, 1995), 3: 309, 423. and 10: 3. This continuity is overlooked by even the most self-critical (former) Left-Heideggerians, including Zizek who persists in periodizing what in Heidegger should not be, and who reads the exoteric Heidegger only. See Slavoj Zizek, *The Ticklish Subject: The Absent Centre of Political Ontology* (London: Verso, 1999), 9–28.
72. Martin Heidegger, "De la nature de la cause," trans. A. Bessey, in *Recherches Philosophiques* 1 (1931/2): 83–124; 115; see also *HGA*, 9: 164.
73. See Martin Heidegger, *Holzwege*, 6th edn (Frankfurt am Main: Klostermann, 1980 [1950]), 30–1.
74. Lefebvre in KMH, 93. See Pierre Bourdieu, *L'ontologie politique de Martin Heidegger*, revised edn (Paris: Minuit, 1988 [1975]), 108.
75. Jacques Derrida, "Faith and Knowledge: The Two Sources of 'Religion' at the Limits of Reason Alone," in *Religion*, ed. J. Derrida and G. Vattimo (Stanford: Stanford University Press, 1996), 1–78; 13.
76. Henri Lefebvre, *De l'État, tome IV: les contradictions de l'État moderne* (Paris: UGE, 1978), 413. Compare the much more nuanced beginning of Theodor Adorno's *Negative Dialectics*, trans. E. B. Ashton (New York: Continuum, 1983 [1966]), 3.
77. Lefebvre, *ibid.*, 416; emphasis added.

78. I adapt from Reiner Schürmann, *Heidegger on Being and Acting: From Principles to Anarchy* [1982], trans. C.-M. Gros (Bloomington: Indiana University Press, 1987), 3–4.

79. Louis Althusser, *Sur la reproduction* (Paris: PUF, 1995), 301.

80. *HGA*, 15: 399; final emphasis added.

81. *Ibid.*, 400 (also *HSZ*, 25).

82. *HGA*, 15: 400.

83. Stanislas Breton, *Philosophie buissonnière* (Grenoble: Millon, 1989), 135, 136.

84. Martin Heidegger, *Gelassenheit* (Stuttgart: Neske, 1959), 58; also *HGA*, 66: 15.

85. *HGA*, 56/57: 40.

86. *HVA*, 146–8.

87. Carl Schmitt, *The Nomos of the Earth in the International Law of the Jus Publicum Europæum* [1950], trans. G. L. Ulmen (New York: Telos, 2003), 78. I thank Ayça Çubukçu for her deep insights into the global ramifications of Schmitt's argument today.

88. Crucial to understanding the necessity "consciously to forget repeatedly" the initiatory violence that founded the democratic πολις is Nicole Loraux, *La cité divisée: l'oubli dans la mémoire d'Athènes* (Paris: Payot & Rivages, 1997).

89. Pindar, Fragment 169 (151).

90. See Martin Heidegger, *Unterwegs zur Sprache* (Pfullingen: Neske, 1959), 37.

91. Henri Lefebvre, *The Urban Revolution*, trans. R. Bononno (Minneapolis: University of Minnesota Press, 2003 [1970]), 21; also see *La production de l'espace* (Paris: Anthropos, 1974), 280–1. Hereafter: *PdE*.

92. The closest Lefebvre comes is *ibid.*, 289.

93. *Ibid.*, 143–4.

94. *Ibid.*, 419.

95. *HSZ*, 220; also see 127, 331–2.

96. Opposed to me, and me to it, is Leo Strauss's master "syllogism" (actually an enthymeme) articulating *mania* with *sophrosyne* (prudence), as stated in "A Giving of Accounts," in *Jewish Philosophy and the Crisis of Modernity*, ed. K. H. Green (Albany: SUNY Press, 1997 [1970]), 457–66; 463.

97. In 1993 Zizek recalled: "In the republic of Bosnia, the Frankfurt school enjoyed a half-official status in the seventies, whereas in Croatia and partially in Serbia 'official' Heideggerians thrived, especially in the army circles." Slavoj Zizek, *Tarrying with the Negative: Kant, Hegel, and the Critique of Ideology* (Durham, NC: Duke University Press, 1993), 228. The year 1993 found radical geographer David Harvey at Oxford seminally albeit tentatively proposing the "bridge between Marx and Heidegger."

98. *HSZ*, 38.

99. See "Politics and Friendship: An Interview with Jacques Derrida," in *The Althusserian Legacy*, ed. E. A. Kaplan and M. Sprinker (London: Verso, 1993 [1989]), 183–231; 190.

100. Marcuse, "Beiträge," 349–50.

101. *Ibid.*, 350; emphases changed.

102. Alain Badiou, *Peut-on penser la politique?* (Paris: Seuil, 1985), 78. See further Louis Althusser, *Solitude de Machiavel*, ed. Y. Sitomer (Paris: PUF, 1998), 31. NB: "impossible possibility" is Karl Barth's name for "God" in *Der Römerbrief (Zweite Fassung 1922)* (Zurich: TVZ, 2005), 229, 345 and the term for "death" is *HSZ*.

103. Friedrich Nietzsche, *Sämtliche Werke: Kritische Studienausgabe in 15 Bänden*, ed. G. Colli and Mazzino Montinari (Berlin: de Gruyter, 1989), 13: 460.

104. Plato, *The Republic*, 533a.
105. Plato, *Sämtliche Werke*, ed. W. F. Otto *et al.*, trans. F. Schleiermacher (Reinbek bei Hamburg: Rowohlt, 1958 [1920s]), 3: 239.
106. Plato, *Epistle VII*, 341c; see *HGA*, 16: 60.
107. Jacques Lacan, *Écrits* (Paris: Seuil/Points, 1969), 1: 288.
108. Lefebvre, *Hegel–Marx–Nietzsche*, 52.
109. Franz Kafka, *Gesammelte Werke*, ed. H.-G. Koch (Frankfurt am Main: Fischer, 1994), 6: 231.

PART II

RHYTHMS OF URBANIZATION
AND EVERYDAY LIFE

7

MARXISM AND EVERYDAY LIFE
On Henri Lefebvre, Guy Debord, and some others
Kanishka Goonewardena

Man must be everyday, or he must not be at all.

Henri Lefebvre

1

Marxism and everyday life. The two seem unlikely bedfellows in the amnesiac age of postmodernism, divulging little of their intimate and revolutionary relationship in the first decades of the last century. According to the politically correct sensibilities of late, the quotidian is too precious and sublime an object to be exposed to the concerns of a doctrine convicted so soundly of (class) essentialism, (economic) reductionism, and (historical) determinism. Better to entrust it to something as pluralist and post-Marxist as cultural studies. Yet it was less than a century ago that the objective of socialist revolution was visible as the radical reconstruction of everyday life. And even—or especially—after attempts to change the world miscarried, the link between this keenly contested level of social reality and the struggle for socialism was not lost on a few thinkers known as Western Marxists. Henri Lefebvre stood out among them when he said: "Marxism, as a whole, really is a critical knowledge of everyday life." Guy Debord and the Situationists agreed, when a talking head in their "detourned" cartoon strip said: "Yes, Marx's thought is really a critique of everyday life!"[1]

2

The ties that bind Marxism and everyday life are old and varied. They go back to Marx's and Engels's early writings, including Marx's *Paris Manuscripts* and Engels's *The Condition of the Working Class in England* (both 1844). In their first collaborative and pivotal work *The German Ideology* (1845/6) a note of "self-clarification" asserts that "[t]he premises from which we begin are not arbitrary ones, not dogmas, but real premises from which abstraction can only be made in the imagination. They are the real individuals, their activities and the material conditions under which they live, both those which they find already existing and those produced by their activity."[2] Several Marxists have taken to heart this methodological point, which is all about being grounded in reality, but also about overcoming existing relations—separations—between abstract processes and concrete life. In this spirit if not letter, the Russian cultural avant-garde—in an instructive moment of alliance with the political vanguard—pursued seriously the task of erasing in particular three separations upon which the bourgeois social order was premised: one between art and life, another between politics and society, and one more between art and politics. In this eminently *practical* "critique of separation," the revolution included aesthetic as well as political dimensions: the "end of art" and the "withering away of the state." Such was the conjuncture of the first influential Marxist theorization of the concept of everyday life—involving art, politics, and their dissolution into a radically democratized daily life.[3]

Referring to this context in his illuminating book *Philosophizing the Everyday*, John Roberts aptly points out that "one should not underestimate the utopian content of the Russian embrace of the 'everyday'" in the aftermath of 1917, which in "Soviet culture was subject to an extraordinary theoretical elaboration and scrutiny,"[4] especially in Trotsky's contributions to *Pravda* in the early 1920s. These writings anticipate Lefebvre's later insistence that everyday life presents the ultimate standard by which socialism's accomplishments must be judged. Although rarely noted in contemporary theory, Trotsky thus ranks as one of the first Marxists to take everyday life as the terrain of revolution and site for building socialism. This is not to say that the notion of everyday life was invented by the Russian Revolution; but instead to note the decidedly positive value accorded an existing concept by one momentous and unexpected historical event. In its pre-revolutionary days, especially in the hands of young Georg Lukács and in Martin Heidegger's critique of the quotidian in *Being and Time*, everyday life reeked of negative connotation, highlighting its "inauthenticity" in the modern world. So the Russian Revolution it was that subjected to "a massive cultural and political haemorrhaging" the "early existential marriage between 'everyday life' and 'inauthentic' experience."[5]

In Lukács's case, unlike Heidegger's, the Soviet experience prompted a more dialectical understanding of everyday life in capitalism, which informs his seminal work and founding text of Western Marxism. True, its concept of reification

(*Verdinglichung*), an original if partial extension of Marx's concepts of alienation and fetishism, condemns everyday life to the foreboding category of "second nature"— one that, like "first nature," works according to its own objective laws, independent of subjective will. But Lukács also sees in the tendency of reification its dialectical other, namely, the "class consciousness of the proletariat." For in *History and Class Consciousness*—key to Debord's concept of the spectacle and Fredric Jameson's theorization of postmodernism—the very dynamic of reification enables Lukács to identify a revolutionary subjectivity emerging from the everyday life of the worker, thanks precisely to the worker's total subjugation by the commodity form. If the key to the secret of capitalism lies in the commodity, argues Lukács, then no one is better placed to make sense of it than the thoroughly commodified worker, the concrete laborer turned into abstract labor power, because the worker's own "lived experience" best embodies—and therefore explains—the social order premised on the commodity: "The self-understanding of the proletariat is . . . simultaneously the objective understanding of the nature of society."[6]

Lukács's immanent critique of everyday life remains as abstract as it is messianic, however. The teleological tone of "Reification and the Consciousness of the Proletariat" seems to stand in compensation for the absence in it of a sufficiently mediated analysis of the formation—and deformation—of working-class consciousness: an adequate account of the transition from the workers' "empirical" existence to their "imputed" consciousness, that is, from the class "in itself" to the class "for itself." This limitation is remarkable, considering Lukács's richly mediated analyses of the "antinomies of bourgeois thought" in this essay and his awareness of the "consciousness of the proletariat" as an immanent tendency of reification, not the actual course of history. Striking also is how closely Lefebvre later echoes him:

> The proletarian "condition" has a dual aspect—more precisely, it implies a dialectical movement. On the one hand it tends to overwhelm and crush the (individual) proletarian under the weight of the toil, the institutions and the ideas which are indeed intended to crush him. But at the same time, and in another respect, because of his incessant (everyday) contact with the real . . . through work, the proletarian is endowed with . . . a sense of reality which other social groups lose in so far as they become detached from practical creative activity. The petty bourgeois, the bourgeois, the intellectuals and the specialists—they all degenerate, decay and wither . . . *The deprivation of the working class is rich in possibilities.* For the individual proletarian to become conscious of the proletariat as a class, of its social reality, and thus of society as a whole, of its action, and therefore of its political future, is to have already superseded the proletarian condition. It is to have achieved a great and true thought: that of the social and human *totality,* of creative labour.[7]

3

In his theory of hegemony, Antonio Gramsci turned to these issues about a decade after Lukács, within a historical context marked by fascism. Here he asked: how did fascism, not socialism, become hegemonic in Italy through the 1930s? Gramsci's interrogation of politics, culture, and ideology with this question proposes the categories of *common sense* and *good sense* designating the contradictory consciousness of everyday life as not only a vital ingredient of bourgeois hegemony but also the substance out of which a revolutionary counter-hegemony of—and for—the subaltern classes must be forged. The consciousness of everyday life remains contradictory, Gramsci opined in the *Prison Notebooks*, because it includes both good sense and common sense. In the everyday life of the worker, he sees not one but "two theoretical consciousnesses . . .: one which is implicit in his activity and which in reality unites him with his fellow-workers in the practical transformation of the real world; and one, superficially explicit or verbal, which he has inherited from the past and uncritically absorbed."[8] The former offers the raw material for a conception of the world that is superior and opposed to the one professed by the latter—the popular view of the world according to the ruling class. Given the durable opposition between the two, Gramsci astutely highlights the dynamic character of everyday life: "Common sense is not something rigid and immobile, but is continually transforming itself, enriching itself with scientific ideas and with philosophical opinions which have entered ordinary life."[9] A counter-hegemonic politics must therefore involve the "criticism of 'common sense,' basing itself initially, however, on common sense in order to show that everyone is a philosopher and that it is not a question of introducing from scratch a scientific form of thought into everyone's individual life, but of renovating and making 'critical' an already existing activity."[10]

4

A seemingly more one-sided treatment of everyday life—recalling the early Lukács and Heidegger's *Being and Time*, but premised on quite different theoretical and political commitments—returns with certain strands of the Frankfurt School as well as the Spinozist Marxism of Louis Althusser. For the former, represented by *Dialectic of Enlightenment* (1944), the everyday life of mass consumerism appears in a mostly depressing light, although Theodor Adorno in particular is too clever a dialectician— and an unrepentant utopian at heart—to be (mis)labeled a pessimist. None the less, the degradation of Enlightenment reason into mass deception emerges as the overarching thesis in this text co-authored with Max Horkheimer, written in the wake of the trauma of fascism, while experiencing the banalities of Los Angeles in exile. Its famous "culture industry" chapter struck a concluding note not of utopia but despair: "the triumph of advertising in the culture industry is that consumers feel compelled to buy and use its products even though they see through them."[11]

This regime of cynical reason—or enlightened false consciousness—anticipates the gist of postmodernism as the cultural logic of late capitalism with indubitable acuity, as does Lukács's reified totality, but suggests no political exit from it.

More than a decade later followed Althusser's powerful definition of ideology as a "representation of the imaginary relationship of individuals to their real conditions of existence."[12] Notwithstanding his structuralist reputation, this positive conception of ideology was no less successful than the "culture industry" thesis in pulling everyday life into questions concerning "ideological state apparatuses" and "the reproduction of the relations of production." Much of its appeal lay, as Jameson perceptively suggests, in the gap it posits between the phenomenological reality of "lived-experience" and the "unrepresentable" totality of social life.[13] But the anti-humanist register within which Althusser inscribes his problematic of ideology tends to be less sharply attuned to the contradictions of lived-experience than either Gramsci's historicism or Lefebvre's own study of the "reproduction of the relations of production": The Survival of Capitalism (1973). On the whole, Althusser excels at explaining how we become ideological subjects in daily rituals. By the same token, however, subjects mired in ideology struggle to produce a mass-based counter-hegemony worthy of socialism.

5

Antithetical in spirit and method to denigrations of everyday life, Walter Benjamin undoubtedly is. As Susan Buck-Morss shows in The Dialectics of Seeing:

> Benjamin's trip to Moscow had convinced him that seizing political power and nationalizing the economy, while [providing] the preconditions for socialist transformation, were not its guarantee, and that so long as the Soviet government repressed cultural innovation, the political revolution was itself in danger of being lost ... Whereas Marx had discovered in the capitalist economic base not only the creation of conditions which would lead to increasing exploitation of the proletariat but also those "that would make it possible to abolish capitalism itself," Benjamin argued that within the superstructure there was a separate (and relatively autonomous) dialectical process, "no less noticeable [. . .] than in the economy," but proceeding "far more slowly." It is this dialectic that makes possible the transition to a socialist society.[14]

This novel theorization of the transition to socialism also enabled Benjamin to see capitalist mass culture in a dialectical perspective, reminiscent of Lefebvre's understanding of everyday life as not just bourgeois but human. His reading of late capitalist modernity, unlike Lukács's, "takes mass culture seriously not merely as the source of phantasmagoria of false consciousness, but as the source of collective energy to overcome it."[15] In so doing he aims "precisely . . . to bridge the gap between everyday experience and traditional academic concerns, actually to achieve that phenomenological hermeneutics of the profane world which Heidegger only pretended."[16]

Benjamin and Lefebvre share not only an interest in everyday life, then, but also a dialectical standpoint on even its most alienated manifestations. And neither, contrary to widespread opinion, offers a critique of modernity that may be termed "nostalgic." Benjamin's betrays rather a profoundly utopian—redemptive—sensibility that enthusiastically greets the new techno-culture ushered in by modernity, the "new nature"; though not the capitalist social relations with which it is gratuitously entangled. But he does not stop at making the vital distinction between the two— productive forces and production relations—within the "base" of the emergent social totality. Benjamin's contribution here lies in discerning a new movement in its "superstructure"—between the "new nature" and collective "fantasy." The latter refers to humanity's "unconscious" yearning for a better life, the material evidence for which he assembled in the incomparable Arcades Project, in the profane place of urban everyday life. On Benjamin's enormously suggestive insight concerning the "superstructural dialectic," Buck-Morss is prescient:

> The relationship between art and technology is a central theme in the *Passagen-Werk* . . . It identifies a structural transformation in the relationship of consciousness to reality—specifically, fantasy to productive forces—that has general theoretical significance, and that is capable of informing every sort of critical cultural practice. It could be said that for Benjamin progressive cultural practice entails bringing both technology and imagination out of their mythic dream states, through making conscious the collective's desire for social utopia, and the potential of the new nature to achieve it by translating that desire into the "new language" of its material forms.[17]

6

"Let everyday life become a work of art! Let every technical means be employed for the transformation of everyday life!"[18] These are Lefebvre's words, uttered in unison with Benjamin's. Their convergence on matters of art and technology avoids the conflation of productive forces with production relations—which is fatal for Marxism, although central to the ideology of modernization. Both Lefebvre and Benjamin take the seduction of mass culture as a problem: a false deliverance of alienated desire that always leaves something to be desired. For Lefebvre, "everyday life is the place of desire, so long as we specify that it is also—indeed primarily— the non-place [u-topia] of desire, the place where desire dies of satisfaction and reemerges from its ashes" in "The Bureaucratic Society of Controlled Consumption."[19] For all this, the "culture industry" à la Adorno and Horkheimer strikes neither Benjamin nor Lefebvre (or indeed even Adorno himself) as just "false consciousness." To the extent that people actively participate in it, rather, it represents for them an unconscious revolutionary desire for an unalienated life sublimated in commodity form—a utopian promise that remains to be redeemed. For Lefebvre, "needs—even if they are provoked and prefabricated—can not all be equally phony and artificial."[20] Accordingly, critics of everyday life

> must . . . start from the fact that they contain within themselves their own spontaneous critique . . . They are that critique in so far as they are other than [bourgeois] everyday life, and yet they are in [human] everyday life, they are alienation. They can thus hold a real content, correspond to a real need, yet retain an illusory form and a deceptive appearance."[21]

This formulation accords clearly with Benjamin's call—as explicated by Buck-Morss[22]—to take mass culture as a *dream*, from which humanity must *wake up*. Benjamin himself here heeds Marx's famous letter to Arnold Ruge of 1843, quoted in the section on method (*Konvolut N*) in the Arcades Project:

> Our motto must . . . be: Reform of consciousness not by means of dogmas, but by analyzing the mystical consciousness unclear to itself, whether it appears religiously or politically. It will then become clear that the world has long possessed in the form of a dream something of which it only has to become conscious in order to possess it in reality.[23]

7

If everyday life is not the first thing that comes to mind when contemplating Marxism, then the historical reasons for this include some afflictions suffered by the socialisms that actually existed: economism, productivism, and evolutionism. These ideologies rooted in the uneven development of capitalism dominated left politics throughout the last century, and thus formed a common enemy against which constructivist critiques of everyday life were issued from within the Marxist tradition. Writing soon after the Second World War, Lefebvre cut an oppositional figure in the French Communist Party (PCF) by explaining why "it is ludicrous to define socialism solely by the development of productive forces" and why "[e]conomic statistics cannot answer the question: 'What is socialism?'" "Men do not fight and die for tons of steel, or for tanks or atomic bombs," he claimed; "they aspire to be happy, not to produce." For him, "socialism (the new society, the new life) can only be defined concretely on the level of everyday life, as a system of changes in what can be called lived experience."[24] Which leads to his poignant question: "What did Marx want?" And response: "Marx wanted to change everyday life," because "to change the world is above all to change the way everyday, real life is lived." And Lefebvre goes "so far as to argue that critique of everyday life—radical critique aimed at attaining the metamorphosis of everyday life—is alone in taking up the authentic Marxist project again and in continuing it: to supersede philosophy and to fulfill it."[25]

The odds stacked against the concept of everyday life came not only from Comintern orthodoxy, however, but also from Western Marxism's institutional bases in academia. The latter afforded no escape from the social division of labor, as it manifested itself in the realm of thought, with some help from narrow-minded professors representing variously bounded disciplines. A notorious attack on them came from Debord, at a (taped) lecture hosted by Lefebvre in 1961, singling out those critics who "are only too inclined to remove from everyday life things that happen to them every day, and to transfer them to separate and supposedly superior spheres." This habit "masks [the] reality [of everyday life] behind privileged conventions"—of politics, economics, culture, and other such *separate* and *superior* activities—all understood within the confines of a "few professional concepts" that are "produced by the division of labour," social and intellectual. Everyday life no doubt exists in relation to *higher* and *specialized* spheres studied by academic experts: the state (the object of political science), the economy (the domain of political-economy), or culture (the province of anthropology). It cannot be reduced, however, to such specialized activities or theoretical objects. "The majority," complains Debord, "recognize specialized activities everywhere and everyday life nowhere." But "[e]veryday life is everywhere," he retorts. Hence the simplest and best-known definition of everyday life that Debord took over from Lefebvre: namely, "whatever remains after one has eliminated all specialized activities."[26]

8

Yet this definition still begs the question: what *is* everyday life? Acknowledging that his "first definition of everyday life is a negative one," Lefebvre invites us to "remove the highly specialized occupations" from our lives and imagine what would be left: "an apparently very scanty residue." This "so-called residue contains a 'human raw-material' which holds hidden wealth," however: a utopian substance that points to *all that is possible* contained and hidden in the *real*.[27] According to him:

> Everyday life, in a sense residual, defined by "what is left over" after all distinct, superior, specialized, structured activities have been singled out for analysis, must be defined as a totality. Considered in their specialization and their technicality, superior activities leave a "technical vacuum" between one

another which is filled by everyday life. Everyday life is profoundly related to all activities, and encompasses them with all their differences and their conflicts; it is their meeting place, their bond, their common ground. And it is in everyday life that the sum total of relations which make the human—and every human being—a whole takes its shape and its form. In it are expressed and fulfilled those relations which bring into play the totality of the real, albeit in a certain manner which is always partial and incomplete: friendship, comradeship, love, the need to communicate, play, etc.[28]

To make sense of this novel conception, several clarifications are in order—concerning the relations between "distinct . . . activities" and everyday life; urban life and everyday life; and revolution and everyday life. Best to begin, then, with the notion of *totality* underlined here, which brings together all of these apparently disparate things in unexpected ways. For as Debord notes, everyday life is a concept "some people are averse to confronting" in spite of its "residual" content precisely "because it at the same time represents the *standpoint of the totality*" involving "an integral political judgment."[29] Wherever "[m]odern society is viewed through specialized fragments that are virtually incommunicable," it comes as no surprise to him that "everyday life, where all questions are liable to be posed in a unitary manner, remains the domain of ignorance," much like "the urban phenomenon" that for Lefebvre "cannot be grasped by any specialized science" or by "bring[ing] specialists (in the fragmentary sciences) together around a table."[30] Everyday life calls for totalization, Debord declares, because "it is the measure of all things: of the fulfillment or rather the nonfulfillment of human relations; of the use of lived time; of artistic experimentation; of revolutionary politics."[31]

9

The centrality of the category of *totality* to the understanding of—and the call to transform—everyday life shared by Lefebvre and Debord signals their fundamental difference from an array of contemporary theoretical fashions. The standpoint of totality invoked here demands not only an account of how the everyday can be conceived of as a *totalizing* phenomenon but also an explication of how it relates to society as a whole. Of crucial import in this regard is Lefebvre's *The Urban Revolution*.[32] For his theorization in it of the *global* (G), *urban* (M-mixed) and *everyday life* (P-private) as levels of social practice related through mediation represents an original contribution to a Marxist theory of totality—the standard structure of which is usually designated by the (in)famous base-superstructure model. Lefebvre makes good *dialectical* use of the latter, but above all to argue here against "the pseudo-Marxist theory" claiming that "the urban and the process of urbanization are simple superstructures of the mode of production" (15, 139, 164). He rejects, that is, the view that "[u]rbanization . . . is the excrescence of the circulation of capital."[33] This reflects in no way any ignorance on his part regarding the political-economic determinants of urban space, which have been elaborated most influentially by David Harvey. Lefebvre writes lucidly about the "role played by urbanism and more generally real estate (speculation, construction) in neocapitalist society" (159): "As the principal circuit [of capital]—current industrial production and the movable property that results—begins to slow down, capital shifts to the second sector, real estate." Anticipating certain post-1973 realities, he also observes how "[i]t can even happen that real-estate speculation becomes the principal source for the formation of capital, that is, the realization of surplus value" (160). Against the excrescence thesis of neoclassical Marxism, however, Lefebvre argues that "[s]pace and the politics of space" not only "'express' social relationships" but also "react against them." In so doing, space "becomes a productive a force, like science." This dialectical perspective also explicates how "[u]rban reality modifies the relations of production without being sufficient to transform them" (15), in the absence of critical interventions from everyday life.

10

Although such observations effectively draw a line between economism and Marxism, they do not indicate with sufficient precision where in the base-superstructure model we may locate the urban as such. If not in the superstructure, then could it be in the base, in-between, or somewhere else? It is in response to this nagging question that Lefebvre approaches totality by means of the concept of level, the choice of which he justifies at some length in his second volume on everyday life.[34] Geographers in particular may find it worthy of note how and why he consciously chooses level over scale, especially in light of Neil Smith's remarks in the foreword to *The Urban Revolution*, when he asserts that Lefebvre's distinction between the levels of G, M, and P represents "an oblique effort to distinguish between scales of socio-spatial reality," that is, "a halting effort at what might now be called a 'politics of scale'" that fails to "allow . . . 'levels' to crystallize into anything approaching coherent spatial entities" (xii, xiv). But Lefebvre himself claims to have had other ideas concerning a path to totality. For a dialectical conception of the latter, he reckons that "[t]he schematic of scale . . . is much too static," whereas "levels can interact and become telescoped, with differing results according to what the encounters and circumstances are." The Hegelian-Marxist notion of mediation, that is to say, works better with levels (possessing "thresholds" discernible by "analysis and experiment") than scales (however "fixed" in space) or other alternatives (instances, stages, aspects, etc.): "the idea of level encompasses the idea of differences between levels," such that "[w]herever there is a level there are several levels, and consequently gaps, (relatively) sudden transitions, and imbalances or potential imbalances between these levels," which however "cannot be completely dissociated" from each other because the "idea of a structural set of precise and separate levels is untenable." The concept of level thus becomes most useful in "expressing a complexity which is differentiated yet structured within a whole (a totality)"; and it "has the merit of uniting mobility and structure" while helping to elaborate the realities of uneven development and contradiction pertaining to the social totality in new ways. The resultant view of totality, moreover, brings to light those (possible and real) conjunctures in which, as Lefebvre puts it, "one level mediates another." Indeed, the revolution, for him as much as for Debord, is premised precisely upon the prospect of level P acting upon M, and M upon G: P>M>G. A revolution is possible, that is, only if "the level of the everyday and the level of the historical can interact."[35]

11

If the highly suggestive "Levels and Dimensions" chapter of *The Urban Revolution* clarifies in essence the mediated relations between everyday life in and of the city, the urban itself, and global neoliberalism (market) and neo-dirigisme (state)— the two foundations, respectively, of what Debord famously identified as the "diffused" and "integrated" moments of the spectacle—then how does Lefebvre differentiate between the everyday level of praxis and what he calls "distinct, superior, specialized, structured activities"? This question recalls the memorable imagery invoked by Lefebvre to draw the shifting line between the everyday and the non-everyday, arguing that all non-everyday (higher) activities derive from everyday (residual) activities, for the former to exist as both critical and alienated expressions of the latter:

> There is a cliché which with a certain degree of justification compares creative moments to the mountain tops and everyday time to the plain, or to the marshes. The image the reader will find in this book differs from this generally accepted metaphor. Here everyday life is compared to fertile soil. A landscape without flowers or magnificent woods may be depressing for the passer-by; but flowers and trees should not make us forget the earth beneath . . .[36]

Lefebvre carries this metaphor through all of his writings on everyday life, with dialectical twists and turns. Everyday life, he says, "surrounds us, it besieges us, on all sides and from all directions"; but "no so-called 'elevated' activity can be reduced to it, nor can it be separated from it." These specialized activities "emerge" out of what is "born" and "grown" in everyday life; and "once they have left the nourishing earth of their native land" to become distinguished as "higher" levels of praxis, "not one of them can be formed and fulfilled on its own account," apart from "this earth" on which "they are born."[37] "Fulfillment" is only possible at the level of the everyday. Nor can any specialized activity—fetishized economy, bureaucratic state, rarefied culture, l'art pour l'art, dominant ideology or urbanism—fully sever its umbilical link to everyday life in (spite of) its alienated form. But then why characterize these "elevated" activities as alienated—indeed, as "those cancerous monstrosities" of "art for art's sake, thought for thought's sake, power for the sake of power over men," whose "disappearance" is the explicit objective of Lefebvre's critique of everyday life as much as Debord's "critique of separation"?[38] This question returns us to the heart of Marx. For alienation, as Lefebvre interprets Marx's early writings, resides in the (relative) autonomy and (incomplete) detachment of "elevated" activities from everyday life, that level of praxis within—or starting from—which "genuine creations are achieved." These last are the "creations which produce the human and which men produce as part of the process of becoming human,"[39] that is, while "appropriating their own nature" in the actualization of the historically produced essence of humanity's "species-being."[40]

12

That Marx's concept of alienation played a leading role in nearly everything that Lefebvre or Debord wrote is widely acknowledged. Less is written about how it clarifies the relationship between the everyday ("fertile soil") and the non-everyday ("flowers and trees"). At the most general—basic—level, Lefebvre's elaboration of alienation deals with the "will to abstract" manifest in capitalist-industrial rationality, which he explicates most forcefully with reference to urbanism. "Innumerable human beings have been tortured by innumerable conflicts," Lefebvre notes, "since abstract (rational) social processes became detached from" the "realm" of "immediate and direct relations between individual people," a "realm" that is "situated within the everyday."[41] And he follows Marx closely with regard to the manifold forms such alienation assume—fetishism, reification, estrangement—all of which involve the confrontation of our "species-being" in the process of being "humanized" with an array of hostile social forces feeding on our own essence while hovering over us rather like a "vampire of the non-human."[42]

> The human, stripped bare and projected outside itself, was and remains at the mercy of forces which in fact come from the human and are nothing but human—but torn apart and dehumanized. This alienation was *economic* (the division of labour; "private" property; the formation of economic fetishes: money, commodities, capital); *social* (the formation of classes); *political* (the formation of the State); *ideological* (religions, metaphysics, moral doctrines). It was also *philosophical*: primitive man, simple, living on the same level as nature, became divided up into subject and object, form and content, nature

and power, reality and possibility, truth and illusion, community and individuality, body and consciousness . . . With its speculative (metaphysical) vocabulary, philosophy is itself a part of human alienation. But the human has developed only through alienation.[43]

In case the demarcation drawn here between the everyday and the non-everyday resembles something like Jürgen Habermas's famous demarcation between "lifeworld" and "system," that impression must be quickly dispelled, along with any moralistic alignment of the former with "good" and the latter with "bad." For the distinction in question, in Lefebvre's case, falls well short of an absolute division; and the link between the everyday and the non-everyday, especially as everyday life in the modern world increasingly involves "social relations more complex than the immediate relations of kinship and primitive economy," turns out to be dialectical.[44] To push his metaphor a little further, we might say that while "flowers and trees" of the (alienated) non-everyday grow out of the "soil" of the (non-alienated) everyday, they also cast long and dark shadows on their native ground, and disintegrate into it, altering its composition and fertility. This "soil" is not virgin; "flowers and trees" enter into it. So, writes Lefebvre, "the non-everyday [appears] in the everyday."[45] By the same token, he eschews every notion of pure alienation. If alienation means "man torn from his self, from nature, from his own nature, from his consciousness, dragged down and dehumanized by his own social products," then we can observe all that in our alienated world, no doubt. But for all that it remains our alienated world: a world that human beings have created in their everyday life, while producing as well whatever actually exists in the name of their own "species-being." To wit: "Man attains his own reality, creates himself through, within and by means of his opposite, his alienation: the inhuman. It is through the inhuman that he has slowly built the human world." "Man has been unable to avoid this alienation" because "[t]he human has been formed through dehumanization— dialectically."[46]

This dialectical perspective complicates the definition of everyday life quoted (from both Lefebvre and Debord) earlier. Although "residual" with respect to "distinct, superior, specialized, structured activities," everyday life cannot be characterized only as such, because a vital, indeed growing, part of it also lives under the shade of those "elevated" activities. Hence the need to define everyday life as "doubly determined"—both as the "residual deposit" and as the "product" of all "elevated" activities.[47] According to philosopher Peter Osborne's penetrating reading, in Lefebvre's concept of everyday life "[t]here is the 'good,' but unrealized universality of an historically produced species-being and the 'bad,' abstract but realized universality of its alienated forms (money, the commodity, the state, etc.)."[48] Lefebvre's own clarification of "everyday life" (la vie quotidienne) aligns "the everyday" (le quotidien) with the former, the incomplete, embattled yet actually existing "species-being," and "everydayness" (*la quotidienneté*) with the latter, "the homogeneous, the repetitive [and] the fragmentary" forms of being-in-the-everyday of modernity.[49]

Roberts sums up this fundamental contradiction of everyday life—between the everyday and everydayness—aptly: *la quotidienneté* represents "the modality of capital's administration of atomization and repetition"; *le quotidien* represents "the modality of social transformation and class resistance."[50] This renders everyday life contradictory to the core: Lefebvre sees it as a "level of levels," or rather two sub-levels locked in tense opposition, one corresponding to its "human" and utopian aspect, the other to the inhuman and "bourgeois" aspect.[51] Debord too defines it as the "frontier between dominated and undominated sectors of life."[52] Indeed, the force of their writings on everyday life lies in the elaboration of it as the most vital terrain of struggle and "the inevitable starting point for the realization of the possible."[53]

13

What remains today of their critique of everyday life? In the world of critical theory, Lefebvre and Debord now represent an alternative to three different yet influential perspectives on the quotidian. The first, perhaps still the most prominent within Western Marxism, is Adorno and Horkheimer's theory of the "culture industry," which amounts to such a devaluation of everyday life under late capitalism that it leaves the first author of *Dialectic of Enlightenment* with little other than autonomous art as the privileged means for opposing a totalitarian world. Adorno's great adversary Heidegger, from an opposed political standpoint, goes even further in his critique of everyday life in the modern world, by equating it with everydayness (*Alltäglichkeit*). The third and more contemporary perspective on the quotidian involves an inversion of both Adorno and Heidegger, most symptomatically in the celebration of everyday life as the realm of "resistance" par excellence by Michel de Certeau. To many he appears as a kindred spirit of Lefebvre and Debord, as often suggested in writings that lump together all three of these authors—sometimes with Gramsci and Benjamin also thrown in for good measure. Aside from being French, however, de Certeau has little to do with either Lefebvre or Debord, given his deeply anti-Marxist and anti-totalizing view of history as much as everyday life.

How, then, does he appeal to some pluralists who also profess fondness for Lefebvre and Debord? It was de Certeau's genius to offer in *The Practice of Everyday Life* an attractive alternative, as Roberts points out, to the "notion of the passive consumer of culture, . . . the mainstay of both 1950s sociologies of mass culture and the Frankfurt School,"[54] and to do so with a concept already popularized by Lefebvre and Debord also stripped of its *totalizing* critique and *revolutionary* subjectivity. For the heroic figure in de Certeau's celebrated work worries less about changing the world, more about becoming a creative consumer. In *Practice*, much of the exalted resistance lies in "walking, reading, decorating, cooking" and so on, that is, in the realm of consumption rather than production, making it easier for not only resourceful subalterns but members of the intellectual establishment to join in the "transgression" of something. De Certeau's inflation of "resistance"—matched appropriately by the intensity of his aversion to "totality"—offers a classic case of the "dissolution of collective politics into cultural politics," a postmodern trend wholly alien to Lefebvre and Debord. Roberts is right:

> de Certeau's . . . *Practice* . . . is paradigmatic . . . in that it contributes to the [laudable] postmodern incorporation of the everyday as a site of complex and differentiated social agency and subjectivity in the "politics of representation" [that is, however, dubiously] separate from any structural engagement with the problems of material distribution and economic justice.[55]

In contrast to the mainstream of contemporary cultural studies, roads not taken yet in the critique of everyday life offer much more promise. One wonders, for example, about the prospects of introducing Dorothy Smith's groundbreaking feminist-socialist exploration of the quotidian—*The Everyday World as Problematic*, accomplished without much engagement to speak of with Western Marxism—to Lefebvre's *Critiques*, which have their own proto-feminist moments; or the potentially global implications of elaborating the relevance of writers like Frantz Fanon and Mike Davis for a non-postcolonial and anti-imperialist critique of everyday life in Age of Empire. While gesturing towards such possibilities in the concept of everyday life proposed by Lefebvre and Debord, however, their basic contribution to Marxism must not be missed: the simple point that there can be no revolution without an urban revolution, no urban revolution without a revolution, and neither without a revolution of everyday life.

NOTES

1. Anselm Japp, *Guy Debord*, trans. D. Nicholson-Smith, foreword by T. J. Clark (Berkeley: University of California Press, 1999), 73.
2. Karl Marx and Friedrich Engels, *The German Ideology* [fall 1845 to mid-1846], <http://www.Marxists.org/archive/marx/works/1845/german-ideology>.
3. See Susan Buck-Morss, *Dreamworld and Catastrophe: Passing of Mass Utopia in East and West* (Cambridge, MA: The MIT Press, 2000).
4. John Roberts, "Philosophizing the Everyday," *Radical Philosophy* 98 (1999): 16–17. For an extended discussion, see also his *Philosophizing the Everyday: Revolutionary Praxis and the Fate of Cultural Theory* (London: Pluto Press, 2006).
5. Roberts, "Philosophizing the Everyday," 16.
6. George Lukács, *History and Class Consciousness*, trans. R. Livingstone (Cambridge, MA: The MIT Press, 1971 [1923]), 149.
7. Henri Lefebvre, *Critique of Everyday Life, Volume I: Introduction*, trans. J. Moore, preface M. Trebitsch (London: Verso, 1991 [1947 and 1958]), 143; emphases added.

8. Antonio Gramsci, *Selections from Prison Notebooks*, trans., ed., and introduction Q. Hoare and G. N. Smith (New York: International Publishers, 1971), 333.

9. *Ibid.*, 326.

10. *Ibid.*, 330–1.

11. Theodor Adorno and Max Horkheimer, *Dialectic of Enlightenment*, trans. J. Cumming (New York: Continuum, 1976 [1944]), 167.

12. Louis Althusser, "Ideology and Ideological State Apparatuses," in *Lenin and Philosophy*, trans. B. Brewster (New York: Monthly Review Press, 1971 [1969]), 127–86.

13. Fredric Jameson, "Cognitive Mapping," in *Marxism and the Interpretation of Culture*, ed. L. Grossberg and C. Nelson (Urbana: University of Illinois Press, 1988), 353.

14. Susan Buck-Morss, *The Dialectics of Seeing: Walter Benjamin and the Arcades Project* (Cambridge, MA: The MIT Press, 1990), 123–4.

15. *Ibid.*, 253.

16. *Ibid.*, 3.

17. *Ibid.*, 124–5.

18. Henri Lefebvre, *Everyday Life in the Modern World*, trans. S. Rabinovitch (New Brunswick: Transaction Publishers, 1984 [1968]), 204.

19. *Ibid.*, 118, 68–110.

20. Henri Lefebvre, *Critique of Everyday Life, Volume II: Foundations for a Sociology of the Everyday*, trans. J. Moore, preface M. Trebitsch (London: Verso, 2002 [1961]), 223.

21. Lefebvre, *Critique*, I, 40.

22. Buck-Morss, *Dialectics of Seeing*, 253–86.

23. *Ibid.*, 281, trans. Buck-Morss.

24. Lefebvre, *Critique I*, 48–9. I must also note here the sloppy tendency in current Lefebvre scholarship to romanticize the heterodoxy of its object of desire. Hardly anyone seems able to acknowledge that Lefebvre reacted repeatedly and opportunistically to the vagaries of the PCF line, citing with approval in his celebrated oeuvre not only Friedrich Nietzsche and Martin Heidegger but also Josef Stalin and his chief ideologue Andrei Zhdanov. See Kevin Anderson, *Lenin, Hegel, and Western Marxism: A Critical Study* (Urbana: University of Illinois Press, 1995), 197, 284 n.50; and Chapter 6, this volume.

25. Lefebvre, *Critique*, II, 35, 23.

26. Guy Debord, "Perspectives for Conscious Alterations in Everyday Life," in *Situationist International Anthology*, ed. K. Knabb (Berkeley: Bureau of Public Secrets, 1981 [1961]), 68–9.

27. Lefebvre, *Critique*, I, 86.

28. *Ibid.*, 97.

29. Debord, "Perspectives," 69, 71; emphasis added.

30. *Ibid.*, 75.

31. *Ibid.*, 69.

32. Henri Lefebvre, *The Urban Revolution*, trans. R. Bononno, foreword by N. Smith (Minneapolis: University of Minnesota Press, 2003 [1970]). All references to page numbers without endnotes refer to this book.

33. Neil Smith, foreword in *ibid.*, xvii.

34. Lefebvre, *Critique*, II, 118–25.

35. *Ibid.*, 119–20.

36. Lefebvre, *Critique*, I, 87.

37. Lefebvre, *Critique*, II, 41.

38. Lefebvre, *Critique*, I, 246; Debord, *Society of the Spectacle*, trans. K. Knabb, §1–34, <http://www.bopsecrets.org/SI/debord>.
39. Lefebvre, *Critique*, II, 44.
40. Karl Marx, "Economic and Philosophic Manuscripts," in *Early Writings*, ed. L. Colletii, trans. R. Livingstone and G. Benton (London: Penguin, 1975 [1844]), 279–400.
41. Lefebvre, *Critique*, II, 210, 214.
42. Lefebvre, *Critique*, I, 183.
43. *Ibid.*, 249.
44. *Ibid.*, 170.
45. *Ibid.*, 40.
46. *Ibid.*, 170, 180.
47. Lefebvre, *Critique*, II, 57; Lefebvre, *Everyday Life*, 32.
48. Peter Osborne, *The Politics of Time: Modernity and Avant-Garde* (London: Verso, 1995), 191.
49. Henri Lefebvre, "The Everyday and Everydayness," trans. C. Levich, *Yale French Studies* 73 (1987): 7–11; "Towards a Leftist Cultural Politics: Remarks Occasioned by the Centenary of Marx's Death," in *Marxism and the Interpretation of Culture*, 75–88.
50. Roberts, "Philosophizing the Everyday," 23.
51. Lefebvre, *Critique*, I, 127, 131; *Critique*, II, 120.
52. Debord, "Perspectives," 72.
53. Lefebvre, *Everyday Life*, 14.
54. Roberts, *Philosophizing the Everyday*, 87–99; "Philosophizing the Everyday," 26–8.
55. *Ibid.*, 28: my view of de Certeau certainly differs from that of the mainstream opinion in contemporary cultural studies, which includes some Lefebvre citers.

8

HENRI LEFEBVRE AND URBAN EVERYDAY LIFE[1]

In search of the possible

Klaus Ronneberger

(translated by Stefan Kipfer and Neil Brenner)

INTRODUCTION

In the Federal Republic of Germany, the works of Henri Lefebvre were read broadly by those informed by materialist theories of culture and socialization. In contrast, his reflections on urbanization and space never became equally popular. Even among urbanists, Lefebvre's unorthodox Marxist theories of space were hardly understood. Largely forgotten for a long time, some of his claims resurfaced recently in German architecture and art criticism.[2] Yet it remains to be seen to what extent Lefebvre's approach can become useful for a contemporary critique of everyday life and urbanism.

In the early years of the Federal Republic, Lefebvre's writings had a kind of "underground" status. This situation changed in the 1970s as social and cultural movements rebelled against the Fordist form of societalization (*Vergesellschaftung*)[3] and demanded more autonomy and participation. In the context of this "cultural revolution," Lefebvre's notion of a "critique of everyday life" attracted increased attention.[4] The "New Left" was drawn, in particular, to Lefebvre's understanding of radical political praxis not only as a transcendence of inherited forms of domination but as a transformation of the everyday.

Lefebvre had, in fact, transcended the programmatic agenda of orthodox Marxism, which was oriented primarily towards a seizure of the state apparatus and the centralized planning of production through the collective power of the working class. By contrast, Lefebvre considered the everyday to be the decisive category linking the economy to individual life experiences. Whereas the economic had long played an overarching role under capitalism, the everyday was now acquiring the same significance. The declared goal of his intellectual project was, above all, a "revalorization of subjectivity"[5] and the quest for spaces that allow for autonomy and creativity. The concept of the *oeuvre* plays a central role in this context; it is intended to replace the much narrower, Marxian concepts of labor. The notion of an *oeuvre* is not only equated with artistic practice but signifies all activities of self-realization or collective self-management (to which Lefebvre referred as *autogestion*). Lefebvre believed that his critique of economistic ideologies—which was directed against an excessively narrow concept of production and a notion of class struggle that was restricted to the factory—contained important implications for the conceptualization of revolution. With the complete urbanization of society, the industrial proletariat found itself in the midst of a process of dissolution that also undermined its role as the agent of transformation. Lefebvre introduced inhabiting (*habiter*) as a new subversive category:[6] this refers to a realm that is essential to everybody but becomes increasingly deficient for its users as social space is integrated ever more directly into processes of capital valorization. On this basis Lefebvre envisioned the emergence of a new revolutionary subject that would revolt not only against the exploitation of labor-power but against the destruction of its entire living environment.

Lefebvre's *Critique of Everyday Life* focused not only upon the sphere of reproduction but took into consideration the processes through which society as a whole is produced. In this manner, his project included a critique of political economy but also simultaneously transcended the latter. In modern industrial societies, the everyday is clearly molded in fundamental ways by economic-technological imperatives that colonize space and time. However, collective social praxis cannot be subsumed completely under this systemic logic: there always remains something that escapes domestication.[7] This ambiguity generates conflicts that configure everyday life as a contradictory relationship between productive activity and passive consumption, between everydayness and creativity. For Lefebvre, therefore, the analysis of the extant must always take into consideration insurgent forces and the question of liberation. Insofar as the critique of everyday life shows how people live, it articulates at the same time an indictment against the strategies from which the everyday emerges and reveals the arbitrariness of the dominant order.[8]

According to Lefebvre, the reproduction of modern everydayness occurs through a threefold movement. First, societalization is accomplished through a "totalization of society." Second, this process is accompanied by an "extreme individualization" which eventually leads to a "particularization."[9] The "bureaucratic society of controlled consumption" is grounded upon the parcelization of social praxis and the shredding of social contexts:

What are the shared features of these realms that have been separated from one another through an inexorable analytical praxis? In the realm of work, it is passivity, the unavoidable acceptance of decisions made elsewhere; in the realm of private life, there are the many forces which manufacture the consumer through the manufacture of objects; in the realm of leisure, it is the transformation of the "world" into images and spectacles. In short, everywhere one finds passivity, non-participation.[10]

Third, capitalist societies atomize people into isolated consumers. The critique of the "society of the spectacle" was grounded upon the premise that this system could not pacify its class contradictions over the long term. Oppositional movements against the banality and homogeneity of the functional city would be unleashed against an alienation process that is no longer confined to the realm of work but increasingly seizes everyday life as well.

Fordist societalization did indeed produce openings in social space. While the extension of the wage relation functioned as a form of social integration, reductions of labor time and more generous vacation benefits helped liberate subjectivity. Enhanced economic security, prolonged socialization within the family and an extension of cultural activities led—at least for certain social groups—to new, increasingly self-determined ways of life. A new "culture of stimulation" emerged, saturated with commodities and distractions and oriented toward self-realization, pleasure and hedonism. As work discipline was gradually corroded by mass consumption, Fordist societalization became increasingly dysfunctional—for it hinged upon the link between the motivation to work and productive performance.[11] Although Lefebvre insisted repeatedly that everyday life represented a site of the "actual and the possible," this tension evaporated in his concrete studies of capitalism. He was able to conceptualize and represent the consolidation of Fordism only as impoverishment, leveling, and flattening. His proposed dialectic of "alienation" and "appropriation" was thus subordinated to a perspective in which collective social praxis appears to be almost completely reified and normalized.

THE PRODUCTION OF SPACE

In the 1960s, Lefebvre detected an epochal shift from the temporal to the spatial. While Foucault analyzed space as an apparatus of political technology and scientific discourse in the transition from absolutist to disciplinary power,[12] Lefebvre relates the dominance of the spatial to the reproduction of capitalism. Space is presented as the result of a concrete production process. For Lefebvre, things are not separate from space. He considers space as social product; the production of space may reveal social relations. Each mode of production produces its own space, albeit not in a linear fashion. The relative fixity of spatial structures produces layering effects.

Changing uses of space and processes of restructuring do not produce radical breaks in spatial patterns but develop within and against existing spatial structures. In principle, capitalist space is characterized by homogeneity and fragmentation. It is based on the separation and subsequent reconnection of space. On the one hand, the abstract logic of state and commodity produces homogenizing effects. On the other, capitalist valorization strategies subdivide, parcellize, and pulverize space.

To define socio-spatial processes further, Lefebvre developed a differentiated schema that distinguishes three dimensions of the production of space.[13] First, *perceived space* refers to the collective production of urban reality, the rhythms of work, residential, and leisure activities through which society develops and reproduces its spatiality. *Conceived space* is formed through knowledge, signs, and codes. Conceived space refers to "representations of space" by planners, architects, and other specialists who divide space into separate elements that can be recombined at will. The discourse of these specialists is oriented toward valorizing, quantifying, and administering space, thereby supporting and legitimating the modes of operation of state and capital. Finally, Lefebvre talks about lived and endured space: "spaces of representation." Users of space experience lived space every day, through the mediation of images and symbols. Lived space offers possibilities of resistance.

With this triadic model of the social production of space, Lefebvre tried to undermine dichotomies of structure and agency, discourse and practice. The schism between subjects' perceived and lived spaces of activity and "objective" scientific-technological spatial structures is bridged by "ideologies of space." According to Prigge,[14] these ideologies articulate science with everyday life, render spatial prac-tices coherent, guarantee the functioning of everyday life and prescribe modes of life.

In The Urban Revolution, Lefebvre reconstructs the history of urbanization, which is shaped by three spatio-temporal "continents": the rural, the industrial, and the urban. He understands these continents as forcefields that represent specific modes of thought, action, and life. They do not simply follow each other in historical sequence but overlap and interrelate in a pattern of parallel spatial coexistence. For Lefebvre, industrialization and urbanization form a dialectical unity. The indus-trialization of society always implies urbanization as well. While industrial dynamics produce spatial agglomerations of labor and means of production, industrialization also requires expanding urban infrastructures. Even though "the city" no longer represents an independent mode of production and life, it does not lose its specific function of centrality. Centrality returns in the form of centers of control and decision-making. The process of urbanization produces a fundamental shift. The industrial and its epistemology defined by disciplines oriented toward capital and labor are replaced by the urban as a "strategic place and strategic object" of social development. The production of space becomes the dominant process of repro-ducing social relations. Even if one does not share Lefebvre's philosophy of history and theory of revolution, his urban work opens up a new perspective on the relationship between city and society.

LEFEBVRE AND THE POVERTY OF GERMAN URBAN STUDIES

Lefebvre's short-lived importance to the New Left in the Federal Republic[15] can be attributed to a specific historical configuration: growing social resistance against the rigid regulatory practices of the Fordist "planning state" (Toni Negri) and its restrictive moral and cultural foundations. This rebellion was provoked "less by the forms of exploitation associated with property relations than by the consequences of industrialization for the lifeworld, less by class oppression than by the modern state's drive towards centralization and sociocultural homogeneity."[16]

While Lefebvre's critique of everyday life attracted a certain following in the Federal Republic during the 1970s, his thesis that the "urban" rather than the industrial represented the foundational tendency of social development did not resonate well. The few exceptions to this include the works by Jansen, Durth, Berndt, Hartmann *et al.*, and Prigge.[17] This can be explained by the fact that the "historical" and the "temporal" dominated postwar German social science while the category of *space* continues to be associated with Nazi-era slogans such as "people without space" (*Volk ohne Raum*) and "territorial expansion policy" (*Großraumpolitik*).

There were still other reasons for the short-lived reception of Lefebvre's work within German urban sociology. The culture industry thesis of the "Frankfurt School" played a central role within studies of socialization and education, and thus provided multiple potential linkages to Lefebvre's critique of everyday life; by contrast, critical theory was hardly acknowledged at all within the registers of urban studies. While some authors did attempt to ground their work upon Marxian terminology, only the economy and the law of value were recognized as universal reference points for understanding urban space (as, for instance, in the German "derivationist" tradition). Lefebvre's rejection of economism, his foundational assumption that the social totality could be experienced and conceptualized only in a fragmented manner as well as the terminological and conceptual inconsistency of his writings (along with a paucity of competent translations) discouraged many critical, anti-capitalist urban sociologists from attempting to integrate his insights into their research.

While Lefebvre's category of the "everyday" was eventually accepted even within the discipline of urban studies, the same cannot be said of his concept of space. In the 1980s, the German translation of an essay by David Harvey presented another, albeit indirect, opportunity for interested readers to acquaint themselves with Lefebvre's complex spatial theory.[18] By this time, German urban studies was in the midst of a paradigm shift, however: political economy approaches were declining in importance and marginalized in favor of a new culturalist approach. The discipline of urban studies opened up to postmodern sociological concepts even as the discourse-theoretical and semiotic methods associated with the latter were largely ignored. German-speaking urban studies remains completely unaware of research on the power-knowledge complex (e.g., Foucault). The "romantic revolutionary"[19] fell through the cracks a second time: with the increasing institutionalization of social movements (e.g., the Greens) and the ebbing of militant struggles, interest in a fundamental critique of state and society likewise diminished. In light of the predominant mentality to accept the state as the unquestioned parameter of life, Lefebvre's reflections on the "state mode of production" no longer had "use-value" for German urban studies.[20] His triadic model of space, which emphasizes the importance of symbolic processes, was once again dismissed by most exponents of the discipline as incomprehensible French prose.

THE NEW SPIRIT OF CAPITALISM

And today? Can Lefebvre's approach help us understand the "contours and convolutions" of post-Fordist everyday life?

First, it is necessary to review the transformations that have unfolded during recent decades. The Fordist growth model experienced a double crisis during the 1970s. On the one hand, the productivity of Taylorism had exhausted itself. On the other, the effectiveness of Keynesian welfare state policies was undermined by increased economic internationalization. Yet changes in everyday life, not only economic crisis, helped undermine the postwar model of societalization. The expansion of social security, rising wages, and the growth of the education system helped free subjectivity in the 1960s. The "children of Fordism" ran up against rigid disciplinary techniques, which at that time dominated school, factory, and family. Expressing these changing attitudes, a series of social movements attacked authoritarian and hierarchical structures and demanded "autonomy" and self-realization. The intensity of struggle and the development of an "autonomous subjectivity" did not however lead to a fundamental change of the system. Instead, capitalism managed to respond to the desires and demands of social movements with new identities and consumption patterns.

The neoliberal project has built upon this critique of the authoritarian welfare state and redirected it against individual subjects. The new technologies of power associated with neoliberalism attempt to individualize social risks, dismantle erstwhile social rights and subject people to self-regulation. Reacting to growing demands for more individuality, neoliberalism "invites individuals and organizations to participate more actively and help solve particular issues and problems which until then had been the responsibility of specialists and authorized state institutions."[21] Whereas a new form of "objective domination" replaced the authoritarian-paternalistic regime at the beginning of the last century, a new form of social regulation grounded in the demand for "controlled autonomy" is currently crystallizing.

Following French sociologists Luc Boltanski and Eve Chiapello, particular regimes of capitalist development are decisively shaped by the forms of critique that develop against them.[22] They suggest that two basic strands of critique have emerged since the mid-twentieth century. Whereas the first is directed against exploitation and inequality (critique sociale), the second foregrounds aspects of autonomy and self-realization (critique artiste). First developed in small intellectual circles, the "artistic critique" criticizes factory discipline and the uniformity of mass society while propagating the ideal of individual autonomy and freedom.

Boltanski and Chiapello argue that capitalism managed to renew itself in the 1980s in part by learning from the radical nature of the "artistic critique," the profound rejection of any form of institution and attachment. While in Fordism the ideal subject is the passive worker who is completely subjected to the thoroughly planned labor process, the dominant virtues under post-Fordism are autonomy and individual initiative. Whereas before the subjectivity of the worker was suppressed, new management approaches now demand "self-organization" and "autonomy." Such managerial models have little in common with Marx's critique of alienation, of course. Rather, the mobilization of subjectivity intends to make productive use of individual capacities for cooperation and communication.

Flexible capitalism managed to absorb the libertarian potential of the "artistic critique" of bureaucracy, uniformity, and dependency. As a result, the conventional "social critique" became increasingly uprooted. During the last few decades, the capacity for collective solidarity, which in industrial society emerged from the common experience of alienated labor, has eroded. Even the social bearers of the old class compromise are in dissolution. Still, in the face of current pressures for flexibilization and deregulation, many critics of neoliberalism long for a return of the "golden age" of Fordism. The social and economic bases for such nostalgia no longer exist, however. Of course, this does not imply that one should give up the struggle for social standards and allow the neoliberals to dispose of the ruins of the welfare state.

To some extent, flexible capitalism has managed to undercut both forms of anti-capitalist critique: one through integration and cooptation, the other by means of a transformation of everyday life into a reality that can no longer be interpreted with the conventional means of social critique. It is here that the limitations of Lefebvre's critique of everyday life become apparent. To be sure, he was able to transcend certain dogmas of the Marxist movement, but he remained locked into a theory of revolution that was grounded in a philosophy of history. Contrary to his belief that a trend toward radical-democratic self-management (or autogestion) was unavoidable, capitalism has become even stronger following the crisis of Fordism: it has proven itself capable of absorbing its critics, taking up oppositional claims for "autonomy" and "creativity" and instrumentalizing them for its own purposes. Following the diagnosis of Gilles Deleuze,[23] the liberated individual represents a particular type of subaltern subject. Once mobilized against capitalism, attributes like "subjectivity" and "creativity" are now important resources for processes of economic valorization.

Despite such qualifications, Lefebvre's concept of everyday life remains visionary. In light of contemporary processes of capitalist societalization, the conventional divisions of paid and unpaid work, production and reproduction have definitely become obsolete. Capital attempts to regulate all aspects of life by commanding not only the capacity to labor (labor-power) but creative potential more generally.[24] Against the "postmodern" technologies and procedures of control, resistance manifests itself in a wide variety of realms: struggles against exploitation and oppression, struggles against exclusion, struggles against predefined subject positions.[25] Confronting the demands of neoliberalism thus requires two tasks. On the one hand, a social critique must be formulated that takes into account contemporary social relations and power structures. On the other, the artistic critique must be kept from being instrumentalized for the purposes of a new kind of productivist subjectivity. Neither task is easy.

THE NEOLIBERAL RESTRUCTURING OF URBAN EVERYDAY LIFE

In his foundational work on Lefebvre, Christian Schmid has demonstrated the meaning of *urban level*.[26] The French philosopher and theorist of space distinguishes three spatio-temporal fields of social reality: the private level, the global or general level, and the level of the "urban" proper, which functions as the mediation between the general and the private. The bottom level Lefebvre also describes as the "near order," which encompasses all of everyday life. Counterposed to the near order is the "far order": state authority and powerful institutions, which organize and regulate society. On this abstract level, one can find general social relations: exchange, industrialization, and so on. With its infrastructures, services, and local systems of power, the urban level works as a relay station between the far order and everyday life. Urban space under capitalism thus has a double character. On the one hand, it functions as a productive force, which helps trigger waves of industrialization; on the other, it represents a social relation, where human everyday life is organized and reproduced.

As a strategic space for social development, the urban level plays as central role for neoliberal restructuring. To understand the relationship between "urban" and neoliberalism, one must highlight the basic features of Fordist spatial strategies.

As the spatial equivalence to the core elements of Fordist processes of societalization (wage labor and nuclear family), the functional separation of work, residence, and leisure became the dominant local conception of space. This resulted in accelerated suburbanization and a growing rationalization of everyday life. In the

Federal Republic of Germany, processes of societalization were also shaped by conceptions of space aimed at eliminating geographical inequalities at a national scale. Based on the assumption that the national territory is the decisive scale, the goal was to create a network of "central places" in order to promote balanced growth and eradicate socio-spatial disparities. The central state tried to limit local initiatives, which were perceived as "narrow-minded particularisms." Individual municipalities had the mere function of "transmission belts" to implement higher-level commands.

This concept of space has been under growing pressure since the 1980s. The erosion of relatively homogeneous social and political spaces transformed existing socio-spatial arrangements. While the Fordist model of development had a long-term tendency toward spatial condensation and a relative cohesion of economy, politics, and ideology at the national scale, economic networks and relationships (affected by globally organized processes of valorizing capital) started to become independent from spatial fixity. It would be wrong to equate this process with a "deterritorialization" of state power. The globalization of national economies led to a restructuring of organizational-territorial structures rather than a loss of significance of the state per se.[27] Whereas under Fordism spatial inequality was meant to be eliminated in favor of national territorial uniformity, central states now increasingly focus on urban–regional scales. This has produced a seeming paradox: while the state is the decisive force in deregulating the Fordist compromise, it seems to undermine its own capacities to act. It is possible, however, to understand this strategy as an attempt to make up for the limited sovereignty of the nation-state by fostering local and regional competitiveness and thus strengthen the state's position within the division of labor. Germany has lagged behind Anglo-American countries in this process. In Germany, the completion of Fordism coincided historically with the secular crisis of this mode of regulation. This tentative consolidation of Fordism was followed by an almost equally tentative move away from the Fordist promise of "everlasting prosperity" and "social partnership." The political climate of the 1970s and 1980s continued to be shaped strongly by Fordist conceptions. In contrast to the United States or Great Britain, neocorporatist strategies of consensus formation remained implicitly committed to the welfare state. Only since the mid-1990s has it become possible to talk about deeper transformations away from the century-old tradition of the German welfare state.

Following Neil Brenner and Nik Theodore,[28] one can identify two forms of neoliberal restructuring. One the one hand, cities face growing economic pressure. Among these are speculative movements of finance and real-estate capital, flexible location strategies of multinational corporations, and increased competitive pressures between metropolitan regions. Most urban administrations try to meet growing economic insecurity by mobilizing all possible resources and initiating city marketing campaigns to attract jobs and investment. On the other hand, neoliberal concepts are brought to bear directly on municipal development strategies. In the transition away from the goal of comprehensive welfare (*Daseinsfürsorge*), that is, the public provision of social infrastructure, the marketization of urban space becomes increasingly important for local state policy. Cities become laboratories for institutional innovation and political-ideological projects: public–private partnerships, lean administration, cross-border leasing, city-management, business improvement districts, and other comparable words of magic. Not only in terminology, "Rhenian capitalism" approximates the Anglo-American model. This implies specific territorial strategies. Municipal actors bank on increasing the commercialization of central cities for high-income groups and tourists. When necessary, the model of the "European city" is mobilized for this purpose. New, dense spaces that in some way combine work, residence, shopping, and entertainment are created on abandoned central city spaces (former railway and port lands). These two forms of city building command the full attention of local planning policy. At the same time, municipal administrations renege on their erstwhile responsibility to look after the city as a whole. Neoliberalism follows a logic of intensified inter-city competition, which hierarchizes urban space by valorizing particular fragments. One can thus speak of a policy of privileged places. Turning away from the statist principle of solidarity and mobilizing space as a strategic resource are the decisive features of the "entrepreneurial city." The "welfare city" (*Vorsorge-Stadt*), which replaced the liberal model of "self-management by property owners" (*Eigentümer-Selbstverwaltung*) of the nineteenth century, is coming to an end. It is too early to tell how deeply the neoliberal project will transform metropolitan social relations. In any case, the task is to search for the breaking points in post-Fordist everydayness. This is not an academic matter. As Lefebvre said: "life is not changed magically by a poetic act, as the surrealists believed. Language liberated from its servitudes plays a necessary role—but it does not suffice."[29]

NOTES

1. This chapter is a substantially revised and rewritten version of a paper previously published as "Contours and Convolutions of Everydayness: On the Reception of Henri Lefebvre in the Federal Republic of Germany," *Capitalism, Nature, Socialism* 13, no. 2 (2002): 42–57.

2. An example is the Berlin-based journal *An Architektur*. It devoted its first issue in 2002 exclusively to Lefebvre.

3. The term *Vergesellschaftung* (societalization) refers to the processes by which practices of production and reproduction (such as those under the Fordist model of development) are generalized and diffused in everyday life.

4. A German translation of Lefebvre's *Critique of Everyday Life* was produced only after a considerable delay. The first volume (and the introduction to the second edition of the first volume) and the second volume (initially published in 1947, 1958, and 1961, respectively) were not translated into German until the mid-1970s as *Kritik des*

Alltagslebens Band I (München: Hanser, 1974) and *Kritik des Alltagslebens Band II* (München: Hanser, 1975). These works were reissued by Fischer in 1987. Other German translations of works by Henri Lefebvre are *Der dialektische Materialismus* (Frankfurt am Main: Suhrkamp Verlag, 1966 [1940]); "Perspektiven der Agrarsoziologie," in *Beiträge zur Marxistischen Erkenntnistheorie*, ed. A. Schmidt (Frankfurt am Main: Suhrkamp Verlag, 1969 [1953]); "Zum Begriff der 'Erklärung' in der politischen Ökonomie und in der Soziologie," in *ibid.*; *Probleme des Marxismus* (Frankfurt am Main: Suhrkamp Verlag, 1965 [1958]); *Aufstand in Frankreich. Zur Theorie der Revolution in den hochindustrialisierten Ländern* (Berlin: Edition Voltaire, 1969 [1968]); *Die Revolution der Städte* (München: Anton Hain Verlag, 1972 [1970]); *Soziologie nach Marx* (Frankfurt am Main: Suhrkamp Verlag, 1972 [1966]); *Das Alltagsleben der modernen Welt* (Frankfurt am Main, Suhrkamp Verlag, 1977 [1968]); *Sprache und Gesellschaft* (Düsseldorf: Pädagogischer Verlag Schwann, 1973 [1966]); *Die Zukunft des Kapitalismus* (München: Paul List Verlag, 1974 [1973]); *Metaphilosophie Prolegomena* (Frankfurt am Main: Suhrkamp Verlag, 1975 [1965]); *Die Stadt im Marxistischen Denken* (Ravensburg: Maier, 1975 [1972]); *Einführung in die Modernität. Zwölf Präludien* (Frankfurt am Main: Suhrkamp Verlag, 1978 [1962]); *Die Revolution ist auch nicht mehr, was sie mal war* (München: Hanser Verlag, 1979 [1978]); "Entwurf einer Theorie der Rythmoanalyse," *Neue Praxis* 2 (1991); "Alltäglichkeit," in *Historisch-Kritisches Wörterbuch des Marxismus*, vol. I, ed. W. F. Haug (Hamburg/Berlin: Arguement, 1994).

5. Lefebvre, *Einführung*, 27.

6. Lefebvre refers to and develops the existentialist term introduced by Heidegger during the Darmstadt Symposium on "Man and Space" in 1951. See Martin Heidegger, "Building Dwelling Thinking," in *Basic Writings*, revised and expanded edn ed. D. F. Krell (New York: Harper and Collins, 1993), 342–63.

7. Ulrich Müller-Schöll, *Das System und der Rest. Kritische Theorie in der Perspektive Henri Lefebvres* (Mössingen-Thalheim: Talheimer Verlag, 1999).

8. Lefebvre, *Kritik des Alltagslebens*, I.

9. Lefebvre, *Einführung*, 340.

10. Lefebvre, *Kritik des Alltagslebens*, II, 120ff. Nearly at the same time, and with direct reference to Lefebvre, the Situationists too spoke of the "colonization" of everyday life—see Guy Debord, *The Society of the Spectacle*, trans. D. Nicholson-Smith (Cambridge, MA: Zone Books, 1995 [1967]). Even the Left in the Federal Republic interpreted the entrenchment of the Fordist welfare state as a process of colonization or as a process of "internalization" (*innere Landnahme*). It is in this sense, for instance, that the social psychologist Peter Brückner criticized Fordist societalization with reference to Lefebvre: "In a second colonization, nearly every subsystem—be it the region, the municipality, education—is being regulated directly in a statist manner. Thanks to new technologies of planning and domination, the state imposes its framework upon all interconnected social processes—for only a homogeneous medium can be governed." *Psychologie und Geschichte: Vorlesungen im "Club Voltaire" 1980/81* (Berlin: Wagenbach, 1982), 266.

11. Rudolf M. Lüscher, *Henry und die Krümelmonster. Versuch über den Fordistischen Sozialcharakter* (Tübingen: Verlag Claudia Gehrke, 1988).

12. Michel Foucault, *Discipline and Punish: The Birth of the Prison*, trans. A. Sheridan (New York: Vintage, 1979).

13. Henri Lefebvre, *The Production of Space*, trans. D. Nicholson-Smith (New York: Blackwell, 1991).

14. Walter Prigge, "Die Revolution der Städte Lesen," in *Stadt-Räume*, ed. M. Wentz (Frankfurt: Campus, 1993), 99–111.

15. Without claiming to be exhaustive, the following list of sources provides an overview of the German-language reception of Lefebvre during the 1970s: Reinhard Bentmann and Michael Müller, *Nachwort zur zweiten Auflage: Die Villa als Herrschaftsarchitektur. Versuch einer kunst- und sozialgeschichtlichen Analyse* (Frankfurt: Suhrkamp Verlag, 1970); Hans-Eckehard Bahr, ed., *Politisierung des Alltags: Gesellschaftliche Bedingungen des Friedens* (Darmstadt and Neuwied: Luchterhand-Verlag,1972); Kurt Meyer, *Henri Lefebvre: Ein romantischer Revolutionär* (Vienna: Europa Verlag, 1973); Horst Arenz, Joachim Bischoff, and Urs Jaeggi, *Was ist revolutionärer Marxismus?* (Berlin: VAS-Verlag, 1973); Gisela Gischner, "Sozialisationstheorie und materialistische Äesthetik," in *Das Unvermögen der Realität. Beiträge zu einem anderen materialistischen Ästhetikum*, ed. C. Bezzel, G. Dischner, and M. Eckelt (Berlin: Wagenbach Klaus GmbH, 1974); Peter Gorsen, "Transformierte Alltäglichkeit oder Transcendenz der Kunst?," in *ibid.*; Rainer Paris, "Befreiung vom Alltag?" *Kursbuch 41* (1975); Thomas Kleinspehn, *Der verdrängte Alltag: Henri Lefebvres Marxistische Kritik des Alltagslebens* (Gießen: Focus Verlag, 1975); Thomas Leithäuser, *Formen des Alltagsbewußtseins* (Frankfurt: Campus, 1976); Alfred Krovoza, *Produktion und Sozialisation* (Köln: Europaische Verlagsanstalt, 1976); Gerburg Treusch-Dieter, "Revolution der Städte?," *Äesthetik und Kommunikation 26* (1977); Werner Durth, *Die Inszenierung der Alltagswelt. Zur Kritik der Stadtgestaltung* (Braunschweig: Vieweg-Verlag, 1977); Lothar Hack, *Subjektivität im Alltagsleben. Zur Konstitution sozialer Relevanzstrukturen* (Frankfurt am Main: Campus, 1977); Heide Berndt, *Die Natur der Stadt* (Frankfurt: Campus, 1978); Hans Joas, "Einleitung," in *Das Alltagsleben. Versuch einer Erklärung der individuellen Reproduktion*, ed. A. Heller (Frankfurt am Main: Suhrkamp Verlag, 1978); Rainer Neugebauer, *Alltagsleben: Zur Kritik einer politisch-historischen und dialektischen Kategorie* (Frankfurt am Main: Haag und Herchen, 1978); Berhard Waldenfels, "Im Labyrinth des Alltags," in *Phänomenologie und Marxismus 3*, ed. B. Waldenfels *et al.* (Frankfurt am Main: Suhrkamp Verlag, 1978); Kurt Hammerich and Michael Klein, "Alltag und Soziologie," in *Materialien zur Soziologie des Alltags*, ed. K. Hammerich and M. Klein (Opladen: Westdeutscher Verlag, 1978); Bernd Dewe, Wilfried Ferchhoff, and Heinz Sünker, afterword, "Perspektiven einer Kritik des Alltagslebens heute," in Henri Lefebvre, *Kritik des Alltagslebens* (Frankfurt: Suhrkamp Verlag, 1987). Lefebvre's work was read above all in a context shaped by materialist approaches to theories of socialization and consciousness, approaches to aesthetic theory and cultural revolution, as well as in the margins of urban studies. In contemporary Germany, he has disappeared from the radar screen; he never became as well known in Germany as Michel Foucault or Gilles Deleuze. His books have disappeared even from the shelves of second-hand bookshops—a fate that Lefebvre shares with Marxists such as Louis Althusser and Nicos Poulantzas.

16. Peter Brückner, foreword in Alfred Krovoza *Produktion und Sozialisation* (Köln: EVA, 1976), 10.

17. Berndt, *Die Natur*; Durth, *Die Inszenierung*; Walter Prigge, *Zeit, Raum und Architektur. Zur Geschichte der Räume* (Stuttgart: Dt. Gemeindeverlag, 1986); Hans G. Helms and Jörn Jansen, eds., *Kapitalistischer Städtebau* (Neuwied: Luchterhand, 1970); Roger Hartmann *et al.*, *Theorien zur Stadtentwicklung* (Oldenburg: Geographische Hochschulmanuskripte, 1986); Walter Prigge, "Hegemonie des urbanistischen Diskurses," in *Die Materialität des Städtischen*, ed. W. Prigge (Basel/Boston, MA:

Birkhäuser, 1987); "Die Revolution" in *ibid*.; "Städte Bauen oder Sätze Bauen?," *Kulturrevolution* 17/18 (1988); *Urbanität und Intellektualität im 20. Jahrhundert. Wien 1900, Frankfurt 1930, Paris 1960* (Frankfurt: Campus, 1996).

18. "Flexible Akkumulation durch Urbanisierung: Überlegungen zum 'Postmodernismus' in den amerikanischen Städten," PROKLA 69 (1987).

19. Meyer, *Henri Lefebvre*.

20. Lefebvre's four volumes on state theory, *De l'État* (1976–8), remain known only among a few specialists. See Martina Löw, *Raumsoziologie* (Frankfurt am Main: Suhrkamp Verlag, 2001); Arno Münster, *Pariser philosophisches Journal. Von Sartre bis Derrida* (Frankfurt am Main: Athenaeum Verlag, 1987); Hajo Schmidt, *Sozialphilosophie des Krieges. Staats- und subjekttheoretische Untersuchungen zu Henri Lefebvre und Georges Bataille* (Essen: Klartext, 1990); Corell Wex, *Logistik der Macht. Henri Lefebvres Sozialtheorie und die Räumlichkeit des Staates*, Ph.D. dissertation, Phillips-Universität Marburg, 1999; Christian Schmid, *Stadt, Raum und Gesellschaft: Henri Lefebvre und die Theorie der Produktion des Raumes* (München: Franz Steiner, 2005). Neil Brenner's innovative essays on Lefebvre's spatial theory and state theory have left no traces within German urban studies ("Die Restrukturierung staatlichen Raums. Stadt- und Regionalplanung in der BRD 1960–1990," PROKLA 109 (1997); "Städte und die Politik des Raumes," *WeltTrends* 17 (1997)).

21. Thomas Lemke, *Eine Kritik der politischen Vernunft. Foucaults Analyse der modernen Gouvernementalität* (Hamburg: Argument Verlag, 1997), 254.

22. Luc Boltanski and Eve Chiapello, *Le Nouvel Esprit du capitalisme* (Paris: Gallimard, 1999).

23. Gilles Deleuze, *Negotiations 1972–1990*, trans. M. Joughin (New York: Columbia University Press, 1997 [1990]).

24. Paolo Virno, *A Grammar of the Multitude: For an Analysis of Contemporary Forms of Life*, trans. I. Bertoletti, J. Cascaito, and A. Casson (New York: Semiotext(e), 2004 [2001]).

25. Michel Foucault, afterword, "The Subject and Power," in Hubert L. Dreyfus and Paul Rabinow, *Michel Foucault: Beyond Structuralism and Hermeneutics* (Chicago: University of Chicago Press, 1983), 208–63.

26. Schmid, *Stadt, Raum und Gesellschaft*.

27. Brenner, "Die Restrukturierung."

28. Neil Brenner and Nik Theodore, "Cities and the Geographies of 'Actually Existing Neoliberalism,'" in *Spaces of Neoliberalism*, ed. N. Brenner and N. Theodore (New York: Blackwell, 2002), 2–32.

29. Henri Lefebvre, *The Explosion: Marxism and the French Upheaval*, trans. A. Ehrenfeld (New York: Monthly Review Press, 1969 [1968]), 90.

9

RHYTHMS, STREETS, CITIES

Kurt Meyer

(translated by Bandulasena Goonewardena)

ON RHYTHMANALYSIS

Henri Lefebvre's incomplete project of rhythmanalysis, closely connected with his critique of everyday life, was published under the title *Elements of Rhythmanalysis* in 1992, a year after he died. It consists of seven loosely connected chapters and a separate study of the rhythms of Mediterranean cities. In 1985, he had published "The Rhythmanalytical Project," co-authored with his wife Catherine Régulier.[1] These rhythmanalytical studies help us penetrate to the inner core—one is tempted to say the holy domain—of Lefebvre's critique of everyday life; that is to say, to those analyses dealing with the temporal order of rhythms in everyday life. In the third volume of *Critique of Everyday Life*,[2] rhythmanalysis is termed an emerging science investigating the complex interactions of cyclic rhythms and linear rhythms.

It was the Brazilian philosopher Lucio Alberto Pinheiro dos Santos who in 1931 coined the term "rhythmanalysis" and developed in his work the physiological principles of this theory. He believed it would be possible by means of rhythm-analysis to cure the mind suffering from occasional mental depression or general apathy. Gaston Bachelard, who in many of his writings spoke of this philosopher's work in admiring terms, considered rhythmanalysis an enlightening and suggestive concept.[3] Like Pinheiro dos Santos, he also thought that rhythmicized living and thinking, alternation of activity and rest, could lead to a cure. The mind that compulsively strives for uniformity should be *disorganized* from time to time, tensed up rhythms relaxed, fatigued rhythms restimulated. Life as a whole should be set to a sensible rhythm. Bachelard considered rhythmanalytical meditations "a kind of philosophical echo of poetic delight."[4] He was so impressed with the Brazilian philosopher's thinking that he wrote: "Rhythm is really the only way of disciplining and maintaining the most distinct energies. It is the basis of the dynamic of life and the dynamic of mind."[5]

In the second volume of *Critique of Everyday Life*, Lefebvre describes for the first time the manifold interplay of *cyclic time* and *linear time*.[6] During the long period before they mastered nature, human beings were exposed to natural and cosmic rhythms from birth to death. The regular recurrence of days, weeks, months, seasons, and years gave human existence a reliable rhythmic order. Strictly speaking, rhythmic time knows neither beginning nor end. "Every cycle is born from another cycle and becomes absorbed in other circular movements. Cyclic time does not exclude repetitive action . . . [N]o genuine cycle returns exactly to its point of departure or reproduces itself exactly."[7] Modern man, integrated into the rational procedures of a techno-industrial world, is subject to the linear flow of time.

> Linear time is both continuous and discontinuous. Continuous: its beginning is absolute, and it grows indefinitely from an initial zero. Discontinuous: it fragments into partial time scales assigned to one thing or another according to a program which is abstract in relation to time. It dissects indefinitely. Techniques which fragment time also produce repetitive gestures. These do not and often cannot become part of a rhythm: the gestures of fragmented labour, actions which begin at any time or cease at any time.[8]

Cyclic time has not simply disappeared even in modernity. In a big city where public transport operates around the clock, certain needs or habits like hunger, sleep, and sexuality have not broken free from deep-rooted cycles. The aim of critical research into everyday life is to investigate the continuity of rhythmic time in the linear flow of time of modern industrial society, to study the interferences between cyclic time and linear time.

Lefebvre commences his posthumously published rhythm theory with a discussion of concepts and categories. It is only later that he proceeds to demonstrate their practical application. He consciously moves from the abstract to the concrete. Thus, he does not begin with particular entities, not with corporeal rhythms: breathing, pulse, blood circulation. First, he shows that the expression *rhythm* is employed differently; in music its significance is different from that of it in history or in economics, where one speaks of epochs, periods, or cycles as moving fast or slow. Cycles that impel a mechanical pace are differentiated from those motions which are organically rhythmacized. The concepts of *measure* and *measure of time*, apparently so clear, lead to special difficulties. What constitutes the measure of the continuous flow of time? The second, or the millionth of a second? Or the year? Every rhythm—be it the heart, breathing, or even the working hour—has its own measure, its own beat. Speed and frequency determine rhythm. The following oppositions help clarify theoretically the concept of rhythm:

- repetition and difference;
- mechanical and organic;
- discovery and creation;
- cyclic and linear;
- continuous and discontinuous;
- quantitative and qualitative . . .[9]

THE RHYTHMANALYST

Lefebvre outlines a suggestive portrait of the future rhythmanalyst, which differs from that of the psychoanalyst. The rhythmanalyst is all ears. He listens not only to words, however, but to everything happening in the world. He hears things that are usually hardly noticed: noise and sound. He pays attention to the babble of voices, but also to silence. The rhythmanalyst is not given to precipitate judgment. Yet, unlike the psychoanalyst, he is not obliged to remain passive. His role as an observer is not that of one lost in thought. He is always listening to his body, to whatever it communicates to him. It is only then that he perceives rhythms coming from outside. The body is, so to speak, his metronome. The rhythmanalyst is master of well-proven techniques: the breathing technique, the rhythms of the heart, the use of muscles and limbs.

Philosophy neglected the body over a long period of time, leaving the subject to physiology and medicine. The body consists of a bundle of rhythms. Under normal conditions, the various rhythms exist in harmony, that is, in a state of eurhythmy. Every organ and every bodily function has a rhythm of its own: acting together they maintain the body in equilibrium. Arrhythmic disturbances coming from without endanger this state of equilibrium. Whatever is found outside the body, whatever is derived from nature and society, also consists of a bundle of rhythms. All these rhythms wish to be "heard."[10]

Nothing is motionless in the eyes of the rhythmanalyst. He hears wind, rain, thunderstorm. In observing a pebble, a wall or a tree trunk, he perceives the slowness of movement of these objects. Their movement is slow only in proportion to our time, our bodies, our rhythms. Even an apparently immobile object—say, a forest— is moving. Such movement is connected to the forest soil, the earth, and the sun; to the atoms and the molecules of which it is composed. A forest is exposed to innumerable aggressions that are resisted by it. The rhythmanalyst strives to rehabilitate sensory perception. He pays attention to breathing, the heartbeat, the words. He is careful to avoid giving priority to any one act of sense perception.

SOME "ELEMENTS" OF RHYTHM THEORY

In Henri Lefebvre's view, there is as yet no general theory of rhythms. Any conception aspiring to uniformity breaks down in the face of the diversity of individual rhythms. Chrono-biologists have attempted to elucidate how living beings are steered by an "inner clock" or by astronomical forces (moon, sun, stars). We can establish that the human body works polyrhythmically—from the blink of an eye to breathing in and out. Lefebvre's ambitious rhythm theory aims not only to found a new science but to draw practical conclusions. Although he is aware that his analyses amount only to the "elements" of a theory, he takes into consideration possible practical applications. Let us now consider some "elements" of this theory.

1. Contemporary everyday life, conforming as it does to the rotating hands of a clock, is oriented to abstract quantitative time. In the West the discovery of clock time led to the introduction of *abstract time*. Its role in structuring public and private life has been increasingly decisive. As homogeneous, profane time, it has provided the time measure for work and subjugated one sphere of life after another: sleeping and waking hours, mealtimes, private life, the relationship of parents to their children, leisure time, times spent at home, and so on. In spite of the merciless rule of the abstract clock time, the immense cosmic rhythms continue to exert influence on everyday life.

   According to Lefebvre, the Marxists have had a restricted view of rhythms from the very beginning. They have investigated them only in connection with labor. Earlier, various collective or work processes were accompanied by rhythms, most frequently by songs. There were the songs of the oarsmen, the reapers, the shepherds, the sailors. Earlier social historians, however, had not noticed that there are rhythms in the collective life of society much older than those of collectively organized labor.

2. We cannot emphasize too strongly that the starting point of rhythm analysis is the body; not the anatomical or functional body but the polyrhythmic, eurhythmic body, the body in its normal state. In a "normal" body the innumerable rhythms form an astonishing harmony, an *isorhythm*. There must be an agent coordinating the various rhythms. Isorhythm or harmony is produced by a higher command. The isorhythm of the human body can be compared to symphonic music. In an orchestra the magic of the conductor's baton sets the rhythm. The human body—like an orchestra—produces isorhythm in an enigmatic way. Today one speaks of the peneal gland, a relatively small cluster of cells in the brain that determines the daily rhythm. Acting as a "conductor," this harmonizes the different rhythms of the organs.

3. Lefebvre also includes *chronobiology* in his concept of rhythm. Chronobiology teaches us that practically all metabolic activities proceed according to a definite

rhythmicity. These activities increase and decrease in the course of twenty-four hours. The rhythms of the liver, kidneys, spleen, heart, blood pressure, and bodily functions are fitted into the twenty-four-hour day; an external timer synchronizes the various physiological functions. Every organ has acquired a certain rhythmic autonomy through its evolution, its own genetic clock that follows an approximately twenty-four-hour rhythm. Invariably recurring processes that hardly change from day to day are called *circadian rhythms*. Apart from them, there are also monthly rhythms: for example, the menstrual cycle, or the skin, which is completely renewed in the course of a month. Altogether there are four frequencies that are repeated periodically and influence nature and life processes: the tides, the alternation of night and day, the rotation of the moon around the earth, and the seasons. In the case of plants, the moon's gravitational influence can be directly proved. In the case of man, direct proof is more difficult. Chronobiology views the entire body as a highly complex rhythm-based organ. Although we live in a high-tech world, the elementary physical needs still constitute the basic conditions of our daily life.

Lefebvre, interested as he was in chronobiology, sees how the ever-increasing night-work runs counter to biological circadian rhythms and poses the question whether the day would not suffice to perform repetitive activity. Life determined by technology effaces natural time structures ever more decisively. An increasing number of workers live contrary to their inner biological rhythms due to contemporary work processes organized around the clock.

4. Music and dance form the core elements of rhythm. The more monotonous the music, the greater the awareness of the need for rhythm. In the chapter "Music and Rhythms," Lefebvre comes to the conclusion that the worldwide spread of new musical rhythms evokes manifold changes. Europe and the West are experiencing a revival through various original and diverse exotic styles of music. According to Lefebvre, *exotic or ecstatic rhythms* produce a greater effect than traditional melodies and harmonies have ever achieved.

5. The political chapter of Lefebvre's book on rhythm bears the title "The Manipulations of Time." The disastrous role of capital does not consist in the first place in its having brought forth rich and poor, propertied and propertyless. It consists rather in its imperious contempt for the body and lived-time. Production and destruction form the rhythm inherent in capital. Capital produces everything: things, human beings, and peoples. It produces destructive effects with wars and brutal interventions, progress, and speculation. The destructive component is on the increase at present. Lefebvre considers it erroneous to personalize the destructive forces of capital. Thus, he does not speak of capitalists or money. "Something" is at work inexorably: political power that understands how to manipulate *time, calendar,* and *daily routine.* It is capable of controlling the possible human development (the rhythms) of all those serving it. This is officially called

mobilization.[11] The word "mobilization" is not necessarily limited to the warlike pervasion of life. There is also mobilization in peacetime—the subjection of life to the rule of the machine. When Lefebvre speaks of mobilization he is thinking of human beings whose lives are totally subjected to the rhythm of technology.

THE COMPLEXITY OF RHYTHMS

Even a simple rhythm—for example, the daily intake of food—depends on several factors. A child takes years to grow accustomed to the regularity of family mealtimes. The human body lives polyrhythmically. It consists of different rhythms. Every single organ or every function has its own. When the human organism exists in equilibrium, the various body rhythms flow interactively. Therefore, Lefebvre names the human body a *bundle* or a *bouquet of rhythms*. An analogous bundle or bouquet of rhythms penetrates the body from outside—from the environment. In order to describe this almost immeasurable complexity of the rhythms overlaying one another—in particular, the impossibility of isolating a single rhythm from the web of all rhythms—Lefebvre and Régulier draw a comparison with the play of ocean waves. They invite the reader to observe the surface of the sea exactly:

> It changes ceaselessly. As it approaches the shore, it takes the shock of the back-wash: it carries numerous wavelets, right down to the tiny quiver that it orientates, but which do not always go in its direction. Waves and wave forms are characterized by frequency, amplitude and displaced energy. Watching waves, you can easily observe what physicists call the superposition of small movements. Powerful waves crash upon one another, creating jets of spray; they disrupt one another noisily. Small undulations traverse each other, absorbing, fading, rather than crashing, into one another.[12]

With a little intuition, the observer can discern a polyrhythmic field or a flexible, fluid frizz of connections. Lefebvre believes the human body is exposed to just such a complex wave structure.

Italo Calvino, too, applies the image of waves to illustrate the rhythmic complexity found in nature. A short piece from the book *Mr. Palomar* is titled "Reading a Wave" and contains all the paradoxical elements that add up to an analysis of rhythms. Lefebvre would have delighted in Mr. Palomar's observations. The amiable Mr. Palomar stands on the seashore and observes a wave that runs out on the sand. He would like to observe a wave, a single wave, and nothing else. Yet this turns out to be extremely difficult:

> [Y]ou cannot observe a wave without bearing in mind the complex features that concur in shaping it and the other, equally complex ones that the wave itself originates. These aspects vary constantly, so each wave is different from

another wave, even if it is not adjacent or successive; in other words, there are some forms and sequences that are repeated, though irregularly repeated in space and time.[13]

Mr. Palomar chooses a new vantage point, a sandbank projecting into the water almost imperceptibly. In order to take an inventory of all the wave movements, he then restricts his field of vision, and observes only those waves running in the opposite direction, reversing time. He is so passionately devoted to unraveling the unending play of the waves that he lapses into a state of mild dizziness.

THE RHYTHMS OF A STREET

In the chapter "Seen from the Window," Lefebvre, the rhythmanalyst, does not move any longer strictly from the abstract to the concrete. In a phenomenological vision, he captures the rhythms of a varied street life that can be observed from the windows of his apartment. He lived at rue Rambuteau for decades. In its immediate neighborhood stand monuments steeped in tradition: the Archives Nationales (where historical documents are preserved), the Hôtel de Ville (city government of Paris), the headquarters of the Banque de France, the Arts et Métiers (Center of Engineering and Industrial Design). The Centre Pompidou—modern Paris—also lies close by. Lefebvre is proud of living at the intersection of tradition and creation, of the active and the inactive Paris. How do these rhythms intersect and overlap in this street?

"In order to grasp and analyse rhythms, it is necessary to get outside them, but not completely: be it through illness or a technique."[14] This sentence opens the *rhythmanalysis* of the rue Rambuteau. The situation of the observer in relation to what is observed is constantly kept in mind. The window overlooking the street is not an abstract location from where the mental eye could, so to speak, abstractly grasp what is happening in the street. It is a real location not only enabling sights but leading to insights. The observer is implicated in what is happening on the street. "To grasp a rhythm it is necessary to have been *grasped* by it."[15]

Lefebvre invites the reader to follow him looking out of the windows, that is, to pay attention to the heterogeneous street rhythms. Down below in the street people keep passing by, in a flood of noise and sounds, exposed at the same time to their own body rhythms. From the window the individual sounds can be distinguished from one another: crowds go their own ways, rhythms respond to each other. Cars stop at traffic lights, pedestrians cross the road. "One does not chatter while crossing a dangerous junction under the threat of wild cats and elephants ready to charge forward, taxis, buses, lorries, various cars. Hence the relative silence in this crowd. A kind of soft murmuring, sometimes a cry, a call."[16]

The signal switches to red: the vehicles stop, one hears steps and words of people. Green light, and the vehicles have the right of way. Human sounds change, no more steps and words. About ten cars start off, they speed up. A bus swerves out. The cars decelerate, slow down the rhythm, and accelerate once again, stepping on the gas. It is unbelievable what one can see and hear from the window.

> Sometimes, the old cars stall in the middle of the road and the pedestrians move around them like waves around a rock, though not without condemning the drivers of the badly placed vehicles with withering looks. Hard rhythms: alternations of silence and outburst, time both broken and accentuated, striking he who takes to listening from his window, which astonishes him more than the disparate movements of the crowds.[17]

Not only motor vehicles but people produce varied rhythms by their coming and going; cyclic, alternating, and arrhythmic. Groups of people who appear daily and regularly at the same time produce slow *cyclic* rhythms: children go to school, residents greet each other in the street, shoppers and tourists arrive regularly from a definite time onward. *Alternating* rhythms mix with cyclic rhythms: motorcars, regulars, employees (white-collar workers), bistro customers come in short intervals. The interaction(s) of these varied rhythms, the repetitive and the alternating, make up, as it is said, the animation of the street or the quarter.

The traffic rhythms slow down during the night without ever coming to a complete standstill. Some vehicles are waiting at red lights even at three or four o'clock in the morning. Once a perhaps tipsy driver approaches the crossing and drives straight through the stop signal. People on the opposite side of the road can be observed at night in arrhythmic intervals:

> Should a window suddenly light up, or on the contrary go dark, solitary dreamer might ask himself—in vain—if it concerns a scene of illness or of love, if it is the movement [geste] of a child who gets up too early or of an insomniac. Never does a head, a face appear in the dozens of windows. Except if there is something going on in the street, an explosion, a fire engine that hurtles by without stopping towards a call for help.[18]

Another window affords a view of the backyards and gardens where a sculptural stillness seems to prevail. There it is the play of sun and shade, of bright corners and dark recesses. Trees and grass appear side-by-side, motionless. On closer and prolonged examination one sees that even plants and trees have their rhythms, which in turn are made up of several rhythms: the leaves and the flowers, seeds and fruits. There is a time for everything. Before leaves sprout the cherry tree is in flower. The tree is first white, then green. In autumn, its leaves and fruits fall; first these, then those. Whoever observes the garden over a certain period of time will notice the polyrhythmic and maybe even the symphonic rhythms in plants. Every single object in the garden has its location, its rhythm, its immediate past, its near or distant future.

The Centre Pompidou, visible from the window, a colorful metal construction built in the 1970s is a child of the 1960s, a visual product of extraordinary events. The earlier decade was under the spell of space travel. In 1961 Gagarin became the first man to be launched into space. There followed the American landing on the moon in 1969. In keeping with the *Zeitgeist*, Lefebvre calls the Palais Beaubourg "meteorites fallen on old Paris," precisely in the middle of the popular center, "from a planet several centuries ahead of our own, and on top of that a complete failure on the market!"[19] Apparently in there is something that attracts crowds of people since they come in multitudes continuously, even at night. Do they come to see the building that has been conceived in order to be seen? The visitors cast an absentminded glance at what is exhibited. "We go around this void (*ce vide*), which fills itself up with things and people in order to empty itself (*se vide*), and so on."[20] It may be that people also come to see each other, to meet each other. It is quite remarkable that the gatherings of people have given back the square its older function—that of coming together and of spontaneous people's theater. "Here on the square, between Saint-Merri and Modernism erupts a mediaeval-looking festival: fire-eaters, jugglers, snake charmers, but also preachers and sit-in discussions."[21]

There are also those roaming about, in search only of themselves, and others trying to forget the dreariness of their homes by visiting the Centre Pompidou. They roam around the area for hours, reappearing at street intersections. While moving around they consume a hotdog, stop occasionally in the big square, and stare ahead helplessly. The trained rhythmanalyst who does not only fix his attention on a single phenomenon but hears the music as a whole sees the following:

> There on the square, there is something maritime about the rhythms. Currents traverse the masses. Streams break off, which bring or take away new participants. Some of them go towards the jaws of the monster, which gobbles them down in order quite quickly to throw them back up. The tide invades the immense square, then withdraws: flux and reflux.[22]

What has the view from the windows of the happenings in the rue Rambuteau and its vicinity been able to capture? A vision of rhythms? The music of the city? A picture which listens to itself? Image in the present of a discontinuous sum? "No camera, no image or series of images can show these rhythms."[23] His view of the street, which certainly has poetic qualities, makes Lefebvre part of a very special tradition. Numerous writers whose works are closely connected to the city's streets and façades, squares and quarters, have lived in Paris. This would apply to the sphere of painting: how many impressionist painters have captured the vivid scenes of life in the grands boulevards at daybreak or at sunset on canvas? When we think of Léon-Paul Fargue, André Breton, Paul Léautaud, Louis Aragon, and many others, it could be said that the city itself whispered to them the text for their stories and diaries. In the center of this free and lively city, on the main boulevards, in front of cafés and bistros, beneath the poster walls, the lonely mass of happy pedestrians enjoy the ever-new spectacle of the street even today. During the enchanting months from March to June, the boulevards were for Guy de Maupassant the only spot on earth where one really lived. When he described the boulevard rhythm in 1884, there was neither radio nor motorcar; neither electronic media nor motorized means of transport.

> A stream of people in black hats flows from the Madeleine to the Bastille. And a continuous hum of voices, just like the sound of the flow of a river, rises and then loses itself in the light spring air. Yet this vague noise is made up of all the thoughts, all the ideas which arise, run their course and disappear everyday in Paris. Like flies, news keep buzzing over the crowd of walkers; they go from one to another, escaping through the streets, flying to the furthest ends of the city.[24]

Henri Lefebvre did not have any literary ambitions in his attempt to read or interpret his street semantically or semiologically. His was free association in modest measure, and the theoretician shines through clearly between the lines. Yet his snapshot of one of the liveliest streets in Paris is much more than a dry socio-cultural sketch.

CITY RHYTHMS

"The city is heard as much as music as it is read as a discursive writing."[25]

Lefebvre and his wife Catherine Régulier co-authored a relatively long treatise entitled "Attempts at Rhythmanalysis of Mediterranean Cities." They make the rhythmanalyst, by now well known to us, crisscross through the streets of a big Mediterranean city—Barcelona, Beirut, Naples, Marseille or Tunis, for example. The rhythmanalyst is more receptive to time than to space. He distinguishes cosmic time from everyday time, time for this or that activity; and he pays attention to the *interferences* between cyclic and linear time. The rhythmanalyst strolling about perceives more the ambience of a city, rather than the image flattering the eye; more the atmosphere than the spectacle. He is all ears but hears not only words and sounds. Being a synesthecist, he can hear a house, a street, a city just as one hears a symphony or an opera. He tries to hear the music that the city plays and to understand its composition. He heeds the tempo, the beat, the repetitions of the tune and the rhythms. He hears the functional interruptions and the arrhythms. His is an attempt to keep the scientific and the poetic apart as little as possible.

Lefebvre and Régulier introduce a fairly long comparative observation: every sea has its own rhythm; that of the Mediterranean is different from that of the oceans. Two distinct city types correspond to the different seas. The oceanic cities are subjected to the cosmic rhythms of the tides, whereas the Mediterranean cities are situated on the shores of a sea that hardly knows ebb and tide. The ocean cities are *lunar* cities (the moon being responsible for the change of ebb and tide). Those in the vicinity of the Mediterranean are *solar* cities (the eternal theme: the sun and the Mediterranean). Equally different are the social and political forms. The Mediterranean cities, originally city-states controlling a small extent of territory, have as solar cities produced a more intensive urban life than the lunar cities, where more contractually regulated but for that reason more confined and abstract forms of community life have developed. In the Mediterranean the state has always been brutal and powerless, violent yet weak, promoting unity yet ruined and imperiled. In the northern oceanic states the political dimension developed with less violence and drama. Yet state power intervened more forcefully in individual and social matters. The rhythmanalyst who pays attention to the everyday lived experiences of the people perceives such differences (and much more). He finds out that in oceanic cities social relations rest more on a contractual-legal basis, on mutual good faith. In Mediterranean cities it is the tacit or explicit alliance that counts: hence affiliation to clans, to the mafia, and so on.

The second part of the essay concerns solely the cities in the Mediterranean region. Lefebvre and Régulier endorse the great historian Fernand Braudel who throughout his scholarly life defended the thesis of the unity of the Mediterranean— the unity of sea, land, and history. As everyone knows, the coasts around the Mediterranean Sea do not constitute a homogeneous whole: they differ from one another according to peoples, ethnicities, and history. The expanses of water not only separate countries and continents but connect them. Islam and Christianity certainly do clash in the Mediterranean region. Equally there are eastern and western centers of economic development. In the last analysis, however, the Mediterranean region forms a compact cosmos, an *économie-monde*, a "world-economy." Entirely in the spirit of Braudel, Lefebvre and Régulier write:

> the Mediterranean itself imposes common characteristics on these towns, insofar as it is a relatively small, enclosed and limited sea . . . The climate also seems to impose a certain homogeneity: olive trees, vines, etc., are found all around the Mediterranean. With regard to Mediterranean ports, they are marked by commercial relations that were the beginning of Greek civilization. The resources available to most of these towns, which they drew from their hinterlands, are limited. Industrialization was accomplished unevenly and with difficulty: it seems to have profoundly altered neither the traditions of exchange nor habits.[26]

They go on to discuss the differences between the public and the private spheres. The description of the private sphere remains as close as possible to the body, to gesture, to behavior, to habits. Hence, close to everyday life (the way the meals are prepared, how one sleeps) and to what is outside everyday routine (the way one dances, sings, makes music). State power and the citizens contend with one another for urban public space. Political power tries to intervene, to dominate space with its own monuments. The monuments and squares, the churches and palaces begin to play a role. Who will emerge victorious? The citizens live their everyday and business rhythms in this struggle for the appropriation of public space. By making this urban public space the place of strolling around, of encounters, of discussions and negotiations, of intrigue and spectacle, they appropriate it spontaneously. The time and rhythms of the people combine with the space these people inhabit.

Around the Mediterranean Sea many cities have been built on hillsides. In these cities one distinguishes a lower and an upper city. The flight of steps plays an important role as an architectonic link. It is not without reason that there exists a significant architecture of steps in the Mediterranean region. The steps connect spaces with times, the house surrounded by a wall with the street, the square, the monument. The steps themselves represent a local time; the minutes required to climb up. In Venice, the steps of the stairway rhythmize the walk through the city. Whoever goes up and down the steps of a bridge crosses the city from one district to another, from one local rhythm to another. The steps of Saint Charles in Marseille are an unavoidable passage for the traveler, almost an irritation as they lead to the city and the sea down below. Their monumentality is passed on to the body and consciousness. The city walker experiences the transition from the rhythm of the steps to another rhythm, clear, yet unknown, still to be discovered.

As in the case of most historic cities, the big cities of the Mediterranean are doomed by virtue of the proliferation of suburbs. And yet historic character seems able to survive better in the Mediterranean than elsewhere—this is Lefebvre and Régulier's cautiously worded thesis. A dogged power of resistance seems to emanate from the everyday lived rhythms and the organization of time. In the Mediterranean region, every form of hegemony or homogeneity is rejected; in the long run, diversity always retaliates. A well-founded, productively applied rhythmanalysis could provide explanations for this.

RHYTHM AS *PRINCIPE ANIMATEUR*

We can distinguish two stages in Henri Lefebvre's late works. A first stage focuses on space, *social space*. A second on time, *social time*. The Production of Space deals with the slow-moving yet deep-going changes of space. In a second stage the focus of research is the multifariousness of time. Lefebvre distinguishes biological or physiological time, psychologically experienced duration, historic and cosmic time—and social time. *Natural time* has a rhythmic character. Rhythm brings about order in time. Sometimes it is perceived only in the form of the fleeting and the variable. Lefebvre's provisional yet magisterial lessons concerning rhythmanalysis revolve around the central point of the relationships between daily life and its rhythms, around the concrete modalities of social time. How often has a philosopher or a meta-philosopher worked out the banal yet misunderstood or mistaken the difference between the cyclical and the linear—between the animating rhythmized time and the repetitive, unchanging time. The *repetitive* produces monotony, satiety, and fatigue. The recurrence of the *cyclical* produces the feeling of a new beginning. A closer examination shows that the new beginning is only a recommencement having the freshness of a discovery or an invention.

"Dawn always has a miraculous charm, hunger and thirst renew themselves marvelously."[27]

Lefebvre's rhythmanalysis appeared at the end of the twentieth century. Let us look at the beginning of the century when a musician (Émile Jacques-Dalcroze) and a painter (Ferdinand Hodler) were looking for rhythmic forms of expression. Jacques-Dalcroze made the children in the cities and villages of the Swiss Romandie sing his new *chansons* and present short dance performances. Then, with the inauguration of the Institute of Rhythmic Gymnastics in Geneva, he initiated a far-reaching reform movement. For Hodler, nature was something integral and harmonious. "Wind, for instance, furnishes an example, which blows across water or over a cornfield. It causes the same wave undulations rhythmically, and the sum of these special individual movements combine into one mighty, stirring over-arching total rhythm."[28] On the occasion of the tenth anniversary of Hodler's death, Jacques-Dalcroze paid tribute to his painter friend's genius and generosity. According to Jacques-Dalcroze, his works bear witness to an unremitting search for the rhythm of life and nature. No one understood better how to combine movements and get them to separate again, to emphasize accents and counterpoints, to treat human feelings symphonically and to orchestrate them with gesture and posture.

Unlike Hodler and Jacques-Dalcroze, who looked for an aesthetic treatment of bodily expression or of nature-sensitivity, Lefebvre directs his attention, at the end of the twentieth century, on to *conflict* zones. The question occupying his mind is how work processes and technology are increasingly breaking away from cyclical nature, and how this has, so far at least, only partly succeeded. Everyday life continues to be tied to the cycles of days, months, and years, to life-cycles, to youth and old age. That the everyday lags behind technology is nothing disadvantageous or deficient. On the contrary. Everyday life becomes a stage upon which the conflict between the indestructible nature-rhythms and the socio-economic processes are played out in dramatic fashion. The Lefebvrist rhythmanalyst armed with a keen ear and a clear mind knows the cyclical and the linear. As a therapist what matters most to him is not healing but prevention. He knows that the destruction of nature-rhythms by the linear has adverse consequences. He knows that the increase of innovative rhythms in music and dance is a reaction to the generally intensified need for rhythm. Rhythm compensates for the inadequacy, deficiency, and wretchedness of daily life.

NOTES

1. Henri Lefebvre and Catherine Régulier, "The Rhythmanalytical Project," [1985] in Lefebvre, *Rhythmanalysis: Space, Time and Everyday Life*, trans. S. Elden and G. Moore (New York: Continuum, 2004).

2. Henri Lefebvre, *Critique of Everyday Life, Volume III: From Modernity to Modernism*, trans. G. Elliott, preface by M. Trebitsch (London: Verso, 2006 [1981]).

3. Gaston Bachelard, *The Dialectic of Duration*, trans. M. McAllester Jones (Manchester: Clinamen Press, 2000), 136–55.

4. *Ibid.*

5. *Ibid.*

6. Henri Lefebvre, *Critique of Everyday Life, Volume II*, trans. J. Moore (London: Verso, 2002 [1961].

7. *Ibid.*, 48.

8. *Ibid.*

9. Henri Lefebvre, "Elements of Rhythmanalysis: An Introduction to the Understanding of Rhythms," [1992] in *Rhythmanalysis*, 9.

10. *Ibid.*

11. *Ibid.*

12. Lefebvre and Régulier, "The Rhythmanalytical Project," 79.

13. Italo Calvino, *Mr. Palomar*, trans.W. Weaver (Toronto: Lester & Orpen Dennys, 1985), 4.

14. Lefebvre, "Elements of Rhythmanalysis," 27.

15. *Ibid.*

16. *Ibid.*, 28.

17. *Ibid.*, 29.

18. *Ibid.*, 30–1.

19. *Ibid.*, 29.

20. *Ibid.*, 34–5.

21. *Ibid.*, 35.

22. *Ibid.*

23. *Ibid.*, 36.

24. Guy de Maupassant quoted in Jean Plumyène, *Trajets parisiens* (Paris: Julliard, 1984), 160–1.

25. Henri Lefebve, "The Right to the City," in *Writings on Cities*, ed., trans. and introduction by E. Kofman and E. Lebas (Cambridge, MA: Blackwell, 1996 [1968]), 109.

26. Henri Lefebve and Catherine Régulier, "Attempts as Rhythmanalysis of Mediterranean Cities," [1986] in Lefebvre, *Rhythmanalysis*, 91.

27. Lefebvre and Régulier, "The Rhythmanalytical Project," 73.

28. Ferdinand Hodler quoted in Carl A. Loosli, *Aus der Werkstatt Ferdinand Hodlers* (Basel: Birkhäuser, 1938), 200.

10

LESSONS IN SURREALISM
Relationality, event, encouter
Sara Nadal-Melsió

A number of Henri Lefebvre's most celebrated conceptualizations can be read as a direct response to the revalorization and revaluation of the aesthetic undertaken by both the philosophical and avant-garde movements of the 1920s and 1930s. I will here connect Lefebvre's rapport with Surrealism to a reconfigured understanding of the aesthetic, whereby the aesthetic becomes an appropriating mechanism rather than autonomous realm of experience. With Surrealism, I will claim, relationality emerges as an expressive event that forces the advent of an encounter between fields of experience that had remained differentiated by the logic of reification and specialization.[1] I will then read Lefebvre's theoretical intervention in May 1968, The Explosion, as his mature formulation of the mechanisms that set relationality, the event, and the encounter to work. The enforced contingency and spontaneity of the events of May will function as correction to both aesthetic and philosophical transcendence.

From very early on in his work, the collaboration, or rather the mutual inclusion, of the aesthetic and the philosophical is key to an understanding of the Lefebvrean project. Lefebvre's critical reading of Surrealism exemplifies the way in which he dealt with his sources and influences: while unveiling the movement's limitations, it also puts to work its potential, its intuitions regarding urban space, the everyday, and the centrality of the work of art. Thus Lefebvre "refunctionalizes" (to use a Russian formalist phrasing) the concept of the everyday by simultaneously blending three of his sources—Marxism, Surrealism, and Heidegger—and pushing them further. Most of all, however, Lefebvre represents a directional shift and a transcritical stance: the question was no longer how to escape everyday life's dullness but how to explore its potential

Lefebvre's critique of Surrealism should be equated with a synthesis of the movement's irreconcilable contradictions. He goes beyond Surrealism; nevertheless, Surrealism remains a starting point. It is therefore useful to stop and analyze the limitations, contradictions, and insights of the movement, with André Breton as its mouthpiece. For better or worse, Lefebvre's understanding of Surrealism, like Benjamin's, was fully mediated by Breton's programmatic texts.

Before entering into an analysis of the Surrealist program, the complicated relationship of Surrealism with Marxism also needs to be briefly recounted. Diehard Surrealists were attracted to Marxism; indeed, Breton had his group join the Communist Party for a while. But the coupling of Surrealism and Marxism did not last. The *affaire* was made possible by the environment of constant intellectual flirtation and experimentation of late twenties Paris, and especially by the desire of the avant-garde to appropriate any discourse of *modernity*. However, not all discourses lend themselves to appropriation in the same way. Marxism's demands on Surrealism threatened the core of the movement: by privileging the collective over the psychological, time over space, and by working toward the eventual destruction of the mechanism that made alienation possible. Despite radical claims, Surrealism betrayed both a fascination *with* and a *dependence on* alienation. The movement fed on the leftovers of capitalism and of the bourgeoisie it set out to attack. Paradoxically, to put it briefly, capitalism could do without Surrealism but the reverse was not true. Breton's programmatic Surrealism, however, was never quite ready to take the leap— to let go of the aesthetic as a privileged category.

Breton's anti-novel *Nadja*, which should be read as Surrealism's political and aesthetic mouthpiece, explores the possibilities of a Surrealist urban historiography. In it, the city emerges as a spatial reality, a collection of forgotten historical sites. In Breton, history is radically spatialized. However, this Surrealist insight also contains an irreducible ahistoricism: Nadja's sites can be pointed at but not experienced— or at least her pathological experience of them cannot be shared. They function as two-dimensional icons that merely quote the past, like the photographs Breton "collaged" into the novel in order to make the descriptions of sites irrelevant. Surrealist photographer Jacques-André Boiffard's images of a deserted Paris, his documentation of revolutionary sites, have the indexical function of postcards. Fetishism overrules history, as the aesthetic overrules experience. Nadja herself is a mere pointer, not a mediator. She lacks agency, because she is mad. Her realm of experience remains alien and inscrutable, her encounter with Breton never really takes place. Differentiation as reification holds its own in the text. The same madness that turns Nadja into an appealing Surrealist object precludes any encounter, whether between past and present, or between her and Breton. The potential of non-synchronicity her remembrances open up remains unused; the event of a fully experienced and relational everyday is absent from Breton's systematic exercise in spatial fetishism.

Once Breton's exercise in Surrealist historiography is over, we are left with a bric-a-brac collection of aestheticized fragments. Paris becomes a city for antiquarians, not historians—to use a Nietzschean typology. The *then* and the *now* fail to be connected, to participate in the incomplete totality that makes historical change, or simply history, possible. Contingency, which proves to be absolutely essential to the Lefebvrean understanding of the event, has no room to upset the Surrealist program. Surrealism does not stand up to the "illuminations" it inspired in Benjamin, and in Lefebvre. The Surrealist city is a dismembered city that can be understood only in paratactic terms, in patterns of substitutions, of repetitions. Surrealism's unveiling of the transformative potential of urban space is left unused. There is neither "inhabiting" nor "dwelling" in the Bretonian city, to use the spatial and phenomenological processes Heidegger was formulating at the time and that Lefebvre would quickly appropriate in a characteristically critical manner.

The Surrealist radical spatialization of the city in the end becomes yet another instance of specialization and abstraction. Similarly, the isolation and preeminence of the aesthetic preclude any access to the alienated reality it sets out to decommodify. The task of overcoming these antinomies, space/time and aesthetics/philosophy, is at the core of Lefebvre's critical production. His concepts of the *everyday*, of the city as a *work of art*, and of the *event* are his critical response to the limitations of his Surrealist sources. Lefebvre's answers are always predicated on a logic of appropriation and refunctionalization. He redirects and blends Georg Lukács and Surrealism in ways reminiscent of Guy Debord and Gil J. Wolman's Situationist practice: "the mutual interference of two worlds of feeling, or the bringing together of two independent expressions, supersedes the original elements and produces a synthetic organization of greater efficacy. *Anything can be used.*"[2] Surrealist insights regarding the potential of the residual, the power of simultaneity—which finds in collage its perfect expression—and even the creativity of desire had a long-lasting effect on Lefebvre. His *everyday* participates in all of these:

> Everyday life, in a sense residual, defined by "what is left over" after all distinct, superior, specialized, structured activities have been singled out by analysis, must be defined as a totality . . . Everyday life is profoundly related to *all* activities, and encompasses them with all their differences and their conflicts; it is their meeting place, their bond, their common ground.[3]

In Lefebvre's synthesis, the everyday will reconstitute itself as a spatio-temporal expression of historicity that takes the form of a relational experience, often without a historiography. Thus, it will recover the lost potential of the Lukácsean totality with a fundamental difference: the everyday is an *incomplete* expression of totality; herein is contained its strength. Expression, as we will see in Lefebvre's intervention in May 1968, is a relational question, a linking mechanism that allows for the temporary emergence of a totality that could not have been deduced from the mere sum of the elements that participate in the encounter that produces it. As Louis Althusser would write, "not all existence is reproduction and the logic of the encounter produces rather than reproduces."[4] *Contingency*—although *spontaneity* is Lefebvre's preferred term—and not *necessity* is the condition of possibility for the encounter, whereby limitations become possibilities.

The Lefebvrean totality contained in the urban everyday is not a given but an encounter between the contingent and the possible. Such an encounter effectively transforms the contingent *into* the possible; a production of a positive content that counteracts the negativity of mere reproduction that is inevitable in a fetishistic market and a cultural economy; an encounter that does not contain necessity because it remains open—it can take place or not take place.

In Lefebvre, "there is no doubt that the knowledge of urban reality can relate to the possible (or possibilities) and not only to what is finished or from the past."[5]

The totality contained in the everyday can thus not be fully accounted for because it contains an as yet unfulfilled potential for change. The future is finally added to the picture, and the picture is all the blurrier because of the addition. The price to be paid is a lack of closure and cohesion that is part flexibility, part vulnerability. The openness of the everyday, as both an expression of permeability and endurance, is a constant in Lefebvre's writings and is often equated to the residual resilience of materiality itself.

The Lefebvrean everyday will recover history as an *incorporated* totality. Lefebvrean history becomes "explosive," eventful; it accelerates and breaks the continuum of time in order to keep pace with experience—it has no Bergsonian *durée*. Explosions are expressions of the spontaneity contained in the appropriation of contingency for history. Spontaneity, a Surrealist principle, defies history as a continuum while at the same time bringing the spontaneous to the level of history. Thus, history comes back in Lefebvre in the form of a "minor history," as the sum of the events that could or could not emerge from the everyday. In this regard, once again, Benjamin and Lefebvre have much in common; their understandings of temporality are virtually identical.[6] They also share an early desire to be overcome by the future, a messianic belief in some form of historical redemption. However, whereas Benjamin remained invested in the redemptive, Lefebvre abandoned the mystical overtones of the "Philosophies" group in favor of the social and the sociological, turning Benjamin's "angel of history" into a socio-historical index, into a possibility.

Because of his attunement with the social, Lefebvre was the only philosopher who was ready for the events of May 1968, prepared to apprehend its "explosion" as an intervention into the social concreteness of everyday life. A self-conscious understanding of everyday life contains the value and potential of an ideological critique of everyday life:

> The day dawns when everyday life also emerges as a critique, a critique of the superior activities in question (and of what they produce: *ideologies*). The devaluation of everyday life by ideologies appears as one-sided and partial, in both senses of the word. A direct critique takes the place of indirect criticism; and this direct critique involves a rehabilitation of everyday life, shedding new light on its positive content.[7]

Disalienation is established as the positive content of a self-conscious everyday life and finds its expression in concrete experience. This means moving beyond the typological and generic understanding of the human: "the critique of everyday life studies human nature in its concreteness."[8]

This commitment to the material, to the human body, rather than the species being, calls for a reappraisal of the spatial. The human body, and its sociological expression in the everyday, takes place in space as well as in time. Relocating bodily experience at the center of the everyday literally means finding a space for it. Lefebvre appropriates here another Surrealist discovery—the city as a relational category—and recovers its mediatory potential. The Lefebvrean city functions like the aesthetic expression of the body in space—a work of art—that produces knowledge as well as history. The city exploits a mediatory and productive potential it had lost after Plato—where the city had originally emerged as the spatio-temporal condition of possibility for political philosophy. Thus, Lefebvre: "The very concept of space has demonstrated its supremely *mediatory* function, in the way in which *its aesthetic formulation* begins at once to entail *cognitive consequences* on the one hand and *sociopolitical consequences* on the other."[9] The city, the "aesthetic formulation" of space, becomes in Lefebvre the ideal intersection of form and content. Temporality is inscribed in space, just as content is inscribed in form. Take, for instance, how the transition from the rural to the urban, the spatial expression of uneven temporalities, which is also the title of one of Lefebvre's sociological studies, is inscribed in the city. The potential contained in Aragon's *Paris Peasant* is eventually set to work. The right to the city will be predicated on hypotactic interrelations that set social and temporal unevenness in motion, rather than merely signal it. Relationality is at the core of urban knowledge as a non-reified experience. The syntactic analogy is useful here: the subordinated clause, rather than behaving like an enclosure within the main sentence, shifts the meaning of the main clause from within it. Paradoxically, it is the synchronicity of the city, its characteristic simultaneity that renders its fundamental temporal unevenness visible through the emergence of relational situations. This is the condition of possibility for Nanterre (see below), both as space and as event.

The emergence of this urban praxis requires not only the simultaneity of space/time but also of philosophy and the aesthetic. The key is not merely discovering reality but finding a means to express and gain access to it, to enter a relational paradigm that will force a shift and create an encounter. This requirement is fulfilled by Lefebvre's unique dialectical blending of the temporal/philosophical in Lukács and Heidegger and the spatial/aesthetic in Surrealism: his concept of the city as an *oeuvre*, a work of art. Both the Lukácsean and Heideggerian movement from the aesthetic into the philosophical and the Surrealist movement from the quotidian/trivial into the aesthetic are reversed in the Lefebvrean "work of art." The concept is used to qualify the city at its moment of greatest relational potential. The city is an *oeuvre* because it brings philosophy closer to concrete social reality through the Surrealist logic of aesthetic appropriation. As we have seen, appropriation is the relational category Lefebvre imported from the aesthetic into the philosophical. It is the spatio-temporal medium through which philosophy relates to the world in its historical and social specificity. The city appropriates the world, contains it in its heteroglossic form, and thus has the potential to change it:

> the philosopher must speak, *say the meaning* of industrial production, as long as he does not speculate on it and use it as a theme to prolong the old manner of philosophizing. Instead he must take it as *means of realizing philosophy*, that is, *the philosophical project* of man in the world: desire and reason, spontaneity and reflection, vitality and containment, domination and appropriation, determinism and liberties. *Philosophy cannot realize itself without art (as model of appropriation of time and space)*, accomplishing itself fully in social practice and without science and technology, as means, not being fully used, without the proletarian condition being overcome.[10]

This decommodification, the overcoming of the proletarian condition, can be effected only through the aesthetic as event. In the moment of its apprehension, the work of art collapses use value and exchange value, recovers use as part of exchange, and retotalizes value—echoes of the Nietzschean "revaluation of all values" can be heard here. The work of art is both work and a product of work. This correction to the logic of production, the logic of capital, recovers the original subversive strain of Duchamp's Surrealist found objects. The found object's blending of the aesthetic and the philosophical, which decommodifies both spheres, together with its interpellation of the social and historical as producers of meaning, provides a good, although partial, example of the Lefebvrean "work of art." The expressive singularity of these objects depends on their lack of differentiation as aesthetic objects. The example of Duchamp is not coincidental. His adoption by the "*nouveau réalisme*" of Pierre Restany and his group and by practitioners of Situationism provides a continuity between Surrealism and realism which has so far not been explored.

As Restany describes the appropriating gesture of Duchamp's "ready-mades," "the object transcends its insignificant, banal everydayness and is liberated: it attains its full expressive singularity."[11] The recovered agency of Duchamp's found objects—they look back at us—is turned into philosophical questioning. What am I? Art? Commodity? Both? The answer undoes the essence of the question: the found object is the relational encounter between these two spheres of experience and the emergence of an event that upsets their previous differentiation.

In a similar vein, the events of May 1968, as apprehended by Lefebvre in his *Explosion*, call for a renegotiation of the urban as a space for the shared practice of citizenship as a relational encounter between student and worker. In the midst of the event, citizens behave as if the void of inequality, to use Jacques Rancière's wording of differentiation,[12] that separates worker from student had already been filled. Equality, a concept that attains its meaning only in the shared space of the public, or what is properly political and social, is not a promise or belief but a reality whose main consequence, in a seemingly retroactive fashion, is the event itself. Equality as a social fact forces a relational shift in the social structure of the city. Equality is by nature polemical; this is at least one possible way to read the violence of the event.

The city as an artwork is both the subject and object of philosophy because it requires experience for its realization, its apprehension as an art of sharing where nothing is missing. The lack of the promise, and the neurotic desire that goes with it, has been transformed into a positive content that fills the void. To put it in very simple and erotic terms, we move from the lack of desire to the transcendent contingency of love. Simultaneously contingent and transcendent, the creative revaluation of what was already there takes the form of political subjectivity.

The encounter brings politics back into the city by breaking the circuit of endless reproduction, of ideology masquerading as politics. It becomes a short circuit in a web of social relations. The city itself becomes the privileged subject/object, rather than mere location, of philosophy: the perception of the city as form, as an expression of "situated knowledge" (the phrase is Bahktin's), constitutes an aesthetic praxis.[13] Since whatever is perceived is perceived in time and space, the work of art becomes the exemplary expression of perception itself, of mediation itself. Lefebvre recovers the utopian potential of aesthetic mediation as a privileged expression and appropriation of the spatio-temporal.

What Bakhtin called the "answerability" of art, in his 1919 essay "Art and Answerability," provides us with an early articulation of the dialectic between art and lived experience that is helpful for the understanding of the cognitive implications of Lefebvre's reclaiming of the city as an artwork:[14]

> I have to answer with my own life for what I have experienced and understood in art, so that everything I have experienced and understood would not remain

ineffectual in my life. But answerability entails guilt, or liability to blame. It is not only mutual answerability that art and life must assume, but also mutual liability to blame [sic]. The poet must remember that it is his poetry which bears the guilt for the vulgar prose of life, whereas the man of everyday life ought to know that the fruitlessness of art is due to his willingness to be unexacting and to the seriousness of the concerns in his life.[15]

Bakhtin here links the decommodifying potential of art to its liability, to the unavoidable responsibility of experience in a non-reified world. One is always accountable for experience. There are no *alibis* in experience, because the events it contains are fully accounted for in the contingencies of space and time. And space and time, in Lefebvre's cognitive remapping, are no longer a priori epistemological categories that make human experience and understanding possible (as a standard reading of Kant would have it) but experiences in themselves. Experiencing the spatio-temporal in everyday life means both re-owning the everyday and being fully accountable for it.

Lefebvre's understanding of the event is an attempt to overcome both philosophy and history and put them in the service of life in its less glamorous embodiment, the everyday life of urban dwellers. His take on the event is never purely epistemological and, I will claim, cannot be separated from the urban praxis of May 1968. Knowledge and experience inform one another in ways only announced by another intervention into urban everyday life: the Paris Commune and its perfect relational synchronicity with the linguistic experimentations and sociological deconstructions of Arthur Rimbaud and Paul Lafargue, respectively.[16] Thus, May 1968 will emerge as the realization, and not just an example, of the Lefebvrean event.

In *Explosion*, Lefebvre embarks on a theoretical intervention that is neither a forecast nor a record of May 1968. He avoids the difficulties of attempting a necessarily reductive representation of the events of the month by being contemporaneous, in the full meaning of the word, with them. His unique strategic answer is contained in the very form of *Explosion*.[17] Lefebvre's text is not a theoretical account of 1968 but a part of its events:

> A theory of the movement has to emerge from the movement itself, for it is the movement that has revealed, unleashed, and liberated theoretical capacities. No contribution to the elaboration of such a theory can lay claim to being an established doctrine; it can never be more than a limited contribution.[18]

Lefebvre's contribution may indeed be partial, as he is well aware, yet it is not self-contained. *Explosion* belongs to the political praxis of May 1968. Lefebvre's voice is embedded in the relational web of the events themselves. The relational web of the events of May 1968 encourages the merging of dissociations/differentiations: theory and praxis, real and ideal, private and public, and so on. Because the dissociation exists, both the event and the theory it unleashes have space to maneuver, to *remplir le vide*. The bringing together of the event is a direct response to unevenness, the emergence of the desire to connect what has been separated:

> Drawn in by the void, spontaneity begins to fill it. It submerges dissociations, overcomes separations. During those days the dichotomies between activity and passivity, between private life and social life, between leisure and work and the places associated with them, between spoken and written language, between action and knowledge—all these dichotomies disappeared in the streets, amphitheaters and factories.[19]

The spontaneity of this desire to connect is unequivocally political and has much in common with the lesser-known Bakhtinian theorizations of the "act" in his unfinished *Toward a Philosophy of the Act*. In Bakhtin's words the act "brings together the sense and the fact, the universal and the individual, the real and the ideal."[20] As we have seen, the revalorization of the everyday, enacted through the aesthetic, as the natural milieu of both the "event" and the "act," as a site for the enactment of being as event, is the prerequisite for both the "act" and the "event" to explode. Experience takes center stage.

Experience entails responsibility because it overcomes the dualism of subject/object and also forces the self to acknowledge the other, by seeing the object as subject and vice versa. The essence of sociability, of a "life in common" as Tzvetan Todorov has put it, is an acknowledging of the other, which is also a way to acknowledge the self, creating a realized moment of reciprocity, an encounter.[21] With the advent of an encounter (which constitutes the core of May 1968 as an event), the individual willingly enters a relational network by assuming its transindividuality as alien, as the product of a subjective interaction with another that has become (unknowingly) reified into a social relation.

Creativity, the expression of change triggered by (and synchronous with) the encounter, emerges from manifested difference. Thus Lefebvre: "with the manifestation of differentiations . . . , there arises a social need for creation or 'creativity.'"[22] And creativity, according to Lefebvre, is always political—in fact, it is the form of political self-consciousness. Manifested difference is at the center of the "creativity" of May 1968, and creativity here incorporates critique. Thus, the student understands her alienation because the space of Nanterre *represents* the alienation of the other, the worker, rendering her own objecthood visible by reflecting it. The periphery brings the alienated nature of the center, Paris, to the foreground by invading and transforming it. The decolonization of Algeria unveils the colonization of France itself. The Algerian reality, as *other*, unveils the French. The relational encounter between two reified political subjectivities brings their reality to light. Urban and political realism emerges as a result of an encounter, as the political creation of something that did not exist before. For once (political) production overrules (ideological) reproduction.

The individual, Lefebvre reminds us, only becomes an agent within a network, the social self as a relation with the other. The potential of such an encounter has been temporarily illuminated by the events of May, but its epistemological and experiential possibilities have by no means been exhausted. The question remains, however, what does the "explosion of urban reality" during May 1968 tell us about the nature of the city? Why does urban knowledge, as political knowledge, emerge as an unparalleled experience of life?

Experience and revaluation go hand in hand in Lefebvre: once values change (Marx) or a revaluation of values (Nietzsche) has taken place, immediacy takes hold of the subject. Things, places, and people are seen for what they are and can be experienced only through the social form of an urban relation. Revaluation can be effected only through a change in relational position, and relationality is nothing but "thereness" (Heidegger). Thus, the city does not merely express the possible, it makes it factually possible; imaginable, because it reveals what is already there ready to be reclaimed. Nothing is missing once urban revaluation takes place. In a moment of heightened relationality and synchronicity urban dwellers were agents both as producers and consumers of the city; they fully appropriated the relationality of their social position within the urban network of production.

Relationality contains a double bind or, more appropriately, what Kojin Karatani has described as a transcritical stance: while it remains contingent it also manages to transcend that contingency through the transindividuality that the encounter brings to the fore.[23] Relationality is both concrete and abstract, contingent and transcendent, historical and philosophical.

Lefebvre's understanding of the role of philosophy and history in the city throws some light on these questions. The double bind of historical and philosophical knowledge can find expression only in the city, where they were both arguably born. Lefebvre's discussion of the discourse of knowledge in Explosion is reiterated in his last writings on the philosophical nature of the city. "Philosophy is thus born from the city, with its division of labor and multiple modalities," as Lefebvre puts it in his late Right to the City.[24] Philosophy, like specialized knowledge in Explosion, has a twofold status: it is both social and theoretical, ideological and political. The relationship between the city and philosophy is complicated; philosophy emerges from an understanding of urban totality and wholeness that it cannot realize because it has simultaneously entered the formal logic of the fragment, of division of labor and specialization. Philosophy retains the content of totality but it cannot express it through form because the connection between the different fragments, form and content among them, has been lost. In philosophy relationality is expressed as a lack. The city produces specialization, that is philosophy, yet it also produces its counterpart, the epistemology contained in urban totality. Somehow the fragment has managed to retain the whole without being able to express it, and thus realize it: "the concept of *totality* is in danger of remaining empty if it is only philosophical."[25] The movement away from specialization is also the movement toward a new understanding of the aesthetic, toward the city as a relational work of art.

Only the expression of the city as a work of art, in its blending of *praxis*, *poiesis*, and *techne*, can recover totality as its content-form. The realization of a non-philosophical totality in Lefebvre is always predicated on the overcoming of specialization, of the science of the fragment. The centrality of the aesthetic emerges from its mediatory and expressive potential. The logic of anti-specialization, the craving for the whole, is the key to Lefebvre's use and understanding of the disciplines he appropriates in his work—philosophy, urbanism, history, sociology, and so on. The case of history is paradigmatic of Lefebvre's appropriating logic and of his critique of knowledge as an enclosed domain.

Both philosophy and history are invested in knowledge and the pursuit of knowledge. Knowledge is a form of specialization "that fulfills neither promises nor needs."[26] The events of May 1968 are a conscious attack on this prevalent form of intellectual specialization. The emphasis on action rather than knowledge is crucial for an understanding of the emancipatory potential of everyday life.

This non-systematic, and non-reductive, understanding of the everyday as the making of history emerges from the unevenness that both produces and masks difference, by condemning each of the uneven parts to isolation and confinement. Nanterre as an event is unleashed by the unevenness expressed in Nanterre as a space. The form of the city successfully represents its reality as a relational product, so that "formerly abstract and incomplete, the dissociations now become complete. Projected onto the terrain, it is here that they can transcend themselves—in the streets."[27] The expressivity of the spatial is at the core of the events of May; it is their condition of possibility. "It was in the streets that spontaneity expressed itself"[28] and "without spontaneity there would be neither event nor movement."[29] Spontaneity takes place and creates events because it has found a form of expression: the city. "It is here [in the streets] that student meets worker, and reason reduced to a function again recovers speech . . . Urban phenomena accompany the withering of the superstructure of industrial growth (including 'urbanism')."[30] In short: a critique of the superstructure, which here takes the form of contestation, can be effected only through the identification of its ideological representations. Production can begin only once reproduction has been short-circuited.

Lefebvre's description of Nanterre as a spatio-temporal reality amounts to a narration of the causality behind May 1968—in Nanterre and *because* of Nanterre. By overturning the ordinary relation between space and time, time is expressed in the shape of space:

This [Nanterre] is a Parisian faculty located outside of Paris. It is not far from the area of *La Défense* (commercial building, truck depots). It may become an urban center by 1980. Right now it contains misery, shantytowns, excavations for an express subway line, low-income housing projects for workers, industrial enterprises. This is a desolate and strange landscape. The Faculty was conceived in terms of the concepts of the industrial production and productivity of neo-capitalist society, but falls short of the implications of such a conception. The buildings and the environment reflect the real nature of the intended project. It is an enterprise designed to produce mediocre intellectuals and "junior executives" for the management of this society, and transmit a body of specialized knowledge determined and limited by the social division of labor. It had from the beginning a well-defined function—topically and typically—which was to reveal itself slowly in its day-to-day activities, but very rapidly once the movement began. Situated in the midst of a civilization which, from the City of antiquity to the historic city of the European West, is based on the City, it may be described as a place of damnation.

The suburbs and their shantytowns are more than a sad spectacle—they constitute a void. *Anomie* and "social marginality" are an integral part of the image projected by this society. Absence is "where unhappiness becomes concrete." This specimen of wall-writing says exactly what it means. In these surroundings work loses all meaning. In the Faculty—a product of industrialization a de-urbanization—the absence of civilization is transformed into obsession. Education can hardly be expected to fill this void, especially in view of the fact that the content and form of knowledge lag behind in the intended project. The City—past and present—assumes a *utopian* value for the boys and girls caught up in a *heterotopia* which generates tensions and obsessive fantasies.[31]

Unevenness and its representation in space as a spatio-temporal and not merely spatial reality are the core of the events of May. Yet, if the events are prompted by an experience of the spatial, they are also directed to the spatial as goal. Recovering the city as the spatial representation of utopian goals meant moving the events of May from Nanterre to the Latin Quarter, and to Paris as a reclaimed city.

The utopia of the city as an event-full space is contained in its form, which is dialogical, caught midway between the imaginary and the real, what it is and what it can be. Its totality is predicated on a new understanding of history and philosophy as tools rather than ends. Urban knowledge cannot be reduced to historical or philosophical categories because it is contained in action and, thus, cannot be reabsorbed into ready-made categories. Indeed, urban knowledge is a concrete expression of political knowledge. In the last lines of *Explosion*, after a thorough exploration of the potential of urban praxis in May 1968, Lefebvre returns to political knowledge as a form of action: "As for the thesis that political knowledge can bring about the unification of compartmentalized knowledge, it will likely continue to be attacked with the same arguments that have been used since philosophy and the pursuit of knowledge began."[32] Political knowledge, in its specificity, returns both philosophy and history to the "here" and "now." And the here and now of May 1968 is the city of Paris as a spatio-temporal reality, whereby political knowledge becomes urban knowledge. Because urban knowledge is urban praxis rooted in concrete experience, it entails action. Action involves a participation in history that is anti-historicist in its refusal to see history as a distinct mode of understanding.

As with Surrealism, changing life, in particular everyday life or the life that we have in common, was the ultimate goal of 1968 as an event. The blending, or rather appropriation, of history and philosophy in the service of life meant the end of the compartmentalized knowledge that rules everyday existence. However, in order for these to take place, a common knowledge and praxis had to fill the void left by specialized knowledge. Urban knowledge came to fill that void. The urban became a common and shared language capable of expressing both goals and realities.

Therefore, the success of May 1968 as an event—which can be understood only as a phenomenon and not an achievement—depended on its realized expressive and relational potential. The urban "event" returned expression to everyday life because it managed fully to represent it: "under the impact of events people and ideas are revealed for what they are."[33] In a privileged moment of synchronicity representation matched reality. The need for representation was fulfilled by the city as a total work of art that included knowledge, praxis, and creation.

We are back to Lefebvre and Bakhtin and their understanding of the mediatory potential of the work of art. Indeed, the Lefebvrean event has a lot more in common with the work of art as a relational event than with history or philosophy. Yet this work of art is not the same one that Breton's Surrealism had championed. Rather, it represents both a return to the aesthetic and an overcoming of the aesthetic as specialization. A creative understanding of the work of art includes a critique of the limitations of the purely aesthetic. Lefebvre's lessons in Surrealism made him well aware of this:

> "To change life—" this defines the meaning of the revolutionary process. But life is not changed magically by a poetic act, as the surrealist believed. Language liberated from its servitudes plays a necessary role—but it does not suffice. The transformation of everyday existence also involves institutions. In fact, it is not sufficient to speak, even less to write. The social practice capable of transcending dissociations and creating new institutions beyond those that affirm dissociations—this social practice has a name, but cannot be reduced to language.[34]

The transformation of everyday life into a relational work of art was successful in May 1968, as it had been during the Paris Commune. Yet, these aesthetic—and therefore, political, historical, and philosophical—interventions could only function synchronically. The city, the mode of expression of these aesthetic interventions, can only contain and represent the memory and history of urban dwellers. Like any work of art, the city exists only in the "here and now" of its inhabitants. However, memory does not travel in space but in time.

In their non-synchronic historicity, in their need for transmission beyond their temporal span, the events of Nanterre pose a challenge to representation. Reconfiguration and representation are as necessary as they are insufficient in their available forms. The void the event opens in the structures of representation was only filled temporally by the city. After the event, the void seems only larger. The challenge is clear: following the spatial model of the city as a relational work of art, what other forms will be capable of reconciling presence and representation, empirical reality and utopian desires?

NOTES

1. Nicholas Bourriaud coined the term "relational aesthetics" in 1998 in an attempt to find a common label that would describe the idiosyncratic artistic practices of the 1990s (of artists such as Rirkrit Tirananija and Gabriel Orozco). See *Relational Aesthetics* (Dijon: Les Presses du réel, 1998). It can easily be argued, though, and Bourriaud seems somewhat aware of it, that relationality goes well beyond this narrow aesthetic category and that it remains fundamentally a Marxian understanding of the human as social. To my mind, Kojin Karatani's use of the same concept in *Transcritique: On Kant and Marx* (Cambridge, MA: The MIT Press, 2003) is much more productive and accurate about its critical emergence.

2. Guy Debord and Gil J. Wolman, "Methods of Detournement," in *Les lèvres nues* 8 (1956). Quoted in the *Situationist Anthology*, ed. and trans. K. Knabb (Berkeley: Bureau of Public Secrets, 1981), 9.

3. Henri Lefebvre, *Critique of Everyday Life, Volume I: Introduction*, trans. J. Moore, preface M. Trebitsch (London: Verso 1991 [1947 and 1958]), 97.

4. Althusser's fascinating "materialism of the encounter" should be read as the beginning of post-Althusserianism and as one of the most touching lessons learned from May 1968. See Louis Althusser, *Philosophy of the Encounter: Later Writings, 1978–1987*, ed. F. Matheron and O. Corpet, trans. G. M. Goshgarian (London: Verso, 2006), 198.

5. Henri Lefebvre, "Right to the City," in *Writings on Cities*, ed. and trans. E. Kofman and E. Lebas (London: Blackwell, 1996), 94.

6. On Benjamin's dialectical understanding of time, see Susan Buck-Morss, *The Dialectics of Seeing: Walter Benjamin and the Arcades Project* (Cambridge, MA: The MIT Press, 1989).

7. Lefebvre, *Critique*, I, 87.

8. *Ibid.*, 97.

9. Henri Lefebvre, *The Production of Space*, trans. D. Nicholson-Smith (London: Blackwell, 1991), 120, emphasis added.

10. Lefebvre, *Writings on Cities*, 176, last emphasis added.

11. Pierre Restany, *Le nouveau réalisme* (Paris: Union Générale d'Éditions, 1978), quoted in Michèle C. Cone, "Pierre Restany and the *Nouveaux Réalistes*," *Yale French Studies* 98 (2000), 63.

12. Jacques Rancière, *On the Shores of Politics*, trans. L. Heron (London: Verso, 1998).

13. This incorporation of praxis distances Lefebvre's city from previous understandings of the city as a metaphor for modern subjectivity and its *malaise*—as is the case in Simmel, Benjamin, and Kracauer. Lefebvre is both more ahistorical, because his city does not belong to modernity, and more historical, because his city is rooted in the sociological. For an analysis of the understanding of the urban as modern in these thinkers, see David Frisby, *Fragments of Modernity: Theories of Modernity in the Work of Simmel, Kracauer, and Benjamin* (Cambridge, MA: The MIT Press, 1988).

14. Bakhtin and Lefebvre have strikingly similar concerns. The decommodifying potential of art is one of them but others include everyday life, the subversive potential of play/carnival, and the theorization of the event/act.

15. Mikhail Bakhtin, *Art and Answerability: Early Philosophical Essays by M. M. Bakhtin*, ed. and trans. M. Holquist and V. Liapunov, notes V. Liapunov (Austin: University of Texas, 1990), 2, emphasis added.

16. See Kristin Ross, *The Emergence of Social Space: Rimbaud and the Paris Commune*, preface by Terry Eagleton (Minneapolis: University of Minnesota Press, 1998).

17. Henri Lefebvre, *The Explosion: Marxism and the French Upheaval*, trans. A. Ehrenfeld (New York: Monthly Review Press, 1969 [1968]), 118. The French title is *L'irruption de Nanterre au sommet*.

18. *Ibid.*, 103.

19. *Ibid.*, 51–2.

20. Mikhail Bakhtin, *Toward a Philosophy of the Act*, trans. Vadim Liapunov (Austin: University of Texas Press, 1993), 29.

21. See Tzvetan Todorov, *Life in Common: An Essay in General Anthropology* (Lincoln, NE, and London: University of Nebraska Press, 2001).

22. Lefebvre, *Explosion*, 93.

23. Karatani, *Transcritique*.

24. Lefebvre, *Writings on Cities*, 88.

25. *Ibid.*, 93.

26. Lefebvre, *Explosion*, 109.

27. *Ibid.*, 98.

28. *Ibid.*, 71.

29. *Ibid.*, 70.

30. *Ibid.*, 98.

31. *Ibid.*, 104–5.

32. *Ibid.*, 157.

33. *Ibid.*, 8.

34. *Ibid.*, 90.

11

LEFEBVRE AND DEBORD
A Faustian fusion
Andy Merrifield

1

A lot of people ask me: "So who influenced whom? Was Henri Lefebvre Guy Debord's mentor, or was it the other way around?" In truth it's impossible to say, because for one brief moment, for about half a decade—between 1957 and 1963—the two men helped shape one another. They were kindred spirits for a while, yin and yang opposites, a dialectical unity of disunity, a thesis and antithesis, an affirmation and a negation all rolled into one, ready to combust internally, to create light, and to catch fire. It was a love affair, Lefebvre said, destined to end badly—very badly. And it did, just as it had for Faust and Mephistopheles in Goethe's great drama. "You cannot do what you desire," Mephisto reminded Faust. "With us the elements conspire,/And ruin reaps your crop at last."[1]

The two men were a classic Faust–Mephistopheles pairing: Lefebvre, the aging scholar, sensing something brewing, gurgling within postwar culture and society, ready to erupt, fraternizing with the devilish powers of Debord, a darker figure, the Prince of Division, a man of the night uniting with Lefebvre's personality of the sun. In rescuing the sun from crucifixion, Lefebvre seemingly summoned up the spirit of darkness. Debord and the Situationists internalized the destructive powers Lefebvre secretly harbored within himself, expressed on the page but never let lose, not quite; they were his catharsis incarnate, his kids of Dionysus. Little wonder the devil's party endured only for a moment.

2

Lefebvre and Debord met through women on a Parisian street. The scene could have been lifted from a great movie, a *Nouvelle vague* black-and-white classic, right out of Godard, one of those phantasmagoric experiences *dans la rue*, glimpsed with a hand-held camera. We can picture Lefebvre, the dandy flirt, who comes on like a Kierkegaard seducer, elegant in his turtleneck sweater and tweed jacket, arm in arm with Évelyne Chastel, a woman young enough to be his daughter; and then, about to cross the street in front of them, there's Michèle Bernstein, Évelyne's friend, with close-cropped hair, a Jean Seberg lookalike from *À Bout de Souffle*, linking arms with Debord, the twenty-six-year-old freelance revolutionary, who sports glasses and his standard Situationist duffel coat. They meet, share *bonjours*, and the two women liaise between the two men.

They are thirty years apart in age. Lefebvre had not long quit the French Communist Party (PCF) while Debord had just assumed the mantle of the Situationist International (SI), a band of militant artists, poets, students, and wannabe students. Lefebvre was working at the Centre National de la Recherche Scientifique (CNRS), and in the midst of *La somme et le reste*, his two-volume, eight-hundred-page auto-biography, manically drafted each morning in an apartment along the rue de la Santé. Debord would read it soon enough. Lefebvre said he had expelled himself from the PCF, departing from the left wing. ("*J'ai quitté le Parti par la gauche*," he enjoyed bragging.) Stalin's misdeeds were now public; the 1956 Soviet invasion of Hungary had disgusted many communists, Lefebvre included. *La somme et le reste* was Lefebvre's heart laid bare, his settling of accounts—with the PCF and with Stalinism—his "inventory" of the epoch: personal reminiscences and stinging rebuttals, historical and political analyses, literary set-pieces, poems that hint at Rimbaud and Mallarmé, portraits of friends and pillories of enemies, all laced with dense philosophical disquisitions and Marxist delineations. Debord, for his part, was happy finally to meet the theorist of everyday life whose books he had read and admired. He himself was already a brilliant theorist as well as a ruthless organizer, a poet and experimental filmmaker, a man who neither worked nor studied conventionally and who seemed to live by night.

He and Bernstein inhabited 180, rue Saint Martin near Les Halles, an apartment of barely thirty square meters. A "miserable place," Lefebvre called it, "a dark room without lights, but at the same time a place where there was a great deal of strength and radiance in the thinking and the research."[2] Bernstein gave an artful glimpse of the nocturnal Debord, a real-life owl of Minerva, in *Tous les chevaux du roi*, her thinly disguised novel.[3] Gilles and Geneviève are dead-ringers for Guy and Michèle. "If Gilles no longer loved the same young women as me," narrator Geneviève muses, "that introduced an element of separation between us."[4]

I know Gilles' taste for spending whole nights wandering, when an open café becomes a precious port of call in streets where night-birds aren't abundant. After 2 a.m., the rue Mouffetard is empty. You need to go back up to the Panthéon to find a bar, rue Cujas. The next stop is near to the Sénat, then rue du Bac, if you have the good taste to avoid what we still call the neighborhood . . . And, at daybreak, to Les Halles, which is a ritual.[5]

Gilles, we hear, seemed to be at once too young and too old for these times. "What do you work as?" somebody asks him. "How do you occupy your time?" "With reification," answers Gilles. "That's very serious work, I imagine, with a lot of thick books and a lot of papers on a grand table," quips his interlocutor. "No," says Gilles. "I wander, principally I wander."[6]

3

Lefebvre and Debord summed up the Earth Spirit together, talked all night, drank, dabbled in soft drugs. "My breast is stirred and feels with youthful pain, / The magic breath that hovers round your train." With Debord, Lefebvre "remembers marvelous moments of warm friendship, free of all mistrust, all ambition, all maneuver . . . These nights were of fervor and passion . . . more than communication—a communion—of which I retain a very vivid memory."[7] They communed about urbanism, shared ideas about Marxism, about praxis, about life and love, about revolution and the city. "I remember very sharp, pointed discussions," Lefebvre recalls, "when Guy said that urbanism was becoming an ideology. He was absolutely right, from the moment that there was an official doctrine of urbanism."

They supped mescal together and read, in concert, Malcolm Lowry's *Under the Volcano*, which immortalized the drink. And like the doomed Consul, Geoffrey Fermin, Lowry's anti-hero abandoned by his wife, Debord and Lefebvre had sympathy for the devil: they loved the magnificent and terrible peace mescal induced. "Nothing in the world was more terrible than an empty bottle!" the Consul says. "Unless it was an empty glass."[8] He wonders, "How, unless you drink as I do, can you hope to understand the beauty of an old woman from Tarasco who plays dominoes at seven o'clock in the morning?"[9] The atmosphere of tropical heat and sweaty bodies, of sapping humidity and overhead fans, of colonial castoffs and quirky barflies steers Lowry toward Gabriel García Márquez; yet Lowry's dramatic tension is more brutal and destructive, more menacing, wrenching him nearer to Faulkner. The volcanoes loom everywhere, adding to the sense of impending doom: "The volcanoes seemed terrifying in the wild sunset."

Under their own volcano, Lefebvre and Debord watch the Consul lean on a Mexican bar, stare into "his second glass of the colorless ether-smelling liquid. To drink or not to drink—But without mescal, he imagined, he had forgotten eternity, forgotten their world's voyage, that the earth was a ship, lashed by the Horn's tail, doomed never to make their Valparaiso."[10] Lefebvre and Debord searched for their Valparaiso, for their eternity, as they downed another mescal, toasting the Consul's memory: "Christ," says Fermin, shot at the end of Lowry's masterpiece, and thrown down a ravine with a dead dog, "this is a dingy way to die." Perhaps the spirit of Nietzsche came to mind as they read, the spirit of Nietzsche of *Gay Science*, the Nietzsche who spoke of "preparatory men," of people of the future, of those, like Lefebvre and Debord, who want "their own festivals, their own weekdays, their own periods of mourning," and whose "greatest enjoyment" is living *dangerously*, sailing into uncharted seas, building a city under Vesuvius, under a volcano?[11]

In one scene, the Consul wonders whether Yvonne, his estranged wife, has read the book he gave her, the letters of Héloise and Abélard, the tragic love story from twelfth-century France. Lefebvre would surely have noticed. "Have I told you," he goads his interlocutor in *Le temps des méprises*, "that I attribute to Abélardian heresy a grand place in the history of philosophy?" Abélard, Lefebvre tells us, is "my philosophical hero." Abélard "hadn't only shattered belief in universals: he shattered Logos itself, the Word of God, the person of Christ."[12] Abélard was one of the most brilliant thinkers of his time, a gifted teacher with an ardent student following, bordering on idolatry. He became a personal tutor of Héloise, niece of the Notre Dame's Canon Fulbert. Héloise was beautiful and gifted, witty with a voracious appetite for knowledge, and twenty years Abélard's junior. They fell in love, she fell pregnant; her uncle was not amused, disapproved entirely of their affair but eventually consented to their marriage. Afterwards the Canon arranged for assailants to work Abélard over.

Embarrassed at his affront, ashamed about his punishment, with his dignity kaput, Abélard fled Paris and became a monk in Brittany. There, he penned his masterpiece *Historia calamitatum* (*Story of My Calamities*); distraught, Héloise similarly took her vows and Abélard's sister took charge of Astrolabe, their son. The couple met only one time again, yet spent the rest of their lives corresponding and remaining "Forever One." Their letters are now legendary, vividly demonstrating how shared love is the reason for human existence. Says Lefebvre, again in *Le temps des méprises*:

> The letters of Abélard and Héloise . . . are their reciprocal adhesion to the theological thesis which is a hurricane blowing, a shattering of the world by reconciling flesh with conscience, Cosmos with Logos, the Father with the Son in a metaphysical and theological trinity . . . I joke. The seriousness in the affair comes from the fact that these heretics awaited, and still await, the incarnation of the Third Person in the Trinity, the Spirit. They admit that the Spirit incarnates in itself intelligence and subversive activity.[13]

4

The Father and the Son, Lefebvre and Debord, Bloom and Stephen Dedalus, each glimpsed the Holy Spirit of anti-Logos, sharing their common penchant for unreason, for minds that understand the necessity of Eros and chaos, of calamity and liberty. In *Introduction to Modernity*, a book that launched the Lefebvrean 1960s, Lefebvre saw in Debord and the Situationists the germ of a "new romanticism," a brazenly utopian response to the problems of technological culture and industrial civilization. In them, he spotted a renewal of both classical and modern romanticism fighting back against the boredom and rationality of a bourgeois modernity run amok, updating the project the French novelist Stendhal announced in the 1820s: "At last," Stendhal wrote in *Racine and Shakespeare* (1823), "the great day will come when the youth of France will awake; this noble youth will be amazed to realize how long and how seriously it has been applauding such colossal inanities." "It requires courage to be a romantic," Stendhal claimed, "because one must take a chance." Stendhal's critical text, insisted Lefebvre 140 years later, is of "vital importance," going far "beyond the limits of literary criticism as such, since it attacked the values of the Restoration (the moral order, imitation of the rich and powerful, pedantry), and spearheaded an alternative direction to French social and political life from 1825 onwards."[14]

In the "Twelfth Prelude" of *Introduction to Modernity*, Lefebvre revivifies the spirit of Stendhal as the antecedent of Guy Debord. This dense, 150-page *dénouement*, expressing guarded, critical admiration for the Situationists as "a youth movement," marked the centerpiece of Lefebvre's inquiry into the "more and more brutal, more rapid, more noisy" march of the modern world. In the Situationists, he recognizes a new avant-garde generation, different from the "Lost" or "Beat" generations, angrier and more realistic than the Surrealists, and less angry and more humorous than Lefebvre's generation of communists. In the thirty years prior to the 1960s, Lefebvre thought that radicalism was all but extinct. Economic growth, material affluence, a world war and a cold war had destroyed, absorbed, bought off, and won over many intellectuals of his generation. Ghettoized or brainwashed, they either died off or killed themselves off, lost themselves or found themselves fraternizing with the mainstream, becoming the self-same bureaucrats and technocrats Lefebvre detested, propping up the institutions of modern power he critiqued—anonymous and depersonalized, clinical and Kafkaesque sorts of power. Lefebvre knew he needed to develop younger friendships, those who could turn up the heat, keep him on his toes, if only to ensure he himself was not another sad victim. "Avant-gardes are forming again," he wrote, "and making their voices heard. It is an observable fact . . . They are perfectly convinced that we are all caught up in a gigantic stupidity, a colossal, dreary, pedantic ugliness, which stands victorious over the corpses of spontaneity, taste and lucidity."[15]

In *Introduction to Modernity*, Lefebvre concludes that there are indications of a "new attitude" drifting in the breeze: revolts, acts of insubordination, protests, abstentions, rebellions are, he says, there to be seen and felt; Stendhal is a man of the late twentieth century. He took the *pleasure principle* as his opening gambit and his romanticism affirmed disparate elements of society: "women, young people, political rebels, exiles, intellectuals, who dabbled in deviant experiments (eroticism, alcohol, hashish), half-crazed debauchees, drunks, misfits, successive and abortive geniuses, *arrivistes*, Parisian dandies and provincial snobs."[16] This ragged, motley array of people attempted to live out, within everyday bourgeois society, their ideal solutions to bourgeois society, challenging its moral order, surviving in its core, "like a maggot in a fruit," trying to eat their way out from the inside. They sought to *reinvent* the world. And using all their powers of symbolism, imagination and fiction, a new subjectivity was born, a new lived experience conceived; outrageous fantasy succeeded in shaping grubby reality. Could, wondered Lefebvre, a "new romanticism" do the same in the 1960s? And where are those maggots eating their way out of our rotten society today?

5

"At present," Guy Debord told his friend André Frankin, in a letter dated February 14, 1960, "I am reading *La somme et le reste*. It is very interesting, and close to us—here I mean: the theory of moments."[17] A week on (February 22), Debord wrote the same Situationist friend a long, detailed letter, analyzing Lefebvre's "theory of moments." Debord's discussion is very technical and very serious: you sense the political stakes are high here, on the cusp of something. He thinks Lefebvre's moments are more durable, more precise, purer than the SI's notion of situations; yet this might be a defect. Situations are less definitive, potentially richer, more open to mélange, which is good—except, says Debord, how can "you characterize a situation"? Where does it begin and where does it end? At what point, and where, does it become a different situation?[18] Could the lack of specificity hamper effective praxis? Could too much specificity turn a situation into a moment? What, Debord asks, is a unique moment (or situation) and what is an ephemeral one?

"We will call 'Moment'," Lefebvre notes in the final chapter of the second volume of *Critique of Everyday Life* (1961), deepening his original take from *La somme et le reste*, "*the attempt to achieve the total realization of a possibility. Possibility offers itself; and it reveals itself. It is determined and consequently it is limited and partial.* Therefore to wish to live it as a totality is to exhaust it as well as to fulfill it. The Moment wants to be freely total; it exhausts itself in the act of being lived."[19] Lefebvre's theory of moments sought to disrupt Henri Bergson's notion of linear real time—his *durée*, or duration. Creation, for Bergson, is like the flow of an arrow on a teleological trajectory. "The line [of the arrow] may be divided into as many parts as we wish,"

Bergson said, "of any length that we wish, and it will always be the same line."[20] Life itself, Bergson insisted, unfolds with similar temporality, and we comprehend ourselves in unbroken, absolute time, not in space: "we perceive existence when we place ourselves in duration in order to go from that duration to moments, instead of starting from moments in order to bind them again and to construct duration."[21]

Lefebvre goes against the grain of time's arrow of progress and builds a framework of historical duration from the standpoint of the moment—from, that is, a position the exact opposite to Bergson's. Time, says Lefebvre, isn't just about evolution but involution: "The duration, far from defining itself solely as linear and punctuated by discontinuities, re-orientates itself like a curl of smoke or a spiral, a current in a whirlpool or a backwash."[22] The Lefebvrean moment was there between the lines, in a certain space, at a certain time. It disrupted linear duration, detonated it, dragged time off in a different, contingent direction, toward some unknown staging post. The moment is thus an opportunity to be seized, and invented. It is both metaphorical and practical, palpable and impalpable, something intense and absolute yet fleeting and relative, like sex, like the delirious climax of pure feeling, of pure immediacy, of being there and only there, like the moment of festival, or of revolution.

Just as alienation reflected an *absence*, a moment empty of critical content, the Lefebvrean moment signified a *presence*, a fullness, alive and connected. Lefebvre's theory of moments implied a certain notion of liberty and passion. "For the old-fashioned romantic," he quips in *La somme et le reste*, "the fall of a leaf is a moment as significant as the fall of a state for a revolutionary."[23] Either way, whether for the romantic or the revolutionary—or the romantic revolutionary—a moment has a "certain specific duration." "Relatively durable," Lefebvre says, "it stands out from the continuum of transitories within the amorphous realm of the psyche." The moment "wants to endure. It cannot endure (at least, not for very long). Yet this inner contradiction gives it its intensity, which reaches crisis point when the inevitability of its own demise becomes apparent."[24] For a moment, "the instant of greatest importance is the instant of failure. The drama is situated within that instant of failure: it is the emergence from the everyday or collapse on failing to emerge, it is a caricature or a tragedy, a successful festival or a dubious ceremony.[25]

The spirit of past revolutions, replete with all their successes and failings, seems near by: of 1789 and 1830, of 1848 and the 1871 Paris Commune, of 1917, 1949, and 1959, of the 1968 "Student Commune." Moments do not just crop up anywhere or at any time. The moment may be a marvel of the everyday, Lefebvre says, but it is not a miracle. Indeed, the moment has its motives, and without those motives it would not intervene in "the sad hinterland of everyday dullness."[26] Still, the chief fault of the Lefebvrean moment, according to Debord, a fault that perhaps anticipates—or provokes—Lefebvre's "spatial turn" to come, is: his moment is "first of all temporal, a zone of temporalization. The situation (closely articulated to place) . . . is completely spatiotemporal." Situations are much more spatial, Debord thinks, and much more urban in orientation than the Lefebvrean moment. Debord told Frankin:

> In the end, for resuming the problem of an encounter between the theory of moments and an operational theory of the construction of situations, we would need to pose these questions: what mix? What interaction? Lefebvre is right in at least this: the moment tends toward the absolute, and devours itself in that absolute. It is, *at the same time*, a proclamation of the absolute and a consciousness of its passage.[27]

6

Faust and Mephisto had found a unity, a moment of absolute togetherness, yet they were equally conscious of its passage, of its ephemerality. This historical moment, that geographical situation, could not endure: its demise was inevitable, its combustibility apparent. Debord and other Situationists were genius agitators and organizers, and, in the run-up to May 1968, their presence was felt, both practically and theoretically. But Debord was ruthless in his sectarianism, invariably falling out with allies—*especially* falling out with allies, being most ruthless with old friends and former comrades. He was the spirit that negated all, and that would later include negating himself. Negation meant dispatching friends and foe into the dustbin of history. Steadily, Mephisto and Faust parted company. Debord pointed the finger at his old Faustian pal Lefebvre, denouncing him as an "agent of recuperation." Lefebvre pointed the finger back, liking Debord's "cult of exclusion" to that of surrealist André Breton's. "I was never part of this group," Lefebvre confessed, almost recanting. "I could have been, but I was careful, since I knew Guy's character and his manner, and the way he had of imitating André Breton, by expelling everyone in order to get at a pure and hard little core."[28]

One wonders whether Lefebvre may have lost his nerve during the 1960s, wavered in front of a student movement intent on destruction and with nothing to lose? As a tenured professor, he had plenty to lose: a career, a reputation, perhaps even a pension. Had the stakes become too high? As the violence erupted in 1968, Lefebvre initially balked from endorsing the revolutionary impulse and unbridled spontaneity. Like Faust, he hedged his bets. (He later wrote The Explosion as a mea culpa, there advocating a sort of compromise, a "cultivated spontaneity.") If you have no head for heights, Mephisto reminded Faust, you should not go flying. Maybe Henri got dizzy or turned giddy? Maybe he felt like Faust near the end of Part II of Goethe's epic drama, after Mephisto burns down the cottage of humble Philemon and Baucis. Faust, like Lefebvre (?), wanted reformism, wanted the old couple moved out peacefully, not eliminated by hardnosed revolution. "Burnt out are the accused flames and done, / And, as is meet and proper, I curse you, every one!" "We brought fuel to where the fire was," Debord explained in his film *In Girum Imus Nocte et Consumimur Igni*. "In this manner we enlisted definitively in the Devil's party—the 'historical evil' that leads existing conditions to their destruction, the 'bad side' that makes history by undermining all established satisfaction."[29] "Destruction," said Debord, citing Mallarmé, was "his Beatrice."

Meanwhile, Mephisto Debord said old Professor Faust had stolen some of the Situationists' ideas. He said Lefebvre's take on the 1871 Paris Commune in the journal *Arguments* (27–8, 1962) was almost entirely lifted from SI's "Theses on the Commune" (1962). "This was a delicate subject," rejoined Lefebvre in a 1987 interview.

> I was close to the Situationists . . . And then we had a quarrel that got worse and worse in conditions I don't understand too well myself . . . I had this idea about the Commune as a festival, and I threw it into debate, after consulting an unpublished document about the Commune that is at the Feltrinelli Institute in Milan. I worked for weeks at the Institute; I found unpublished documentation. I used it, and that's completely my right . . . I don't care at all about these accusations of plagiarism. And I never took the time to read what they wrote about the Commune in their journal. I know that I was dragged through the mud.[30]

Curiously, Lefebvre thanks Debord in *La proclamation de la Commune* for his friendship and support "in the course of fecund and cordial discussions." (In a typesetting howler [or a Lefebvre practical joke?], Debord is cited as M. Guy Debud![31]) Both men believed the Commune a historical antecedent of 1968. For seventy-three days, between March and May 1871, Paris, surrounded by warring Prussian forces, had become a liberated zone of people power. The barricades went up, even across Haussmann's mighty boulevards, amid the carnivals and pranks. Freely elected workers, artists, and small business owners were suddenly at the helm. Their rally cries were territorial and urban; their practice was festive and spontaneous. For the first time, a working-class revolution was not merely possible but imminent. The Situationists said the "Commune was the biggest festival of the nineteenth century" (Thesis #2). In *La proclamation de la Commune* (1965), Lefebvre said the Commune's style "was, first of all, an immense, grandiose festival . . . Festival at springtime, festival of the disinherited, revolutionary festival and festival of revolution, free festival, the grandest of modern times."[32] "Underlying the events of that spring of 1871," the SI said, "one can see the insurgents' feeling that they had become the masters of their own history, not so much on the level of 'governmental' politics as on the level of their everyday life."[33] The Commune, Lefebvre claimed, was at once "grandeur and folly, heroic courage and irresponsibility, delirium and reason, exaltation and illusion."[34]

An urban revolution had made its glorious debut, reenergizing public spaces and transforming everyday life, touting victory while it wobbled in defeat. It was condemned to death at birth, despite the gaiety of its baptism. "The Commune," the SI's Thesis #7 said, "represents the only realization of a revolutionary urbanism to date." It "succumbed less to the force of arms, than to the force of habit." "Theoreticians who examine the history of this movement," continued Thesis #11, "can easily prove that the Commune was objectively doomed to failure and could not have been fulfilled. They forget that for those who really lived it, the fulfillment *was already there*" (emphasis in original). "The audacity and inventiveness of the Commune," continued Thesis #12, "must obviously be measured not in relation to our time, but in terms of the prevailing political, intellectual and moral attitudes of its own time, in terms of the interdependence of all the prevailing banalities that it blasted to pieces." "The social war of which the Commune was one moment," concluded the penultimate Thesis #13, "is still being fought today. In the task of 'making conscious the unconscious tendencies of the Commune' (Engels), the last word is still to be said." "The success of the revolutionary movement," said Lefebvre, "masked its failings; conversely, its failures are also victories, openings on to the future, a standard to be seized, a truth to be maintained. What was impossible for the Communards stays until this day impossible, and, by consequence, behooves us to realize its possibility."[35] "We are thus compelled," he reasoned, "to rehabilitate the dream, otherwise utopian, and put to the forefront its *poetry*, the renewed idea of a *creative praxis*. There resides the experience of the Commune and its style."[36]

Ninety-seven years later, during the equally turbulent "May-days" of 1968, history repeated itself on Paris's streets. In 1968, Debord and Lefebvre dueled for an answer. The Nanterre sociologist claimed the Situationists

> proposed not a concrete utopia, but an abstract one. Do they really imagine that one fine day or one decisive evening people will look at each other and say, "Enough! We're fed up with work and boredom! Let's put an end to them!" and they will then proceed into eternal Festival and the creation of situations? Although this happened once, at the dawn of March 18, 1871, this combination of circumstances will not occur again.

"The '68 movement didn't come from the Situationists," insisted Lefebvre, years later. "The movement was made up by students . . . It was an energetic group that took form as the events developed, with no program, no project—an informal group, with whom the Situationists linked up, but it wasn't they who constituted the group."[37]

7

And yet, doctrinal tiffs and accusations of plagiarism were only one part of this Goethean drama. Another aspect was Gretchen. If Henri's womanizing brought him and Debord together, it was the former's libido that equally drove the two men apart. One tale is recounted by Michèle Bernstein, whose friend Nicole Beaurain, a young student, Faust's Gretchen, was bearing Lefebvre's child (after he had split with Évelyne). Lefebvre was already "so old," Bernstein said, "and already several times a father." Bernstein was dead against the pairing, and, according to Lefebvre, she and Debord sent an envoy, another of Michèle's friends, Denise Cheyre, down to Navarrenx to persuade Nicole to abort. Lefebvre accused Debord of meddling; Debord apparently insulted Lefebvre on the phone. "I didn't see Guy mixing himself up in this affair," Bernstein remembered, years later. "It wasn't his style."[38]

But even this scene from Gretchen's Garden falls short of the whole truth about Lefebvre and Debord. In the end, the two men danced to a different drum, embodied contrasting character traits and had different psychic needs. They were creatures of the day and night, figures who either basked in the sunshine or hid themselves in the shadows. One of them, Lefebvre, wanted to rescue the sun from crucifixion: "They've crucified the sun! They've crucified the sun!" a young Henri had wailed years earlier, resting under a giant crucifix during a long country walk in his native Pyrenees. It was he, of course, who had been crucified. He recounts the incident in *La somme et le reste*.[39] The sun had been nailed to the cross and he wanted to undo the nails, to release the sun, and to wreck the cross. In so doing, he would release himself, reclaim his body, taste forbidden fruit, feel warmth, bare flesh, affirm himself as a young romantic. "I was the nailed sun and the tortured cross," Lefebvre says. "I'd seen my image. I vowed to extirpate those mortal nails, to deliver the principle of the sun, to smash up the cross of death."[40]

On the other hand came Debord, the prince of darkness, the owl of Minerva, whose self-knowledge and critical-negative powers came only at the fall of dusk. "In the midwinter nights of 1988, in the square des Missions Étrangères," as Debord drafted his *Comments on the Society of the Spectacle* at his nearby rue du Bac apartment, "an owl would obstinately repeat his calls . . . And this unusual run of encounters with the bird of Minerva, its air of surprise and indignation, did not in the least seem to constitute an allusion to the imprudent conduct or various aberrations of my life." So wrote Debord in his autobiography *Panégyrique*.[41] Debord liked owls and seemed to identify himself with them. Their secrecy, their wisdom, their nocturnal qualities, their melancholy, their consecration by Hegel, all somehow inspired him. In his *Correspondance*, currently stretching to five hefty volumes, he often alludes to their calls. At Champot, his rural retreat in the Auvergne, "every evening," he wrote Gérard Lebovici (March 8, 1978), "one hears in a wood that surrounds us the call of the bird of Minerva. Given that 'knowledge will never come,' it's comforting to know that at least it doesn't reside too far away."[42]

If Debord was a night owl, then Lefebvre was a brightly colored butterfly. As a wayward youth he collected them in Pyrenean meadows; as a young apprentice dreamer he came to their rescue. Butterflies were as flighty and as frivolous as

Lefebvre himself, so light and breezy as to float away, to flit from flower to flower, to pollinate and come alive in the sunshine, in mid-summer. The butterfly reigns as a powerful romantic metaphor in *La somme et le reste*, even as a symbol of Lefebvre's anarchist tendencies! Lefebvre recalls an incident from his military service in 1926, out on an infantry exercise one early summer's morning, "I glimpsed ten steps ahead of me, at the side of the lane, a lovely butterfly whose rose wings where damp; this prevented him from flying. I hastened myself, took him as delicately as possible and placed him down on the embankment." Three seconds later, a corporal sticks a rifle butt in Henri's back. The captain on horseback shouts: "Chasseur Lefebvre! 8 days in police detention." "This lad announces himself as a dangerous subversive element . . . a soft dreamer, a saviour of butterflies . . . an intellectual anarchist."[43]

The spirit of the night owl and wandering butterfly negate and create, are both pessimistic and optimistic, the moon and the sun. In their dialectical antithesis they express the critical and constructive powers of Marxism itself, of negating and destroying, of the phoenix rising out of the ruins, of a utopia based upon a dystopia. "What acceptable paradise can we extract from so many ruins," an adolescent Debord asked, "without falling into them?" How can Marxists paint a society like Matisse, with gorgeously evocative primary colors, without devouring their children as in Goya's dark paintings, where blackness overwhelms everything? Like Matisse, Lefebvre thrived in the sunshine—after he had released the sun from the nails of the holy cross. He relished the dawn just as Debord anticipated dusk. In Goya, Debord knew there is no light only lightening.[44] He knew that night meant security and that it is the dawn one should fear, for then the enemy closes in. "Up! Or you are lost," Mephisto warns near the end of Part I of *Faust*. "Prating and waiting and pointless wavering./My horses are quavering,/Over the sky creeps the dawn . . . What did the darkness spawn?/He! He! Send him away!"[45]

Banishing the darkness is to negate Marxism. In their sympathy for the devil, Lefebvre and Debord recognized the elemental power of darkness. The ruling powers always want to send away darkness, to condemn it as "evil," to flood it with artificial light and climatized air, with a false brightness of lies. But to forget natural light, to ignore the butterfly, the will-o'-the-wisp, to downplay frivolity and warmth, is also to condemn the Marxist life-spirit, to deny its ability to create and engineer photosynthesis. So, in a book about Henri Lefebvre, let us give the last word to Henri Lefebvre, a person who lived to ninety rather than killed himself at sixty-two. It is a passage written in July, in summer, 1973—the summer of his retirement—in a fresh preface to his masterpiece, *La somme et le reste*. He describes his own process of photosynthesis, inspirationally and instructively for us all:

This book speaks of deliverance and happiness regained. Liberated from political pressure, like fleeing a suffocating place after a long, long period of asphyxiation, a place of delusion and concealed disappointments, someone starts to live and to think again. Look at him: he exits from the abyss. Strange animal. A little flattened by heavy pressures, he surges from the depths, surfaces. He breathes in the sunshine, opens himself, displays himself, comes alive again.

NOTES

1. Johann Wolfgang von Goethe, *Goethe's Faust*, trans. W. Kaufmann (New York: Anchor Books, 1963), 467.
2. Henri Lefebvre, "Interview: Henri Lefebvre on the Situationist International," *October* 79, Winter (1997), 69–70.
3. Michèle Bernstein dedicated the text to Debord. In 2004, Éditions Allia republished Bernstein's debut novel from 1960, adorned with a youthful picture of its author.
4. Michèle Bernstein, *Tous les chevaux du roi*, trans. A. Merrifield (Paris: Éditions Allia, 2004), 19.
5. *Ibid.*, 22.
6. *Ibid.*, 26.
7. Henri Lefebvre, *Le temps des méprises*, trans. A. Merrifield (Paris: Stock, 1975), 158.
8. Malcolm Lowry, *Under the Volcano* (New York: Plume Books, 1971), 86.
9. *Ibid.*, 50.
10. *Ibid.*, 287.
11. Friedrich Nietzsche, "The Gay Science," §283, in *The Portable Nietzsche*, ed. and trans. W. Kaufmann (New York: Viking Press, 1954), 97. Toward the end of his life, Guy Debord increasingly came to resemble Geoffrey Fermin, the doomed Consul. With a tragic cast, he too would brood, under the Massif Central's volcanoes, reclusive yet majestic in the Auvergne, where he would experience "grandiose isolation" and "impressive and pleasing solitude." In *Métaphilosophie*, what Lefebvre said of Lowry seemed accurate for Debord. Lowry took "auto-destruction" to its apogee in *Under the Volcano*, "to the degree that auto-destruction of an oeuvre and auto-destruction of an artist become a supreme work of art." See Henri Lefebvre, *Métaphilosophie* (Paris: Les Éditions de Minuit, 1965), 244 n1.
12. Lefebvre, *Le temps des méprises*, trans. A. Merrifield, 60.
13. *Ibid.*, 61.
14. Stendhal, *Racine and Shakespeare*, cited in Henri Lefebvre, *Introduction to Modernity: Twelve Preludes: September 1959–May 1961*, trans. G. Moore (London: Verso, 1995), 239. Stendhal (1783–1842) was the penname of Marie-Henri Beyle, whose romantic novels, especially *Scarlet and Black* (1830) and *The Charterhouse of Parma* (1839), brought him fame and a following. Stendhal dedicated his works to "the happy few," and coined the term "Beylism" as his philosophical credo for the pursuit of happiness. His dedication may have been an allusion to Shakespeare's *Henry V*: "We few, we happy few, we band of brothers." Interestingly, and unbeknown to the Lefebvre of *Introduction to Modernity*, Shakespeare's phrase would feature in Guy Debord's film version of *The Society of the Spectacle* (1973). Following the caption of "we happy few," the frame flashes to wall graffiti at an occupied Sorbonne, around the late 1960s: "Run quickly, comrade, the old world is behind you!"
15. Lefebvre, *Introduction to Modernity*, 343.
16. *Ibid.*, 302.

17. Guy Debord, *Correspondance, tome I: juin 1957–août 1960*, trans. A. Merrifield (Paris: Librairie Arthème Fayard, 1999), 313.
18. *Ibid.*, 318.
19. Henri Lefebvre, *Critique of Everyday Life, Volume II*, trans. J. Moore (London: Verso, 2002), 348, emphasis in original.
20. Henri Bergson, *Creative Evolution* (New York: The Modern Library, 1944), 337.
21. *Ibid.*, 393.
22. Henri Lefebvre, *La somme et le reste* (Paris: La Nef de Paris Éditions, two volumes, 1959), I, 234.
23. *Ibid.*, II, 647.
24. Lefebvre, *Critique*, II, 345.
25. *Ibid.*, 351.
26. *Ibid.*, 356.
27. Debord, *Correspondance*, I, 318, emphasis in original.
28. Lefebvre, "Interview," 69–70.
29. Guy Debord, "In Girum Imus Nocte et Consumimur Igni," in *Oeuvres cinématographiques complètes, 1952–1978* (Paris: Gallimard, 1994), 253. Debord's 1978 threnody to Paris, and his finger to the established film world, has a Latin palindrome title with an English translation: "We go round and around and are consumed by fire."
30. Lefebvre, "Interview," 81.
31. Henri Lefebvre, *La proclamation de la Commune*, trans. A. Merrifield (Paris: Gallimard, 1965), 11/n1.
32. *Ibid.*, 20–1.
33. Guy Debord, Attila Kotányi, and Raoul Vaneigem, "Theses on the Paris Commune," in *Situationist International Anthology*, ed. and trans. K. Knabb (Berkeley: Bureau of Public Secrets, 1981), 314. (All subsequent quotes from this work are taken from the same page.)
34. Lefebvre, *La proclamation*, trans. A. Merrifield, 21.
35. *Ibid.*, 39.
36. *Ibid.*, 40.
37. Lefebvre, "Interview," 81.
38. Quoted in Christophe Bourseiller, *Vie et mort de Guy Debord* (Paris: Plon, 1999), 258–9. Nicole gave birth to Lefebvre's sixth child, a daughter called Armelle, in 1964. In 1978, at the age of seventy-seven, Lefebvre married Catherine Régulier, then a twenty-one-year-old communist militant. Estranged from her parents because of her relationship with Lefebvre, Catherine stayed with Henri until the end of his life.
39. Lefebvre, *La somme*, I, 252.
40. *Ibid.*, 253.
41. Guy Debord, *Panégyrique, Volume I* (London: Verso, 1991), 51.
42. Guy Debord, *Correspondance, tome V: janvier 1973–décembre 1978* (Paris: Librairie Arthème Fayard, 2005), 452.
43. Lefebvre, *La somme*, II, 428.
44. See Debord, *Panégyrique*, I, 49.
45. The Project Gutenberg EBook of Faust (2005), <http://www.gutenberg.org/files/14591/14591-h/14591-h.html#/>.

PART III

DIFFERENCE, HEGEMONY,
AND THE RIGHT TO THE CITY

12

HOW LEFEBVRE URBANIZED GRAMSCI[1]

Hegemony, everyday life, and difference

Stefan Kipfer

INTRODUCTION

This chapter traces the problematic of hegemony in Henri Lefebvre's work. This search for Gramscian resonances in Lefebvre may seem surprising since the relevance of Gramsci's Marxism for contemporary oppositional politics is hotly contested. For some, an overreliance on Gramsci can contribute to a stifling intellectual pessimism among radicals. Certain theorizations of hegemony in the Anglo-American academy (including those associated with some post-marxist readings of Gramsci) may have undermined a search for intellectual hope and utopia, thus promoting the very political passivity and intellectual fatalism that Gramsci himself never tired of criticizing.[2] In addition, one-sided adaptations of the problematic of hegemony can blind us to the often unmediated coercion, violence, and dispossessions of contemporary imperialism.[3] These reservations about the current relevance of Gramsci are sometimes echoed by autonomist and anarchist observers of anti-globalization movements such as Toni Negri, Michael Hardt, and John Holloway. Close to anarchist currents within these movements, Richard Day declares Gramsci "dead."[4] Forms of political practice inspired by Gramsci have exhausted themselves, he argues, because they are too wedded to Leninist state-centrism. Such state-centrism runs counter to what Day sees as the base-democratic sensibilities of a new genera-tion of anti-capitalist activists, who have energized mobilizations from Seattle to

Genoa and carried these energies of mobilizations into projects like social centers and self-managed enterprises.

Rather than providing a direct defense of Antonio Gramsci's theory and practice, this chapter intends to underline the contemporary relevance of Gramscian problematics by foregrounding Gramscian resonances in Lefebvre's work. I have argued elsewhere that linking Lefebvre to Gramsci is politically and theoretically plausible even though in Lefebvre's work references to the Sardinian marxist were sparse and usually cursory. There are clear affinities between the two intellectuals' respective "open" and "integral" understanding of marxism.[5] In this chapter, I will not compare Gramsci and Lefebvre but outline how Lefebvre extended and redirected Gramsci's Marxism while making productive use of Gramsci's theory of hegemony. The first section outlines Lefebvre's sympathetic, but crucial epistemological and political critique of the Italian communist. Much of this critique follows Lefebvre's exit from the French Communist Party (PCF) in the late 1950s and draws from the lessons of "1968." The bulk of this chapter takes Lefebvre's question from the opening pages of *The Production of Space* (is it "conceivable that the exercise of hegemony leaves space untouched"?[6]) as an invitation to urbanize Gramsci's theory of hegemony *thoroughly*. This search for an urban conception of hegemony will force us to link Lefebvre's urban and spatial writing to his critique of everyday life and his conception of difference. As I will argue in the conclusion (against those who have proclaimed the death of Gramsci-inspired theory and politics), Lefebvre's dialectical and anti-statist redirection and differential urbanization of Gramsci lends the problematic of hegemony much of its contemporary salience.

GRAMSCI IN LEFEBVRE'S MARXISM

Antonio Gramsci has been omnipresent in critical intellectual debates within the Anglo-American academic world of the last three decades. His writing has been applied in many fields of research, from state and regulation theory and global political economy to cultural studies, literary theory, and radical geography. The dominant (but by no means exclusive) interpretations of Gramsci within these fields of debate have been those influenced by structuralism (Althusser) and deconstruction (Derrida). This is most evident in those Gramscians (Stuart Hall, Ernesto Laclau, and Chantal Mouffe) whose own work has undergone a metamorphosis from structuralism to post-structuralism and thus had a profound influence on Gramsci readings in cultural studies, post-colonial theory, and more recent versions of subaltern studies. Research undertaken within this intellectual lineage (such as the analyses of racism, articulation and authoritarian populism by Hall, different from both Laclau and Mouffe) represents a crucial contribution to Gramsci scholarship. But reading Gramsci into the specific linguistic turn defined by structuralism and its deconstructive critics jives only uneasily with key aspects of Gramsci's Marxism: his very particular historicism, his historical-relational notion of language, and his nuanced understanding of internationalism and social difference.[7]

This chapter intervenes into these debates only indirectly, by pointing out that Lefebvre's own (very selective) reading of Gramsci is also difficult to reconcile with an Althusserian and Derridean rendering of Gramsci. Just as Gramsci used particular strands of Italian linguistic theory to theorize hegemony, Lefebvre was profoundly interested in using linguistic concepts and metaphors for his critique of everyday life and his theory of production of space. But like Gramsci's, Lefebvre's interest in language was based on a rejection of one-sidedly abstract conceptions of language as formal structure, notably those inherent in the (post-)structuralist deployments of de Saussure's linguistic theory. As I will stress in the section on difference, Lefebvre's persistent critique of structuralist linguistic theory demonstrates a qualitative distance between his use of hegemony and that espoused by post-marxists Ernesto Laclau and Chantal Mouffe. The lineage between Gramsci and Lefebvre rests not on the alleged affinity of both with the particular linguistic and cultural turn of post-theory but on their respective attempts to move beyond Leninism and forge an open marxism attuned to the uneven development of metropolitan capitalism in all its multidimensional (economic, political, cultural) forms.

Lefebvre's comments on Gramsci are few compared to his continuous engagement with Marx, Hegel, Nietzsche, and Heidegger, and his tension-ridden, but explicit relationships to Breton, Nizan, Sartre, Merleau-Ponty, Bachelard, Axelos, Debord, Barthes, and Althusser. Lefebvre was tied to Gramsci through shared orientations, not direct links and connections. One of the few sustained discussions of Gramsci can be found in Lefebvre's *De l'État*. There, Gramsci appears (together with Rosa Luxemburg) as the marxist linchpin of Lefebvre's project for a spatialized political theory. For Lefebvre, Gramsci's theory of hegemony pointed beyond a Leninist conception of marxism as philosophy of praxis. In contrast to Lenin, Gramsci considered hegemony a project to be built patiently through interplays of "wars of position" and "wars of movement." As Lefebvre points out, this entails a sense of political organization and intellectual practice as active, constitutive forces within the historical process. Instead of instrumental factors to be brought to bear on class formation and revolutionary politics *from the outside*, as it were, intellectual practice, moral leadership, truth claims, and political passion must be considered immanent to the dynamics of history itself.[8]

Lefebvre stressed how Gramsci developed a sensitivity to the artistic and intuitive aspects of political knowledge by developing Marx's own analysis of Bonapartism. In Lefebvre's eyes, Gramsci's political theory implies a "severe critique of Lenin"[9] and leads to an open-ended, non-objectivist understanding of marxism similar to his own. If knowledge in all its cognitive and sensual aspects (*connaissance*, in Lefebvre's vocabulary) is itself a historical force, it is no longer possible to uphold objectivist distinctions between base and superstructure. As Lefebvre points out, base and superstructure become fused in the tension-ridden formations of what Gramsci called historic blocs.[10] This leads to a self-reflexive, historicized conception of marxism itself, according to Lefebvre. Marxism cannot be considered as an already-formed, ready-made body of theory and strategy. It is rather contingent upon successful engagements with hegemonic forms of life and thought in bourgeois society.[11] For Lefebvre, Gramsci's refusal to fix his writing in a "system," a doctrinaire "gramscianism,"[12] thus resonated with his own view of Marx and marxism as a formally and substantially open-ended, even contradictory totality. Indeed, like Gramsci's, Lefebvre's work does not lend itself to a *Lefebvreanism*. It resembles a moving constellation of concepts tied together by dialectical method rather than instrumental party doctrine (of Thorez's French Communist Party, for example) or formalistic protocols (in Althusserian structuralism).[13]

Lefebvre wanted to rescue Gramsci from being the iconic figure he had become for the Stalinist leadership of the Italian and French communist parties. But in his autobiographical *La somme et le reste*, written after his expulsion from the PCF, Lefebvre warned, with specific reference to Gramsci, that collapsing marxism as theoretical orientation with marxism as political-organizational strategy easily reduces intellectual practice to an instrument of political strategy.[14] Gramsci, Lefebvre argues in *De l'État*, rehabilitated Machiavelli's Prince (Gramsci's figure for the communist party) only at great cost. The Prince, for whom all means are adequate and political strategy is essential, strives to "annex science and scholarship" and marshal knowledge to political authority.[15] As a result, the validity of knowledge claims threatens to become synonymous with their political success. According to Lefebvre, Gramsci did not fully anticipate the danger of fusing intellectual practice to the imperative of the Stalinist party-state in waiting (to which Lefebvre sometimes succumbed himself, notably with his officious critique of Sartre in his 1946 book *L'existentialisme*). In contrast to Lefebvre, Gramsci made no clear distinction between critical, embodied forms of knowing (*connaissance*) and rationalist, instrumental, disciplinary (and thus ultimately state-dependent) knowledge (*savoir*). For Lefebvre, this distinction (as well as the distinction between political theory and political action), was essential to safeguard critical knowledge at a time when the proletariat (ossified in Stalinist and statist social democratic parties) no longer functioned as a revolutionary pole of negativity vis-à-vis totality.[16] Partly against Gramsci (and resonant with German critical theory) Lefebvre retained a distinction between critical knowledge and political expression, political thought and political activism, more decisive than Gramsci's own.[17]

Because of Gramsci's epistemological limitations (and his optimistic view of French Jacobinism as a recipe to unify Italy), Lefebvre argued that Gramsci's political theory never went beyond a "statist critique of the State."[18] With reference to Marx's early work, Lefebvre never tired of stressing that Marx's thought is "fundamentally directed against the state."[19] Writing in Gaullist France, with full knowledge of real (state) socialism, he could harbor no illusions about the prospects of a "revolutionary state," even in transitional form.[20] Lefebvre thus proposed to read Gramsci's insights on hegemony (from the *Prison Notebooks*) through his earlier writing about the workers' uprising in 1919 Turin (in the socialist weekly *Ordine Nuovo*). This was to learn from the legacy of Stalinist state doctrine, which effectively disconnected two of Lenin's key revolutionary notions: the "dictatorship of the proletariat" (immortalized in state socialism) and the "withering away of the state" (postponed indefinitely).[21] For Lefebvre, the latter notion becomes the imperative of a dynamically conceived counterhegemonic perspective. In this view espoused by Lefebvre, counterhegemonic projects are long-term quests to form "dual power" in all areas of life, "from the economy to pedagogy, culture and knowledge."[22] Following this Lefebvrean adaptation of Gramsci, the declining dominant class holds onto and perfects the state while the ascendant revolutionary class establishes itself from below, "in councils, soviets, community of interests, users' groups etc.," pointing toward the "end of an all-pervasive, perfected state."[23] One might say that with his critique of a lurking statism in Gramsci, Lefebvre approximates the Gramscian perspective of counterhegemony to the new left problematic of *autogestion* (self-management) as continuous process of transformation (see Chapter 4, this volume).

Lefebvre mobilized Gramsci not only for an analytically more promising theory of the state as a relatively autonomous condensation of power (as his contemporary, state theorist Nicos Poulantzas did).[24] He redeployed Gramsci for a radical critique of all things state-like (l'*étatique*). More than Gramsci, Lefebvre insists that the state itself is an "instrument, site, result (product) of the struggle for hegemony."[25] As a totalizing form of institutions and apparatuses and a doctrine for a hierarchy of functionaries (*bureaulogie*), the state embodies a logic of equivalence, hierarchy, and functional dissociation that is central to the organization of the commodity form itself and as such transcends distinct political ideologies. The state as state-like form becomes diffuse, penetrating all aspects of society, threatening to become identical with life and "imprisoning" oppositional forces.[26] For Lefebvre, the state (as well as civil society, in Gramsci's terminology) is itself central to hegemony to the extent that everyday life (across increasingly anachronistic divides between city and countryside) is suffused by the state-like. Lefebvre's critique of the state as potentially hegemonic form thus returns to the critique of everyday life. For the Lefebvre of the late 1970s, it was equally clear that the role of the state-like in the formation of everyday life was mediated spatially. The state-like helps institute the everyday in and through the urban.[27] The state takes on hegemonic ("consensual") aspects as a familiar social space everyone can identify with: the post office, city hall, the train station, the bistro, the grocery store.[28] This is why Gramsci must be redirected toward an anti-statist, urbanized form of critical theory.

URBANIZING HEGEMONY: EVERYDAY LIFE . . .

In Lefebvre, Gramsci continues to be an important reference point. For him, Gramsci's concept of hegemony remains relevant "as an interpretation of historical materialism"[29] and a theory of the role of passion and intuition in the art of politics.[30] In late and after-Fordist capitalism, however, the problematic of hegemony must be disentangled from its statist aspects. Indeed, one can argue that in this vein, Lefebvre critically reformulated analyses of hegemony as a differential analysis of everyday life mediated by the production of urban space. This argument rests on two assumptions. First, Lefebvre met Gramsci's analyses of hegemony as lived reality (common sense, in Gramsci's terminology) most clearly in the critique of everyday life, as has been pointed out by John Roberts and in the early works of Ed Soja.[31] The critique of everyday life was Lefebvre's most enduring concern and thus the linchpin to his conception of marxism as metaphilosophy and critique of political economy.[32] Second, Lefebvre's urban writing refracts his critique of everyday life. Just as his critique of everyday life was of epistemological importance for his view of marxism as metaphilosophy, so too were Lefebvre's urban writings.[33] As Kristin Ross has argued most forcefully, the link to the critique of everyday life represents the most explosive aspect of Lefebvre's urban turn.[34] In Lefebvre, Gramsci's problematic of hegemony thus becomes explicitly urbanized.

As we will see below, the degree to which the production of abstract space takes on hegemonic importance stands and falls with its capacity to incorporate everyday life (the immediate level of totality, or lived space, as Lefebvre calls it in his urban and spatial writings). Lefebvre's critique of everyday life was developed from his work on "mystification" with Norbert Guterman, published in 1933 and 1936.[35] From early on, Lefebvre's approach to everyday life revealed a Gramscian "suspicion vis-à-vis the stratosphere of society" (the abstract aesthetic distinctions of the culture of the bourgeoisie) and a penchant for analyzing the contradictory, mundane tenacity of the daily round.[36] Lefebvre's Critique of Everyday Life (published in three volumes between 1947 and 1981) effectively reformulated the critique of alienation and commodity fetishism in an analysis of separation, fragmentation, and naturalization in the new "sectors" of postwar capitalism: leisure, radio and TV, café life, advertising, popular literature.[37] The critique of everyday life signaled a shift in the production of consent from the explicit cultural and intellectual leadership exercised by intellectuals of particular ruling-class factions to a more pervasive diffusion of bourgeois culture through commodification in intensive, and, particularly in the French case, heavily state-administered regimes of accumulation. Neo-capitalism (Gramsci's Americanism and Fordism) undermined the bourgeois culture of the nineteenth century. In an era when capitalism "extends into the slightest details of ordinary life,"[38] cultural distinctions by bourgeois class fractions became part of a more diffuse "bourgeois society."[39]

Lefebvre stressed that as a particular level of totality, everyday life is fraught with its own contradictions. In this, Lefebvre was closer to Gramsci (who distinguished between common and good sense) than to Lukács (whose treatment of everyday life Lefebvre considered lofty and aristocratic)[40] or non-marxists (who saw everyday life one-sidedly, as lowly banality—Heidegger—or source of popular ingenuity—de Certeau).[41] Lefebvre contrasted daily life (la vie quotidienne) with the everyday (le quotidien), and everydayness (la quotidienneté).[42] Everyday life is where dominated, accumulative sectors (everyday, everydayness) meet undominated, non-accumulative sectors (daily life), "where both richness and poverty of modern life become evident."[43] Everyday life is central to the reproduction of capitalism[44] insofar as it is saturated by the routinized, repetitive, familiar daily practices that make up the everyday in all spheres of life: work, leisure, politics, language, family life, cultural production.[45] Everyday life is the best "guarantee of non-revolution"[46] because it refers to what we take for granted, what seems self-evident ("that's how it is") and inevitable ("it can't be any different"), irrespective of whether we like it or not.[47] Effective because of our "taste of solidity and durability" as a defense against the uncertainties of modern life,[48] the everyday becomes a "seat of power," the "very soil on which the great architecture of politics and society rise up."[49]

The installation of everydayness and the diffusion of power in neo-capitalism reduced the degree to which classes opposed each other as demarcated blocs.[50] But Lefebvre refuted Herbert Marcuse's thesis of the one-dimensionality of the subaltern subject to insist on the contradictions and promising potentials within postwar everyday life.[51] Indeed, he never tired of stressing the role of intellectuals to extricate the possible within the real rather than to reify the systemic coherence of capital.[52] The dialectical methods that permeate his work—transduction, dialectical humanism, spectral analysis, differential theory, conjunctural analysis—were all meant to excavate possibilities latent in commodified and administered everyday life. Never completely engulfed by the dull constraints of the everyday, daily life—as symbolized in neo-capitalism by such novelties as the car, the mass-produced bungalow, the popular beach resort, women's magazines, TV ads—includes utopian promises for non-instrumentalized, playful, and non-alienated futures. Contradictions emerge because these promises are denied by the very regressive forces of administered consumption and gendered, phallocentric planning that spread them.[53] As he argued in his analysis of May 1968, radical or even revolutionary political claims can emerge from within these everyday contradictions.

The extent to which contradictions within everyday life are tied up with matters hegemonic becomes clearer in Lefebvre's urban and spatial writing, which he saw as a rearticulation of the critique of everyday life.[54] In The Production of Space, Lefebvre explicitly links the problematic of hegemony to the production of space. He agrees with Gramsci that "hegemony implies more than an influence, more even than the permanent use of repressive violence."[55] Hegemony includes the exercise of bourgeois influence over culture and knowledge, institutions and ideas as mediated by policies, political leaders, parties, intellectuals, and experts. Most importantly, he underlines the importance of the production of space for analyses of hegemony. If it is true that space can no longer be treated as "the passive locus of social relations," the production of space "serves" hegemony. This suggests, among other things, that "the actions of the bourgeoisie, especially in relation to space" may be analyzed under the rubric of hegemony. Of course, hegemony is not an immutable thing but a contingent set of processes and strategies which are far from being "purged of contradictions" and have no "legitimate claim to immortality." Treating hegemony as an incomplete, produced totality thus excludes views of capitalism as a "closed system" or "an aggregate of individual decisions."

How can the production of space be said to be hegemonic? It is useful to recall that Lefebvre analyzed the production of space as a three-dimensional process. In a materialist development of phenomenological categories (see Chapter 2, this volume), Lefebvre insisted that produced space has perceived, conceived, and lived dimensions. To put it differently, processes and strategies of producing social space can be looked at in their material (perceived) aspects, their representational, institutional, and ideological (conceived) aspects, and their affective-symbolic (lived) aspects. The production of urban space contributes to hegemony insofar as it fuses the contradictory immediate realm of lived space with processes and strategies of producing conceived and perceived space.[56] The dominant form of produced space under capitalism is abstract. It is shaped by the relentless forms of repetition (linear time), homogenizing abstraction, and alienating separation of the commodity, the state, technocratic knowledge, and patriarchy (phallocentrism). Although structurally violent, abstract space is hegemonic to the degree that it envelops and incorporates the daily aspirations, desires, and dreams of subaltern populations. Key examples of this are two spatial forms of neo-capitalism: the bungalow and the high-rise tower. While standardized industrial products, they also embody hopes for social reform, domestic harmony, and a reconciliation with nature in the after-industrial city.

The serialized abstract space and repetitive linear time of state, capital, phallo-centrism become part of the everyday through a combination of daily repetition and the appeal to popular aspirations in an alienated world. Lefebvre had already articulated this insight in his urban writings. There, Lefebvre treated the urban as a *level* of analysis. As the middle level of analysis (level M) between the general level of the social order (level G) and the "private" level of everyday life (level P), the urban mediates totality.[57] Urban social space is of strategic importance in binding everyday life (the immediate, near order) to macro-structures (the far order of life).

> Abstract, formal, supra-sensible and transcending in appearance, it [the far order] is not conceptualized beyond ideologies (religious and political). It includes moral and juridical principles. This *far order* projects itself into the

practico-material reality and becomes visible by writing itself within this reality. It persuades through and by the *near order*, which confirms its compelling power. It becomes apparent by and in immediacy.[58]

As a product of industrialization, commodification, real estate capital, and everyday symbols (such as phallic images) urbanization is abstract space, a multidimensional "projection of society" that is vital for the solidification of capitalism.[59] To the extent that this projection has coercive and persuasive aspects, it may be said to be hegemonic. The persuasive character of the urbanization process derives not only from the "self-evident" habits of daily repetition but from the process by which inhabitants actively and affectively identify with the symbolic promise of privatized urban life.

The production of space is not agent-less. It is, at least in part, a result of concerted strategies. Key agents in making the production of space hegemonic are specialists of *urbanisme*: architects, planners, developers, specialized academics.[60] Given Lefebvre's broader claim about the centrality of the urban as a mediation of neo-capitalist totality, urbanists take on a strategic role as organic intellectuals in an urbanizing, neo-capitalist order. Urbanists give meaning to the practical-material aspects of city-building with disciplinary, fragmented knowledge (*savoir*) and through symbolic forms (monuments, advertising images). Both forms of conceived space assume and promote the political passivity *and* the affective involvement of users of space. The specialized, state-dependent knowledge of architects, planners, and urban designers treats urban space as a reified, thing-like object that imposes itself on the urban inhabitants from the outside, as it were. In turn, carefully researched and marketed symbols of "good urban life" captured by urban forms (the apartment and single-family dwelling, for example) invite inhabitants to identify their dreams and desires with regressive, myth-like utopias caught within the bounds of the nuclear family, private property, and segregated "community." By promoting the simultaneous (symbolic) integration and (political) demobilization of inhabitants, *urbanisme* had, by mid-century, significant success in temporarily preempting qualitatively different ways of producing space.[61]

. . . AND DIFFERENCE

The processes and strategies by which abstract space becomes hegemonic are highly differential. The production of abstract space homogenizes *through* separation. Neo-capitalist urbanization is explosion/implosion. It undermines city centers by scattering urban life into isolated parcels: bungalows (*pavillons*), districts of high-rise towers (*grands ensembles*), factory and university compounds, and resort towns on the beach. Demarcated by property divisions, transportation routes, and lines of functional and social segregation, these parcelized social spaces (planned in vulgar modernist fashion) represent forms of minimal difference. As specified in Le manifeste différentialiste, The Production of Space, and The Critique of Everyday Life (Volume III), minimal or "induced" difference is alienated particularity (individualism or group particularism) that tends toward "difference-as-sameness" and "formal identity."[62] Akin to the "diversity between villas in a suburb filled with villas" and the patriarchal "family cell,"[63] minimally differential space dissociates everyday life, peripheralizes the working class, imposes much of the weight of reproduction onto women,[64] and banishes new immigrants to "neocolonial" shantytowns and the worst public housing tracts.[65] But minimally different spaces such as beach resorts extend "bourgeois hegemony to the whole of space."[66] Like bungalows, they promise a different, erotic appropriation of nature and body, embody hopes for non-instrumental human relationships, and nurture daydreams about freedom from repetitive drudgery even as they are managed with "identical plans" and strategies to foster predictable "rituals."[67]

In contrast to post-marxists Ernesto Laclau and Chantal Mouffe, Lefebvre did not consider hegemony a discursive form of articulation, a linguistic way of "fixing" the interminable flux of signs that is, in this view, language.[68] In Lefebvre's view, hegemonic productions of space have a strong linguistic dimension: the symbolism of lived experience. But Lefebvre insisted that the particular theories of language inspired by (post-)structuralist readings of de Saussure, which form the philo-sophical basis of Laclau's and Mouffe's post-marxist Gramscianism, is a form of "semantic reductionism" that separates formal language structure (langue) from speech (parole) and thus detaches language as a whole from lived experience.[69] Lefebvre's difference is not Derrida's différance, a term meant to highlight the necessarily fluid, unstable modality of language that is given by the irreducible temporal delay and spatial distinction between signs.[70] For Lefebvre, difference is a multidimensional (not-just-linguistic) "struggle concept," emerging from particular political struggles rather than the quasi-ontological, a priori conception of linguistic différance which Laclau and Mouffe import from Derrida.[71] To conflate Lefebvre's differential method with the deconstructive différance and contain differential method within the modernist, self-referential world of signs of Derrida's philosophy of language would be to restrict one's field of engagement to the very decorporealized world of linguistic abstraction that also informs the logic of equivalence in the commodifed, state-bound abstract space of neo-capitalism.[72]

For Lefebvre, abstract space is hegemonic precisely not because it denies différance through hegemonic articulations of identity, as is claimed by those who have tried to spatialize Laclau and Mouffe's post-marxism.[73] Instead, the potentially hegemonic character of abstract space rests on a successful production and incorporation of (minimal) difference in all its dimensions (linguistic and otherwise). Harnessing minimally different social space is, of course, fraught with tension. The very urbanist practices of planners, architects, and developers that established neo-capitalist "dreamscapes" negate the aspirations associated with postwar everyday spaces by reducing them to industrialized, neo-colonial, and patriarchal spaces. In his study "habitat of the bungalow" (*habitat pavillonnaire*), Lefebvre described this tension as a disjuncture of perceived, conceived, and lived aspects of abstract space: a schism between the bungalow as mode of practical appropriation (of urban space by private property), ideology (the nuclear, privatized family), and utopian hope for harmony with nature embodied in the symbolism of built form.[74] The chaotic-differential side of the production of urban space thus also functions as an achilles heel of capital, revealing the bourgeoisie's ultimate inability to reduce "the body," "the practico-sensory realm" to abstract space.[75] While providing grounds for hegemonizing urbanisms, the "explosion of the city" may also produce "breaking points"[76] where minimally differential aspirations clash with other realities of daily life and may lead to claims for *maximal* difference.

From the perspective of Laclau and Mouffe, counterhegemony implies an almost impossible, Sisyphian task. For them, there can be "no 'beyond hegemony'" since hegemony (as an articulation of identity/difference) rests on an ontology of language as play of signs. All that remains is a perennial (reformist) project to mobilize a (linguistic) "logic of difference" to dis- and rearticulate and "pluralize" hegemony as discursively fixed identity.[77] To the extent that Lefebvre shared a skepticism of identitarian politics, it was rooted not in deconstructive linguistic theory but a differential understanding of marxism. Within that understanding, differential method is informed by a dialectical quest of *transformation*. Lefebvre points to this with his distinction between minimal and maximal difference. In contrast to minimal difference, *maximal*, or *produced*, difference implies a "shattering of a system."[78] It points to festive, creative, affective, unalienated, fully lived forms of plurality and individuality that assume rich social relations unfettered by forms of "indifference" (individualism, pluralism, imitation, conformism, naturalized particularism).[79] Maximal difference is incompatible with the alienations of private property, the state-like, decorporealized knowledge, linguistic abstraction, phallocentrism, and neo-colonialism.[80] Sources for maximal difference can be found both within the interstices of everyday life and in the midst of uprisings.

Asserting a (maximal) right to difference implies a two-pronged quest for revolutionary transformation. In the more general sense, asserting a right to difference means laying claim to a *different*, no longer capitalist world defined by use-value relationships and generalized *autogestion*: the self-determination of all aspects of life, from workplaces to territorial units.[81] This general differential quest is tied to a commitment to strip existing social differences of the very alienating, often state-sanctioned aspects (productivism, sexism, racism) that make them minimal in the here and now. Differentialist theory is intended to help move from affirming oppositional manifestations of difference to transforming these manifestations in a dialectically humanist fashion:[82]

The distinction between particularities and differences, and the dynamic it displays, form part of the theory [of difference]. Neglecting it leads to confusions with serious consequences. To assert particularities as such under the guise of differences sanctions racism, sexism, separations, and disjunctions. This is what differentialist theory, its methodology and concepts, precludes.[83]

The purpose of dialectical, differentialist theory is thus not to reify difference by deploying a linguistic imperative (différance) or by affirming essentialized particularities ("natural distinguishing characteristics").[84] To lay claim to naturalized, false "authenticity,"[85] or to affirm particularities without clarification, leaves politics firmly within the realm of minimal difference. Instead, a quest for maximal space is contingent on the possibility that, in their quest for a different, socialist world, struggles to "establish differences" in class struggle and the "political action of minorities"[86] transform the very alienated forms of social difference that originally formed their point of departure.

For Lefebvre, claims to "the right to the city" are the prism through which minimal difference may be transformed into maximal difference and fragments of abstract space may be connected in a quest to differential space. It helps to recall that Lefebvre treated the urban not only as a mediation of far and near order of totality. He also saw it as a (fleeting) form of centrality and difference, a point of convergence and "an ensemble of differences."[87] The right to difference is thus simply the flipside of asserting the right to the city (centrality/power). Affirming the right to the city/difference does not mean celebrating actually existing manifestation of diversity per se, however. The liberal-pluralist diversity refers to reified forms of minimal difference (individualism, group pluralism).[88] For Lefebvre, the Commune of 1871 and May 1968[89] were calls for the right to the city because they combined revolutionary assertions to power and spatial centrality with a plurality of particular aspirations of segregated groups (workers, students, immigrants).[90] This implies a process by which claims of particular, peripheralized social groups "against discriminatory and segregative organization" are transformed into maximal claims to the "city" as "the centres of decision-making, wealth, power" and spatial centrality ("meeting places, gatherings," etc.).[91] This process of transformation takes on a spatial dialectic whereby dissociated, peripheralized spaces (popular suburbs) are reconnected in mobilizations to reclaim central spaces (Paris's Left Bank). In the disruptive moments[92] created by this spatial dialectic of mobilization, experiences of comradeship, festivity, and democratic community may liberate "parodies" of minimal difference and shatter the homogeneous-fragmented world of abstract space and linear time. In these moments, a "different"—creative, self-determined, fully lived—urban society is tangible.[93]

In retrospect, the claims to the city/difference of "1968" functioned more as a force of capitalist modernization than as a stimulus of counterhegemony. The mobilizations ultimately failed to energize potentially counterhegemonic (urban) strategies with longer time horizons.[94] Lefebvre anticipated this failure to some extent when he warned of the danger of reifying moments of spontaneity in street revolts. Without a capacity to transform the energies of short-term mobilization into a sustained urban strategy of transformation, differentialist claims could thus be appropriated by the state, the bourgeoisie, and urban specialists for a process of commodifying the very form of the urban as centrality/difference (see Chapter 17, this volume). Since the 1970s, calls for centrality, difference, and the ludic have reappeared as commodified traces in those areas of central Paris that have been gentrified and turned into "diversified museums" in yet another phase of cleaning up and reclaiming the central city.[95] The French state helped commodify the urban by combining its (increasingly) punitive arsenal of intervention with "softer" strategies of replanning suburbs, restructuring citizenship rights, and promoting "social inclusion" (and this sometimes with explicit reference to Lefebvrean concepts like centrality and festivality).[96] As a result of the displaced effects of oppositional claims, (minimal) difference under neo-Fordism has been a focal point in the reorganization of hegemony not only through the continuously decentralizing fragmentation of our conurbations but through bourgeois claims and lifestyles of urbanity as gentrified centrality/difference.[97] In this situation, oppositional strategies have counterhegemonic potential only if they transform (rather than only assert) the minimal differences of commodified festivality, multiculturalized ethnicity, and racialized suburban marginality.

CONCLUSION

From Lefebvre, we can gather a new, urbanized understanding of hegemony. While Gramsci saw hegemonic projects implicitly as alliances spanning socio-spatial divides at multiple scales (city and countryside, Italy's North and South, an unevenly developed international order), Lefebvre invites us to make an explicit link between hegemony and the production of space. Following Lefebvre, one may submit that, in advanced capitalism, hegemony is an incomplete, never fully total result of multidimensional (perceived, conceived, lived) processes and strategies of pro-ducing abstract space. The central, contradictory arena for potentially hegemonic projects of producing space is everyday life, or, more precisely, the point at which dominated aspects of lived space become integrated into the linear-repetitive rhythms of state, commodity, and technocratic knowledge. Processes of producing space (shaped by urban specialists) are potentially hegemonic insofar as they integrate the affective-symbolic sides of everyday life (lived space) into the practical-material (perceived) and institutional-ideological (conceived) dimensions of abstract space. This process of producing and incorporating lived space into abstract space can be hegemonic not by homogenizing diversity or denying différance, as post-marxists have it, but by incorporating particular kinds of minimal difference into the alienations of property, segregation and reified particularisms. Hegemonic projects in an urbanizing world are thus best captured as ways of absorbing everyday life and "minimizing" difference through the production of abstract space and linear time. In turn, oppositional projects become counterhegemonic to the extent that they connect revolutionary claims to decision-making and strategies that transform segregated, minimally different peripheries into quests for spatial centrality and maximally different, non-capitalist forms of everyday life.

How do these arguments demonstrate the relevance of a Gramsci-inspired theory and politics today? In light of Lefebvre's redirection of Gramsci, what are we to make of those arguments that contrast Gramsci's allegedly stodgy, state-centered legacy to the cutting-edge of contemporary anti-capitalist practice? Is it not true that within the range anti-globalization campaigns, Gramsci lives on in the least inspiring formations: the left-social democratic milieus or party-based alliances represented most prominently by French-based Attac and Brazil's Workers Party? This is certainly the implication of Michael Hardt and Antonio Negri's work, for whom the Gramscian legacy is necessarily tied to the very state-socialist, top-down, and productivist party communist trajectory Negri himself confronted in the form of the Italian Communist Party.[98] Going beyond Hardt and Negri's claim about the hegemony of immaterial labor within the "multitude," Richard Day counterposes the state-centrism of Gramsci (as well neo-Gramscians such as Laclau and Mouffe) to what he sees as more vibrant practices of self-organization, direct action, cultural subversion by the Black Bloc, the Earth Liberation Front, the Zapatistas, and the Argentinian Unemployed Workers Union. Day interprets these practices as expressions of a distinctly minoritarian, postmodern "ethic of affinity" that lends itself to building micro-political experiments in the here and now but abdicates horizons of large-scale, centered forms of revolutionary transformation.[99]

As we can see from Lefebvre, however, Gramscian themes are not inexorably state-centric (let alone Leninist). Like some exponents of contemporary anti-globalization politics, Lefebvre's socialism, while critical of anarchism, had an anarchist twist (un socialisme anarchisant). He was also uncomfortable with the officious use of Gramsci by the Stalinist parties of his time. But Lefebvre wanted us to take Gramsci into a decidedly non-Leninist direction. He refused to throw out the baby (a problematic of hegemony) with the bathwater (lingering state-centrism) and insisted that the former be tied to a critique of all things state-like and rallied to autogestion as an incarnation of revolutionary spontaneity and continuous projects of changing everyday life.[100] Lefebvre's view of hegemony as a complex combination of integration-homogenization and separation-fragmentation is thus sociological extension and politico-theoretical redirection of Gramsci. His reframing of hegemony as a production of urban space is tied to his epistemological critique of Gramsci's lack of distinction between marxism as dialectical method and marxism as party-dependent strategy. In Lefebvre, Gramsci lives on in clearly dialectical, differential, and anti-statist form. It is within this new left theoretical context that Lefebvre's urbanization of Gramsci's problematic of hegemony may be of promise for those hostile to Gramscian themes but otherwise committed to a marxist-influenced perspective of "changing the world without taking power."[101]

As other current voices against capitalist globalization have argued,[102] dissociating radical, alternative practices of self-determination from the question of hegemony is dangerous, however. Over the last decade, moments of mobilization (Los Angeles, 1992; Seattle, 1999; Genoa, 2001), social fora (Porto Alegre, Mumbai) and alternative micropractices (centri sociali, squats, self-managed enterprises) have provided only uneven counterweight to the forces of neo-imperial capitalism. Whether this indicates that in metropolitan centers of decision-making, power is based not only on coercion but on persuasion, as Lefebvre suspected long ago,[103] we cannot really know without linking the subjectivities of radical politics to an urbanized problematic of hegemony. While radical moments of mobilization demonstrate the possibility of revolutionary change, they can also provide the socio-cultural material for renewed hegemonic projects. The differential claims of 1968 and its aftermath, for example, now live on in the culturalized neo-racisms and commodified centralities of metropolitan life. More explicitly than during Fordism, the minimal differences of the current postmodern "era of difference" are central for hegemonic projects in a neo-imperial world that is otherwise characterized by a shift from consent to coercion (unilateralism, militarism, repression, exclusion). Tackling both consensual and coercive aspects of neo-imperial capitalism requires a protracted, dialectical urban strategy to link spectacular protests or promising subterranean practices with each other. Otherwise, radical spaces of experimentation risk being confined to the acutely segmented experiences that mediate the rapidly urbanizing world order today.

NOTES

1. This chapter is a substantially revised and rewritten version of a paper previously published as "Urbanization, Everyday Life and the Survival of Capitalism: Lefebvre, Gramsci and the Problematic of Hegemony," *Capitalism, Nature, Socialism* 13, no. 2 (2002): 117–49.
2. David Harvey, *Spaces of Hope* (Berkeley: University of California Press, 2000), 17; Leo Panitch and Sam Gindin, "Transcending Pessimism: Rekindling Socialist Imagination," *Socialist Register* (2000): 1–29.
3. David Harvey, *The New Imperialism* (Oxford: Oxford University Press, 2003).
4. Richard Day, *Gramsci Is Dead: Anarchist Currents in New Social Movements* (Toronto: Between the Lines, 2005).
5. Stefan Kipfer, *Urbanization, Difference, and Everyday Life: Lefebvre, Gramsci, Fanon and the Problematic of Hegemony*, Ph.D. dissertation, Department of Political Science, York University, Toronto (2004); and "Urbanization, Everyday Life and the Survival of Capitalism."

6. Henri Lefebvre, *The Production of Space*, trans. D. Nicholson-Smith (Oxford: Basil Blackwell, 1991), 10.

7. Esteve Morera, *Gramsci's Historicism* (New York: Routledge, 1990); Colin Sparks, "Stuart Hall, Cultural Studies and Marxism," in *Stuart Hall*, ed. D. Morley and Kaun-Hsing Chen (New York: Routledge, 1996); Himani Bannerji, "Pygmalion Nation: Towards a Critique of Subaltern Studies and the 'Resolution of the Women's Question,'" in *Of Property and Propriety*, ed. H. Bannerji, S. Mojab, and J. Whitehead (Toronto: University of Toronto Press, 2001); Peter Ives, *Language and Hegemony in Gramsci* (London: Pluto, 2004); Timothy Brennan, "The Southern Intellectual," in *Wars of Position* (New York: Columbia University Press, 2006), 233–72. But see Gillian Hart, "Changing Concepts of Articulation," *Review of African Political Economy* 111/85 (2007), 85–101.

8. Henri Lefebvre, *De l'État, tome II* (Paris: Union Générale d'Editions, 1976), 352–3, 63, 380–1.

9. *Ibid.*, 381.

10. *Ibid.*, 378–80.

11. For Lefebvre, this leads to an anti-ontological conception of communism and marxism not as being but as possibility and movement. See *Conversation avec Henri Lefebvre*, ed. P. Latour and F. Combes (Paris: Messidor, 1991), 65–6; *La somme et le reste* (Paris: Bélibaste, 1973), 341–2.

12. Lefebvre, *De l'État*, II, 378.

13. Henri Lefebvre, *Le Matérialisme Dialectique* (Paris: Presses Universitaires de France, 1971), 80, 105; *The Explosion: Marxism and the French Upheaval*, trans. A. Ehrenfeld (New York: Monthly Review Press, 1969 [1968]), 24, 34; *Le manifeste différentialiste* (Paris: Gallimard, 1970), 175–6, 186; *Introduction to Modernity*, trans. J. Moore (London: Verso, 1995), 3–5; "Toward a Leftist Cultural Politics," in *Marxism and the Interpretation of Culture*, ed. C. Nelson and L. Grossberg (Chicago: University of Illinois Press, 1988), 76.

14. Lefebvre, *La somme*, 189–91; also, *The Sociology of Marx*, trans. Norbert Guterman (Harmondsworth: Penguin, 1968), ch. 2.

15. Lefebvre, *De l'État*, II, 379, 383.

16. Henri Lefebvre, *Métaphilosophie* (Paris: Syllepse, 1997), 114–15; "State" (from *Le retour de la dialectique*, [1986]), in *Key Writings*, ed. S. Elden, E. Lebas, and E. Kofman (New York: Continuum, 2003), 61.

17. John Roberts, "Philosophizing the Everyday: The Philosophy of Praxis and the Fate of Cultural Studies," *Radical Philosophy* 98 (1999): 18–19.

18. Henri Lefebvre, *De l'État, tome III* (Paris: Union Générale d'Editions, 1977), 381–2.

19. Henri Lefebvre, *The Sociology of Marx*, trans. N. Guterman (New York: Columbia University Press, 1982), ch. 5.

20. Henri Lefebvre, *De l'État, tome IV* (Paris: Union Générale d'Editions, 1978), 402.

21. Henri Lefebvre, "Une interview d'Henri Lefebvre – débat sur le Marxisme: Leninisme–Stalinisme ou autogestion?," *Autogestion et socalisme* 33/4 (1976): 119–20.

22. Lefebvre, *De l'État*, II, 387.

23. *Ibid.*

24. Lefebvre took Poulantzas to task for his emphasis on the logical coherence of the state (*De l'État*, IV, 336–9).

25. *Ibid.*, 381.

26. *Ibid.*, 381–2, 393–5; see also "The State and Daily Life," in *The Critique of Everyday Life, Volume III*, trans. G. Elliott (London: Verso, 2005), 122–8.

27. Lefebvre, *De l'État*, IV, 270–1.

28. *Ibid.*, 261.

29. *Ibid.*, 381–2.

30. *Ibid.*, 388.

31. Roberts, "Philosophizing the Everyday," 19, 28; Edward Soja, *Postmodern Geographies* (London: Verso, 1989), 90–2.

32. Lefebvre, "Toward a Leftist Cultural Politics," 78; *La pensée marxiste de la ville* (Paris: Casterman, 1972), 52–8, 70, 106–7.

33. Lefebvre, *Métaphilosophie*, 115; David Cunningham, "The Concept of Metropolis: Philosophy and Urban Form," *Radical Philosophy* 133 (2005): 13–25.

34. Kristin Ross, "French Quotidian," in *The Art of the Everyday: The Quotidian in Postwar French Culture*, ed. L. Gumpert (New York: New York University Press, 1997), 26; Rémi Hess, *Henri Lefebvre et l'aventure du siècle* (Paris: Métailie, 1988), 288.

35. Henri Lefebvre and Norbert Guterman, "Mystification: Notes for a Critique of Everyday Life," in *Key Writings*, 71–83; Norbert Guterman and Henri Lefebvre, *La conscience mystifiée* (Paris: Syllepse, 1999).

36. Lefebvre, *La somme*, 271.

37. Henri Lefebvre, *The Critique of Everyday Life, Volume I*, trans. J. Moore (London: Verso, 1991), 14–22, 39, 61–2, 145–75, 98–9; *Everyday Life in the Modern World*, trans. S. Rabinovitch (Harmondsworth: Penguin, 1971), 33–7.

38. Lefebvre, *La pensée marxiste*, 79.

39. Henri Lefebvre, *L'idéologie structuraliste* (Paris: Anthropos, 1971), 192–3.

40. Lefebvre, *La somme*, 180, 263–4.

41. Roberts, "Philosophizing the Everyday," 18–19; see also Michael Gardiner's effective engagement with recent populist critics of Lefebvre's critical but nuanced, dialectical approach to everyday life, "Everyday Utopianism: Lefebvre and his Critics," *Cultural Studies* 18, no. 2/3 (2004): 228–54.

42. Lefebvre, "Toward a Leftist Cultural Politics," 87.

43. *Ibid.*, 262–3, 266.

44. Lefebvre, *Critique*, I, 89; *Critique of Everyday Life, Volume II* (London: Verso, 2003), 335.

45. *Ibid.*, 11, 14–15, 18, 21, 26, 132; *La somme*, 262.

46. Lefebvre, *Critique*, I, 32.

47. Lefebvre, *Everyday Life*, 109, 187.

48. *Ibid.*, 109.

49. Henri Lefebvre, *The Survival of Capitalism*, trans. F. Bryant (London: Alison and Busby, 1976), 66–7, 83, 88–9.

50. Lefebvre, *La somme*, 272.

51. Lefebvre, *Everyday Life*, 66.

52. Lefebvre, *Explosion*, 83.

53. Lefebvre, *Everyday Life*, 86–90, 98–106; *Critique*, I, 3, 21, 32–41, 206, 207, 187–8.

54. Henri Lefebvre, *Writings on Cities*, ed. and trans. E. Kofman and E. Lebas (Oxford: Blackwell, 1996), 185.

55. Lefebvre, *Production of Space*, 10. All other quotes in this paragraph are from pp. 10–11 of this translation.

56. *Ibid.*, 33–9, 41–3.

57. Lefebvre, *The Urban Revolution*, trans. R. Bononno (Minneapolis: University of Minnesota Press, 2003), 100–1; *The Survival*, 348–50.
58. Lefebvre, *Writings on Cities*, 101.
59. Lefebvre, *La pensée*, 128–30, 145–7; *The Survival*, 65–6.
60. Lefebvre, *Urban Revolution*, chs. 7, 8.
61. Lefebvre, *Urban Revolution*, 181–8.
62. Lefebvre, *Production of Space*, 395.
63. *Ibid.*, 372, 53.
64. *Ibid.*, 49–50; *Du rural à l'urbain* (Paris: Anthropos, 1970), 102.
65. Lefebvre, *Explosion*, 92–4.
66. Lefebvre, *Production of Space*, 383–4.
67. *Ibid.*, *Critique*, I, 7–10; *Everyday Life*, 150–1; *Le manifeste*, 141–3, 172–8, 233–4.
68. Ernesto Laclau and Chantal Mouffe, *Hegemony and Socialist Strategy: Towards a Radical Democratic Politics* (London: Verso, 1985), 139, 141, 143.
69. Lefebvre, *Métaphilosophie*, 228.
70. Jacques Derrida, "Différance," in *Margins of Philosophy*, trans. A. Bass (Chicago: University of Chicago Press, 1982), 7–13.
71. Eleonore Kofman and Elizabeth Lebas, "Lost in Transposition," in Lefebvre, *Writings on Cities*. Peter Osborne has brilliantly captured Derrida's linguistic essentialism that animates Laclau and Mouffe. See "Radicalism without Limit?," in *After the Fall: Socialism and the Limits of Liberalism*, ed. P. Osborne (1991), 213–17.
72. Lefebvre, *Le manifeste*, 162–6.
73. Edward Soja, *Thirdspace* (Oxford: Blackwell, 1996), 86–7; Doreen Massey, "Thinking Radical Democracy Spatially," *Environment and Planning D* 13 (1995): 283–8.
74. Lefebvre, *L'idéologie*, 86–8.
75. Lefebvre, *Production of Space*, 63.
76. *Ibid.*, 385.
77. Laclau and Mouffe, *Hegemony and Socialist Strategy*, 30–1; Chantal Mouffe, *On the Political* (New York: Routledge, 2005), 118, 17.
78. *Ibid.*, 372.
79. Lefebvre, *Le manifeste*, 70, 134, 145–51.
80. *Ibid.*, 84–91, 97–9, 127–9, 159, 161–6; *Explosion*, 92–5.
81. Lefebvre, *Le manifeste*, 122–9, 172–3; *Production of Space*, 370–91; *Writings on Cities*, 196, 231, 239.
82. Lefebvre, *Production of Space*, 373–4.
83. Lefebvre, *Critique*, III, 111–12.
84. Lefebvre, *Production of Space*, 64.
85. *Ibid.*, 373.
86. *Ibid.*, 64, 55.
87. Lefebvre, *Urban Revolution*, 117–20.
88. Attempts by scholars of citizenship to pluralize the notion of "the right to the city" into "rights to the city" are incompletely dissociated from such group pluralist views (which paradoxically return to a form of state-dependence by short-circuiting the all-pervasiveness of the state-like against which Lefebvre's term was also directed). The concept right to the city (in the singular) does not deny the possibility of a plurality of struggles but proposes that the spatial form of struggle (dialectical relationships of centrality and periphery) may be crucial in linking and transforming such a plurality of claims for social power and against segregation.

89. See *Explosion* and *La Proclamation de la Commune* (Paris: Gallimard, 1965).

90. Lefebvre, *Critique*, III, 105–10; *Explosion*, 94; *Le manifeste*, 42–5; *Writings on Cities*, 196.

91. *Ibid.*, 195; *Explosion*, 91–100, 104–10, 116–19, 137–9.

92. On moments as disruptions of linear time (which is a spatialized sequence of reproducible time-fragments, "instants"), see Lefebvre, *La somme*, 295–313, and *Critique*, II, 340–58).

93. Lefebvre, *Urban Revolution*, 99–100; *De l'État*, III, 373–4.

94. Lefebvre, *Explosion*, 74–4. Lefebvre repeatedly insisted that if revolution is to be conceived also as a revolutionary change in everyday life and lived space/time, it must adopt such a patient, longer-term strategy to deal with the tenacity and thickness of everyday life; see *Critique*, I, 49, 56–7, 151; "Space: Social Product and Use Value," in *Critical Sociology*, ed. J. W. Freiberg (New York: Irvington, 1979), 285. His call for an urban strategy against the political and epistemological dimensions of urbanism in *The Urban Revolution* (ch. 7) reflects this rather Gramscian sense of revolutionary change as an interplay of multiple temporalities.

95. Lefebvre, *Critique*, III, 105–9, 161; *Writings on Cities*, 209–11.

96. Jean-Pierre Garnier, "La vision urbaine de Henri Lefebvre: des prévisions aux révisions," *Espaces et Sociétés* 76 (1994): 123–45; Kofman and Lebas, "Lost in Transposition," 35–6; Liette Gilbert and Mustafa Dikeç, this volume.

97. Walter Prigge, "Hegemonie des Urbanistischen Diskurses," in *Die Materialität des Städtischen*, ed. Prigge (Basel: Birkhäuser, 1987), 177–96.

98. Michael Hardt and Antonio Negri, *Empire* (Cambridge, MA: Harvard University Press, 2000), 383; Michael Hardt, "Porto Alegre: Today's Bandung?," in *New Left Review* 14 (2002), 112–18.

99. Day, *Gramsci Is Dead*.

100. Lefebvre, "Problèmes théoriques de l'autogestion," *Autogestion* 1 (1966): 59–70.

101. John Holloway, *Change the World without Taking Power: The Meaning of Revolution Today* (London: Pluto, 2005).

102. Ulrich Brand, *Gegenhegemonie: Perspektiven globalisierungskritischer Strategien* (Hamburg: VSA, 2005).

103. Lefebvre, *Writings on Cities*, 161.

13

TOTALITY, HEGEMONY, DIFFERENCE
Henri Lefebvre and Raymond Williams[1]
Andrew Shmuely

TRACING THE CONSTELLATION

Henri Lefebvre and Raymond Williams died within a few short years of one another.[2] Having lived through most of what Eric Hobsbawm was later to call "the short twentieth century,"[3] they spent the duration of their lives trying to come to terms with the immense social, political, and cultural shifts ushered in through the arrival of the "modern world." At a glance, despite the geographic and contextual gulf between them—Lefebvre escaping his Jesuit upbringing in the south of France to study philosophy at the Sorbonne in Paris; Williams, the working-class son of a railway signalman, leaving the Welsh border town he grew up in for Cambridge as a "scholarship boy"[4]—their biographical similarities prove striking.

To begin with, it can be noted that both thinkers were significantly marked by the experience of war. As Lefebvre was helping the resistance movement to "derail enemy trains" and hunt down Nazi "collaborators,"[5] Williams was serving as an anti-tank captain in the British army. It is likely that these circumstances contributed not only to their spirited activism—recall their shared interest in anti-colonial politics (Algeria and Vietnam) and parallel engagements with May 1968—but also to their mutual distrust of unwieldy and oppressive state structures and concomitant preference for some form of "self-management."

It can also be claimed that both scholars were "men of frontiers." Eleonore Kofman and Elizabeth Lebas have pointed out that Lefebvre must have been thinking of himself when he wrote that "only the man apart, the marginal, the peripheral

. . . has a creative capacity . . . [as] he is both inside and outside, included and excluded."[6] Similarly, David Harvey has alluded to the unique insights harnessed by Williams as a result of the both literal and metaphorical "borderland space" he inhabited.[7] This common sense of critical distance pushed them to look all the more vigilantly for the contradictory relations that bind social reality together: instilling in both thinkers a profound commitment to the concept of *totality* in all of its many guises.

This, of course, brings us to the place of Marx in each of their respective oeuvres. If Lefebvre's adherence to a distinctly open brand of Marxism was established early on in his career—in the late 1920s, through an affair with Hegel and the Surrealists, and his involvement with the *Philosophies* group[8]—then Williams's relationship with Marx was more gradual in its evolution, and sober in its tone. Accordingly, while Lefebvre was heralding the "explosive" arrival of urban society,[9] Williams was contemplating a much different form of "long revolution":[10] one that shied away from a Marxian emphasis on "confrontation" and "struggle."[11] From the 1970s onwards, however—as Williams became more familiar with the works of the likes of Lucien Goldman and Antonio Gramsci—we find him engaging with a series of theoretical and practical concerns in a manner that dovetails with Lefebvre's own sensibilities in ways that this chapter will attempt to map in some detail.

After commencing with an exposition of the idea of *totality* through the eyes of Lefebvre, this chapter will unfold by considering how he and Williams made use of this crucial notion to, first, surmount the problems posed by the base-superstructure model, and, second, come to a (decidedly open and contingent) theory of *hegemony*. After dwelling on their respective understandings of this decisive concept, it will proceed by assessing how their schematics come together in a dialectic of *difference* and *recuperation*. Lastly, it will offer an evaluation of their shared perspectives on the problem of *counterhegemony*: aiming to illuminate not only their common aspirations, but also their penetrating reflections on the existing state of (what's left of) the "left."

It has been made apparent by the editors of this volume that this book seeks to offer something of a "third reading" of Lefebvre's work: one that clears a path between an entirely admirable, if somewhat limiting *political-economic* interpretation on the one hand, and a rather less inspiring *post-structuralist* appropriation on the other. Of course, this division is in no way arbitrary; it speaks volumes about the polarized coordinates of the contemporary left as a whole. On this matter, consider Terry Eagleton's assessment:

> It would sometimes seem today that a commitment to class struggle on the one hand, and a celebration of difference and plurality on the other, have been linked up on opposite sides of the left political fence. Yet both ways of thinking

would seem to have subtly coexisted in your own work almost from the beginning. You've always deeply suspected closed, monolithic theories and strategies, and from the outset your socialism has stressed difficulty, complexity, variety.[12]

While these remarks were made explicitly of Williams, they could just as easily have been made of Lefebvre. Both thinkers were unwavering in their attempts to supersede the false binary that would situate an allegiance to class politics over and against a devotion to difference; and more than anything, it is this underlying point of convergence that I hope most forcefully emerges in the exposition below.

TOTALITY, LEVELS, MEDIATION

Lefebvre can be found engaging with the concept of totality in the two fundamental senses it has generally assumed throughout the history of Marxist thought.[13] On the one hand, he deploys it *normatively*, as a type of utopian longing for a radically different way of being.[14] On the other, he employs it *descriptively*, as an epistemological sensibility, in order to grasp the complexity and interrelatedness of social life under global capitalism. "Without this concept," he observes in the second volume of his *Critique of Everyday Life*, "there can be no frame of reference; no generality, and even more, no universality."[15]

Lefebvre is as vehemently opposed to the fragmentation of *knowledge* as he is to the specialization of practical and aesthetic activity. If the social division of labor is found to impose an alienating and reductive force on the individual human subject, then it is also seen to bring about similar results in the realm of thought itself. We thus find him lamenting the compartmentalized nature of disciplines and studies that would carve up human phenomena into "myriad isolated, empirical facts."[16] Accordingly, he is equally dismayed by the concomitant *relativism* that inevitably follows from such "anti-totalizing" approaches, noting that in "an empiricism without concepts, one fact is as good as another."[17] In losing sight of the "whole," what is lost is nothing less than the very "object" of investigation itself: "[w]hen we try to particularize knowledge, we destroy it from within."[18]

While it should be obvious that the idea of totality occupies a fundamental place in Lefebvre's conceptual arsenal, it would be wrong to infer—as so many "post-thinkers" have been inclined to do—that its use somehow precludes an adequate understanding of the contingent nature of social reality. Completely refuting the notion of a preexisting or inevitable historical telos,[19] Lefebvre's "metaphilosophical" approach appropriates the concept of totality both *critically* and *dialectically*. Noting its tendency "to absorb particularities and specificities, and therefore to neglect differences and types,"[20] he readily acknowledges the "almost insurmountable difficulties" behind its deployment, asking:

Are we *inside* a totality? Which one? Bourgeois society? Industrial society? Technological society? Society in transition (but to where)? How can we determine a totality *from inside*? . . . In any event, how could we determine a totality if we take up a position *outside* of it, be it from this side or that?[21]

But if the amount of philosophical resilience required to face these challenging questions head-on made it all the more inviting for some to consign them to the dustbin of history, it only pushed Lefebvre to think them through all the more rigorously. He developed an increasingly *partial* and *open-ended* understanding of the social totality, coming to view it as a never-ending and dynamic spatio-temporal process of creation-negation. This is briefly implied in the second volume of his *Critique* by the shorthand formula, "realization/fragmentary totalization/breaking of the totality";[22] but it is more sufficiently developed in *The Production of Space*, wherein it is alleged:

The notion of *centrality* replaces the notion of *totality*, repositioning it, relativizing it, and rendering it dialectical. Any centrality, once established, is destined to suffer dispersal, to dissolve or to explode from the effects of saturation, attrition, outside aggressions, and so on. This means that the "real" can never become completely fixed, that it is constantly in a state of mobilization.[23]

In this manner, we find Lefebvre preserving a necessarily *relational* understanding of complex phenomena *while at the same time* avoiding the pitfalls of overly systemic thinking.

At this point, however, a decisive, if deceptively banal, methodological question immediately suggests itself: how might we effectively explore a particular avenue of inquiry without abandoning a commitment to totality? Lefebvre found his answer in the idea of the *level*. In the midst of a detailed consideration in the second volume of his *Critique*—possibly his most steadfastly analytical work—he tells us that levels "contribute towards expressing a complexity which is differentiated and yet structured within a whole (a totality)."[24] "Wherever there is a level," he writes, "there are several levels, and consequently gaps, (relatively) sudden transitions, and imbalances or potential imbalances between those levels."[25] While refuting the idea of a "continuous field"—such as the supposedly "smooth space of Empire" in the work of Michael Hardt and Antonio Negri[26]—Lefebvre nevertheless underscores the fact that "[l]evels cannot be completely disassociated one from the other."[27] Regarding the crucial notion of *mediation*—in this context, a reference to both the "interpenetration" *between* levels and also *within* any given level—he asserts that "levels can interact and become telescoped, with differing results according to what the encounters and circumstances are."[28] Finally, and most critically, Lefebvre posits that "[a]t one particular moment of becoming . . . *one level can dominate and incorporate the others.*"[29]

REARTICULATING THE BASE: FROM TOTALITY TO HEGEMONY

The idea that one level of social reality could come to dominate another has loomed large in the history of Marxist theory, particularly in the form of a vulgar, but regrettably widespread, (mis)interpretation of Marx regarding the relationship between a society's "determining" base (often synchronically reified at the level of the economy alone) and its "determined" superstructure (usually perceived as a mixed bag of political, ideological, and juridical apparatuses that some have even attempted to rank in relation to the base itself). Of course, it should be obvious that this form of "systematization" is not quite what Lefebvre had in mind regarding the relationship between the levels of a given totality; and it is on these grounds that we find his thoughts converging with the equally nuanced efforts of Raymond Williams.

Opposing the "totality of social practices" to the "layered notion of a base and a superstructure"[30] in order to focus on the irreducible role of "real cultural activities"[31] in the production and reproduction of social life, Williams observed that while Marx's truncated elaborations on the base-superstructure theme were ambiguous at best, they were always rooted in a *relational* context: a fact that was surely lost on those who attempted to develop them into a static model that allowed for the *separation* of human activity into discrete categories. In the resulting "transition from Marx to Marxism,"[32] the "base" became a fixed and inflexible concept that betrayed "Marx's central emphasis on productive *activities*."[33] To correct this error, Williams transformed it back into a dynamic *process* that Marx would have recognized. In so doing, he included within it a much broader array of social forces and practices, in effect reclaiming a substantial degree of phenomena once deemed to be "merely" superstructural.

It is in this sense that we find Williams turning toward a theory of totality, save for one important caveat: the idea of *determination*. Although this was a concept he substantially reworked—leaving behind the idea of "an external cause which totally predicts or prefigures" in favor of "a notion of determination as setting limits, exerting pressures"[34]—it was nonetheless one he refused to dispose of. "If totality is simply concrete," he argued, "if it is simply the recognition of a large variety of miscellaneous and contemporaneous practices, then it is essentially empty of any content that can be called Marxist."[35] What he therefore endeavored to attach to the concept of totality was a more acute emphasis on *social intention* and the *class character* of certain practices, forms of knowledge, and "structures of feeling";[36] and it was with this "synthesis" in mind that he came critically to appropriate Gramsci's notion of *hegemony*.

Before going any further, however, it should be acknowledged that Lefebvre employed a strategy that is in many ways comparable, if not outright equivalent, to the one depicted above. Indeed, we have already seen how Lefebvre utilized the idea of totality without sacrificing the problematic of domination; but we have yet to explore how he too rearticulated the base to focus on a much broader segment of lived experience. To do so, we need to turn to the subject that preoccupied him more than any other: (the critique of) *everyday life*. The profundity of this level in Lefebvre's oeuvre can perhaps best be illustrated through a fundamental image he utilized on many occasions: that of the *soil* upon which all other levels of social reality are rooted. While we find this crucial metaphor deployed as early the first volume of his *Critique*,[37] it would be some thirty years before it ripened to full maturity.

In *The Survival of Capitalism*, first published in 1973, we come across an illuminating reference to the everyday as "the greatest weight" and "the very soil on which the great architectures of politics and society rise up,"[38] along with the more direct assertion that "[t]he everyday, and not the economic in general, is the level at which neo-capitalism has been able to establish itself."[39] By the time of the third volume of his *Critique*, he presents his (much evolved) thesis with heightened clarity and vigor. The passage is worth quoting at length, as it not only captures the affinities he shares with Williams, but also paves the way to his own distinctive approach to the problematic of hegemony:

> The state is now built upon daily life; its base is the everyday. The traditional Marxist thesis makes the relations of production and productive forces the "base" of the ideological and political superstructures. Today—that is to say, now that the state ensures the administration of society, as opposed to letting social relations, the market and blind forces take their course—this thesis is reductionist and inadequate . . . Daily life and people in daily life still perceive the institutional edifice above their heads . . . In daily life, these believers do not realize that they *are* the soil on which the edifice rests and bears down. With all their gestures, words and habits, they preserve and support the edifice.[40]

If Williams expanded the base by subsuming within it a number of social and cultural practices from the domain of lived experience, Lefebvre proceeded analogously by equating the base with the level of everyday life itself. And while it would be careless to wrest the above remarks from the historical context in which they emerged (France on the eve of the "technocratic" left's rise to power), it can nevertheless be claimed that they described a situation general enough to the conditions of advanced capitalism that Williams was able to make similar comments from the viewpoint of an entirely separate national context.

DOMINANT, RESIDUAL, EMERGENT

For Williams, the idea of hegemony conveys how dominant social groups maintain their ascendancy over subordinate classes in the lived experiences of everyday life, *while at the same time* referring to the way in which those subordinate classes consent to their being ruled as such in the first place. Accordingly, he is careful to separate hegemony from *ideology*, because "[w]hat is decisive is not only the conscious system of ideas and beliefs, but the whole lived social process as practically organized by specific and dominant meanings and values."[41] Thus, hegemonic relations are not simply produced by—or are the result of—a decidedly *idealist* phenomenon like "false consciousness." Instead, they are implicated *materially* in the relations of power that permeate every aspect of lived experience.

Of course, Williams's dynamic view of the social totality—an undeniably similar outlook to Lefebvre's—kept him from envisioning the hegemony of any given dominant group as hermetically sealed. As a contingent network of social relations and productive forces, he tells us that hegemony "does not just passively exist as a form of dominance. It has continually to be renewed, recreated, defended, and modified."[42] This remark proves crucial; because if the hegemony of a dominant group is always, to a certain extent, in a state of flux, then it follows that it can be "resisted, limited, altered, [and] challenged by pressures not at all its own."[43] We here find Williams implicitly agreeing with Lefebvre's recoding of totality in terms of *centrality*, as he tells us that "in any society, in any particular period, there is a central system of practices, meanings and values, which we can properly call dominant and effective."[44] Meanwhile, what the center denies—that is to say, what it cannot *incorporate*—remains confined to the margins "outside" its purview of dominance.

Williams creates two intersecting ideal-type dichotomies to refer to those marginalized elements that manage to "slip through the cracks," as it were. In the first, *residual* and *emergent* cultures are contrasted, with the former described as "survivals" from previously dominant social formations, and the latter based on "new meanings and values, new practices, [and] new significances and experiences [that] are continually being created."[45] In the second, *alternative* cultures are portrayed as those that deviate from a given dominant group—but nevertheless do so without challenging their place in the social hierarchy—whereas truly *oppositional* cultures are those that attempt to engage directly with the hegemonic formation for a position of centrality.

To give a somewhat unorthodox example of how these categories relate to the domain of lived experience, they can fruitfully be applied to Lefebvre's short but lucid *Notes on the New Town*, wherein he offers a poetic juxtaposition of two social and spatial formations.[46] The first, Naverrenx, a quiet and antiquated village near the Pyrenees where Lefebvre came of age, can be labeled *residual-alternative*. The second, Mourenx, a Corbusian industrial settlement that appeared in the 1950s to house those working in the oil fields at nearby Lacq, can be called—with some reservations—*emergent-oppositional*. Describing the dynamic of the former, Lefebvre likens it to that of the "natural" relationship between a seashell and the creature housed within: an organic and spontaneous secretion of space through time. "Look closely," he tells us, "and within every house you will see the slow, mucous trace of this animal which transforms the chalk in the soil around it into something delicate and structured: a family."[47] And yet, despite this apparently nostalgic, *Gemeinschaft*-like outlook, he is quick to emphasize that the social and cultural context from which Naverrenx emerged has *itself* become residual: "ever more distant from us as the years pass by."[48] While the boredom that has settled over Naverrenx is still infused with the sounds and smells of a life worth living, its time is seen to have passed: "[t]he expiring seashell lies shattered and open to the skies."[49] Increasingly irrelevant in a rapidly changing world, it is content to lumber on, "vegetating and emptying, like so many other dying towns."[50]

Conversely, while many commentators have pointed out Lefebvre's unrepentant hostility toward the stifling urbanism that Mourenx so vividly represents, they are often less inclined to notice that the dialectical subtleties behind his critical analysis generally betray an *affirmative* stance to the forces of modernity in general. Thus, we are told that it is the boredoms of the *new town* that are "pregnant with desires, frustrated frenzies, [and] unrealized possibilities."[51] It is in this experimental "laboratory," he thinks, that new forms of social existence will emerge to "face up to the challenge" of our era.[52] And while this is not to say that the new town is "oppositional" in its own right, it is to suggest that the new town creates the conditions from which an oppositional culture could arise. "[W]e will not find a style for our age in a place like this," alleges Lefebvre, "[b]ut we will find the way towards it."[53]

Before leaving behind Williams's topology of hegemony, it is vital that we introduce a final, critical component in the notion of *incorporation*. Aside from brute force—which would, in any case, fall outside the jurisdiction of hegemony in the strict sense[54]—history has surely revealed that a dominant formation's most successful strategy regarding those who would "question or threaten its dominance"[55] can be found in the attempt to incorporate their views and practices in a manner that effectively diffuses them of their revolutionary potential: a perverse "negation of the negation" that allows the reigning relations of power to remain fundamentally unaltered. And so much the better, notes Williams, if this can be accomplished *ideologically*, so as to conceal the instrumental nature of the incorporation behind a façade of recognition and acceptance.[56]

A salient example of the phenomenon in question materializes in Kristin Ross's incisive account of May 1968,[57] wherein she describes how capitalist society in France subsumed the myriad and vociferous demands to *changer la vie* by presenting itself not as their brutal and repressive negation—a more accurate representation, in any case—but, instead, as the triumphant culmination of their very aspirations. In this way, the "official story" depoliticized the event and rendered it both familial and pathological; it eventually came to serve as an "affirmation of the status quo," thereby banishing the tumultuous occasion's social and political contradictions to the outermost margins of historical memory.[58]

Of course, this particular occurrence resonates strongly with Williams's rather sobering observation that

> the dominant culture reaches much further than ever before in capitalist society into hitherto "reserved" or "resigned" areas of experience and practice and meaning. The area of effective penetration of the dominant order into the whole social and cultural process is thus now significantly greater.[59]

To use the language of Guy Debord, we could say that Williams is here speaking of the dominant culture's "colonization of social life":[60] a strategy of inward-facing imperialism that emerged as a supplemental alternative on the eve of decolonization. In fact, this was a diagnosis that Lefebvre also emphatically proposed. In the second volume of his *Critique*, we find him speaking approvingly of Debord's use of the colonization motif in the context of everyday life under the thumb of state capitalism.[61] It would thus seem that Lefebvre and Williams are essentially in agreement here; but in order to avoid overstating the case, it is necessary to consider just how they might differ.

SPATIAL DIALECTICS: FROM HEGEMONY TO THE RIGHT TO DIFFERENCE

The foremost divergence between Williams and Lefebvre on the hegemonic process turns on the different levels of emphasis they each place on space and time. While the former conceived of the antagonistic relationship between dominant, residual, and emergent cultures in a basically temporal framework,[62] the latter moved to connect the notion of hegemony explicitly to the bourgeoisie's prevailing *spatial* practices,[63] asking:

> Is it conceivable that the exercise of hegemony might leave space untouched? Could space be nothing more than the passive locus of social relations, the milieu in which their combination takes on the body, or the aggregate of procedures employed in their removal? The answer must be no.[64]

Perhaps overemphasizing the severity of the transition—Neil Smith has rightly noted that he "is always suggestive, reaching, pushing his argument farther than he would later want to go in order to get a point out"[65]—we find Lefebvre making this radical, almost scandalous truth claim: "[T]*he dialectic is no longer attached to temporality* . . . To recognize space, to recognize what 'takes place' there and what it is used for, is to resume the dialectic; analysis will reveal the contradictions of space."[66] On this matter, Kanishka Goonewardena provides us with a fruitful way to proceed in his insightful reading of *The Urban Revolution*, wherein he discusses the pivotal, mediating role played by the specifically "urban" level (M) in the two (conflicting) socio-spatial trajectories—from "global" (G) to "private" (P) and back again— that ultimately demarcate the very horizons of hegemonic struggle in Lefebvre's oeuvre.[67] On the one hand, we bear witness to the uneasy alliance between capital and the state at level G: a strategic assemblage that attempts to dominate everyday life at level P by controlling the urban "battlefield" at level M. On the other hand, we are reminded that in Lefebvre's "vision of the struggle for socialism," level P's revolutionary capabilities and practices can affect level G "primarily but not exclusively" through the occupation and defense of level M (hence the provocative title he gave to his book).[68]

Regarding the first of these trajectories, Lefebvre provides a series of paradoxical metaphors to illuminate its underlying dynamic. The most suggestive of these falls under the rubric of "implosion–explosion,"[69] but there are numerous variants throughout all of his explicitly spatial works.[70] Confined to the urban alone, this formula implies a benign and predominantly descriptive significance, entailing both a *concentration* of various phenomena ("people, activities, wealth, goods, objects, instruments, means, and thought") as well as their simultaneous *dispersion* into space (in the form of "peripheries, suburbs, vacation homes, [and] satellite towns").[71] But taken in conjunction with the motivations of the global, this process unfolds its patently *ideological* dimensions, unveiling "neo-capitalism's" two-pronged strategy of *internal colonization* (the invasion of everyday life by "the bureaucratic society of controlled consumption"),[72] and *external segregation* (the "expulsion of whole groups towards the spatial, mental, and social peripheries").[73]

Like Williams, Lefebvre is quick to emphasize just how much further the forces of state capitalism have managed to penetrate into the stronghold of the everyday; but in positing the urban as the central intermediary between them, the latter highlighted the irreducibly spatial nature of their struggle. Consequently, he gave the term *abstract space* to refer to those "lethal" territories that obliterate "the historical conditions that give rise to [them]," including even their "own (*internal*) differences, and any such differences that show signs of developing, in order to impose an abstract homogeneity."[74] Indeed, he posited as their endgame nothing less than "the removal of every obstacle in the way of the total elimination of what is different."[75]

For Lefebvre, this is the absolute "ground zero" of hegemony, as abstract space "depends on consensus more than any space before it."[76] Through the "reproduction of the relations of reproduction,"[77] it preemptively attempts to quash whatever differential ruptures might arise in order to secure its rule indefinitely. However, by way of an abrupt shift in subject-positions, Lefebvre turns this problem on its head:

> If it is true that [the] reproduction of the relations of production is the result of a strategy and not of a preexisting system, and that it is an attempt to constitute this system rather than to ratify it, then it follows that the "real" cannot be enclosed . . . There can be no reproduction of social relations either by simple inertia or by tacit renewal.[78]

Once again, we find his observations in agreement with those of Williams, who maintains that "[t]he reality of any hegemony, in the extended political and cultural sense, is that, while by definition it is always dominant, it is never either total or exclusive."[79]

Ascendant social formations—and the abstract spaces they seek to maintain—are never wholly successful in achieving their ultimately reductive aims; because within those areas of human activity they inevitably attempt to normalize, there are "other forces on the boil,"[80] and "[t]hese seething forces are still capable of rattling the lid of the cauldron . . . for differences can never be totally quieted. Though defeated, they live on, and from time to time they begin fighting ferociously to reassert themselves and transform themselves through struggle."[81] Indeed, for Lefebvre, the very concept of "difference" is all but fused to the notion of (counterhegemonic) "struggle." As Kofman and Lebas note, "[h]e insists that difference is not based on particularity, originality, or individualism; it emerges from struggle, conceptual and lived."[82] Accordingly, in Lefebvre's own, prescient words, we are told that "[t]he right to difference implies no elements that do not have to be bitterly fought for."[83]

DIFFERENCE AND RECUPERATION; OR, REINTEGRATING THE TEMPORAL

It needs to be emphasized that Lefebvre's way of dealing with difference is worlds apart from the (in)famous articulations of his post-structuralist counterparts. While many of the latter have tended to conceive of difference as something like a quasi-transcendental, a priori category that establishes the conditions of possibility for virtually anything that might contingently emerge, Lefebvre maintains that difference can *never* be posited at an ontologically constitutive level. On the contrary, it is something that emerges *dialectically*—after the fact—in the struggle between any number of *particularities*.

Lefebvre tells us that particularities "are defined by nature and by the relation of the (social) human being to this nature";[84] they are always already-existing distinctions that are understood as "given and determinate."[85] Differences, in contrast, are thought never to be isolated in and of themselves. Emerging from the antagonistic articulations between the various particularities within a given totality, they are purely *social* and entirely *relational*. Consider this passage from the third volume of Lefebve's *Critique*:

> Particularities confront one another in struggles which run through history, and are simultaneously struggles between ethnic groups, peoples, and classes or class fractions. It is in the course of these struggles that differences are born out of particularities; they *emerge*.[86]

It should be understood that Lefebvre here utilizes the word "emerge" in a sense that is entirely analogous to Williams's idea of "emergent" formations. He was, in fact, overstating the case when he claimed that the dialectic had abandoned time in favor of space, as there is a definite *diachronic* dimension inherent to the break he poses between particularities and differences.

Lefebvre is also quick to point out that particularities can *suppress* differences, noting that "[t]he victory of a particularism abolishes difference and replaces it with a return to the natural, the original, affirmed and valorized as such."[87] Moreover, he claims that "[t]o assert particularities as such under the guise of differences sanctions racism, sexism, separations and disjunctions."[88] In this context, it needs to be stressed that dominant formations effectively "function" as veiled particularities, as they, first, attempt to eliminate even the possibility of difference by presenting themselves as natural and thus inevitable; and, second, assert particularities as such under the guise of differences by incorporating the latter into their homogeneous structure of rule, thus emptying them of whatever differential "content" they might have possessed in the first place. While we have already seen precisely how this occurs in Williams's conceptual schema, it should prove instructive to see just how close Lefebvre comes to reflect his views in toto.

Stefan Kipfer has rightly dwelled on Lefebvre's distinction between *minimal* (or *induced*) differences, on the one hand, and *maximal* (or *produced*) differences, on the other.[89] The former are strictly analogous to what Williams deems *incorporated*, or having been brought under the control of a dominant power, while the latter remain *non-incorporated*, as alternative or oppositional practices that have managed to elude its hegemonic grasp. Viewed synchronically, this is all well and good; however, taken diachronically, especially in relation to once disruptive but now subdued events like May 1968, the key question becomes: *how are produced-maximal differences effectively transformed into induced-minimal ones?* Lefebvre responds by inflecting his spatial schematic of hegemony with a more temporally anchored dialectic of difference and recuperation.

Specifically defining the phenomenon of *recuperation*, Lefebvre alleges that it is what occurs when an idea or project regarded as irredeemably revolutionary or subversive—that is to say, on the point of introducing a discontinuity—is normalized, reintegrated into the existing order, and even revives it. Shaken for a brief moment, the social relations of production—that is to say, domination—are reinforced.[90]

After implicating Marxism, the urban question, and difference in general, Lefebvre cites as the most exemplary case of recuperation nothing other than *the critique of everyday life itself*:

This formula—which, to start off with, was disturbing and subversive, albeit vague—was then adopted and adapted on all sides, banalized, recuperated by advertising as well as political parties, and ended up being blunted and flattened into "quality of life" . . . In lieu of changing life, the image of life was changed![91]

And is this not entirely aligned with what Williams has termed *incorporation?* In each case, we are faced with the exact process by which an emergent-oppositional formation is swallowed up and rendered ineffectual by the hegemonic order. On this matter, we find Lefebvre and Williams in staunch accord: both *theoretically*—with the former claiming that "[d]ifferences are replaced by differential signs, so that produced differences are supplanted in advance by differences which are induced,"[92] and the latter warning that "[e]lements of emergence may indeed be incorporated, but just as often the incorporated forms are merely facsimiles of the genuinely emergent cultural practice"[93]—and *empirically*, given their mutual focus on changes to the domain of *leisure* as a vital incorporative-recuperative gesture on behalf of state-capitalist hegemony.[94]

A QUESTION OF ALLIANCES: MOVING BEYOND THE (MILITANTLY) PARTICULAR

Differences endure or arise on the margins of the homogenized realm, either in the form of resistances or in the form of externalities . . . Sooner or later, however, the existing centre and the forces of homogenization must seek to absorb all such differences, and they will succeed if these retain a defensive posture and no counterattack is mounted from their side. In the latter event, centrality and normality will be tested as to the limits of their power to integrate, to recuperate, or to destroy what has transgressed.[95]

How, then, to conceive of—and properly *actualize*—the "counterattack" alluded to above? For his part, Lefebvre was relentless in asserting the need for a "total project" that "expressly proposes a radically different way of living."[96] This inevitably entailed "a critique of politics in general, of politics and parties in particular, of the existing state and every state."[97] It meant the (critical) affirmation of "self management," and it strived to establish both "the right to the city" and the "right to difference" on an unprecedented scale. As for Williams, he too believed in "the distinctive principle of *maximum self management*."[98] He put his faith in a "socialist democracy . . . built from direct social relations," wherein power would be located "in the base" and "at the grassroots."[99]

What both thinkers have in mind here, then, goes against the grain not only of state capitalism in all of its reactionary variations, but also of two entirely separate strands of the so-called leftist alternative: namely, a heavily bureaucratized, "technocratic socialism" as exemplified by Mitterand's France; and those social and theoretical formations that would refute any conception of totality, choosing instead to focus on the fragments at the margins alone. In the first instance, they strongly object to state socialism's uncritical acceptance of the ideology of "development" and "growth."[100] In trying to outplay capitalism at its own game, it is seen to have displayed "a monstrous lack of vitality, imagination, or social creativity."[101] As for the second case, Lefebvre's critique is sympathetic but incisive, as he observes how the "anti-totalizing" strategy on which they inevitably rely brings about

> a lot of pin-prick operations that are separated from each other in time and space. It neglects the centres and centrality; it neglects the global . . . So long as the centres and centrality remain stable or reconstitute themselves, the pin-prick operations can be beaten off one by one.[102]

Of course, Lefebvre is *deeply* concerned with "those groups which central power has rejected and thrown back into the mental, social, and spatial peripheries,"[103] considering their struggles to be "of the greatest possible interest."[104] But his intervention here is to ensure that they do not retreat upon their own *particularities* in the midst of their concrete efforts at fighting back.

On this point, we find Lefebvre approximating Williams's critique of "militant particularism": a phenomenon that occurs when "[i]deals forged out of the affirmative experience of solidarities in one place get generalized and universalized as a working model for a new form of society that will benefit all of humanity."[105] The problem here arises when—due to level G's successful strategies of division and expulsion—marginalized groups are forced to develop their own utopian visions in isolation from all the others. Under these circumstances, when such formations *are* able to come together, it is usually in order to establish temporarily and instrumentally "an alliance of negatives, the priority being to unite against an immediate evil rather than concentrating upon the development of a truly popular programme with mass support from below."[106] This is a recipe doomed to failure;

because, as Williams rightly warns us, "you can't make much of an alliance out of negatives; the only real basis of alliances is agreement on positive proposals for transcending the negatives."[107]

Here, we return to the question of the *conjuncture*. "Apart from one or two exceptional moments," claims Lefebvre, "it is a question neither of a working 'class' as a structure nor of a predetermined historical bloc, but *a question of alliances*."[108] Thus, he would insist on the importance of "[a] strategy which would join up the peripheral elements with elements from the disturbed centres" in a "kind of global project" that "can only be linked to a diversified, qualitative ensemble of movements, demands and actions."[109] Out from the multitude of *anti*-hegemonic struggles, what is required is a perspective that, while respecting the right to difference of those particular interests articulated within, could properly bring them together in the form of a *counter*hegemony that could effectively challenge and overcome the power of state capitalism by removing it from its privileged position at the center indefinitely.[110]

As for the specifics of such a strategy, it would be wrong to offer anything more than an *orientation*: "a direction that may be conceived, and a directly lived movement progressing towards the horizon."[111] But I would like to conclude with at least *one* powerful suggestion. Recall, for a moment, the Janus-faced tactic described at length regarding Lefebvre's level G: with one side working to reduce and recuperate, the other aiming to divide and marginalize. With this in mind, Lefebvre once claimed that "[t]he answer to separation and dispersion is unification, just as the answer to forced homogenization is the discernment of differences and their practical realization."[112] Through these patently dialectical reversals, he rightly emphasized the futility in applying a logic of "either–or" to the question of unity and difference on the part the counterhegemonic subject-in-becoming.

Which brings us right back to where we began: to the fracture delineated by Eagleton regarding the left's dissolution into two separate camps. Indeed, given the fact that it has become nothing more than "an aggregate of divergent attitudes beneath the appearance of unity, or of convergent attitudes beneath an appearance of diversity,"[113] is it not due time to leave such inadequate appearances behind and become, at one and the same time, an *actually existing unity-in-difference*? Should the contemporary left—like neo-capitalism itself—not make the most of its contradictions? The impassioned and articulate writings of Lefebvre and Williams would seem to suggest that, contrary to the prevailing Zeitgeist, there is still much we can learn from the dialectic after all.

NOTES

1. I would like to thank Kanishka Goonewardena, Stefan Kipfer, and Gavin Smith for providing such attentive readings of drafts of this chapter. Their insightful comments and suggestions have been incorporated into the final version.

2. 1991 and 1988, respectively.
3. See Eric Hobsbawm, *The Age of Extremes* (London: Abacus, 1994).
4. Dennis Dworkin, *Cultural Marxism in Postwar Britain: History, the New Left, and the Origins of Cultural Studies* (Durham, NC: Duke University Press, 1997), 82.
5. Andy Merrifield, *Metromarxism: A Marxist Tale of the City* (New York: Routledge, 2002), 72.
6. Eleonore Kofman and Elizabeth Lebas, "Lost in Transposition—Time, Space, and the City," in Henri Lefebvre, *Writings on Cities*, ed. E. Kofman and E. Lebas (Oxford: Blackwell, 1996), 36–7.
7. David Harvey, *Justice, Nature, and the Geography of Difference* (Oxford: Blackwell, 1996), 101–2.
8. See the ninth chapter of Martin Jay, *Marxism and Totality* (Berkeley: University of California Press, 1984), 276–99.
9. See Henri Lefebvre, *The Urban Revolution*, trans. R. Bononno (Minneapolis: University of Minnesota Press, 2003 [1970]).
10. See Raymond Williams, *The Long Revolution* (Harmondsworth: Penguin, 1961).
11. This was E. P. Thompson's diagnosis. See Dworkin, *Cultural Marxism*, 101–5.
12. Raymond Williams, "The Practice of Possibility," in *Resources of Hope*, ed. R. Gable (London: Verso Press, 1989 [1987]), 318.
13. Jay, *Marxism and Totality*, 23–4.
14. As a lucid example, consider Lefebvre's passionate attachment to the idea of the "total man." See especially his *Dialectical Materialism*, trans. J. Sturrock (London: Cape, 1968 [1939]).
15. Henri Lefebvre, *Critique of Everyday Life, Volume II*, trans. J. Moore (London: Verso, 2002 [1961]), 180.
16. *Ibid.*, 181.
17. *Ibid.*
18. *Ibid.*
19. See, especially, Lefebvre's critique of "finalism" in *Urban Revolution*, 67–8.
20. Lefebvre, *Critique*, II, 185.
21. *Ibid.*, 186–7.
22. *Ibid.*, 183.
23. Henri Lefebvre, *The Production of Space*, trans. D. Nicholson-Smith (Oxford: Blackwell, 1991 [1974]), 399.
24. Lefebvre, *Critique*, II, 119. For a congruent deliberation on the idea of the level, see Frederic Jameson, "The Brick and the Balloon: Architecture, Idealism and Land Speculation," in *The Cultural Turn* (London: Verso, 1998), 164–5.
25. *Ibid.*
26. Michael Hardt and Antonio Negri, *Empire* (Cambridge, MA: Harvard University Press, 2000). See, for example, p. 190.
27. Lefebvre, *Critique*, II, 119.
28. *Ibid.*
29. *Ibid.*, emphasis added.
30. Raymond Williams, "Base and Superstructure in Marxist Cultural Theory," in *Culture and Materialism* (London: Verso, 2005 [1973/1980]), 35.
31. *Ibid.*, 32.
32. Raymond Williams, *Marxism and Literature* (Oxford: Oxford University Press, 1977), 77.

33. *Ibid.*, 81.
34. Williams, "Base and Superstructure," 32.
35. *Ibid.*, 36.
36. For an elaboration of this central concept in Williams's work, see his *Marxism and Literature*, 128–35.
37. Henri Lefebvre, *Critique of Everyday Life, Volume I*, trans. J. Moore (London: Verso, 1991 [1947/1958]), 87.
38. Henri Lefebvre, *The Survival of Capitalism*, trans. F. Bryant (New York: St. Martin's Press, 1976 [1973]), 88–9.
39. *Ibid.*, 58.
40. Henri Lefebvre, *Critique of Everyday Life, Volume III*, trans. G. Elliot (London: Verso, 2005 [1981]), 122–3.
41. Williams, *Marxism and Literature*, 109. It should be obvious that he is here relying on a more or less "traditional" (i.e., pre-Althusserian) definition of ideology in making this contrast.
42. *Ibid.*, 112.
43. *Ibid.*
44. Williams, "Base and Superstructure," 38.
45. *Ibid.*, 41.
46. Henri Lefebvre, *Introduction to Modernity*, trans. J. Moore (London: Verso, 1995 [1962]), 116–26.
47. *Ibid.*, 116.
48. *Ibid.*
49. *Ibid.*, 117–18.
50. *Ibid.*, 117.
51. *Ibid.*, 124.
52. *Ibid.*, 125.
53. *Ibid.*, 126.
54. As Williams notes, this is precisely the distinction that Gramsci posited between hegemony and rule (*dominio*) in the first place. See Williams, *Marxism and Literature*, 108.
55. *Ibid.*, 113.
56. *Ibid.*, 125.
57. Kristin Ross, *May '68 and its Afterlives* (Chicago: University of Chicago Press, 2002).
58. *Ibid.*, 6.
59. Williams, *Marxism and Literature*, 125–6.
60. Guy Debord, *The Society of the Spectacle*, trans. D. Nicholson-Smith (New York: Zone Books, 1994 [1967]), paragraph 42.
61. Lefebvre, *Critique*, II, 11.
62. Williams explicitly states that "[w]e have to see, first, as it were a temporal relation between a dominant culture and on the one hand a residual and on the other hand an emergent culture." See Williams "Base and Superstructure," 41.
63. In making this contrast, I have left myself open to the valid objection that Williams was also a keen observer of spatial dynamics: especially in celebrated works like *The Country and the City* (London: Chatto and Windus, 1973) and *People of the Black Mountains* (London: Chatto and Windus, 1989). That this is the case is beyond dispute; my intention here is simply to point out that Williams prioritized *time* over space in his understanding of hegemony specifically, while the opposite would seem to hold true for Lefebvre.

64. Lefebvre, *Production of Space*, 10–11.
65. See Neil Smith, foreword to Lefebvre, *Urban Revolution*, xxii.
66. Lefebvre, *Survival of Capitalism*, 17.
67. Kanishka Goonewardena, "The Urban Sensorium: Space, Ideology and the Aestheticization of Politics," *Antipode* 37, no. 1 (2005): 46–71.
68. *Ibid.*, 67.
69. Lefebvre, *Urban Revolution*, 14.
70. For example, "totalization-fragmentation" (Lefebvre, *Introduction to Modernity*, 121), "integration-segregation" (Lefebvre, "Right to the City," in *Writings on Cities*, 144), "gather[ing]-dispers[ing]" (Lefebvre, *Production of Space*, 386), and "joined-disjoined" (Lefebvre, *Survival of Capitalism*, 79).
71. Lefebvre, *Urban Revolution*, 14.
72. See the second chapter of Henri Lefebvre, *Everyday Life in the Modern World*, trans. S. Rabinovitch (New York: Harper and Row, 1971 [1968]), 68–109.
73. Lefebvre, *Survival of Capitalism*, 23.
74. Lefebvre, *Production of Space*, 370.
75. *Ibid.*, 371.
76. *Ibid.*, 57.
77. See especially Lefebvre, *Survival of Capitalism*, ch. 2.
78. *Ibid.*, 90.
79. Williams, *Marxism and Literature*, 113.
80. Lefebvre, *Production of Space*, 23.
81. *Ibid.*
82. Kofman and Lebas, "Lost in Transposition," 26.
83. Lefebvre, *Production of Space*, 396.
84. Lefebvre, *Critique*, III, 111.
85. *Ibid.*
86. *Ibid.*, emphasis added.
87. *Ibid.*
88. *Ibid.*, 111–12.
89. See Stefan Kipfer, "Urbanization, Everyday Life and the Survival of Capitalism: Lefebvre, Gramsci and the Problematic of Hegemony," *Capitalism, Nature, Socialism* 13, no. 2 (2002): 117–49.
90. Lefebvre, *Critique*, III, 105.
91. *Ibid.*, 108.
92. Lefebvre, *Production of Space*, 389.
93. Williams, *Marxism and Literature*, 126.
94. See Lefebvre, *Production of Space*, 383–5, and Williams, *Marxism and Literature*, 110.
95. Lefebvre, *Production of Space*, 373.
96. Lefebvre, *Survival of Capitalism*, 34.
97. *Ibid.*, 35.
98. Williams, "Democracy and Parliament," in *Resources of Hope*, 273.
99. *Ibid.*, 274.
100. See Lefebvre, *Survival of Capitalism*, 102–19, and Williams, "Towards Many Socialisms," in *Resources of Hope*, 295–313. It should be noted here that Lefebvre and Williams were not simply *against* growth either. Both preferred the idea of "limiting" or "monitoring" growth with the intent of subordinating it to the needs of the social.
101. Lefebvre, *Survival of Capitalism*, 126.
102. *Ibid.*, 116.

103. *Ibid.*, 36.

104. Lefebvre, *Production of Space*, 379.

105. This is David Harvey's definition. See his *Justice*, 32.

106. Williams, "Decentralism and the Politics of Place," in *Resources of Hope*, 240.

107. *Ibid.*, 239.

108. Lefebvre, *Survival of Capitalism*, 38, emphasis added.

109. *Ibid.*, 119.

110. I am here essentially paraphrasing a memorable statement of Williams—dwelled on extensively by David Harvey—which asserts "that the defense of certain particular interests, properly brought together, are in fact the general interest." See Harvey, *Justice*, 32.

111. Lefebvre, *Production of Space*, 423.

112. *Ibid.*, 418.

113. Lefebvre, *Survival of Capitalism*, 126.

14

HENRI LEFEBVRE'S CRITIQUE OF STATE PRODUCTIVISM[1]

Neil Brenner

INTRODUCTION

The mid-1970s was a remarkable phase of Henri Lefebvre's intellectual and political career. Having published *La production de l'espace* in 1974,[2] he embarked upon an ambitious project on the theory and historical geography of the modern state on a world scale. The result of this inquiry, which appeared in France between 1976 and 1978, was a sprawling, four-volume treatise entitled *De l'État*.[3] In significant part because it has never been translated into English, *De l'État* has been largely ignored in the rediscovery of Lefebvre's work on urbanism and capitalist spatiality during the last decade within Anglo-American geography. Yet *De l'État* arguably represents an essential pillar within the corpus of Lefebvre's mature writings on sociospatial theory.

As in previous decades, Lefebvre developed many of his seminal ideas of the 1970s in conjunction with his involvement in political struggles and debates within the French Left. The interaction of Lefebvre's theoretical and political projects is particularly apparent in his writings on state theory of the late 1970s, in which issues of conceptualization, interpretation, strategy, and praxis are explored in an exceptionally immediate relation to one another. Although Lefebvre had previously published scholarly commentaries on the political sociology of Marx and Lenin,[4] *De l'État* represented, simultaneously, the culmination of his own theoretical reflections on the modern state, an important extension and concretization of his writings on the production of space, and, perhaps most importantly, an impassioned call to arms in the name of an anti-Stalinist *and* anti-social-democratic form of radical-democratic political praxis. Indeed, in *De l'État* and his other writings on the state of the 1970s, Lefebvre developed theoretical foundations for a number of political projects that he had begun to elaborate in his earlier writings, including radical political decentralization, grassroots democratic governance, and the transformation of everyday life. Lefebvre's writings on the state during this period can thus be read as an expression of his sustained efforts to clarify both theoretically and practically the possibility for transformative political praxis under the highly fluid global, European, national, and local conditions of that tumultuous decade.

Particularly in light of the lively interest in Lefebvre's work among Anglo-American geographers, the aforementioned reasons would probably suffice to justify a contemporary reengagement with Lefebvre's state-theoretical and political writings of this period. However, there is an additional, and more immediate, justification for such an exercise: it can be argued that a number of Lefebvre's central preoccupations of the 1970s—in particular, his conception of radical democracy as a process of *autogestion*; and his concern to develop a left-radical critique of the capitalist state—remain essential to the work of critical social theorists in the contemporary conjuncture of neoliberal globalization.

MARXISM EXPLODED: LEFEBVRE, 1968, AND THE FRENCH LEFT

As Stefan Kipfer has argued, Lefebvre's politics were forged under the influence of four key experiences:

(1) the critique of Stalinism in France and Eastern Europe before and after his expulsion from the PCF [French Communist Party] at the end of the 1950s; (2) a critical engagement with Situationist avant-gardism in the 1950s and 1960s; (3) a brief flirtation with the alternative Communism of Yugoslavia and China; and (4) his contribution to New Left politics in France both before and after 1968.[5]

This fourth layering of Lefebvre's political identity was articulated most powerfully and systematically during the 1970s as his relation to politics shifted—in the words of his biographer Remi Hess—"from [an embrace of] grassroots militantism to a critique of the state."[6]

The post-1968 period witnessed a number of dramatic transformations within the French Left that significantly conditioned Lefebvre's outlook. He would subsequently describe these transformations as an "explosion" (*éclatement*) of Marxism in which the dogmatic unity of Marxian theory associated with Stalinism was splintered into a multitude of strands and currents.[7] Although, as Lefebvre noted, this explosion of Marxism had begun as early as the late nineteenth century in the bitter debates between Marx, Ferdinand Lassalle, and Mikhael Bakunin, it continued well into the late twentieth century.[8] In the post-1968 period, the explosion of Marxism occurred in sites scattered throughout the world, from Prague, Belgrade, London, Chicago, and Berkeley to Mexico City, Calcutta, and Beijing, but Paris was arguably one of its most vibrant global flashpoints. Here, as Sunil Khilnani remarks, "[t]he 'long decade' between the revolutionary efflorescence of May 1968 and the Socialist Party's election to government in 1981 produced the most dramatic and decisive realignment in the political affiliations of French intellectuals that has occurred in recent times."[9] Since many of Lefebvre's state-theoretical and political writings of the 1970s can be viewed as attempts to decipher these realignments, it is worth reviewing some of their main contours here.

The SFIO (Section Française de l'Internationale Ouvrière), which had been the major political organ of the non-communist Left in France since 1920, had entered a process of terminal decline by the early 1960s and was dissolved following the defeat of the traditional left parties in the 1968/9 national elections. Soon thereafter, the PCF emerged from the political ghetto to which it had been consigned since the outbreak of the Cold War: following the example of the Italian Communist Party (PCI), it embraced the project of Eurocommunism by abandoning its commitment to a dictatorship of the proletariat and its rigid support for the Soviet model. Major segments of the non-communist Left were reconstituted under Mitterrand's leadership at the Epinay Congress of 1971 to form a revived Socialist Party (PS). Although some segments of the post-1968 New Left subsequently affiliated with the PS, other *gauchiste* thinkers such as Lefebvre, André Gorz, and Cornelius Castoriadis continued to seek an alternative, radically democratic socialism that circumvented the rigidified orthodoxies of the PCF as well as the feeble reformism of the social-democratic model.[10]

In July 1972, the newly formed PS, the PCF, and the Left-Radicals forged a political alliance under the "Common Program of Government" (*Programme commun du gouvernement*) in which they committed themselves to a somewhat inchoate mixture of communist/socialist/*gauchiste* political goals (demand-led growth, nationalization of major industrial sectors, increased corporate taxation, extension of social protection and civil liberties) and traditional liberal ideology (acceptance of political pluralism, multiple political parties, and the parliamentary system of the Fifth Republic). During the ensuing decade, as the electoral base of the PCF dwindled under Georges Marchais's foundering chairmanship, Mitterrand's pragmatic, power-hungry PS acquired an unprecedented political influence as it strategized to expand its constituency by appealing to the anti-communist Left. Although the unified Left lost the parliamentary elections of March 1978, the socialists obtained more votes than the PCF for the first time since 1936. Indeed, in contrast to the "popular front" of the 1930s, which had benefited the communists, the "popular front" of the 1970s was a major boon to the PS and "signaled the beginning of the end for French communism."[11] Through its embrace of the *Programme commun*, the PS managed to gain credibility as a left-wing reformist party. As of the late 1970s, the PS surpassed all other parties of the Left in strategic political importance, paving the way for its landslide electoral triumph in 1981. The PCF, meanwhile, refused to accept its increasingly subordinate role as a mere junior partner within the unified left alliance and withdrew from the *Programme commun* following the March 1978 elections. Throughout the subsequent decade, the PCF retreated from its earlier Euro-communist stance but its electoral base continued to decline.

In the midst of these unpredictable shifting political tides, *autogestion*—an idea "whose vagueness was its strength"[12]—became a central topic of political debate and ideological struggle throughout the French Left. Literally, *autogestion* means "self-management," but its specific connotation in the French context of the 1960s and 1970s may be captured more accurately as "workers' control." The project of *autogestion* can be traced to the anti-statist socialist movements of the nineteenth century; it was subsequently debated among contributors to Castoriadis's journal *Socialisme ou Barbarie* in the 1950s and again in the 1960s in discussions within the French Left of the Yugoslav system of industrial democracy and the Algerian independence movement. During the events of May 1968, *autogestion* became a popular rallying cry for the non-communist and anarchist Left, including Lefebvre himself, who discussed it enthusiastically in a number of texts and interviews during this period and afterwards.[13]

As of the early 1970s, the concept of *autogestion* was reappropriated by a range of left-wing intellectuals, organizations, and movements to characterize very different, and often fundamentally opposed, political projects within universities, factories, trade unions, localities, and municipal and regional administrations.[14] The main non-communist trade union federation CFDT (Confédération Française Démo-cratique du Travail), guided by the editor and philosopher Pierre Rosanvallon, promoted *autogestion* as a means to enhance workers' control at the site of produc-tion.[15] The dissident socialist Michel Rocard and the CFDT trade unionist Edmond Maire advocated autogestion as a form of radical democratic political mobilization to counteract the hierarchical, state-centered orientations of both the PCF and the PS. Meanwhile, various urbanistic and regionalist strands of the autogestion discussion emerged which advocated a radical decentralization of political power, enhanced local control over basic economic and administrative tasks and an abolition of the divide between governors and governed. At its founding congress, the PS likewise embraced the slogan of autogestion, albeit primarily on opportunistic grounds as a means to gain trade union support, to maintain its alliance with the PCF and to recruit *soixante-huitards*.[16] Finally, despite its entrenched *étatiste* tendencies, even the PCF tentatively adopted a politics of *autogestion* in conjunction with its experiments with Eurocommunist ideology, particularly between 1975 and 1978. In short, as Lefebvre quipped in *The Survival of Capitalism*, autogestion was the ideological focal point for "a great outburst of confusion."[17] By the mid-1970s, the concept of *autogestion* had come to operate as a strikingly vague, internally contradictory semantic placeholder, an "infinitely plastic idea" which encompassed, at one and the same time, anti-statist and statist political projects, anti-productivist and productivist visions of modernization, and radical-grassroots and traditional liberal forms of political participation.[18]

Nowhere in his writings of this period does Lefebvre explicitly invoke the *Programme commun* or its abrupt dissolution in 1978, and he only fleetingly alludes to the PCF's confused appropriation of a politics of *autogestion* just prior to the Twenty-third Congress. None the less, several of Lefebvre's key political writings of the 1970s allude to the changing ideological landscape of the French Left, in particular to the evolving positions of the PCF and the PS, in relation to one another, in relation to French civil society, and in relation to the state apparatus itself.[19] As Lefebvre notes, the political conjuncture of the late 1970s was strongly reminiscent of the 1930s in France. In both cases, an organizationally fragmented and ideologically divided Left was struggling to articulate and defend a common ground of political positions against its opponents in the midst of a systemic capitalist crisis; and in both cases, the communist and non-communist factions of the socialist Left were engaged in frenzied internal debates as they attempted to clarify their ideological positions, political commitments, and practical strategies in response to that crisis. It was a moment in which established political choreographies were being unsettled as an atmosphere of heightened uncertainty—but also of possibility—swept across the European Left.

While insisting upon the superiority of a critique "from the left," Lefebvre distances himself from both "the so-called Socialist Party" and the "so-called Communist Party."[20] In his fascinating 1979 intervention, "Comments on a New State Form" (hereafter "CNSF"), Lefebvre quickly dispenses with the political positions of the PCF, confining himself to the observation that it had yet to break sufficiently with its Stalinist legacy and that its approach to political strategy in the Fifth Republic was "dangerously empirical" due to a consistent failure to ask the question, "What kind of state do we want?"[21] Elsewhere Lefebvre argued that the PCF and other "worshippers of the total state economy" were "just playing with words" in their adoption of the slogan of *autogestion* in the 1970s.[22] In CNSF, Lefebvre devotes a more extensive commentary to the evolving agendas of the PS, particularly to the work of the social-democratic economist and theoretician Jacques Attali, whose widely discussed book *La nouvelle économie française* had appeared the previous year.[23] Against the traditional communist position, Lefebvre rejects the instrumentalist interpretation of social democracy as the "principal social support of capital," emphasizing instead the ideological heterogeneity of the Parti Socialiste in contrast to the social-democratic parties of Germany and Northern Europe. Despite their tendency to sprinkle their texts with certain Marxian-inspired categories, social-democratic theoreticians such as Attali ultimately conceived the state in traditional liberal-pluralist terms, as a neutral institutional framework for the articulation of societal interests. Lefebvre scornfully dismisses this view as a "peevish negation of politics."[24]

Albeit in qualitatively different ways, both the PCF and the PS had proposed to strengthen civil society through a decentralization of political power. Lefebvre had likewise endorsed such an agenda in his earlier writings on cities and on territorial *autogestion*, but here he expresses extreme skepticism about its viability in the absence of a systematic critique of the state. Alluding to de Gaulle's cynical use of political decentralization as a weapon of central state steering, Lefebvre suggests that this project has all too frequently amounted to no more than a "simulacrum" of democratization in which administrative problems and fiscal burdens are merely reshuffled without qualitatively modifying the balance of power. More generally, Lefebvre argues that society-centered projects of political transformation have, since Hegel, been tightly intertwined with a de facto enhancement of state control. Hence, Lefebvre maintains, any viable approach to the democratization of civil society must be linked to a sustained critique—and radical democratization—of the modern state form itself.

LEFT PRODUCTIVISM: SOCIAL DEMOCRACY AND THE STATE MODE OF PRODUCTION

Here Lefebvre arrives at one of his core politico-theoretical arguments of the 1970s: the real historical significance and political danger both of Stalinism and of social democracy consists in their role in facilitating the consolidation of a "new state form" (*une nouvelle forme étatique*), a hyperproductivist politico-institutional ensemble to which he refers as the state mode of production (SMP). Clearly, Lefebvre considered the ideological nuances within the French Left to be of paramount strategic and political importance, but he developed his analysis at a higher level of abstraction in order to interrogate theoretically the very institutional field within which the sociopolitical forces of the Left were situating themselves. The dispersed threads of Lefebvre's analysis of the French Left thus converge around the politico-theoretical problem of the SMP.

For Lefebvre, the structural essence of the SMP is the state's increasingly direct role in the promotion and management of capitalist industrial growth. The concept of the SMP is intended primarily as a means to describe what might be termed *state productivism*: "A qualitative transformation occurs from the moment in which the State takes charge of growth . . . from this moment forward economic failures are attributed to the State."[25] In volumes three and four of *De l'État*, Lefebvre examines the dynamics, geohistory, and consequences of state productivism at some length, with reference both to the Stalinist state apparatuses of the East and to the neocapitalist state apparatuses of Western Europe and North America. In CNSF, Lefebvre focuses more closely upon the role of social-democratic political regimes in the reconstitution of the SMP in Western Europe during the 1970s. According to him, the social-democratic model of the state is but one specific politico-institutional form in which the SMP has been articulated historically.

Lefebvre interprets the social-democratic form of the SMP as the long-term historical outcome of the Lassallian political project that had been promoted by reformist social-democratic parties during the early twentieth century. Since this period, when social-democratic parties first gained access to the national parliamentary systems of Western European bourgeois democracies, social-democratic control over the machinery of state power has been deployed consistently, if unevenly, as a means to redistribute the social surplus to the working class on a national scale. This social-democratic politics of national redistribution, Lefebvre suggests, has in turn masked a profound transformation of state/economy relations, in which the state has become imbricated in ever more complex ways in producing, maintaining, and reproducing the basic socio-institutional and territorial preconditions for capital accumulation. The conception of social democracy as a deradicalizing form of collaboration with the capitalist class enemy dates to Marx's 1875 *Critique of the Gotha Program* (a text which Lefebvre frequently cites) and to the subsequent debates between Lenin, Karl Kautsky, Eduard Bernstein, and Rosa Luxemburg within the Second International.[26] However, Lefebvre's central concern over a half-century later is to assess the politico-institutional *consequences* of this strategy of social-democratic redistribution and aggressive state productivism. From his vantage point in the late 1970s, the key issue is less the role of social democracy as a reformist political strategy than its long-term structural impacts upon the nature of state power and everyday life within neocapitalism. Lefebvre maintains, in short, that the social-democratic strategies that were deployed during the first half of the twentieth century have now been inscribed directly onto the very structure and logic of the capitalist state. State productivism appears to reign supreme, independently of fluctuations of political regime or ruling coalition, within the bureaucratic society of controlled consumption of the late twentieth century. Throughout Western Europe, Lefebvre argues, the social-democratic class compromise has served as a key political anchor for the consolidation of state productivism. One of Lefebvre's specific politico-theoretical concerns of the 1970s was to articulate an uncompromising critique of the French Left for its failure critically to interrogate its own role in the creation of this social-democratic crystallization of the SMP.

Lefebvre considers this task particularly urgent because, in his view, the SMP was being reconfigured in a number of disturbing ways during the 1970s. In *De l'État*, he examines the role of the SMP in the production of the socio-territorial infrastructures for successive historical regimes of capital accumulation. In Lefebvre's framework, state institutions play an essential role in the production, regulation, and reproduction of a vast range of capitalist spaces—from factories, industrial farms, housing estates, commercial zones, suburban enclaves, and large-scale urban ensembles to roads, canals, tunnels, port facilities, bridges, railway networks, highway grids, airports and air transport corridors, public utilities systems, and diverse techno-institutional infrastructures for communication and surveillance. According to Lefebvre, the state's unparalleled capacities to channel large-scale, long-term investments into the built environment for industrial production, collective consumption, commodity circulation, transportation, and communication—coupled with its sovereign legal power to plan and regulate the social uses of such investments—give it a privileged institutional position in the production of capitalist spatiality. As he notes, "Only the state can take on the task of managing space 'on a grand scale.'"[27]

In CNSF, Lefebvre extends this analysis by focusing upon three emergent realms in which the SMP is attempting to protect and promote capitalist growth: the regulation of energy; the control of computers and information technology; and the mediation of national and worldwide market relations.[28] In each of these spheres, Lefebvre argues, state institutions have been extending their power over everyday life, at a range of spatial scales, causing civil society in turn to be threatened with obliteration.

Lefebvre's remarks on each of the aforementioned aspects of the modern state are abbreviated but suggestive. For instance, he suggests that the real danger of nuclear power lies less in its environmental impacts than in its role in further insulating the techno-infrastructures of the modern state from democratic deliberations. Lefebvre's apparent anxiety, at the moment when the French formation of Fordism was being systematically dismantled, that the power of the modern state was being still further entrenched may appear rather unfounded in the contemporary period of global neoliberalism, in which major utilities infrastructures are being privatized and in which information technology is more frequently equated with an erosion of state regulatory capacities than with their oppressive extension.[29] Lefebvre's more general point, however, is less to engage in speculative futurology than to emphasize the profoundly political implications of these apparently technocratic developments within diverse fields of state power. In this sense, Lefebvre's remarks bear direct comparison to the critique of instrumental rationality and technology developed by the early Jürgen Habermas and other writers in the Frankfurt School.

Lefebvre's analysis of the role of the SMP in mediating national/global interactions remains particularly salient in the contemporary period insofar as it questions both left-wing and right-wing forms of "global babble." Lefebvre rejects instrumentalist understandings of the state, such as that embraced by the Red Brigades in Italy, as a direct tool of manipulation by multinational corporations. At the same time, he dismisses state-decline arguments and conceptualizes the national state as the major institutional framework in and through which the contemporary round of globalization is being fought out. Much like Nicos Poulantzas—whose final book *State, Power, Socialism* was published during the previous year (1978)—Lefebvre insists that the state is a contested institutional arena in which diverse sociopolitical forces struggle for control over everyday sociopolitical relations. Consequently, Lefebvre argues, the relation of national states to multinational capital is never predetermined but is the object and expression of nearly continual sociopolitical contestation, conflict, and struggle. If the risk persists that the state might be subordinated to the demands of global corporations, so too, according to Lefebvre, does the possibility of a state controlled by an anti-imperialist, popular-democratic coalition oriented toward radically anti-productivist goals.

AUTOGESTION, RADICAL DEMOCRACY, AND THE CRITIQUE OF THE STATE

These considerations enable Lefebvre to articulate two central political conclusions. First, he argues that a critique of the modern state form is a crucial prerequisite for any viable radical-democratic political project:

> Such is the danger that menaces the modern world and against which it is necessary to struggle at all costs. There is no "good State"; today there is no State which can avoid moving towards this logical outcome: the state mode of production; that's why the only criterion of democracy is the prevention of such an outcome.[30]

Lefebvre's claim is not that a critique of the SMP could or should somehow replace the Marxian project of a critique of political economy. Rather, he is suggesting that, in an era of entrenched state productivism, the former project has today become a particularly essential *component* within any viable critique of capitalism. According to Lefebvre, therefore, there is today a direct contradiction between state productivism—which is increasingly premised upon what Poulantzas termed "authoritarian statism"[31]—and the existence of substantive forms of democracy and democratic participation. Second, Lefebvre advocates a generalized project of *autogestion* through which all social institutions—including those of capital, the modern state, political parties, urban and regional administration, and everyday life—would be systematically democratized. As noted previously, Lefebvre recognized the degree to which *autogestion* had become a "hollow slogan" within the French Left as it was appropriated by pseudo-radical political organizations that were committed substantively neither to democratization nor to democratic socialism.[32] Nonetheless, Lefebvre insists that *autogestion* is the "one path and the one practice" through which the SMP—in both its Stalinist and its social-democratic forms—might be opposed and transcended.[33]

Particularly in light of his critique of the mainstream left-wing political parties within France, this is a provocative assertion. For Lefebvre, *autogestion* is not only a project of democratic governance but a conflictual process through which participants continually engage in self-criticism, debate, deliberation, and struggle; it is not a fixed condition but a process of intense political engagement and "revolutionary spontaneity"[34] that must "continually be enacted" (*se gagne perpétuellement*).[35] Lefebvre therefore distances himself from the various meanings that were linked to projects of *autogestion* within France, Yugoslavia, and elsewhere: *autogestion*, Lefebvre insists, is not a magic formula, a system, a model, or a panacea; it is not a purely technical or rational operation; it will not solve all the workers' problems; it encounters countless obstacles and threats; and it is in constant danger of degenerating or being assimilated into considerably less radical projects of "co-management" (*co-gestion*). In this manner, Lefebvre promotes *autogestion* less as a fully formed post-capitalist institutional framework than as a political orientation through which various sectors of social life—from factories, universities, and political associations to territorial units such as cities and regions—might be subjected to new forms of decentralized, democratic political control through the very social actors who are most immediately attached to them.

The roots of Lefebvre's approach to *autogestion* during the 1970s lie in his lifelong concern to elaborate a critically revised Marxian approach to the philosophy of praxis in the context of twentieth-century industrial capitalism.[36] Lefebvre had articulated the foundations for this project in his writings on the critique of everyday life, in his detailed historical analysis of the Paris Commune of 1871, in his interpretation of the French student revolts of 1968, as well as in his various critical commentaries on Marxian theory.[37] His remarks on *autogestion* in the 1970s illuminate the ways in which this philosophy of praxis may be extended to include a critique of the modern capitalist state: *autogestion*, in this sense, is a form of grassroots political practice that "is born spontaneously out of the void in social life that is created by the state."[38] To the extent that the apparatuses of the SMP are redefined into mechanisms of grassroots democratic political practice, Lefebvre argues, the state is "withering away in the Marxist sense."[39] The issue here, however, is less the erosion of state power as such than the possibility of its qualitative transformation into a non-productivistic, decentralized, and participatory institutional framework that not only permits social struggles and contradictions, but actively provokes them.[40] The political utopia envisioned by Lefebvre is one in which the state would serve not as an instrument for capital accumulation, bureaucratic domination and everyday violence but rather as an arena for—as he puts it at the end of *De l'État*—"spatial (territorial) *autogestion*, direct democracy and direct democratic control [and the] affirmation of the differences produced in the course of and through this struggle."[41]

Unfortunately, Lefebvre provides few clues about how such a project might be pursued under contemporary conditions, and he left to others the complex task of translating this vision autogestionnaire into viable, sustainable social institutions and practices.[42] Apparently, Lefebvre's concern in his major discussions of autogestion was to suggest that the concept can and should be reappropriated from the social-democratic and communist Left in the name of an alternative socialist project grounded upon anti-productivism and radical grassroots democracy. In this general sense, Lefebvre's remarks on autogestion can be read as a spirited defense of utopian thinking during a period in which, as Habermas would argue a few years later, the utopian energies associated with classical Marxism appeared to have been "exhausted."[43]

However, as Kipfer has noted, Lefebvre's political utopianism was profoundly dialectical, grounded upon the method of "transduction" which "entails detecting and transforming the possible within the real, the symbolic forms and fragments of an alternative future within everyday life."[44] Lefebvre's interest in the diverse experiments in autogestion that were percolating throughout French society during the post-1968 period—in factories, schools, universities, trade unions, cities, regions, and so forth—stemmed from his conviction that they represented the elements of a "social pedagogy"[45] within everyday life that pointed beyond the extant and towards alternative futures grounded upon more progressive, democratic, and egalitarian ways of organizing social space and time: "In political thought and political theory, the category (or concept) of the 'real' should not be permitted to obscure that of the possible. Rather, it is the possible that should serve as the theoretical instrument for exploring the real."[46] To proceed otherwise, Lefebvre believed, would be to engage in a fetishism of the present that perpetuates the unquestioned power of capital and the state to foreclose political possibilities and to dominate everyday life.[47]

BEYOND FORDIST MARXISM? LEFEBVRE IN THE AGE OF NEOLIBERALISM

The Eurocommunist movements of the mid-1970s in France, Italy, and Spain may be viewed as the high point of a distinctively Fordist form of Western Marxism that prevailed throughout much of the postwar period. In Western Europe and North America, the main reference point for this Fordist crystallization of Marxist theory and practice was the framework of political-economic organization that was consolidated between the early 1950s and the early 1970s: the critique of capitalism was articulated, under these conditions, as a critique of the Fordist regime of accumulation, the bureaucratic apparatuses of the Keynesian welfare national state, and the entrenched patterns of everyday power, class domination, and popular alienation with which those institutional forms were intertwined.[48]

Like many of the major critical theorists of the postwar period, Lefebvre's most important works were tightly embedded within the theoretical grammar of Fordist Marxism. Whereas Lefebvre's initial analyses of the bureaucratic society of controlled consumption were explicitly focused upon the political-economic order of the 1950s and 1960s, even his later studies of neocapitalism implied that the restructuring processes of the 1970s represented an entrenchment of the postwar capitalist order rather than its destabilization. In his mature works, Lefebvre occasionally mentions the politics of neoliberalism, but in so doing he is more frequently referring to a specific ideological strand within the French Right than to the worldwide capitalist class offensive that has underpinned the successive waves of state retrenchment and economic restructuring of the post-1970s period. Although De l'État was published while the institutional foundations of French "state Fordism" were being dismantled, Lefebvre does not attempt in these works to examine the global economic crises of the 1970s or their ramifications for the forms, functions, and territorial organization of the modern state.

These contextual limitations of Lefebvre's theoretical framework have not been acknowledged by many of his commentators and arguably deserve to be examined much more closely. None the less, a recognition of the contextual boundedness of Lefebvre's theoretical framework also points toward a number of potentially fruitful questions about its possible applications and redeployments under the after-Fordist conditions of the present day.[49] What, we might ask, would a Lefebvre-inspired interpretation of the current round of global sociospatial restructuring entail? In what ways might Lefebvre's political writings help illuminate the strategic dilemmas of the radical-democratic Left under conditions of global neoliberal domination and authoritarian statism? In the present context, I consider four possible ways in which the specific arguments developed by Lefebvre in his state-theoretical and political writings of the 1970s remain relevant to the concerns of left-radical scholars and activists.

Neoliberalism as a new form of the SMP

Lefebvre's analysis of the SMP can be fruitfully redeployed to decipher the neoliberal forms of state restructuring that have been unfolding on a world scale throughout the last two decades. As we have seen, Lefebvre interprets the social-democratic form of the SMP as the outgrowth of a historical class compromise that was consolidated during the mid-twentieth century and grounded upon a complex combination of aggressive state productivism and a class-based politics of redistribution and decommodification. The post-1970s round of state restructuring can be understood as an assault upon the state's redistributive functions coupled with an intensification of the productivist, commodifying aspects of the SMP—its role in promoting, financing, and managing capitalist growth. Indeed, as contemporary analyses of "competition states"[50] imply, we may currently be witnessing the emergence of a historically new form of the SMP in which the state's function as an agent for the commodification of its territory—at once on national, regional, and urban scales—has acquired an unprecedented supremacy over other regulatory operations within the state's institutional architecture. Although this productivistic function of state power was already evident within the social-democratic form of the SMP, the newly emergent, neoliberal form of the SMP appears to signal: an intensified role for the state in "developing the productive powers of territory and in producing new spatial configurations";[51] an increasing dissociation of state productivism both from mechanisms of social redistribution and from historically attained relays of democratic accountability;[52] and a deepening of uneven geographical development within and between national territories as states target specific cities, regions, or technopoles as globally competitive development areas to the detriment of others.[53] From this point of view, currently emergent patterns of authoritarian statism entail a significant enhancement of the state's role in mobilizing space as a productive force, coupled with a major recalibration of the social power relations that are mediated in and through the state apparatus. In an era when public discourse on the state is dominated by the neoliberal utopia of free, deregulated markets, powerless states, hypermobile capital, and unlimited exploitation, Lefebvre's theory of the SMP provides a powerful analytical lens through which the evolving political, institutional, and geographical dimensions of actually existing state productivism can be critically decoded.

Beyond left productivism

The social-democratic form of the SMP was grounded upon the assumption that redistributive goals could be attained within the parameters of a political system that was structurally dependent upon capital for its own reproduction. However, as the current period of worldwide capitalist restructuring has brutally illustrated, this assumption was deeply problematic insofar as it was premised upon historically and geographically contingent socio-institutional conditions and power relations that appear now to have been largely superseded through the destructive forward movement of capital. Whereas many traditional left-wing political parties struggled throughout the 1970s and into the 1980s to defend the redistributive arrangements associated with the Fordist–Keynesian settlement, much of the centrist or mainstream Left today appears to have embraced some version of the so-called Third Way, whose economic policy repertoire is almost indistinguishable from that of the neoliberal Right. Under these conditions, Lefebvre's analysis of the SMP provides a timely warning against the tendency—which is quite rampant even within contemporary left-wing political discourse—to narrow the field of political discussion to the issue of how to promote capitalist growth and thus to vacate the problematic of criticizing the logic of capitalism itself as an objectified form of abstract domination. Clearly, the politico-institutional frameworks within which capitalist growth occurs have massive ramifications for everyday life and must remain a key focus of any progressive, egalitarian, and democratic politics. None the less, from a radical-democratic socialist perspective, it would be fatal to accept the capitalist form of development as an unquestioned feature of contemporary social existence. In an era in which putatively left-wing parties across Europe and North America have become agents, enforcers, and apologists for various kinds of soft neoliberalism, Lefebvre's dissident critique of the French Left over two decades ago provides a welcome reminder of one essential ingredient within any radically democratic socialist politics: the ruthless critique of the capitalist growth dynamic in the name of alternative frameworks for the production of everyday life.

Radical democracy and the critique of the state

Whereas the project of a critique of the state was a central agenda of left-wing, socialist, and radical theory throughout the 1970s, this project today appears to have been monopolized by the neoliberal and neoconservative Right. In a paper originally published in 1979, shortly after the completion of Lefebvre's De l'État, Claus Offe noted the apparent convergence between leftist and neoconservative accounts of the crisis of the Keynesian welfare state.[54] At that time, the critique of the state was one of the major ideological battlegrounds on which the politics of capitalist restructuring were being fought out in Western Europe. Today, over two decades later, the right-wing critique of the state in the name of efficiency, lean-management, fiscal discipline, market rationality, and the putative rights of capital has become the dominant political response to the most recent round of capitalist globalization. Meanwhile, the left-wing critique of the state seems to have all but disappeared as progressives struggle to salvage the vestiges of the Keynesian settlement and to manage the polarizing socioeconomic effects of neoliberal policies. Such struggles no doubt remain significant, even essential. However, as Lefebvre's analysis indicates, they need not be premised upon a wholesale retreat from the project of a critique of the state. Indeed, as we observe state institutions becoming leaner, meaner, and increasingly undemocratic in their quest to promote territorial competitiveness, a critique of the state must surely remain central to any radically democratic politics. Although Lefebvre's conceptualization of *autogestion* is multifaceted, one of its core components is the affirmation of grassroots democracy as an ongoing project at all geographical scales and within all sectors of social and political life—including, crucially, within state institutions themselves. During the last three decades, neoliberal regimes have undermined mechanisms of democratic accountability that were won during many centuries of popular struggle. Currently, this US-dominated "new constitutionalism" of corporate capitalist power, fiscal austerity, heightened social polarization, and financial speculation is being extended onto a global scale through the initiatives of autocratic institutions such as the IMF, the World Bank, the WTO, the OECD, and the World Economic Forum.[55] These trends have been further complicated through the consolidation of new forms of militarism and imperialism in an increasingly volatile, post-9/11 geopolitical system.[56] Under these circumstances, the project of a democratization of the state at all spatial scales remains particularly urgent. Lefebvre's sustained critique of the state in the name of a politics of social and territorial *autogestion* could potentially provide a normative reference point for the rejuvenation of political struggles oriented toward a redemocratization of state institutions and other governance institutions.

Toward a dialectical utopianism

One of the hallmarks of neoliberal politics is the appeal to the supposed external constraints of the global economy, which are generally represented as being quasi-natural forces that are independent of human control. This neoliberal political program is most concisely expressed in the infamous Thatcherite dictum, "There is no alternative" (TINA). A number of left intellectuals have recently written stinging critiques of this neoliberal politics of "false necessity"[57] with its "utopia of unlimited exploitation."[58] Lefebvre's critique of the state likewise questions this necessitarian logic while emphasizing the need to excavate everyday life for political possibilities that could point toward more democratic, egalitarian, and humane futures. For Lefebvre, the formation of the Paris Commune in 1871 and the French student revolts of 1968 represented defining political conjunctures within capitalist modernity that revealed such latent possibilities for radical democracy and *autogestion*, even if they were realized only fleetingly and incompletely.[59] In an epoch in which the apparent "exhaustion of utopian energies"[60] continues to plague the radical Left, Lefebvre's dialectical utopianism[61] provides a salient reminder that everyday life under capitalism is permeated with utopian possibilities and strivings—of both reactionary and progressive variants, and with foreboding, benign, or emancipatory ramifications. Whether we look to the anti-WTO protests in Seattle, to the ongoing grassroots mobilizations around the World Social Forum, to the living-wage and justice for janitors campaigns in a number of major US cities, to the anti-sweatshop movement in North American universities, to the efforts of European progressives to establish a Europe-wide welfare net, or to the struggles of left-wing urban social movements to create more socially just, democratic, and sustainable forms of urbanism, there is plenty of evidence to suggest that progressive, potentially emancipatory forms of everyday utopianism, grounded in and expressed through diverse forms of political struggle, persist unabated in a broad range of institutional sites and spaces within contemporary capitalism. Against the background of these ongoing struggles, Lefebvre's dialectical utopianism continues to provide an extraordinarily useful orientation for the activities of radical scholars, even in a dramatically different political conjuncture than that to which his critique of the state was a response.

NOTES

1. This chapter is a substantially revised and rewritten version of a paper previously published as "State Theory in the Political Conjuncture: Henri Lefebvre's 'Comments on a New State Form,'" *Antipote* 33, no. 5 (2001): 738–808.

2. Henri Lefebvre, *La production de l'espace* (Paris: Éditions Anthropos, 1974).

3. Henri Lefebvre, *De l'État, tome IV: les contradictions de l'état moderne* (Paris: Union Générale d'Editions, 1978); *De l'État, tome III: Le mode de production étatique* (Paris: Union Générale d'Editions, 1977); *De l'État, tome I: l'État dans le monde moderne* (Paris: Union Générale d'Editions, 1976); *De l'État, tome II: De Hegel à Marx par Staline* (Paris: Union Générale d'Editions, 1976).

4. Henri Lefebvre, *The Sociology of Marx* (New York: Columbia University Press, 1968), 123–86; *Pour connaître la pensée de Lénine* (Paris: Bordas, 1957), 311–24.

5. Stefan Kipfer, *Marxism, Everyday Life and Urbanization*, unpublished manuscript, Department of Political Science, York University, (1996), 34.

6. Rémi Hess, *Henri Lefebvre et l'aventure du siècle* (Paris: Éditions A. M. Métailié, 1988), 284.

7. Henri Lefebvre, *Une pensée devenue monde* (Paris: Fayard, 1980).

8. *Ibid.*, 21.

9. Sunil Khilnani, *Arguing Revolution: The Intellectual Left in Postwar France* (New Haven: Yale University Press, 1993), 121.

10. Bernard Brown, *Socialism of a Different Kind: Reshaping the Left in France* (Westport, CT: Greenwood Press, 1982); Khilnani, *Arguing Revolution*, 121–54; Donald Sassoon, *One Hundred Years of Socialism: The West European Left in the Twentieth Century* (London: I. B. Tauris, 1996), 534–71.

11. Sassoon, *One Hundred Years*, 541.

12. *Ibid.*, 538.

13. See Lefebvre, *De l'État*, IV, 438–9; *The Survival of Capitalism*, trans. F. Bryant (New York: St. Martin's Press, 1976 [1973],) 40–1, 120–4; "Interview – débat sur le Marxisme," *Autogestion et socialisme* 33/4 (1976): 115–26; *Everyday Life in the Modern World* (London: Transaction, 1971), 294–306; *The Explosion* (New York: Monthly Review, 1969); "Problèmes théoriques de l'autogestion," *Autogestion* 1 (1966): 59–70.

14. Brown, *Socialism*; J.-P. Cot, "Autogestion and Modernity in France," in *Eurocommunism & Eurosocialism*, ed. B. Brown (New York: Cyrco Press, 1979), 67–103.

15. See Pierre Rosenvallon, *L'âge de l'autogestion* (Paris: Seuil, 1976).

16. Sassoon, *One Hundred Years*, 538–40.

17. Lefebvre, *Survival*, 40.

18. Khilnani, *Arguing Revolution*, 182.

19. See Henri Lefebvre, "Comments on a New State Form," *Antipode* 33, no. 5 (2001 [1979]): 769–82. Originally published as "À propos d'un nouveau modèle étatique," *Dialectiques* 27 (1979): 47–55.

20. Lefebvre, *Survival*, 40.

21. Lefebvre, "Comments," 771–2.

22. Lefebvre, *Survival*, 120.

23. Jacques Attali, *La nouvelle économie française* (Paris: Flammarion, 1978).

24. Lefebvre, "Comments," 769.

25. *Ibid.*, 773.

26. Adam Przeworski, *Capitalism and Social Democracy* (New York: Cambridge University Press, 1985).

27. Lefebvre, *De l'État*, IV, 298.

28. Lefebvre, "Comments," 775–8.

29. See, for instance, Manuel Castells, *The Rise of the Network Society* (Cambridge, MA: Blackwell, 1996).

30. Lefebvre, "Comments," 774.

31. Nicos Poulantzas, *State, Power, Socialism* (New York: New Left Books, 1978).

32. Lefebvre, *Survival*, 120.

33. Lefebvre, "Comments," 779.

34. Lefebvre, "Problèmes," 62.

35. Lefebvre, "Comments," 780.

36. Horst Müller, *Praxis und Hoffnung: Studien zur Philosophie und Wissenschaft gesellschaftlicher Praxis von Marx bis Bloch und Lefèbvre* (Bochum: Germinal, 1986); Stuart Elden, *Understanding Henri Lefebvre* (New York: Continuum, 2004).

37. See, for example, Henri Lefebvre, *Critique of Everyday Life, Volume I: Introduction*, trans. J. Moore (New York: Verso, 1991 [1958]); *La proclamation de la Commune* (Paris: Editions Gallimard, 1965); as well as *Explosion* and *Sociology of Marx*.

38. Lefebvre, *Survival*, 120.

39. Lefebvre, "Comments," 778.

40. *Ibid.*, 778, 780; see also Lefebvre, "Problèmes," 68–9.

41. Lefebvre, *De l'État*, IV, 324. There are some interesting parallels between Lefebvre's position and the arguments developed by Poulantzas in his final work, *State, Power, Socialism*, likewise published in 1978. Both authors reject the traditional binarism of reform versus revolution, as well as the established opposition between top-down (statist) versus bottom-up (civil society-based) strategies of political transformation. However, Poulantzas (*State, Power, Socialism*, 255–6) explicitly argued that the institutions of representative democracy, as inherited from the epoch of bourgeois rule, must be radicalized rather than replaced, and subsequently combined with multiple forms of direct, rank-and-file democracy and *autogestion*. For Poulantzas (*ibid.*, 260–1), therefore, the preservation of certain achievements of bourgeois/liberal democracies—such as universal suffrage, political and civil liberties, and ideological pluralism—is an essential precondition for the realization and protection of any substantively democratic form of *autogestion*. By contrast, Lefebvre remained ambivalent about the institutional framework of representative democracy, which he analyzed and criticized extensively in the fourth volume of *De l'État* (pp. 97–170). As Lefebvre notes in a footnote to that chapter (p. 170), he had not originally planned to include an analysis of political representation in *De l'État* but decided to do so following his discussions of the issue with various audiences during a visit to post-Franco Madrid in autumn 1976. For Lefebvre, one of the major operations of the modern state is to impose and enforce an equivalence upon non-equivalent social relations; representational democracy and bourgeois law are said to play constitutive roles in this "homogenizing" and "identitarian" dynamic of state domination. See *De l'État*, III, 19–36; *Le retour de la dialectique* (Paris: Messidor, 1986), 27–30. Consequently, in his accounts of social

transformation, Lefebvre emphasizes the need to democratize existent state institutions but consistently deploys the language of *autogestion* rather than that of representation. Lefebvre may well have believed that an effective radicalization and decentralization of liberal-democratic institutions would eventually reach a socialist "threshold," at which point they would be qualitatively transformed into a framework for large-scale territorial *autogestion*. However, many of his formulations seem to recycle a version of the Leninist notion of dual power, in which the bourgeois state apparatus is to be superseded entirely by workers' councils or other units of *autogestion*. In short, despite his explicit disdain for Stalinism and his consistent endorsement of a politics of radical-democratic pluralism, Lefebvre's remarks on this quite crucial issue are tantalizingly ambiguous. Whereas Jessop has examined Poulantzas's left-Eurocommunist approach to socialist strategy at considerable length (see Bob Jessop, *Nicos Poulanzas* (London: St. Martin's Press, 1985)), a more detailed inquiry into Lefebvre's unorthodox positions on these matters—including his critical appropriations of theoreticians such as Lenin, Luxemburg, and Gramsci—remains to be pursued. To my knowledge, the only sustained analyses of Lefebvre's political theory are in Elden's excellent book and Hajo Schmidt's doctoral thesis, *Sozialphilosophie des Krieges* (Essen: Klartext, 1990), 283–304.

42. Lefebvre's most detailed discussion of these issues is in his little-known essay "Problèmes théoriques de l'autogestion," published in 1966 in the inaugural issue of the journal *Autogestion* and now translated in *Henri Lefebvre: State, Space, World* ed. Neil Brenner and Stuart Elden (Minneapolis: University of Minnesota Press, 2008). This appears to be the first publication in which Lefebvre discusses revolutionary praxis in the terminology of *autogestion*. It also anticipates many of the central themes of his work on urban theory and state theory that he addressed during the subsequent fifteen years.

43. Jürgen Habermas, *Die neue Unübersichtlichkeit* (Frankfurt am Main: Suhrkamp Verlag, 1984).

44. Kipfer, "Marxism," 37–8.

45. Lefebvre, *Survival*, 121; *Explosion*, 86.

46. Lefebvre, "Comments," 769.

47. See also Elden, *Understanding Henri Lefebvre*; Andy Merrifield, *Metromarxism* (New York: Routledge, 2002).

48. The term "Fordist Marxism" is derived from Bernd Röttger, *Neoliberale Globalisierung und eurokapitalistische Regulation* (Münster: Westfälisches Dampfboot, 1997). It can be argued that Fordist Marxism also assumed distinctive politico-ideological forms in Eastern Europe, where it culminated in the Prague Spring and in the work of dissident writers such as Rudolf Bahro; and in the imperialist/postcolonial periphery, where it was expressed in the form of left critiques of the national-developmentalist projects associated with the Bandung alliance.

49. Neil Brenner and Stuart Elden, "Henri Lefebvre in Contexts," *Antipode* 33, no. 5 (2001): 763–8.

50. Philip Cerny, "Paradoxes of the Competition State," *Government and Opposition* 32, no. 2 (1997): 251–74; Bob Jessop, "Towards a Schumpeterian Workfare State?," *Studies in Political Economy* 40 (1993): 7–40.

51. Erik Swyngedouw, "Territorial Organization and the Space/Technology Nexus," *Transactions, Institute of British Geographers* 17 (1992): 431.

52. Stephen Gill, "New Constitutionalism, Democratisation and Global Political Economy," *Pacifica Review* 10, no. 1 (1998): 23–38.

53. Neil Brenner, *New State Spaces* (Oxford: Oxford University Press, 2004).

54. Claus Offe, "Ungovernability," in *Contradictions of the Welfare State* (Cambridge, MA: The MIT Press, 1984), 65–87.

55. Gill, "New Constitutionalism."

56. David Harvey, *The New Imperialism* (Oxford: Oxford University Press, 2004).

57. Roberto Unger, *False Necessity* (New York: Cambridge University Press, 1987).

58. Pierre Bourdieu, *Acts of Resistance* (New York: New Press, 1998).

59. Lefebvre, *Explosion*; *La proclamation*.

60. Habermas, *Die neue Unübersichtlichkeit*.

61. On which, see David Harvey, *Spaces of Hope* (Berkeley: University of California Press, 2000).

15

RIGHT TO THE CITY
Politics of citizenship[1]
Liette Gilbert and Mustafa Dikeç

INTRODUCTION

In January 1991, the Chief of Land-use and Planning Operations at the French Ministry of Equipment and Housing invited various researchers and academics to discuss a new law in preparation.[2] The law in question was the *Urban Development Act* (*Loi d'orientation pour la ville*, hereafter LOV), also known as the "anti-ghetto law," with the major concern to fight against social exclusion and spatial segregation. The ensuing seminar spawned lively debates that generated difficult questions, particularly concerning the opening article of the law, which read:

> In order to realize *the right to the city*, urban districts, other territorial collectivities and their groupings, the State and its public institutions assure to all the inhabitants of cities the conditions of living and dwelling in favor of social cohesion as to avoid or abate the phenomena of segregation.[3]

The invocation of "the right to the city" seemed, as one of the participants suggested, merely "a homage to the work of Henri Lefebvre."[4] Indeed, the inclusion of the catchphrase, without deliberate elaboration and careful consideration of larger structural issues, appeared unable to deliver on its promises. Besides, it was unclear what this "right" would mean for inhabitants of cities—especially for the marginalized and those without legal citizenship or "proper" papers.

Étienne Balibar was also present at the seminar. The LOV, Balibar argued, failed to take into consideration the implication of any notion of right, that is, "defining and instituting the balance between equality and freedom."[5] There was no reference to freedom; it was largely presupposed under the conditions of the free market. The allusion to equality, on the other hand, was ambiguous. It was not clear whether it implied an "egalitarian redistribution of a service or an indivisible good, situated beyond individual property, that in sum would be the urban as such, or the quality of urban life," or a conception of equality that would "attribute each individual or group a good corresponding to its rank; that is, to its financial means, and material and cultural needs."[6] This ambiguity, Balibar maintained, undermined the viability of LOV, particularly in its reference to the right to the city. What he had in mind was a third notion of equality, neither distributive nor participatory, but openly civic. Informed by such a conception, "talking about the right to the city would be a way of indicating that the city becomes as such a polis, a political collectivity, a place where public interest is defined and realized."[7]

Adopted on July 13, 1991, the LOV (with the right to the city as its opening article) was to encourage diversity through the provision of social housing: agglomerations with more than 200,000 inhabitants were obliged to provide a minimum of 20 percent social housing.[8] A letter was circulated on July 31, 1991 to clarify the articles of the law, which stated that the opening article—the right to the city—had "no normative nature."[9]

The LOV envisioned the construction of some form of community with the objective of social cohesion. But "in which space-time does this community have to be constituted?"[10] The ultimate horizon that the law implicitly presupposed was the nation-state. In a period in which the local and the global seem to be intertwined, creating new human geographies and new frameworks of action, "would it not be necessary," Balibar asked, "to formulate the questions of right, equality, and democracy in terms of global flows?" In other words, "[w]ould it not be necessary that the framework in which the urban questions are approached be a space of flow of populations and not simply an administrative and financial space?"[11]

Why did the French urban policymakers prefer to repudiate Lefebvre's notion rather than attempt to develop some normative content for it? Such an attempt would have raised at least two major issues: the terms of membership and the structural dynamics articulating society and its space; and the dialectical relationship between them. It would, in other words, have had to be confronted by a reconsideration of immigration policy and principles of citizenship, and the ethics and politics of urban society, including the socio-spatial dynamics that make the city.

Our aim in this chapter is to argue that the notion of right to the city, if it is to go beyond a catchphrase, has to be considered within a larger framework. One way to reflect on the implications of the right to the city is to consider it in relation to the current debates about immigration and citizenship, of which absolutely no mention was made in the aforementioned law. In attempting to push the conceptual boundaries of the right to the city, we shall particularly focus on Lefebvre's *Right to the City* (1968), and on *Du contrat de citoyenneté* (1990), written in collaboration with the Navarrenx Group.[12] We contend that it is particularly relevant to revisit Lefebvre's writings, which have been consistently concerned with the structural dynamics of urban society and space in an era of increased immigration and undermined citizenship.

Three decades later, Lefebvre's right to the city as a practice and argument for claiming rights and appropriating social and physical spaces of the city resonates loudly in the streets of many French and North American metropolitan areas (among others). It might be argued that the notion of new citizenship has always been (if not explicitly) part of Lefebvre's insistent call for the practice of the right to the city and the right to difference by urban inhabitants. But Lefebvre's thinking on the notion of citizenship became more explicit in his later writings, where he argued for a new citizenship linked to a new societal ethics. We are certainly not pretending to resolve his thoughts on the "social contract" (*pacte social*) and "new citizenship" that were cut short by his untimely death. It is our aim to interpret Lefebvre's writings on the right to the city and citizenship together against the backdrop of the recent urban debates revolving around immigration and citizenship.[13]

IMMIGRATION AND THE QUESTION OF CITIZENSHIP

The growing literature on the questions of immigration and citizenship is articulated around three major currents. First, immigration and citizenship directly call into question the sovereign and unitary capabilities of the nation-state, and consequently the issues of membership and its borders. Second, the notion of citizenship occupies a considerable place in current debates revolving around globalization and its unsettling impacts on the nation-state. While the flows of migrant labor have secured economic production, such new spatializations are still lacking social and political recognition of citizenship. Third, the effects of immigration, and the practices of citizenship mainly unfold at the urban level. This provides a link between Lefebvre's right to the city as elaborated in the revolutionary political context of the 1960s and the current formulation of rights-claims of urban citizenship.[14] While these three arguments are developed separately below, it is important to recognize their interrelatedness and their influences on the everyday practices of the city.

Immigration is not only an important part of the processes of economic and cultural globalization but, as Catherine Wihtol de Wenden states, the "ultimate symbol of the exercise of state sovereignty," and, therefore, "the object of tension between market logic, state logic, and human rights."[15] Usually regarded as a "threat to sovereignty and national identity," migratory movements do not enjoy the same ease of mobility of capital, goods, information, and knowledge.[16] These movements nevertheless challenge the territorial borders of the nation-state, while also probing the national boundaries of membership and its ostensible homogeneity. The immigration question, with regard to the social, economic, and political status of the immigrant, formally and informally touches on the question of citizenship, another domain in which the state exercises its sovereign powers by controlling who has access to membership. For the nation-state, the challenge is not only to ensure official citizenship provisions but to facilitate the equal practice of citizenship rights of its members, since the provision of citizenship rights does not necessarily mean that each member will equally enjoy the fruits of these rights.[17] Moreover, as the gap between provision and performance is contested, the state is confronted with the task of reconsidering the political status of the "non-citizen residents" within its borders.

Second, the citizenship literature has recently received its share of arguments about the eradicating powers of deterritorialization, either in the form of denation-alization as (the transformation of the nation-state) or of post-nationalization as a "call for global civil society and citizenship."[18] Both arguments "invoke a world without borders in which nation-states play a diminished role."[19] But these arguments eschew the difficult questions of defining the political community to which one belongs, as well as the multiple conceptions and scales of citizenship. Post-national forms of cosmopolitan or transnational citizenship have accurately emphasized the emergence of practices of citizenship outside the national realm.[20] These trends, resulting from the current processes of globalization, certainly do represent a challenge to the nationally conceived notion of citizenship, but these practices of citizenship are predominantly grounded at the sub-national level of cities. As Saskia Sassen has argued, global cities have become the strategic sites for localized practices of globalization, immigration, and citizenship.[21] What we are therefore witnessing is a gap between the terms of economic development and participation, and social and political development. In other words, low-skilled and deskilled workers become the victims of social and political alienation and the agents of new claims of citizenship.

Finally, these claims and other aspects of substantive or performative citizenship are shaped to a large extent at the urban level. Holston contends that "many cities have experienced political mobilization through local civic affiliation, which in turn resulted in a reformulation of principles of membership and distribution of resources."[22] From this argument, Holston identifies three forms of urban citizen-ship based on, first, the city as the "primary political community," second, "urban residence as the criterion of membership and the basis for political mobilization," and, third, the formulation of "right-claims addressing urban experiences and related civic performances."[23] These conceptions of urban citizenship, emphasizing the struggles over the conditions and inequities of globalization and urban life, resonate particularly well with Lefebvre's notions of the right to the city and the right to difference. The civil rights movements of the 1960s demanded equality and recognition of difference by national minority groups. More recent social mobilizations around the struggles of the *sans-papiers* in France and the current protests to regularize millions of undocumented workers in the United States invoke new conceptions of citizenship conceived on the basis of residence, of inhabiting the city.[24] These efforts, although responding to national policies, occur in the streets of cities, and the protesters constitute themselves as political subjects in and through the spaces of the city even if they are not officially recognized as citizens. Such efforts may be read as a recognition of the urban as a new spatial level where the practice or performance of citizenship unfolds through local affiliations, in contradistinction to a notion of citizenship conceived merely at an abstract level and national scale. Moreover, recent struggles of urban citizenship are also based on claiming a just access to resources, but this time by people who are not necessarily national citizens. Hence, revisiting Lefebvre's notions of the urban, of the right to the city, of the right to difference, and of new citizenship, brings urban social and political engagement to the forefront of the current debates on immigration and citizenship.

REARTICULATION OF THE URBAN

Writing in France in the mid-1960s, Lefebvre could not have envisioned the most recent intensification and diversification of international migrations, and the multiple claims and scales of citizenship related to full-blown globalization. Yet, for Lefebvre, immigrants and their marginalized positions were important (if perhaps underdeveloped) reference points for the notion of the right to the city as early as the late 1960s. Just a few decades later, the internationalization of labor has become an inherent aspect of globalization—even though the mobility of capital and goods remains far greater than the mobility of people (particularly the mobility of low-skilled workers).

Immigration has typically concentrated in cities, and, as a result, cities have become increasingly heterogeneous and culturally diverse. While cities are reemerging as more salient sites for citizenship (hence challenging the modern construct of national citizenship itself built upon the obliteration of the historical primacy of urban citizenship), claiming the right to the city does not simply translate into a relocalization of claims from the national to the urban level. Urban citizenship does not necessarily replace or negate national citizenship. The right to the city, or what Lefebvre also referred to as the right to urban life, is a claim upon society rather than a simple claim to territorial affiliation. For Lefebvre, the urban is not simply limited to the boundaries of a city, but includes its social system of production. Hence the right to the city is a claim for the recognition of the urban as the (re)producer of social relations of power, and the right to participation in it. In the words of Engin Isin, "[r]ethinking rights that arise in the age of the global city requires the articulation of the right to the city rather than rights of the city as a container of politics."[25] Thus, any attempt to frame citizenship in merely formal and territorial terms rather than substantive and structural terms will fail to recognize the role of the city as a political community that reflects the urban society and its social relations of production and power.

Lefebvre's reflection on the disjuncture between economic and social development was initially guided by a practical question relating housing to the notion of *habitat* in France in the 1960s. Postwar public housing policy attempted to deal with housing shortages and the need to accommodate an unprecedented number of foreign-born (mainly Algerian) workers. New suburban neighborhoods of public housing, commonly referred to as *grands ensembles*, led to the social and spatial peripheralization of immigrants/workers. The *grand ensemble* "had both objective (as a response to a completely new situation) and normative considerations (as an ideal of collective stability)."[26] In spite of their inclusionary intents, these housing projects led to severe problems of social exclusion and spatial segregation of immigrant workers and their families from the center of the city and society, which has been made manifest by recurring revolts in such areas, of which the incidents of fall 2005 remain a particularly striking example in terms of magnitude. This, roughly, was the context in which Lefebvre first conceived the notion of the right to the city as a way to legitimate "the refusal to allow oneself to be removed from urban reality by a discriminatory and segregative organization."[27]

Immigrants and workers were subject to discriminatory and segregated organization not only of urban space but of society. This, as Brian Turner argues, reflects the inherently contradictory nature of citizenship, which

> can be seen as (1) an inclusionary criterion for the allocation of entitlements, and (2) an exclusionary basis for building solidarity and creating identity. In this sense, national citizenship is constructed around institutionalized racism because it excludes outsiders from access to entitlements, characteristically on the basis of a racial or national identity.[28]

Marginalized from the city and its activities, immigrants and workers were, and still are, seen as a double challenge to integration in the city and to the integrity of the state, even though immigration has long provided the necessary labor force for economic development. This process of integration inevitably questions the capacity of the state and the willingness of the dominant society to define acceptable terms of admission.

Despite a façade of humanism, immigration policy in Canada and the United States has long been complicit with corporate interests and was historically institutionalized with labor or employment departments. Whether through recurrent support for guest-worker programs or through unenforced employers' sanctions and the targeting of professional qualifications, low-skilled immigrants have found themselves caught between economic and political alienation (i.e., in low-paid jobs, and with temporary or "illegal" status). Immigrant workers are consistently the scapegoats for worsening social conditions and economic instability, even though the exploitation of the immigrant labor force directly aids economic growth. But the so-called immigrant problem is not just one of marginalization of people; it is about access to affordable and decent housing, to living-wage jobs, to basic services, and to official papers. However, work permits and passports do not automatically move someone up the economic and social ladder. Immigrants have been, and continue to be, victims of economic, political, and social segregation, captive in the production system, excluded from the benefits, and marginalized from, or even denied, full participation in society.

Many people find themselves between national borders. The forces of economic and political displacement are such that some people are caught in situations where they can afford neither to stay in their countries of origin nor migrate elsewhere. The opposite condition is sometimes also true: that is, some people who manage to leave often find themselves in the precarious situation of struggling to stay while not necessarily being able to return. Think of the estimated twelve million undocumented workers/citizens living in the United States and imagine the whole population of a city like Mumbai, Shanghai, or São Paulo being completely denied its everyday existence.

Unprecedented demonstrations of support for immigrants' rights mobilized millions of people in street protests in many North American cities in spring 2006. In Chicago, Los Angeles, Washington, D.C., Milwaukee, Phoenix, and Atlanta, among many others, these demonstrations not only mobilized immigrants and immigration advocates but received the support of unions, religious and community organizations, Spanish-language media, and business groups.

Longtime and newly arrived residents marched together to oppose the HR 4437 *Border Protection, Anti-terrorism, and Illegal Immigration Control Bill* of 2005 that would make living in the United States without legal documents a felony (rather than a violation of civil law), persecute people for assisting undocumented immigrants, expand police powers over immigrants, and lead to the construction of a 698-mile security wall on the U.S.–Mexican border. This bill, also known as the Sensenbrenner Bill, was awaiting Senate approval at the time of writing, and has been the catalyst for other immigration reform proposals. Many immigration reform bills have recently been debated, including the bipartisan proposal by Senators J. McCain (Republican, Arizona) and Ted Kennedy (Democrat, Massachusetts) known as the *Secure America and Orderly Immigration Bill* of 2005. The McCain–Kennedy proposal would potentially regularize more than ten million undocumented immigrants and create a temporary worker program (long favored by President George W. Bush). Like no others, the issue of immigration has divided the Republicans between supporters of this bill and those in fear of alienating the Latino vote and business owners who are pressing for more laborers to fill jobs in construction and service industries. Another unexpected effect has been the convergence of the progressive left and corporate America in the regularization of undocumented immigrant workers.

In addition to the many controversial anti-immigration proposals and militia activities toughening border security and immigration laws, anti-immigration drives are under way in many states. Measures seeking to deny state services to undocumented immigrants have been spurred by the passage of *Proposition 200* in Arizona (in 2005) and *Proposition 187* in California (in 1994). The "effect and likely goal of *Proposition 187*," as Honig states, was "not to prevent illegal immigration but to render aliens politically invisible, to quash their potential power as democratic actors, labor organizers, and community activists."[29] Indeed, *Proposition 187* (eventually declared unconstitutional by the Supreme Court on the basis that immigration is under the sole jurisdiction of the federal government) gave rise to an impressive mobilization of "illegal" and "legal" citizens defending the right of immigrants to be part of the city where they work and live.

It is unclear what the 2006 street protests and legislative debates will yield but the explosion of protests, often the largest street demonstrations many U.S. cities have ever witnessed, is exposing the blatantly hypocritical immigration policies and recasting the debate in the media and public opinion. These claims, formulated on the basis of residence and participation in the economy, offer a "display of public citizenship in performance," claiming the right to live where one labors, and therefore demanding recognition of the immigrant contribution to the global economy and society.[30]

Some cities have been more preemptive in their approach to immigration issues. San Francisco and Cambridge, among others, declared themselves sanctuary cities for undocumented immigrants in the 1980s and have reaffirmed, in the light of the recent anti-immigration rhetoric and legislative measures, their sanctuary policy prohibiting the use of city funds to enforce the civil provisions of federal immigration law. Some mayors have supported the recent protests by immigrants and immigration activists. Antonio Villaraigosa, Mayor of Los Angeles, addressed a crowd estimated at one million, stating that "we cannot criminalize people who are working, people who are contributing to our economy and contributing to the nation."[31] Richard Daley, Mayor of Chicago, affirmed that "those who are undocumented, we are not going to make criminals out of them. Everyone in America is an immigrant."[32] In fact, as early as 2000, when momentum for regularization was building nationally (but was subsequently halted in the aftermath of 9/11), the City Council of Chicago adopted a resolution "wholeheartedly support[ing] a new legalization program to allow undocumented immigrants to obtain legal residency in the United States."[33] The resolution also support[ed] the abolition of the present system of employer sanction and . . . join[ed] ICIRR, AFL-CIO and other leading business, religious and civic leaders and organizations in urging the United States Congress to establish such a new legalization program to ensure the rights of undocumented immigrants and to insure that it is justly applied to all peoples of African descent.[34]

This municipal initiative supported the regularization of immigrants as well as the recognition of their citizenship as both a status and a practice.

However, ensuring justice in the workplace for immigrants as well as for people of African descent raises the question of practices of substantive and normative citizenship rights. The majority of the so-called minorities in the United States, as in the case of people of African descent, are national citizens. The tension between possessing rights and being able fully to practice them is exemplified by the distinction between formal status and substantive practices of citizenship. Formal citizenship is a legal category whose terms are defined by the nation-state. Each citizen, in this framework, is granted certain rights (e.g., welfare, political participation), and expected to fulfill certain obligations (e.g., paying taxes). The specifics and combinations of these rights and obligations vary according to the political community (the nation-state) in question. Yet, such official rights continue to fail a large sector of the population disadvantaged by social and economic conditions. Performative or substantive citizenship, on the other hand, refers "to the ability to act as a citizen and to be respected as one," and is "shaped by the material and ideological conditions in a society that enable people to function with some degree of autonomy, to formulate political ideas, and to act on those ideas."[35]

While a regularization program would allow undocumented immigrants to obtain legal citizenship, residence and labor rights on paper are not sufficient by themselves if they do not translate into the exercise of rights and participation in the society.[36] "Tolerating" or "legalizing" immigrant workers in the fields, factories, and kitchens of restaurants is not enough if they cannot move freely on the streets, in the media, in universities, in government positions, and in society at large. Substantive practices of citizenship emphasize the difference between rights and the ability to enjoy and perform such rights.

Lefebvre's reflections on the right to the city and the right to difference, as a right not inscribed on paper but cultivated through sharing space, could make a specifically urban contribution to the debates of citizenship rights. Normative rights provide citizens with a political voice (i.e., voting) but do not prevent social, cultural, and economic marginalization. Yet, while being officially included in a polity, this marginalization may very well prevent political representation. Even as legal citizens, people may not have their say in decisions that affect their lives. The full and effectual participation in the society in which they live might be denied, but still can be claimed. If one considers the city as the utmost site of social interaction and exchange, every person has the right to the city. Hence, the notions of the right to the city and urban citizenship connote a sense of engagement in the public and urban realm. Citizenship is acquired through public participation, and is enacted through participatory democracy. As Eleonore Kofman argues, the right to the city "was about the right to appropriate space and participate in decision making, a situation in which exchange values had not usurped use values, and where the city could be added to other abstract rights of the citizens."[37] Street protests, whether in the suburbs of Paris or in the streets of Los Angeles, act as reality checks on the marginal living conditions of people imposed by the norms of prevailing political praxis and social spatialization. For Lefebvre, the potential transformation of the dominant political culture by more inclusive or alternative social relations expressed a new citizenship.

THE RIGHT TO THE CITY AND NEW CITIZENSHIP

For Lefebvre, the right to the city represents the right to participate in society through everyday practices (e.g., work, housing, education, leisure). For him, everyday life and the urban were inextricably connected. The realization of urban life becomes possible only through the capacity to assert the social in the political and the economic realms in a way that allows residents to participate fully in society. Lefebvre's right to the city is established through social relationships, and, once claimed, it gains its own value affirming new ways of life, new social relations, and possibilities for political struggles. In this sense, the right to the city

> becomes a claim upon society for resources necessary to meet the basic needs and interests of members rather than a kind of property some possess and others do not . . . [I]n terms of rights to the city and rights to political participation, right becomes conceived as an aspect of social relatedness rather than as an inherent and natural property of individuals.[38]

Lefebvre's rights, then, were at once ethical and political projects. They were not rights to be granted from above, but rather rights to be defined and redefined through political action and social relations. Such rights were enacted through the right to difference that Lefebvre considers as resistance to centrality through and ultimately against marginalization. The complementary right to difference was "the right not to be classified forcibly into categories which have been determined by the necessarily homogenizing powers."[39] The right to the city and to difference were aimed at fighting discrimination and repression through a reinvention of the political and the development of a new societal ethics.

The implications of these rights would figure later in Lefebvre's writings with the Navarrenx Group. There is, in the collective work of Lefebvre and the Navarrenx

Group, an explicit recognition of the necessity for a new expression of citizenship. First, Lefebvre observes a discrepancy between human rights and citizen rights. He argues that human rights have been an important contribution to the rights discourse by inscribing rights to mobility, opinion, the vote into national and international institutions and constitutions. However, the discrepancy emerges from the capacity of the citizen to claim and enact human rights in a changing democratic society. Acknowledging the global transformations redefining political and economic systems, Lefebvre insists on the redefinition of new relations of dependence and interdependence which not only challenge the meaning of representative democracy but emphasize the multiple and often contradictory identities and sense of belonging now characterizing the globalized citizens. Citizens are no longer strictly defined in terms of family, origin, or place with a rather direct and simple claim of representation. Their diverse identities and affiliations reposition the question of citizenship in political, as well as ethical and philosophical terms. The new citizen is the "synthesis of the political citizen, the producing citizen and the user and consuming citizen."[40] Furthermore, in the preface of *Du Contrat de citoyenneté*, Armand Ajzenberg writes:

> The New Citizenship can be defined, for each individual and for each social group, as a possibility (as a right) to recognize and master (individually and collectively) its own conditions of existence (material and intellectual), and this simultaneously as a political actor, as a producer, as a citizen-user-consumer, in its place of residence, its city and its region, its professional and non-work related activities, as well as in its nation and in the world.[41]

Implicit in this new contract of citizenship are a new ethics and new ways of living. Such a contract implies new relationships between individuals and the state, as well as between individuals themselves. While such relations are certainly made more complex by the construction and contradiction of changing rapports between institutions and people, such a definition of new citizenship emphasizes that the citizen plays an active role in shaping this new rapport. Lefebvre calls this essential participation in society self-management (*autogestion*). In his words, self-management describes a situation where "each time a social group refuses passively to accept its conditions of existence, of life or of survival, each time such a group attempts not only to learn but to master its own conditions of existence."[42] Thus the idea of new citizenship and the project of a contract of citizenship have profound practical and political implications for the ways in which individuals participate in the processes that affect their lives. It is the formulation of this new social and political contract that holds the promises of a new societal ethics. The new rights of citizenship would be directly linked to the experiences and exigencies of everyday life.

Lefebvre's new citizen rights evidently exceed an understanding of citizenship as the nationally defined bundle of rights (e.g., voting) and obligations (e.g., paying taxes). For Lefebvre, there is a series of additional rights crucial to fully participating in society. Such rights include the right to information, to express ideas, to culture, to identity in difference (and equality), to self-management. The right to the city provides a terrain for the assertion and exercise of these rights:

> The right to the city, complemented by the right to difference and the right to information, should modify, concretize and make more practical the rights of the citizen as an urban citizen (*citadin*) and user of multiple services. It would affirm, on the one hand, the right of users to make known their ideas on the space and time of their activities in the urban area; it would also cover the right to the use of the center, a privileged place, instead of being dispersed and stuck in ghettos (for workers, immigrants, the "marginal" and even for the "privileged").[43]

CONCLUSION AND OPENING: RIGHT TO THE CITY AS SOCIETAL ETHICS

We have tried to advance three main arguments on the nature of the right to the city and its relation to contemporary debates and issues around citizenship. First, as Balibar's remarks on the LOV imply, the advancement of a right to the city calls for major changes in the structural dynamics that produce urban space. Unless the forces of the free market, which dominate—and shape to a large extent—urban space, are modified, the right to the city would remain a seductive but impossible ideal for those who cannot bid for the dominated spaces of the city; those, in other words, who cannot freely exercise their right to the city.

Second, the notion of the right to the city implies a change not only of spatial conceptions, but of society, for the ways in which the notion is conceived and justified depend very much on society itself. As May Joseph reminds us, "[t]he citizen and its vehicle, citizenship, are unstable sites that mutually interact to forge local, often changing (even transitory) notions of who the citizen is, and the kinds of citizenship possible at a given historical-political moment."[44]

Finally, there is a continuing unbundling of "the postwar political-geographical consensus" on the principle of citizenship.[45] Anti-immigration and regularization legislative proposals exposed the limits of citizenship conceived merely in abstract terms, revealing the ways in which racism is institutionalized. There obviously is a need to complement formal rights of citizenship with an ethics cultivated by living together and sharing space. The right to the city may be seen in this perspective, and recognized as a new societal ethics. This is why Lefebvre's right to difference and right to the city, years later, resonate so loudly in the recent protests offering more radical conceptions of the city.

NOTES

1. A previous version of this chapter was published as "Right to the City: Homage or New Societal Ethics?," *Capitalism, Nature, Socialism* 13, no. 2 (2002): 58–74.

2. The invitation to the seminar was made by Agnès Desmarest-Parreil, Chief of Land-use and Planning Operations at the Ministry of Equipment and Housing of France. The minutes of the seminar were later published as "Loi d'orientation pour la ville: séminaire chercheurs décideurs," in *Recherches* 20 (Paris: Ministère de l'équipement, des transports et du logement, 1991).

3. *Journal Officiel de la République Française,* July 19, 1991, trans. the authors.

4. Comment made by Véronique de Rudder, *Recherches* 20, 36.

5. Étienne Balibar, *Recherches* 20, 65, trans. the authors.

6. *Ibid.*

7. *Ibid.,* 66.

8. The implementation, however, was ineffective. Moreover, the Carrez Law of January 21, 1995 would slacken the obligation to build social housing.

9. Ministère de l'équipement, des transports et du logement, "Direction de l'architecture et de l'urbanisme, Direction de la construction," in *Circulaire no. 91–57 relative à la loi d'orientation pour la ville no. 91–662 du 13 juillet 1991* (Paris: Government of France).

10. Balibar, *Recherches* 20, 68.

11. *Ibid.*

12. Henri Lefebvre, *Le droit à la ville—espace et politique* (Paris: Editions Anthropos, 1968); Translated as "Right to the City," in Lefebvre, *Writings on Cities,* trans. and intro. E. Kofman and E. Lebas (Cambridge, MA: Blackwell, 1996); Henri Lefebvre and Le Groupe de Navarrenx, *Du contrat de citoyenneté* (Paris: Syllepse and Editions Périscope, 1990).

13. Throughout the chapter we used examples from France and the United States to illustrate our points but they are not intended to be directly comparative.

14. See, for example, Engin Isin, ed., *Democracy, Citizenship and the Global City* (London: Routledge, 2000); James Holston and Arjun Appadurai, "Cities and Citizenship," *Public Culture* 8, no. 2 (1996): 187–204.

15. Catherine Wihtol de Wenden, *Faut-il ouvrir les frontières?* (Paris: Presses de Sciences Po, 1999), 9–10, trans. the authors.

16. *Ibid.,* 10.

17. See Susan E. Clarke and Gary L. Gaile, *The Work of Cities* (Minneapolis: University of Minnesota Press, 1998).

18. Lynn A. Staeheli, "Globalization, National Cultures and Cultural Citizenship," *Geography Research Forum* 19 (1999): 60.

19. *Ibid.*

20. See Brian S. Turner, *Citizenship and Social Theory* (London: Sage, 1993); Michael P. Smith and Luis E. Guarnizo, *Transnationalism from Below* (New Brunswick: Transaction, 1998); Yasemin N. Soysal, *Limits of Citizenship* (Chicago: University of Chicago Press, 1994).

21. Saskia Sassen, "Whose City Is It? Globalization and the Formation of New Claims," *Public Culture* 8, no. 2 (1996): 205–23.

22. James Holston, "Urban Citizenship and Globalization," in *Global City-Regions: Trends, Theory, Policy,* ed. A. J. Scott (Oxford: Oxford University Press, 2001), 326.

23. *Ibid.*

24. See Étienne Balibar et al., *Sans-papiers: l'archaïsme fatal* (Paris: La Découverte,

1999); and Johanna Simeant, *La cause des sans-papiers* (Paris: Presses de Sciences Po, 1998).

25. Engin Isin, "Introduction: Democracy, Citizenship and the City," in *Democracy*, ed. Isin, 15.

26. Rémi Baudouï, "Building the Third Millennium City," trans. A. B. Hedjazi and L. Gilbert, *Critical Planning* 7 (2000): 118.

27. Lefebvre, *Writings on Cities*, 195.

28. Brian Turner, "Cosmopolitan Virtue: Loyalty and the City," in *Democracy*, ed. Isin, 137.

29. Bonnie Honig, "Immigrant America? How Foreignness 'Solves' Democracy's Problems," *Social Text* 56, no. 3 (1998): 5.

30. May Joseph, *Nomadic Identities: The Performance of Citizenship* (Minneapolis: University of Minnesota Press, 1999), 15.

31. Teresa Watanabe and Hector Beccerra, "500,000 Pack Streets to Protest Immigration Bills," *Los Angeles Times*, March 26, 2006. Available at: <http//www.latimes.com/news/local/la-me-immg26mar26,0,7628611.story?coll=la-home-headlines>.

32. Illinois Coalition for Immigrant and Refugee Rights, "People Unite! March against H.R. 4437," March 10, 2006. Available at: <http://www.icirr.org>.

33. Sasha Khokha, "Paper Chase," *Colorlines* 4, no. 2 (Summer 2001): 26–9.

34. James J. Laski, "City Clerk's Office, City of Chicago," *Chicago City Council Resolution for Legalization*. Available at: <http://www.icirr.org/newsandaction/citycouncilresolution.htm>, 2. Acronyms stand respectively for Illinois Coalition of Immigrant and Refugee Rights, and American Federation of Labor-Congress of Industrial Organizations.

35. Staeheli, "Globalization," 64.

36. David Bacon, "Which Side Are You on?," *Colorlines* 4, no. 2 (Summer 2001): 32.

37. Eleonore Kofman, "Whose City? Gender, Class, and Immigrants in Globalizing European Cities," in *Cities of Difference*, ed. R. Fincher and J. M. Jacobs (New York: Guilford, 1998), 291.

38. Holston and Appadurai, "Cities and Citizenship," 197.

39. Henry Lefebvre, *The Survival of Capitalism: Reproduction of the Relations of Production*, trans. F. Bryant (London: Allison & Bushy, 1976 [1973]), 35.

40. Armand Ajzenberg, "Henri Lefebvre: la société au point critique ou de l'individu écartelé," *Regards* (September 1998), trans. the authors. Available at: <http://www.regards.fr/archives/1998/199809/199800ideo1.html>.

41. Armand Ajzenberg, "Avant-propos," in *Du contrat de citoyenneté*, ed. H. Lefebvre and Le Groupe de Navarrenx (Paris: Syllepse and Editions Périscope, 1990), 13, trans. the authors.

42. Henri Lefebvre quoted in *ibid*.

43. Lefebvre, *Writings on Cities*, 170.

44. Joseph, *Nomadic Identities*, 3.

45. John Agnew, "The Dramaturgy of Horizons: Geographical Scale in the 'Reconstruction of Italy' by the New Italian Political Parties, 1992–95," *Political Geography* 16, no. 2 (1997): 100.

16

LUCIEN KROLL
Design, difference, everyday life[1]
Richard Milgrom

In order to create a type of politics unrealizable at present, we are trying out in advance the different methods which might one day bring about the political situation we have in mind. This is simply a matter of suggesting prototypes . . . and taking note of their possibilities and drawbacks. We have never imagined that we could bring about revolution with pockets of alternative architecture, which to make a revolutionary impact, would have to infiltrate the existing constraints. The familiar question is: "If tomorrow morning we woke up to find the earth taken over by local authorities, how would we change our way of planning and constructing the built environment?"

Lucien Kroll, 1980[2]

INTRODUCTION

Henri Lefebvre argues against the *abstract* space of capitalism, space that tends toward homogeneity and suppresses difference rather than attempting to accommodate the representational spaces and spatial practices of diverse populations.[3] He suggests, however, that a new *differential* space will emerge, one that embraces and enhances difference. In *Spaces of Hope*, David Harvey notes that Lefebvre leaves few clues as to how this space might be realized—except that it will rise from the contradictions in abstract space—or how its physical manifestations might be configured.[4] Harvey suggests that this new space cannot be imagined in the manner of the "utopias of spatial form" proposed in conventional architectural models.[5] Instead, he calls for the articulation of utopias of space and utopian processes "to build a utopianism that is explicitly spatiotemporal."[6]

The work of Belgian architect Lucien Kroll provides an example of how utopian processes (or at least thinking about them) might influence the production of urban space.[7] Rather than starting with abstract ideas about urban space, Kroll starts with the everyday lives of human populations. Describing himself as a *situationist*, Kroll works in a non-hierarchical manner, addressing concerns as they are identified, rather than assigning priorities to issues.[8] He suggests that the configuration of urban spaces must adapt to meet the changing needs of dynamic populations and recognizes that design is an integral part of the processes of habitation that should involve all human urban dwellers. The urban forms resulting from Kroll's work accentuate the differences present in the resident communities and the particularities of local contexts, while inviting change over time.

The genesis of this chapter stems from my concerns with sustainability and the particular roles that architects could play in the production of sustainable urban space. I start, therefore, with a brief discussion of architectural visions of sustainable cities. Sustainability, in design circles, tends to be uncritically accepted as an approach that emphasizes ecological processes while making few connections between social and environmental conditions. My particular concern here is with the social structures and processes that are assumed in designs that purport to address ecological issues and conditions of human health. I contend that these proposals generally fall into Lefevbre's category of *abstract space*—overlooking aspects of inhabitants' everyday lives, suppressing the diversity of populations and assuming a standardized and static social structure. In addressing the possibility of another approach to the design of cities, one that embraces the diversity of urban dwellers and assumes that ever-changing populations continually produce urban space, I place the architectural process within Lefebvre's "conceptual triad" of the production of space. Based on this analysis, I suggest that Kroll's approach to design, atypical in terms of all three of triadic elements, represents an attempt to envision differential space that includes the possibility of embracing both ecological *and* social diversity.

DESIGN, SUSTAINABILITY, AND SOCIAL DIVERSITY

For the most part, in the fields of design, sustainability has been viewed as a physical or ecological problem—the search for urban configurations that promote human physical health by providing access to light and clean air and by preserving the ecological processes that support human life. This is not a particularly new endeavor. Although not specifically identified as such, the iconic city designs of Modernism generally addressed the physical health of urban dwellers. The most frequently cited of these, like Le Corbusier's Ville contemporaine (1922) and Frank Lloyd Wright's Broadacre City (1932)[9] were developed in reaction to the congestion, pollution, and poor living conditions that had become common in the industrial cities of the late nineteenth and early twentieth centuries. Although the term was not in use at the time, they were addressing what would now be understood as issues of sustainability. In hindsight, and from an ecological point of view, these designs were badly flawed. But as Richard Ingersoll notes, Le Corbusier's towers in the park were intended to save land and concentrate services; and Wright's sprawling utopia provided agricultural land for all inhabitants, integrating the production of food into everyday lives.[10] A generation later, Paolo Soleri provided his own utopian vision of a sustainable city, in which millions would be housed in mega-structures with relatively small physical footprints.[11] While conserving most land for "nature," the ecological feasibility of Soleri's proposals, relying heavily on automated industries and energy-intensive construction techniques, were just as questionable.[12]

The Modernist visions mentioned here can be placed within Harvey's category of "utopias of spatial form." The spaces that are proposed are not the result of social processes that have occurred over time, nor do they suggest that form might change significantly if the social profile of the inhabitants changes over time. Harvey is more concerned with the

> relationship proposed between space and time, between geography and history. All these forms of Utopia can be characterized as "Utopias of spatial form" since the temporality of the social processes, the dialectics of social change—real history—are excluded, while social stability is assured by a fixed spatial form.[13]

For Harvey, a strictly aesthetic vision also risks authoritarianism as the price for stability.

Some versions of these utopian forms have been realized—certainly many North American urban renewal projects were derived from Le Corbusier's vision of towers in the park. The resulting environments provide clear illustrations of Lefebvre's concerns with abstract space:

> Formal and quantitative, it erases distinctions, as much those that derive from nature and (historical) time as those which originate in the body (age, sex, ethnicity). The signification of this ensemble refers back to a sort of super-signification which escapes meaning's net: the functioning of capitalism . . . The dominant form of space, that of the centres of wealth and power, endeavours to mould the spaces it dominates . . . and it seeks, often by violent means, to reduce the obstacles and resistance it encounters there.[14]

This description mirrors the history of urban renewal and the resulting projects that applied universal templates to a wide range of contexts and populations. Although there were forces lobbying for the provision of better housing in urban areas, economic concerns of capital, for example the need to clear slums from inner cities to maintain a safe environment for investment, were the deciding factors in the reshaping of the inner cities.[15] The bulldozing of neighborhoods illustrates the violent means employed in these efforts. The strict rules imposed on residents, particularly in public housing projects, also belie the diversity of the resident populations, imposing rules of tenure that do not acknowledge, for example, the cultural diversity of the resident populations, and deny them significant roles in the management of the neighborhoods that they occupy.

This critique should not be limited to Modernist visions, however. With rare exceptions, the recognition by some of the need to integrate understandings of ecological processes into the design of cities has not in itself managed to overcome the universal design templates used by city planners and developers.[16] Building on the environmental awareness that emerged in the 1960s and 1970s, designers developed more detailed understandings of ecological processes and the impacts that urban forms have on the environment.[17] As a result of this new knowledge, proposals for "green cities"[18] and "sustainable communities"[19] have been developed. Green city advocates have laudably made proposals for more environmentally benign technologies and green infrastructure to support urban life, but, while addressing issues of biodiversity, have not addressed the social diversity and social change present in all cities. For example, David Dilks, reporting on a workshop addressing sustainability indicators, suggests that the environmental component of urban sustainability "implies dynamic, changing [ecological] processes (rather than a steady state),"[20] while the social component "connotes social stability and encompasses equity."[21] While I have no trouble with the idea of equity, hoping to achieve social stability in the near future seems unrealistic and possibly undesirable, if for no other reason than the fact that most of the world's cities are going to continue to grow as the world's population increases. And realized examples of sustainable communities—built neighborhoods[22] and "eco-villages"[23]— are generally accessible only to those with the capital to buy into the vision by purchasing property. These visions of sustainability remain rather exclusive.

The most recent discussions about urban form have centered on the possible sustainability of the compact city.[24] Although this discourse encompasses a broad range of concerns, much of its analysis is based on questions of density, distributions of resources, questions of energy conservation, and efficiency of transportation links. Kevin Lynch argues that "functional theory," like that often found in the compact city discourse, abstracts space "in a way that impoverishes it, reducing it to a neutral container, a costly distance, or a way of recording a distribution." For Lynch, this type of approach fails to deal with the "rich textures of the city form and meaning."[25] While it may provide valuable tools for analysis of existing and proposed forms,

I suggest that it has generally failed to deal with the experience of the urban inhabitants.

For some, the idea of the compact city is being realized in the works of New Urbanists.[26] This popular design trend, based on the model of the pre-1940s American town,[27] purports to address sustainability by reducing reliance on the automobile and preserving agricultural land by building at greater densities. However, the aesthetic predilection of the designers and developers is culturally (and economically) exclusive.[28] Many of the realized neo-traditional neighborhoods include aesthetic regulations intended to maintain the appearance of a common and homogeneous culture. While the most widely published examples of built projects have been made available as a new consumption choice for the suburban market,[29] the model is now also being imposed on inner-city redevelopment, to accommodate populations that have little choice in the housing they can afford. This vision of a homogeneous community, however, is at odds with the increasing cultural diversity of urban areas in North America[30]—the social composition of the turn-of-the-millennium city bears little resemblance to that found in the early twentieth century.

Stren and Polèse provide a more satisfactory approach to understanding social sustainability, taking into account the complexity of urban social relations. Their understanding of human interactions in cities is drawn from Henri Lefebvre's concepts of the social production of space (see below) and theorists like Jordi Borja and Manuel Castells, who argue that policy-makers must accept the multicultural nature of cites. Borja and Castells argue: "Learning to live with this situation, succeeding in managing cultural exchange on the basis of ethnic difference and remedying the inequities arising from discrimination are essential aspects of the new local policy in the new conditions arising out of global interdependence."[31] Stren and Polèse provide their own definition of social sustainability, one that addresses social difference:

> Social sustainability for a city is defined as *development (and/or growth) that is compatible with the harmonious evolution of civil society, fostering an environment conducive to the compatible cohabitation of culturally and socially diverse groups, while at the same time encouraging social integration, with improvements in the quality of life for* all *segments of the population.*[32]

In architectural visions, this harmony and social integration have most frequently found physical expression in the similarity of the accommodation provided for residents in particular neighborhoods—difference is tolerated only insofar as it fits within the overall vision of the designer. Wright, for example, suggested different dwelling models for different household types in Broadacre City, but all would have conformed to a common aesthetic.[33] Implicit in the design is an understanding that the dwellers share a common culture, not only among themselves but with the architect. In Lefebvre's terms, the variety permitted is "minimal" difference that "remains within a set or system generated according to a particular law"[34]—in this case the designer's law. He uses particularly apt illustrations suggesting that minimal difference might include "the diversity of villas in a suburb filled with villas; . . . or . . . variations within a particular fashion of dress, as stipulated by that fashion itself."[35]

Harvey also identifies the need to accommodate difference, but defines the "variety of spatio-temporalities" as a central problem for the production of urban space: "accommodating a variety of spatio-temporalities, varying from that of the financial markets to those of immigrant populations whose lives internalize heterogeneous spatio-temporalities depending upon how they orientate themselves between place of origin and place of settlement."[36]

In this, Harvey is suggesting the need for the coexistence of greater differences encompassing wide ranges of cultural and spatial experience. This comes closer to Lefebvre's understanding of "maximal" or "produced" differences within which "a given set gives rise, beyond its own boundaries, to another, completely different set."[37]

Rising to this challenge would, for Lefebvre, constitute the production of a new type of space in reaction to abstract space that "carries within it the seeds of this new space"—differential space.[38] Lefebvre writes extensively about the contradictions that exist in abstract space—between, for example, use and exchange values, quality and quantity, production of objects in space (commodities) and the production of space.[39] He suggests that "inasmuch as abstract space tends towards homogeneity, towards the elimination of differences or peculiarities, a new space cannot be born (produced) unless it accentuates differences."[40]

ARCHITECTS AND THE PRODUCTION OF SPACE

Henri Lefebvre's conceptual triad provides a framework within which to address an alternative role for architects attempting to engage sustainability within the field of ecological and social diversity. For Lefebvre, space is a social product consisting of three elements: *representations of space*, or "conceived space," which for my purposes includes not only the drawings and images produced by the designer but the material manifestations of those designs in the built environment (i.e., urban form); *representational space*, "lived space" or the symbolic values produced by the inhabitants; and *spatial practice*, "perceived space" or the ways in which spaces are used.[41] These elements are not independent, and it is the interaction between them that results in the production of space (see Figure 16.1).

It is important to note, however, that while the interaction of these three elements produces space, they are also produced in space—Lefebvre notes that space is a

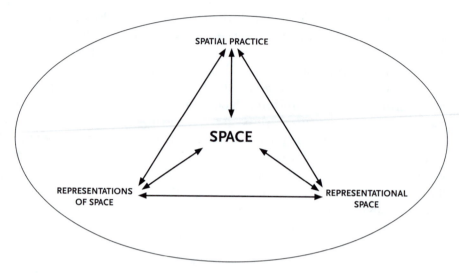

Figure 16.1 Lefebvre's conceptual triad

product of and a precondition for social processes: "space is at once result and cause, product and producer."[42] This added dimension means that space itself is not a neutral container but plays a role in shaping the social processes that determine representations of space, spatial practice, and representational space. While this appears at first glance to be a circular argument, it is actually an acknowledgment that the production of space is a continual process, and that space is always changing as conceptions, perceptions, and lived experiences change. This point further explains the "heterogeneous spatio-temporalities" that Harvey refers to as a result of moving from a place (or space) of origin to a new place (space) of settlement.

In attempting to define roles for architects and designers in the production of urban spaces, I refer to the comments of Peter Davey, made in an introduction to Lucien Kroll's work. Davey asserts that "architecture must have social effects in at least three areas: direction, production and image."[43] While he applies rather narrow definitions to these terms, I am suggesting here that they are more or less congruent with the corners of Lefebvre's triad, and as such can help develop an understanding of an architect's participation in the production of differential space.

Lefebvre designates representations of space as the dominant space in any society. It is the "space of scientists, planners, urbanists, technocratic subdividers and social engineers, as of a certain type of artist with a scientific bent—all of whom identify what is lived and what is perceived with what is conceived."[44] Clearly this is the realm within which the architect is most comfortable. By *direction*, Davey means that architecture has an influence on how people behave in space (he does not want to fall into environmental determinism, but notes that the form of urban space must have some influence on the way spaces are used). More broadly speaking, designs suggest "how people might live."[45] The designer's direction is, therefore, a representation of space—not only is it a prescription for the configuration of urban form, but it makes assumptions about the spatial practices of the users, their understandings of space, and the symbolism carrying the designer's intentions.

Because of the interrelated nature of the three elements of the triad, it is not enough to know that architects produce representations of space. Although designers may place themselves firmly in that corner, their activities are influenced by the spatial practices around them, and their own understandings of representational spaces. Spatial practice, for Lefebvre, "embraces production and reproduction, and the particular locations and spatial sets characteristic of each social formation."[46] For Davey, the second area of architectural influence is that of production. Davey's narrow interpretation here takes in social consequences of design in terms of those who produce building from designers' instructions. While this alone is a spatial practice, a broader interpretation might take into consideration the design process itself, the practice of architecture and the "social formations" involved. Clearly, the nature of these formations has an influence on the designs produced. Thomas Dutton, for example, criticizes "drawing-room" architects who, rather than engaging with social movements, practice an "aestheticized politics" in suggesting alternative urban forms.[47] In eschewing engagement and maintaining their autonomy, Dutton suggests that this practice "cannot help but generalize and universalize their discourse, in other words, to speak for the people instead of with them."[48] Although the designers in question (Leon Krier and Lebbeus Woods) base their designs on a critique of existing urban spaces, the isolated spatial practice retains an abstract nature.

Representational space, for Lefebvre, is the space of the users. It is "space as directly lived through its associated images and symbols . . . This is dominated space— and hence passively experienced—space which the imagination seeks to change and appropriate. It overlays physical space, making symbolic use of its objects."[49] Davey argues that the architect has a role to play in "their choice of imagery."[50] Moreover, he notes that at the time of writing (the early days of architectural post-Modernism), clients and architects were just starting to escape from the aesthetic dogma of Modernism and a new freedom of image-making was emerging. He is careful to add, however, that these images were often associated with particular lifestyles, and that these choices were political decisions.

While Davey talks about the designer's choices, Lefebvre's insistence that this is the realm of the user suggests it is the interpretation of the choices made that is of primary importance in the production of space. Despite the attempts by some theorists, influenced by semiotics, to develop an understanding of architecture as a language that could clearly communicate designers' meanings to the users,[51] misunderstandings have persisted. Lefebvre observes that "architects seem to have established and dogmatized an ensemble of significations, as such poorly developed and variously labeled as . . . functionalism, formalism, and structuralism. They elaborate them not from the significations perceived and lived by those who inhabit, but from their interpretation of inhabiting."[52] It is difficult to image how Dutton's "drawing-room" architects can appreciate the spaces of the users if they do not engage with them.

LUCIEN KROLL AND THE PRODUCTION OF DIFFERENTIAL SPACE

[T]here are two ways of organizing social space. The first aims at a single, predetermined objective. It is authoritarian, rational, and reductive. It corresponds to the desire to control events and people on the part of those whose task it is to conceive, organize, and produce . . . Some people like this. It corresponds to a wish to manipulate and be manipulated.

The other way of making social space . . . is a living process which imparts only key centers of activity in a clear spatial configuration and with an intensity of form and meaning that favors (and expresses) what we believe essential: living relationships and activities that spring from diversity, unexpected initiatives, and above all, that something in social man that leads to the creation of community.[53]

There are a number of striking similarities between Lefebvre's concerns with the production of space and the architectural work and supporting writings of Lucien Kroll. The quote above from Kroll, for example, more or less parallels Lefebvre's descriptions of abstract and differential space. Although Kroll met Lefebvre, he claims that he was not directly influenced by him.[54] *The Production of Space* was first published in 1974, while Kroll's best-known work, a student residence for L'Université Catholique de Louvain on the outskirts of Brussels (see Figure 16.2), was initiated in the late 1960s. It appears that the similarities are based more in common concerns, and similar experience of political events and times.

Like Lefebvre, Kroll was influenced by the student uprisings of 1968. In fact, his appointment as architect for the university residence was at the insistence of the students. The university administration's own ideas for the university campus were already partially realized; following a strict Modernist segregation of functions, an anonymous mass-production aesthetic (abstract), and an institutional image. The students found this environment overwhelming and alienating, and "demanded that the project be broken up and mixed in with the functions and families in the adjacent neighbourhoods."[55] The university agreed to the students' choice of architect, thinking that the design team would assume the typical hierarchical role of the expert and that ultimately the university's agenda would be served by the conventional practice of architecture. But Kroll contrasts the "authoritarian,

Figure 16.2 Student residence, L'Université Catholique de Louvain, Brussels

paternalistic order" of the pre-existing institution and its architecture with his team's approach that moved toward "diversity, everyday culture, decolonization, the subjective, toward an image compatible with the idea of self-management, an urban texture with all its contradictions, its chance events, and its integration of activities"[56] (see Figure 16.3). He claims that this approach is political rather than aesthetic, and compares his work with the complexity of ecological systems.[57] While Lefebvre criticizes the focus on "things in space" (commodities) rather than a broader understanding of production of space,[58] Kroll suggests that his practice has "moved far from the traditional role of the architect as maker of isolated objects." Instead, Kroll's emphasis is on the "relationships between people in space that suits them . . . Construction finds its meaning only in the social relations that it supports."[59]

Kroll insists that his commissions should allow the designers to work directly with the present and/or future users, adamantly believing that the relations of users and the environments of their everyday lives can be understood only if the users themselves are as engaged as possible in the design process. In this engagement Kroll attempts to address one of the fundamental challenges presented by abstract space— what Lefebvre has referred to as the "silence of the users." He asks: "when the interested parties—the 'users'—do not speak up, who can speak in their name or in their place?" There have been some attempts within the design professions to address this problem, and Lefebvre singles out "advocacy planning" in the United States as

Figure 16.3 Kroll's work contrasted with other campus architecture of the period

an example.[60] He states: "The notion was that . . . 'users' and 'inhabitants,' as a group, would secure the services of someone competent, capable of speaking and communicating—in short an advocate—who would negotiate for them with political or financial institutions."[61] In Lefebvre's thinking, these attempts to speak for the users were bound to fail "because no one has the right to speak for those directly concerned here. The entitlement to do so, the concepts to do so, the language to do so are simply lacking. How would the discourse of such an expert differ from that of the architects, 'developers' or politicians?"[62] Although these practitioners were well intentioned, their efforts ultimately fell short because they did not give voice to the silent users, choosing instead to speak for them, interpreting their needs.[63]

Kroll attempts (with varying degrees of success) to work with the users, and also to take into account how future users might be involved in producing their own environments, even after the architects are no longer engaged in the project. In addressing the present *and* future concerns of users, Kroll has drawn heavily on the work of SAR (Stichting Architecten Research) and John Habraken,[64] particularly their research on the concepts of "supports" and "infill."[65] Habraken's approach suggested that a system of key structures could be placed permanently in the urban environment, to support the infill elements provided by future residents. The idea was to provide accommodation that would meet the needs of future generations, as well as those who first occupied the sites, since infill could be changed with no negative effects on the structural integrity of the whole.

One of the best examples of an application of these principles (apart from Kroll's work) is, surprisingly and maybe inadvertently, in a project designed originally by Le Corbusier. In the 1920s, the architect was commissioned to design a new neighborhood in Pessac, a suburb of Bordeaux. His vision consisted of Modernist flat-roofed houses, featuring clean, machine-like geometries and an artistic interplay of open and closed spaces. The development is best known, however, not for Le Corbusier's architectural vision, but for the modifications that the residents have made to the buildings over time. Occupied, the structures bear little resemblance to the blueprints as residents have added decorative elements that many architects would claim undermine the purity of the original design. Lefebvre, however, in the preface to a case study of Pessac, praises the residents for their initiatives as well as the architect for designing structures that could so easily accommodate the desires of the users:

> Instead of installing themselves in their containers, instead of adapting to them and living in them "passively," they decided that as far as possible they were going to live "actively." In doing so they showed what living in a house really is: an activity. They took what had been offered to them and worked it, converted it, added to it. What did they add? Their needs. They created distinctions . . . They introduced personal qualities. They built a differentiated social cluster.[66]

There is also a parallel in the connections of both Lefebvre and Kroll with Situationism. Lefebvre's work had a well-documented influence on the Situationists and their concerns with the disruptions imposed by capitalism and Modernism on the spaces of everyday life in the mid-twentieth century. In the early days of the movement, the search for alternative urban visions, a "unitary urbanism," was presented in terms like those used to describe differential space, acknowledging "no boundaries; it aims to form a unitary human milieu in which separations such as work/leisure or public/private will finally be dissolved."[67]

One of the methods employed by the Situationists in their interrogation of and interaction with the city was referred to as the "drift" (dérive). Their search for the valuable elements of the city, those not degraded by capitalism, was undertaken by wandering through the city following a spontaneously determined path. Simon Sadler relates Situationist Guy Debord's explanation of this as

> "playful constructive behavior" that . . . should not be confused . . . with "classical notions of the journey and the stroll"; drifters weren't like tadpoles

in a tank "stripped . . . of intelligence, sociability and sexuality," but were people alert to "the attractions of the terrain and the encounters they find there," capable as a group of agreeing upon distinct, spontaneous preferences for routes through the city.[68]

Supporting this Situationist approach, Kroll argues against the methods of "functional spatial organizers" and their imposed hierarchies with similar vocabulary:

The approach of the "Situationist" in architecture . . . consists of pre-occupying oneself with the first object one comes across, at random and carefully noting its personal characteristics in order to be able to integrate it into a general context without destroying it or reducing it to a semi-abstraction.[69]

In this manner, Kroll hopes to embrace differences that are encountered, whether they are in architectural form, the symbolic values of users, or the spatial practices of everyday life. Rather than ignoring differences or placing them in, and suppressing them with, a preconceived hierarchy, Kroll understands difference as an opportunity to engage with users and to allow them to engage with the environments that they inhabit.

While there were strong links between Lefebvre and the Situationists in the late 1950s, they parted company in the early 1960s. According to Mary McLeod, he had been attracted to their "active engagement in spatial experimentation, their focus on urban transformation, and their global critique." However, he "never accepted the Situationists' belief in the revolutionary potential of situations or short-term events. He believed that revolutionary change was a slower and more comprehensive process, less theatrical and individualistic, necessitating a more historically grounded engagement with everyday life."[70]

Writing about Lefebvre's *Critique of Everyday Life*, McLeod goes on to note that in his understanding of utopia, "only by proposing alternative possibilities, conducting endless experiments, and constructing new futures could individuals and groups actively initiate the process of social transformation"; and that his notion of utopia "precluded any totalitarian synthesis or controlling a priori vision."[71] Closely paralleling Kroll's statements that his process is "simply a matter of suggesting prototypes . . . and taking note of their possibilities and drawbacks," Lefebvre asserts in *Right to the City* that utopia should be

considered experimentally by studying its implications and consequences on the ground. These can surprise. What are and what would be the most successful places? How can they be discovered? According to which criteria? What are the times and rhythms of daily life which are inscribed and prescribed in these "successful" spaces favourable to happiness? That is interesting.[72]

CONCLUSION

Kroll acknowledges that his work is utopian. As he notes in the quote at the beginning of this chapter, his work addresses "a type of politics unrealizable at present." But, unlike most other architects, who have been content to conceive new representation of space in isolation, Kroll recognizes that, in order to have any chance at implementation, a new vision must be based in an understanding of the social processes that would be involved in realizing that vision. As David Harvey has argued, utopian visions must be derived from utopian processes, and it is in this regard that Kroll's work is remarkable. He is perhaps best known for his attempts at participatory design (and has been known to insist on community involvement before accepting commissions), but he also realizes that his desire for full participation, for giving voice to all the users, is an unrealistic expectation within current social structures.

Returning to the conceptual triad (as modified by Davey's architectural concerns), Kroll's work is atypical in all three areas. His representations of space are different, diversified, complex, and maybe even cluttered, yet they appear to invite change. Rather than imposing an order on the built environment, Kroll hopes that a complex ecological order will emerge from the needs and desires (spatial practices and representational spaces) of the users. In this sense, his vision is part of a process rather than the result of one.[73]

Kroll's own spatial practice, that is the design processes he initiates, differs significantly from conventional and Modernist architectural practices. His insistence on the participation of users is rare in design fields (but not unheard of), and he has taken involvement further. Recognizing that the future users of the building are not the only people affected by its design, and following Davey's logic that the architect has social effects in determining how buildings are constructed, Kroll's work on the university residence is particularly unusual in that he left some design decisions to the builders. The pattern of the window openings, the changes of wall materials, and the brick sculptures were often left to the discretion of the workers. This involvement of the workers as users makes Kroll's spatial practice still more inclusive and adds yet another layer of complexity to the built environment.

Finally, it is through this inclusive spatial practice that Kroll hopes to address the representational spaces of the users. In most cases, designers and their clients have very different sets of values and understandings of space. Kroll acknowledges and embraces these differences. On the cover of his book *Enfin chez soi* (*Home at Last*)[74] a garden gnome has a prominent place. He makes this symbolic statement in recognition that the elements that constitute home, the symbolic values of the user, may differ significantly from those of the designer. Kroll welcomes symbolic as well as practical interventions of users.

Unlike most other designers, Kroll acknowledges that difference in environments that humans inhabit and create does not fit into fixed sets. His methods seek differences rather than working to suppress it, and present the possibility of addressing Lefebvre's "maximal" difference. Lefebvre argues that the resulting "produced difference presupposes the shattering of the system; it is born of an explosion; it emerges from the chasm opened up when a closed universe ruptures."[75] While Kroll does not imagine that his individual projects "could bring about a revolution,"[76] his work provides a glimpse of what might happen if the contradictions of abstract space were acknowledged and addressed in the design of human environments.

NOTES

1. A previous version of this chapter was published as "Realizing Differential Space? Design Processes and Everyday Life in the Architecture of Lucien Kroll," *Capitalism, Nature, Socialism* 13, no. 2 (2002): 75–95.
2. Lucien Kroll, "Architecture and Bureaucracy," in *Architecture for People*, ed. B. Mikellides (New York: Holt, Rinehart and Winston, 1980), 162–3.
3. Henri Lefebvre, *The Production of Space*, trans. D. Nicholson-Smith (Cambridge, MA: Blackwell, 1991).
4. David Harvey, *Spaces of Hope* (Berkeley: University of California Press, 2000), 183.
5. *Ibid.*, ch. 8.
6. *Ibid.*, 182.
7. For a monograph of works, see Lucien Kroll, *Buildings and Projects*, trans. J. Masterson (New York: Rizzoli, 1987).
8. Lucien Kroll, "The Soft Zone," *Architectural Association Quarterly*, December (1975): 54.
9. Robert Fishman, *Urban Utopias in the Twentieth Century: Ebenezer Howard, Frank Lloyd Wright, Le Corbusier* (Cambridge, MA: The MIT Press, 1982).
10. Richard Ingersoll, "Second Nature: On the Social Bond of Ecology and Architecture," in *Reconstructing Architecture: Critical Discourses and Social Practices*, ed. T. Dutton and L. H. Mann (Minneapolis: University of Minnesota Press, 1996).
11. Paolo Soleri, *Arcology: The City in the Image of Man* (Cambridge, MA: The MIT Press, 1969).
12. For a discussion of physical versus ecological footprints of urban areas see Mathis Wackernagel and William Rees, *Our Ecological Footprint: Reducing Human Impact on the Earth* (Gabriola Island, BC: New Society Publishers, 1996).
13. Harvey, *Spaces of Hope*, 160.
14. Lefebvre, *Production of Space*, 49.
15. Michael Goldrick, "The Anatomy of Urban Reform in Toronto," in *The City and Radical Social Change*, ed. D. I. Roussopoulos (Montreal: Black Rose, 1982), 267.
16. See Michael Hough, *Out of Place: Restoring Identity to the Regional Landscape* (New Haven, CT: Yale University Press, 1990); and Eran Ben-Joseph, *The Code of the City: Standards and the Hidden Language of Place Making* (Cambridge, MA: The MIT Press, 2005).

17. Much of this improved understanding builds on works like Ian McHarg, *Design with Nature* (Garden City, NY: The Natural History Press, 1969); Anne Whiston Spirn, *The Granite Garden: Urban Nature and Human Design* (New York: Basic Books, 1984); and Michael Hough, *Cities and Natural Process: A Basis for Sustainability*, 2nd edn (New York: Routledge, 2004).

18. For example, David Gordon, ed., *Green Cities: Ecologically Sound Approaches to Urban Space* (Montreal: Black Rose Books, 1990); Richard Register, *Ecocity Berkeley: Building Cities for a Healthy Future* (Berkeley: North Atlantic Books, 1987); Nancy Jack Todd and John Todd, *From Eco Cities to Living Machines: Principles of Ecological Design* (Berkeley: North Atlantic Books, 1994).

19. Sim van der Ryn and Peter Calthorpe, eds., *Sustainable Communities: A New Design Synthesis for Cities, Suburbs and Towns* (San Francisco: Sierra Club Books, 1986).

20. David Dilks, *Measuring Urban Sustainability: Canadian Indicators Workshop, June 19–21 1995, Workshop Proceedings* (Ottawa: State of the Environment Directorate, Environment Canada Centre for Future Studies in Housing and Living Environments, Canada Mortgage and Housing Corporation, 1996), 21.

21. *Ibid.*, 23.

22. Judy Corbett and Michael N. Corbett, *Designing Sustainable Communities: Learning from Village Homes* (Washington, DC: Island Press, 2000).

23. Gaia Trust and Global Eco-Village Network, *The Earth is Our Habitat: Proposal for Support Programme for Eco-Habitats as Living Examples of Agenda 21 Planning* (Copenhagen: Gaia Trust, 1996).

24. Michael Breheny, ed., *Sustainable Development and Urban Form* (London: Pion, 1992); M. Jenks, E. Burton, and K. Williams, eds., *The Compact City: A Sustainable Urban Form?* (London: E. & F. N. Spon, 1996); Katie Williams, Elizabeth Burton, and Mike Jenks, eds., *Achieving Sustainable Urban Form* (London: E. & F. N. Spon, 2000).

25. Kevin Lynch, *Good City Form* (Cambridge, MA: The MIT Press, 1981), 39.

26. Michael Neuman, "The Compact City Fallacy," *Journal of Planning Education and Research* 25, no. 1 (2005).

27. Peter Katz, ed., *The New Urbanism: Towards an Architecture of Community* (Toronto: McGraw Hill, 1994); Alex Krieger, Andres Duany, and Elizabeth Plater-Zyberk, *Towns and Town-Making Principles* (New York: Rizzoli, 1991).

28. Ute Angelika Lehrer and Richard Milgrom, "New (Sub)Urbanism: Countersprawl or Repackaging the Product," *Capitalism, Nature, Socialism* 7, no. 26 (1996); Ivonne Audirac and Anne Shermyen, "An Evaluation of Neotraditional Design's Social Prescription: Postmodern Placebo or Remedy for Suburban Malaise?," *Journal of Planning Education and Research* 13 (1994).

29. See Jill Grant, *Planning the Good Community: New Urbanisms in Theory and Practice* (New York: Routledge, 2005).

30. Leonie Sandercock, ed., *Making the Invisible Visible: A Multicultural Planning History* (Berkeley: University of California Press, 1998).

31. Jordi Borja and Manuell Castells, *Local and Global: Management of Cities in the Information Age* (London: Earthscan, 1997), 89.

32. Richard Stren and Mario Polèse, "Understanding the New Sociocultural Dynamics of Cities: Comparative Urban Policy in a Global Context," in *The Social Sustainability of Cities: Diversity and the Management of Change*, ed. M. Polèse and R. Stren (Toronto: University of Toronto Press, 2000), 15–16, emphasis in original.

33. Frank Lloyd Wright, *The Living City* (New York: Horizon Press, 1958).

34. Lefebvre, *Production of Space*, 372.
35. *Ibid.*
36. David Harvey, "Cities or Urbanization," *City* 1/2 (1996): 52.
37. Lefebvre, *Production of Space*, 372.
38. *Ibid.*, 52.
39. *Ibid.*, ch. 6.
40. *Ibid.*, 52.
41. Lefebvre uses the term perceived to mean the "practical basis of the perception of the outside world," the use of the body, the "gestures of work and those not related to work." *Ibid.*, 40.
42. *Ibid.*, 142.
43. Peter Davey, "The Political Angle," *The Architectural Review*, October (1981), 203.
44. Lefebvre, *Production of Space*, 38.
45. Davey, "The Political Angle," 204.
46. Lefebvre, *Production of Space*, 33.
47. Thomas Dutton, "Cultural Studies and Critical Pedagogy: Cultural Pedagogy and Architecture," in *Reconstructing Architecture: Critical Discourses and Social Practice*, ed. T. A. Dutton and L. H. Mann (Minneapolis: University of Minnesota Press, 1996).
48. *Ibid.* 194.
49. Lefebvre, *Production of Space*, 39.
50. Davey, "Political Angle," 204.
51. See Geoffrey Broadbent, Richard Bunt, and Charles Jencks, eds., *Signs, Symbols, and Architecture* (Toronto: John Wiley and Sons, 1980); Geoffrey Broadbent, Richard Bunt, and Tomas Llorens, eds., *Meaning and Behaviour in the Built Environment* (Toronto: John Wiley & Sons, 1980); Charles Jencks and George Baird, eds., *Meaning in Architecture* (London: Barrie and Rockliff, The Cresset Press, 1969).
52. Henri Lefebvre, "The Right to the City," in *Writings on Cities*, ed. E. Kofman and E. Lebas (Cambridge, MA: Blackwell, 1996), 152.
53. Lucien Kroll, "Anarchitecture," in *The Scope of Social Architecture*, R. Hatch, ed. (New York: Van Nostrand Reinhold, 1984), 167–9.
54. Lucien Kroll, interview with the author, Brussels, May 25, 2000.
55. Kroll, "Anarchitecture," 167.
56. *Ibid.*
57. Kroll, interview.
58. Lefebvre, *Production of Space*, 410.
59. Kroll, "Anarchitecture," 167.
60. Lefebvre, *Production of Space*, 364–5. See also the "community architecture" movement in Britain: Graham Towers, *Building Democracy: Community Architecture in the Inner Cities* (London: UCL Press, 1995); Nick Wates and Charles Knevitt, *Community Architecture: How People Are Creating Their Own Environments* (London: Penguin, 1987).
61. Lefebvre, *Production of Space*, 364.
62. *Ibid.*
63. Allan David Heskin, "Crisis and Response: A Historical Perspective on Advocacy Planning," *American Institute of Planners Journal*, January (1980); Lisa R. Peattie, "Reflections on Advocacy Planning," *American Institute of Planners Journal*, March (1969).
64. Kroll, "Anarchitecture," 171.

65. N. J. Habraken, *Supports: An Alternative to Mass Housing*, trans. B. Valkenburg (New York: Praeger, 1972).

66. Henri Lefebvre, preface to Phillipe Boudon, *Lived-in Architecture: Le Corbusier's Pessac Revisited*, trans. G. Onn (London: Lund Humphries, 1979 [1969]).

67. Guy-Ernest Debord, "Situationist Theses on Traffic," *Internationale Situationniste #3 (November 1959)*, trans. K. Knabb. Available at: <http://www.cddc.vt.edu/sionline/si/traffic.html>.

68. Simon Sadler, *The Situationist City* (Cambridge, MA: The MIT Press, 1999), 77–8.

69. Lucien Kroll, "The Soft Zone," 54.

70. Mary McLeod, "Henri Lefebvre's Critique of Everyday Life: An Introduction," in *Architecture of the Everyday*, ed. S. Harris and D. Berke (New York: Princeton Architectural Press/Yala Publications on Architecture, 1997), 21.

71. *Ibid.*, 16.

72. Lefebvre, "Right to the City," 151.

73. On an ironic note, the university in Brussels has decided that the residence, designed to be changed by each generation of students and with the understanding that materials age naturally, is a building of architectural importance and has now started to initiate measures to preserve it. So while the designers looked forward to changes like the weathering of materials, sealants are now being applied to limit further change. (Dag Boutsen, Atelier Kroll, comments on tour of residence building, May 24, 2000.)

74. Lucien Kroll, *Enfin chez soi . . . Réhabilitation de préfabriqués: écologies & composants propositions* (Paris: Editions l'Harmattan, 1994).

75. Lefebvre, *Production of Space*, 372.

76. Kroll, "Architecture and Bureaucracy," 162.

PART IV

CONCLUSION

17

GLOBALIZING LEFEBVRE?

Stefan Kipfer, Christian Schmid,
Kanishka Goonewardena,
and Richard Milgrom

INTRODUCTION

This book presents in many respects a different Henri Lefebvre. Whereas, in the English-speaking context, the most influential Lefebvre readings have centered on urban marxist political economy and postmodern geographical interpretations, most of the contributors to this volume go beyond these views. Some of them reconstruct Lefebvre's epistemological basis in order to understand his theoretical concepts, such as *space*, *difference*, and *everyday life*. Others trace links between Lefebvre and a number of his intellectual contemporaries, such as Axelos, Bachelard, Breton, Debord, Gramsci, Heidegger, Kroll, Lukács, and Merleau-Ponty. While noting the limitations of Lefebvre's theoretical life-project, most authors in this volume understand Lefebvre as an important source of inspiration for their work and have stressed the importance of "translating" his work for today's world and political conjuncture.

In this sense, it is possible to point to a "third" constellation of Lefebvre scholarship, one that links his urban-spatial contributions to the most promising, dialectical aspects of his broader theoretical projects and political commitments. This is in no way intended to open up a new "Lefebvre School," nor to develop a unifying perspective. Contributors in this collection see Lefebvre's work serving as a promising starting point, and they try to go beyond it to open up new perspectives for analytical interpretation as well as political action.

Attempts to interpret authors in their historical-geographical context are by necessity an excavation for the present and the future. Any contemporary engagement with past writing implies that the meaning of a text is not fully exhausted by its historical context. As we know from various theorists, including Lefebvre, every particular historical and geographical situation is tied to the past and the future by multiple temporal rhythms. The rhythms of cultural practice (including intellectual work) are not neatly synchronized with other temporalities. Translating past intellectual work, to echo Walter Benjamin, is an active intervention into multiple temporalities and depends on strategies of de- and re-contextualization.

As Neil Brenner and Klaus Ronneberger remind us in this volume, Lefebvre's life's work was strongly shaped by the formation and crisis of Fordism as well as the social struggles in French marxist debates responding to this context. In this sense, Lefebvre's work is limited in ways not dissimilar to those of other Western Marxists. Still, he continues to be relevant today, partly because there are historical continuities between postwar capitalism and the contemporary world order, partly because elements of Lefebvre's work can be fruitfully brought to bear on contemporary intellectual debates. Most prominently, contributors to this volume highlight Lefebvre's relevance for theorizations not only of space, difference, and everyday life, but of time, modernity, hegemony, state, scale, urbanization, architectural practice, and radical political strategy.

How is it possible to make Lefebvre "live" today by more decisively "globalizing" the insights in his life's work? We start by linking Lefebvre's thinking about the protorevolutionary urban "moments" of 1871 and 1968 to the contemporary worldwide conjuncture of politics. The entry point to this discussion will be the wave of urban uprisings in the France of late 2005 and early 2006. Next, we sketch how Lefebvre's work holds considerable promise for analyzing transnational urbanization and attendant social struggles. Central to Lefebvre's relevance in this regard are his multi-scalar notions of *centrality*, *periphery*, and *colonization*. Finally, we reflect upon the possibilities of incorporating and rearticulating Lefebvre's meta-philosophy into a "global" formation of radical theory. In all sections, we underline the importance of fusing Lefebvre's European perspective with anti-colonial and feminist traditions. In this regard, Lefebvre's persistent critique of specialized and academic knowledge remains crucial.

THE URBAN REVOLT OF 2005 IN PARIS

On October 27, 2005, two boys, Zyed Benna and Buna Traoré, were killed by electrocution in a transformer station while trying to escape police harassment in Clichy-sous-Bois, an eastern suburb of Paris. For three weeks after that, youths in popular suburbs around Paris and then across the country engaged the police in street battles and burned cars, schools, and shops. Most of the rioters were apparently young male French citizens without criminal records and with familial links to France's former colonies. The then Interior Minister Nicolas Sarkozy described them as "scum" (racaille) and demanded the "mopping up" of popular suburban housing projects. While the deaths sparked the actions, the uprising was in fact a reaction to the Chirac government and its politics of intensified neoliberalism, aggressive law and order campaigns, and "culture wars" aimed at demonizing Islamic culture. In this sharpening conjuncture, the uprising articulated three pre-existing structural conditions: socio-economic inequality, precariousness, and structural unemployment; racialized exclusion coupled with experiences of daily humiliation at the hands of authorities; and a growing gulf between all forms of organized politics and third-generation residents of the popular suburbs (la génération de cité).[1]

The right to the city

Some commentators insisted that the uprising of 2005 was difficult to understand without recourse to Henri Lefevbvre's urban work.[2] It helps to recall that Lefebvre's political orientation strongly hinged upon his path-breaking analysis of the role of spatial relations in the revolutionary moments of 1871 and 1968. As Andy Merrifield, Sara Nadal-Melsió, and Stefan Kipfer point out in this volume, Lefebvre's work on everyday life, the state, the city, and space was shaped by May 1968 and the decades on either side of those events. As a professor in Strasbourg (1961–5) and Nanterre (after 1965), Lefebvre supported student struggles before and during May 1968. Elements of his work (on marxism, everyday life, autogestion) were known among activists at the time.[3] Indeed, Lefebvre's own reading of 1968 captured the key aspects of the mobilizations.[4] He saw May 1968 as a twentieth-century version of the Commune of 1871, a specifically urban interruption of the linear time and abstract space of postwar capitalism and its colonial aspects. This protorevolutionary rupture was produced by a spatial dialectic of struggle that linked the segregated suburban social spaces of students, workers, and immigrants with Paris's Left Bank in calls for the right to the city. The result was an experience of the city as a collective work of art (see Nadal-Melsió, this volume).[5]

Lefebvre's perspective, which is at odds with the revisionist view of 1968 as a mere counter-cultural movement of spoiled middle-class kids,[6] invites us to draw parallels between 1968 and 2005. Both events were part of a history of urban struggle against spatial peripheralization that dates back at least to the Commune. They suspended the normal course of daily life. Rioters and resident bystanders of different generations and genders intermingled in festive scenes and seemed to say: "the city is ours."[7] The uprising of 2005 was a struggle for the right to the city also because it rebelled against socio-spatial peripheralization and threatened to overtake the central cities. Such a spatial dynamic linking city and suburb was prevented only by the efforts of paramilitary forces and state of emergency legislation that allowed the state to deport rioters and suspend freedom of association. The deportation measure was first used to expel strikers in 1934 and dissidents during the 1930s. The emergency laws date back to efforts to stop decolonization in 1955 (in Algeria) and 1985 (in New Caledonia).

A lost generation?

The uprising of 2005 emerged from the most segregated parts of the suburbs where colonial aspects were more prominent than in 1968. It was rooted in a history of suburban riots against exclusion and police brutality dating back to the late 1970s.[8] While novel in terms of scale, duration, and intensity of mobilization, it was also shaped by the racialized experience of "apartheid à la française."[9] Young people with family connections to the former French colonies were the clear majority of the rioters. Unlike their grandparents and parents, they are no longer seen as "immigrant workers" or beurs (second-generation North African immigrants) with at least one foot in the world of the organized left and struggles for immigrant rights, fair rents, and workplace justice. Instead, they conjure up the media image of racialized, demonized "youth" with no perspective other than violence and chaos.

After three decades of socio-spatial polarization and segmentation, the postwar suburbs that are their home are no longer considered the "red belt" (couronne rouge), the organized "red" (communist) threat to bourgeois city centers, as they had been from the 1920s until the 1960s. They are also no longer as strongly shaped by left-leaning struggles for equality and against racism—represented by events like the annual Marche pour l'égalité et contre le racisme in the mid-1980s.[10] The social spaces of the third and fourth suburban generations are now treated as social pathologies that associate unemployment and immigration with crime and rampant male violence.[11] Ghettoization, disappointment with left governments, and resurgent racism have distanced these generations from formal political channels and left organizations.[12] As a result, the uprising did not originate with formal political organizations, nor was it articulated in left-wing terms. Even local associations, organized Islam, and anti-racist groups have no or only fleeting relationships with the rioters.[13] Without an organized voice, the movement of 2005 appeared on the scene ghost-like, visible and invisible at the same time.[14]

The segmentation of social movements

Following 1968, Lefebvre pointed to the difficulties associated with connecting distinct social groups (students, workers, immigrants in the north, peasants and slum dwellers in the south), whose experiences of peripheralization were rooted in distinct processes.[15] Today, the segmentation of social movement mobilization is hard to overlook. The uprising of 2005 had only weak links to other strands of mobilization. It occurred in the period immediately following the successful referendum campaign against the constitution of the European Union in May 2005, which had been spearheaded by unions and anti-globalization forces on the left of the Socialist Party. Shortly after the uprising—in February and March 2006— students and unions staged a series of strikes, road blockades, and mass demon- strations against "precarious" work. This led to the withdrawal of a law that would have removed young workers from the "hire and fire" protections provided by French employment law. Most clearly in the tradition of French anti-globalization (alter-mondialiste) politics, these student/labor mobilizations overlapped only marginally with the milieus of youth rioters and, in some cases, actually clashed with youth for whom education no longer offers any hope of social advancement.[16] They also overlapped only partly with the (unsuccessful) efforts of immigrant rights activists to block another punitive response to the uprising: a harsh reform of French immigration laws that will make permanent the precarious status of migrants without papers.[17]

Importantly, the social spaces of popular suburbs have strong material and symbolic ties to transnational migrant networks and associated subcultural practices.[18] In this transnational context, geopolitical concerns about imperialism often come into direct contact with experiences of socio-spatial exclusion in the banlieue. Today, it is not uncommon for suburban youth to link their experience of segregation and racism in France to the occupations in Iraq, Palestine, Haiti, and the Ivory Coast.[19] Such anti-imperial and anti-colonial sentiment is much less central within the networks of student and labor mobilization that shaped the protests in the winter of 2006. This bifurcation between "social" and "anti-colonial" struggles—a distinction often made in France—highlights the difficulty of linking points of mobilization positioned differentially vis-à-vis dynamics of socio-spatial peripheralization. This difficulty was in evidence back in 1968.[20] But today, more than ever, the uneven development of anti-systemic politics suggests the need for a differentially articulated globalization of calls for the right to the city.[21]

CENTRALITIES AND PERIPHERIES IN A GLOBALIZED WORLD: A RESEARCH AGENDA

These reflections on recent urban struggles in France indicate a need to deepen our understanding of the links between the "colonial management of the planet" and the "colonial management of the neighborhood," to cite a Paris-based anti-racist organization.[22] Lefebvre's conception of urbanization, as an articulation of central and peripheral social spaces that mediates the social order, appears promising here.

Transnational urbanization

Lefebvre's hypothesis of the "complete urbanization of the world" is more relevant today than ever.[23] Just think of the exploding literatures on transnational urbanization: global and globalizing cities, scale and globalization, transnational urbanism, cosmopolis, colonial and Third World cities, imperial and postcolonial urbanization. Nevertheless, Lefebvre offers a view of the urbanization process that is distinct from most others. He analyzes the urban not as accomplished reality but as possibility, a potential that is inherent in existing urbanization but can be realized only through fundamental social change: an urban revolution. The peculiar quality of this analysis is that it does not limit itself to a critique of the urbanization process but thinks through the implications of this process to lay bare its social possibilities. This reveals a potential that Lefebvre programmatically calls "urban society."

In order to grasp the specific character of the urbanized world, a fundamental reorientation of analysis is required: the city has to be embedded in the context of society as a whole. Seen from this perspective, the focus of the analysis changes, from the city as an object to the process of urbanization and its implications. As Ronneberger, Schmid, Kipfer, and Kanishka Goonewardena remind us in this volume, Lefebvre saw the urban at the same time as form and as level of analysis.

Level: mediation

Lefebvre identifies the urban as a specific level or order of social reality. It is a middle or mediating level situated between the private level, the nearby order, the realm of everyday life, on the one hand; and the global level, the distant order, the realm of the global market, of the state, of knowledge, of institutions, and of ideologies, on the other. The urban is the middle level of analysis and thus mediates micro- and macro-levels of social reality in the modern world. In urbanized society, however, the urban level is at risk of being eroded between the global and private levels. A universal rationalism is undermining the particularities, the specificities of places. At the same time, space is parceled up and subjected to the individualist logic of private enterprise. The hypothesis of the disappearance of the city as mediating reality can, however, reveal the significance of the urban. The city should be understood as a social resource: it represents an essential device for organizing society; it brings together widely disparate elements of society.

The urban is not reducible to a scale. Lefebvre's hypothesis about complete urbanization was meant to apply to the world as a whole. The urban as level of social reality is thus subject to analysis at multiple scales: the scale of metropolitan regions, national urban systems, and transnational, potentially global urban networks and strategies.[24]

Form: centrality

Under conditions of complete urbanization, "the city" is permanently undermined as a distinct social space physically demarcated from the (pre-capitalist) countryside. The old opposition between town and countryside is dialectically transcended into the contradictory relationship of center and periphery.

From a Lefebvrean point of view, the urban can be analyzed as a fleeting and historically contingent social form that connects various fragments of modern life. It is a social product of centralization of power and oppositional struggles against its dominant spatial and social forms. Centrality is defined by the association and encounter of whatever exists together in one space at the same time. Thus it corresponds to a logical form: the point of encounter, the place of coming together. This form has no specific content. Its logic stands for the simultaneity contained within it and from which it results: the simultaneity of everything that can be brought together at one point.

Centrality eliminates peripheral elements and condenses wealth, means of action, knowledge, information, and culture. Ultimately it produces the highest power, the concentration of powers: the decision. In *The Right to the City*, long before the discussions about "global cities" and "world cities," Lefebvre argued that urbanization signaled the advent of new forms of global centrality: today's cities are centers of design and information, of organization and institutional decision-making on a global scale. They are centers of decision and power that unite all the constitutive elements of society in a limited territory.

> The ideal city, the New Athens, is already there to be seen in the image which Paris and New York and some other cities project. The centre of decision-making and the centre of consumption meet. Their alliance on the ground based on a strategic convergence creates an inordinate centrality. We already know that this decision-making centre includes all the channels of information and means of cultural and scientific development. Coercion and persuasion converge with the power of decision-making and the capacity to consume. Strongly occupied and inhabited by these new Masters, this centre is held by them. Without necessarily owning it all, they possess this privileged space, axis of a strict spatial policy. Especially, they have the privilege to possess time. Around them, distributed in space according to formalized principles, there are human groups which can no longer bear the name of slaves, serfs or even proletarians. What could they be called? Subjugated, they provide a multiplicity of services for the Masters of this State solidly established on the city.[25]

Lefebvre identifies new centralities with centers of decision-making that facilitate the globalization of the state (the experts of "technicity"), capital ("new masters") and servant-laborers ("new slaves"). They do so with technical infrastructures (airports, hotels, expressways), modes of reproduction, and consumption and strategies of segregation that reserve central places to "directors, heads, presidents of this and that, elites, writers, artists, well-known entertainers and media people," "executives, administrators, engineers," "scholars and intellectuals" while banishing workers and surplus populations to "planned suburbs," "satellite cities," and "residential ghettos."[26]

Lefebvre's conception of the urban incorporates relationships between centers and peripheries. This relationship is not fixed in physical form. Once central social spaces (imperial capitals at the global scale or historic city centers at the scale of urban regions) can lose their status as centers of decision-making and control. At the regional scale, central functions of city centers can "implode" socially and economically while cities "explode" into far-flung metropolitan agglomerations. In turn, new centralities can emerge: new business districts, newly powerful urban centers of finance and state control. In all cases, the formation of centralities is predicated on processes of peripheralization—displacement, enclosure, segregation, exclusion. This takes place through both "coercion" and "persuasion," incorporation and domination.

Space–time: difference

Against the perspective of the city as a totalizing control center, Lefebvre developed the concrete utopia of an urban society as a differential space–time. Seen from this point of view, the city can be defined as a place in which differences know, recognize, test, confirm, or offset one another: space–time distances are replaced by contradictions, contrasts, superimpositions, and juxtapositions of different realities.

Differences must be clearly distinguished from particularities: they are elements of active connection, while particularities remain mutually isolated, external, and can easily turn into antagonism toward other particularities. Over the course of history, however, they come into contact with one another. Their confrontation evolves into mutual "understanding," and hence into *difference*, a concept that obtains its content not only by means of logical thought but along a variety of paths, that of history and those of the manifold dramas of everyday life. In this way, and under these circumstances, particularities become differences and produce difference.

As Kipfer, Milgrom, and Andrew Shmuely remind us in this volume, there is also an important distinction between *minimal* and *maximal* difference. Minimal or *induced* difference tends toward formal identity that fragments everyday life and peripheralizes social groups. Maximal or *produced* difference implies a fundamental social transformation. Sources for maximal difference can be found both within the interstices of everyday life and in the midst of uprisings. For Lefebvre, difference is a multidimensional concept emerging from political struggles. It has to be understood as an active element that is constantly produced and reproduced. Differences can only present and re-present themselves within their reciprocal relationships.

In this context, Lefebvre's famous call for a *right to the city* has to be reconsidered as the *right to difference*.[27] It means essentially the right not to be forced into a space that was produced only for the purpose of discrimination. It refers to a renewed centrality, to the places of meeting and exchange, to life rhythms, and a use of time that enable a full and complete—maximal—use of these places. This right cannot be simply interpreted as the right to visit or to return to traditional city centers. It can only be formulated as the right to a transformed, renewed urban life. Lefebvre's grand project envisions a possible path to this urban world in which unity is no longer opposed to difference, where the homogeneous no longer conflicts with the heterogeneous, and gatherings, encounters, and meetings—not without conflicts— will replace the struggle of individual urban elements that have become antinomies as a result of divisions: this urban space would provide the social basis for a radically transformed daily life that is open to possibility.

The commodification of the urban

In recent years, the city has been reinvented as a positive socio-cultural category. Claims to oppositional centrality (street life, central-city living, festivity) and difference (multiculturalism, ethnic and sexual diversity, avant-garde cultural practice) can be traced to various urban movements since the 1960s. Today, superficial versions of these claims are integral components of bourgeois urbanism and gentrification[28]—the result of the integration and cooptation of parts of the oppositional milieus into the metropolitan mainstream. At the same time, they represent a "rediscovery of the city," a process that was initiated by innovative social groups and then spread out into wider social milieus. These processes could also be understood as more or less successful attempts of powerful social groups to appropriate and monopolize the urban as a productive force through various urban strategies which reduce maximal difference to minimal difference. From a general point of view, this demonstrates a fundamental contradiction within the dialectic of the urban. On the one hand, the productivity of the city brings into contact and mutual reaction the most variegated elements of society. On the other hand, access to the resource that is the city tends to be controlled and appropriated by powerful interests. This both limits the productivity of the city and denies some the right to the city.

Furthermore, these processes entail a new tendency: the incorporation of the urban into the process of valorizing capital. During this process, the urban itself becomes a commodity. One may describe this form of incorporation as *the commodification of the urban*.[29] Not only is urbanization subjected to top-down forces of privatization, marketization, and competitive entrepreneurialism. But the very form of centrality and difference that is the urban for Lefebvre is also incorporated into the commodity form. Urban space itself is mobilized as a commodity, and becomes the ultimate object of exchange: "The deployment of the world of commodities now affects not only objects but their containers, it is no longer limited to content, to objects in space. More recently, space itself has begun to be bought and sold. Not the earth, the soil, but *social space*, produced as such, with this purpose, this finality (so to speak)."[30] As a consequence, space itself becomes the very general object of production, and consequently of the formation of surplus value. For Lefebvre, this strategy goes far beyond simply selling space, bit by bit. It not only incorporates space in the production of surplus value but attempts to reorganize production completely as something subordinate to the centers of information and decision-making.[31]

The colonization of everyday life

Hand in hand with the commodification of the urban go a variety of forms of exclusion and control of marginalized spaces. Lefebvre used the term *colonization* to describe relationships between central and peripheral spaces.[32]

In the 1960s, Lefebvre framed his critique of everyday life as a critique of colonization to draw attention to the unevenness of everyday experiences. Notably, he wanted to alert us to the process by which colonial techniques of subjection and accumulation were reimported from the former colonies to the metropolitan heartlands,[33] thus shedding light on how "the modern city . . . is seat, instrument and centre of action of neo-colonialism and neo-imperialism all at once."[34] In his work on the state, Lefebvre articulated these insights with a more systematic intervention in theories of imperialism, suggesting that "wherever a dominated space is generated and mastered by a dominant space—where there is periphery and centre—there is colonization."[35] Rather than a delimited historical era of European (and Japanese) territorial expansion, colonization refers to the role of the state in organizing territorial relationships of center and periphery, with all the alienating, humiliating, and degrading aspects such relationships entail. It can be analyzed at multiple scales: geopolitical formations, interregional relationships within a national context, and relationships between social spaces within metropolitan areas. Lefebvre proposes that in any historical period, colonial spatial forms can be compared directly across scalar divides, thus making it possible to compare colonization in formally occupied territories to peripheralized regions or segregated areas in advanced capitalist countries.

At the scale of metropolitan regions in the imperial core, new forms of colonial core–periphery relations can be detected in the polarizing effects of gentrification and exurbanization. This has resulted in highly visible forms of "advanced marginality" and hyper-ghettoization[36] as well as more easily hidden forms of micro-segregation in both old and new suburbs. In global and capital cities, as well as in dependent metropoles, strategies of keeping peripheralized spaces apart from spaces of bourgeois urbanism—surveillance, policing, walls and fences—have seen a marked increase.[37] In some parts of the urbanizing Third World, one might stress accentuated depeasantization, the rise of the "global slums," and associated strategies of spatial control.[38] Among the latter are strategies of urbicide: forms of military planning aimed at undermining capacities for resistance to colonization by destroying urban infrastructure and collective social space.[39]

Lefebvre's conception of urbanization as a worldwide process and strategy articulating central and peripheral social spaces with colonial undertones is of ongoing relevance to resurging debates about imperialism.[40] The colonial aspects of global urbanization highlighted by Lefebvre point to what Mike Davis has called the "urbanization of Empire."[41] Compared to other, geographical interventions into these debates on empire and imperialism, Lefebvre's concept has distinct advantages. His concept of colonization as state strategy of organizing center–periphery relationships at multiple scales avoids the reified view of empire as a deterritorialized "smooth space."[42] Also, it takes us closer to everyday life and beneath the macro-political economic analyses of imperialism as crisis-driven accumulation strategy and interstate conflict, which dominate current neo-marxist debates.[43]

The thrust of Lefebvre's concept is to hone in on the colonial dimensions of spatial relations in metropolitan centers themselves. He suggested that the mid-century project of homogenizing and separating inhabitants in large-scale reservations—the "native quarters" in colonized cities and the vast high-rise housing tracts of advanced capitalist centers—was a "model of isolated units" informed by vulgar modernist strategies: urban renewal, standardized public housing, and mass suburbanization. With the help of comparative research on strategies of segregation,[44] we may venture the hypothesis that this "model of isolated units" of the Fordist and late colonial era is being supplanted by strategies of dispersal and decentralized re-segregation (euphemistically called "social mixing"). In this view, it is possible to compare strategies of displacing slum dwellers to make room for new middle-class suburban enclaves in the expanding metropoles of India, China, and South Africa; military strategies of urbicide in Iraq, Lebanon, Somalia, and Palestine; and the more confined and selective cases of destroying, gentrifying, and privatizing ghettoized spaces (public housing districts, racialized enclaves) in Paris, Chicago, and Toronto. The case of Hurricane Katrina—widely seen by policy-makers as an opportunity to permanently expel poor African American residents and lay the groundwork for large-scale gentrification in New Orleans—clearly highlights processes of military occupation, forced displacement, and urbicide that also operate in formally occupied Iraq.[45]

Oppositional centralities

The transformation of cities into polarized centers of decision-making and marginalization does not, however, proceed uncontested. Centrality becomes a political question; cities become contested terrain. Research on transnational urbanization thus also includes a search for oppositional centralities that emerge from alternative and subaltern networks and strategies of mobilization. These express the demands of homogenized and segregated groups and refract the everyday contradiction between the cosmopolitan promise of capitalist globalization and its reduction to minimally differential capitalist urbanization. However, oppositional strategies have counter-hegemonic potential only if the minimal differences of commodified festivity, multiculturalized ethnicity, and racialized suburban marginality are themselves transformed in the process of the political struggle.

Such alternative and oppositional claims for difference can take on very different forms and ways of expression: small-scale resistances, counter-projects, anti-imperial insurgencies, rebellions of the dispossessed in metropolitan centers such as the recent uprisings in Paris, as well as well-documented anti-globalization struggles and networked encounters. Struggles of peripheralized social groups against segregation and for empowerment can produce their own forms of centrality. Here, one can think of alternative social spaces created by sub- and counter-cultural groups or the oppositional centralities produced through mass mobilization (strikes, demonstrations, uprisings). The search for new centralities in a context of trans-national urbanization thus leads not only to global and capital cities (New York and London) but also to central places produced by counter-networks and mobilizations (Porto Alegre and Bamako).

The ultimate political promise of Lefebvre's perspective on the colonial territorial relations within global urbanization processes is to establish closer contact between what he called "far" and "near" peripheries: Paris and Dakar; New York and Fallujah; Toronto and Kingston.[46]

KNOWLEDGE FOR A MULTI-POLAR WORLD

Lefebvre's concern for the global has become increasingly prominent since the 1960s. In French, this concern—the worldwide—is usually captured not by *global* (which stands for general) but by *mondial, mondialité,* and *mondialisation.* However, in Lefebvre's work, the term *mondial* is used with a certain ambiguity. As Elden and Waite point out from opposite perspectives in this volume, Lefebvre's notion of *mondial* was meant to be also of philosophical significance, and thus not only an analytical term to grasp processes of "globalization," that is the role of the global scale in social processes and human action. We would submit that the *worldwide* functions as a concept of critique to think about the relationship between knowledge and the world. Lefebvre deployed *mondial* also as a synonym for totality or, more specifically, the difficulty of grasping totality, which, in a world defined by homogenization, fragmentation, and hierarchy, comes to us only in bits and pieces.[47] Given the fragmentation of the modern world, no shortcuts—speculative philosophy, scientific system building, false claims to authenticity (including Heideggerian ones)[48]—can lead to knowledge of the world as a whole, however. The world (totality, *mondialité*) is knowable only as incomplete totality: *possibility*. This, Lefebvre proposed to achieve with a critique of positive totality and attempts to reconnect the fragments of experience left by the production of abstract space.[49] Skeptical of premature intellectual totalizations, he insisted on the *contingency* of lived experience and embodied politics as key sources to distinguish the real from the possible (see Nadal-Melsió, this volume).

Lefebvre's worldwide perspective owes much to political conditions. He suggested that the contingent possibility of knowing and experiencing the world as a whole was clarified to him not least by the worldwide conjuncture of multiple, unevenly developed points of revolt and revolution that was "1968."[50] To globalize (make worldwide) meta-philosophy as a politically informed critique of totality thus means to think through the relationship between particularity and universality, negative and positive reality. In this respect, Lefebvre's skepticism about totalizing knowledge claims cautions us against conceiving of the globalization of knowledge as a unilateral quest for intellectual unification. As he argues in the last volume of *De l'État*, the notion of "*mondialité* denies the existence of one, unique centre and affirms the *differential* multiplicity of centers, as well as their relative (moving, precarious, uncertain) character."[51] Knowledge (*connaissance*) understood in world-wide terms implies also a recognition of a certain epistemological relativity. Connecting knowledge and the world is thus not about claiming the world as a whole only from one fixed and absolute center. Such unilateral claims to the worldwide Lefebvre considered potentially complicit with strategies of globalizing the state and enveloping the world in a web of rationalist, state-bound knowledge (*savoir*).[52] Globalizing knowledge is about connecting multiple centers of knowledge creation from a range of possible vantage points. What emerges from this is something akin to an incomplete historical intellectual praxis with multiple centers of gravity, each of which is caught in a dialectic of universality and particularity.

Globalizing Lefebvre

Taking Lefebvre's meta-philosophy seriously means also applying these insights to his work, which was laced with Eurocentrism. As in the works of most Western Marxists,[53] questions of colonization and imperialism appeared only as secondary concerns in Lefebvre. As a consequence, his understanding of "colonization" (as one aspect of urbanization and the production of space) still remains under-mediated historically, geographically, and socially. It does not pay adequate attention to the distinction between *different varieties* of "colonization" and their *particular forms of determination*. In order not to gloss over the specificities of distinct forms of "colonization" ("far" or "near"), Lefebvre's work needs to be complemented by other radical approaches that can shed light on the specifically imperial, patriarchal, racialized, and class-specific aspects. His critique of the "colonial model of isolated units" is insufficient without other influences, such as Frantz Fanon's understanding of everyday racism and geopolitical colonization *as spatial relations*.[54] Recent debates about the colonial aspects of center–periphery relations in metropolitan France point in the same direction.[55] Lefebvre's concept of colonization must be complemented with explicitly anti-racist and feminist analyses of the relationship between urbanization and imperialism.

It is possible that Lefebvre's own view of critical theory as an incomplete, contradictory, open-ended, and multiple formation, and his program for a multi-polar critical knowledge point beyond the intellectual universe of postwar Europe. His heterodox work may be fruitfully opened up to a number of globalizing intellectual formations today. Among these—and there are many others—we would like to point to certain strands of postcolonial theory and transnational feminism. We submit that these links provide the emphases on the globally unequal conditions of knowledge production and the fatal cognitive blockages produced by Eurocentric social theory, a twin emphasis that is necessary for a truly plural conception of marxism or critical theory.[56]

In postcolonial studies, a number of authors have recently distanced themselves from more orthodox marxists and tried to redirect, rather than dismiss, this sprawling field away from its formerly hegemonic postmodern philosophical bases.[57] They have attempted to rescue key postcolonial concerns—with Euro-centrism, subalternity, legacies of colonial culture, and anti-colonial nationalism—without replicating the postmodern philosophical assumptions of key postcolonial theorists.[58] For this purpose, they propose to fuse marxism and critical theory with those anti-imperial and anti-racist traditions that differ from the structuralist or "post-structuralist" underpinnings of much postcolonial theory.[59] This theoretical project also entails research projects to reconstruct and learn from existing points of contact between European and anti-colonial critical theory. In the French context, examples for this include the links between communist, surrealist, and radical Black and *négritude* circles in the inter-war period and the connections between anti-colonial movements and various maoist, trotskyist, situationist, and existentialist currents in the French New Left from the 1950s to the early 1970s. Lefebvre's own (limited) ties to these two moments of worldwide anti-colonial solidarity[60] make it plausible to suggest that his critique of everyday life is vital in linking analyses of (post-)colonial formations with critiques of modernity and global capitalism.[61]

Another rapidly globalizing intellectual formation to which we may connect Lefebvre is transnational feminism. Authors in this research paradigm are forging a global perspective on feminist theory and practice that is confined neither to Eurocentric lineages nor to strictly national(ist) articulations of anti-racist or anti-colonial feminism. In this, transnational feminists are informed in no small measure by nodes of centrality produced by diasporic experiences of displacement, alternative cultural practices, and, most centrally, an internationalist or transnational understanding of feminist, anti-imperial, and indigenous politics. Transnational feminism is theoreti-cally highly heterogeneous. Some voices within it promisingly link materialist feminist legacies, anti-imperial currents, and marxist method-ologies.[62] What makes these globalized intellectual voices particularly interesting in our context is an overarching concern with, first, rooting social difference in a dialectical understanding of everyday life as a contradictory experience, and, second, linking considerations of everyday life to a broad critique of the imperial and patriarchal aspects of capitalist world order. Despite the obvious distance between transnational feminism and Lefebvre's European perspective on critical theory, such a double concern does allow for fruitful points of contact with Lefebvre's own project to link a critique of privatized, gendered everyday life with analyses of the "far" social order.[63]

Intellectual labor in cosmopolitan times

Consistent with his view of meta-philosophy as the sublation of philosophy, Lefebvre considered the globalization of philosophy simultaneous with its "withering away."[64] A project to "globalize" Lefebvre thus presupposes a critique of rarefied intellectual practice. Lefebvre was neither a traditional nor an organic intellectual in Gramsci's sense of these terms. He was wary of the hyperactivism he detected in leftist politics, such as that embodied in his one-time allies, the Situationists (see Merrifield, this volume). Partly to avoid instrumentalizing political thought for the benefit of an ossified Communist Party (who had laid claim to Gramsci) or the daily imperatives of avant-garde interventions, he repeatedly insisted on a (notably contingent) distinction between political action and political theory, and this in part against Gramsci himself (see Kipfer, this volume). At the same time, Lefebvre was no conventional academic. Much of his more visible intellectual contributions rested on a life of engagement in often subterranean debates in and against communist and avant-garde circles.[65] In Lefebvre, theory is thus not a function of individual philosophical genius or specialized scientific insight but something akin to a work of art with strong sensual and collective dimensions. For him, to separate theory from everyday life and political passion was to impoverish intellectual cognition itself. Without strong links to daily experience and political strategy, political thought is vulnerable to being enveloped by the specialized, objectivist character of thinking (*savoir*). The rationalism in such knowledge forms is also subject to the pressures of intellectual "accumulation" that, homologous with the commodity form, subordinates intellectual practice to an acquisitive thirst for never-ending, incremental, purely quantitative growth.[66]

Lefebvre's notion of knowledge as creative, sensual practice is more pressing than ever in our times, when "more and more, academic labour is up for sale and there for hire, . . . evermore alienated, increasingly judged by performance principles, by publisher sales projections—or by their ability to justify the status quo."[67] Lefebvre scholars are well advised to turn Lefebvrean criticism onto themselves, analyzing their own daily life and space at the same time as they analyze global capitalism. As Merrifield suggests,

> Hence, a universal capitulation to the conceived over the lived hasn't just taken place in the world: it has taken place in those who should know better, in those who read Lefebvre's work, in those who edit and contribute to radical journals. When scholars write about emancipation, about reclaiming space for others, we might start by emancipating ourselves and reclaiming our own work space, giving a nod to disruption rather than cooptation, to real difference rather than cowering conformity. Yet before imagination can seize power, some imagination is needed: imagination to free our minds and our bodies, to liberate our ideas, and to reclaim our society as a lived project . . . It's a project that can begin *this afternoon*.[68]

Breaking down the boundaries between academic and other forms of labor opens up a horizon of social transformation. It promises to reconnect critical theory to everyday life and political interventions in the social order.

Today, traditional intellectual practice is sustained by the "fast," hyper-commodified sensibilities of transnational jet-set life. Centered on transnational (but US-centered) publishing networks, conference circuits, and "fly-by" research operations, such sensibilities are most likely to sustain liberal-cosmopolitan intellectualism.[69] The latter one-sidedly celebrates our age of transnational mobility, prefers comfortable "complexity" over radical critique, and screens out the contradictions of territorially mediated politics. Lefebvre's own critique of traditional intellectual practice stands at an unambiguous distance from jet-set intellectualism, which, despite its critique of cultural nationalism, has failed to provide a counterpoint to the fundamentalisms and colonizations of today's world. Lefebvre's insistence on worldwide but plural strategies to embed knowledge creation in lived experience and radical political commitment urges us to combine a worldwide perspective of emancipation with territorially more limited (continental, national, regional, local) practices.[70] This requires a willingness to work through (instead of bypass or ignore) the mystifications, separations, and hierarchies which structure such practices.[71] Only in this way is it possible to realize difference globally—as a worldwide revolution.

NOTES

1. Among the vast literature, we draw in particular on Clémentine Autain *et al.*, *Banlieue, lendemains de révolte* (Paris: La Dispute, 2006); Hugues Lagrange and Marco Oberti, eds., *Emeutes urbaines et protestations* (Paris: Les Presses Sciences Po, 2006); and the special journal issues of *Contretemps* 13 (2005), *Mouvements* 44 (2006), *Annales* 61, no. 4 (2006), and *Le Monde Diplomatique—Manière de Voir* 89 (October–November 2006).

2. Alain Bertho, "Bienvenue au 21e Siècle," in *Banlieue, lendemains de révolte* (2006): 33; Matthieu Giroud, "Résister en habitant," *Contretemps* 13 (2005): 50–1; Jean Harari, "Ségrégation territoriale: l'effet des politiques foncières et des stratégies d'aménagement," *ibid.*, 120–1. *Le Monde Diplomatique* reprinted an article by Henri Lefebvre originally published in 1989 as "Métamorphoses planétaires": *Le Monde Diplomatique—Manière de Voir* 89 (2006): 54–6.

3. Michael Trebitsch, preface to Henri Lefebvre, *Critique of Everyday Life, Volume III*, trans. G. Elliott (London: Verso, 2005), viii–xxii; Andy Merrifield, *Henri Lefebvre: A Critical Introduction* (New York: Routledge, 2006), 40–53.

4. Kristin Ross, *May '68 and Its Afterlives* (Chicago: Chicago University Press, 2002), 95–6, 145, 191.

5. Henri Lefebvre, *The Explosion: Marxism and the French Upheaval* (New York: Monthly Review Press, 1969).

6. Ross, *May '68*; Michael Scott Christofferson, *French Intellectuals against the Left: The Antitotalitarian Moment of the 1970s* (New York: Berghahn Books, 2004).

7. Alain Bertho, "Nous n'avons vu que des ombres," *Mouvements* 44 (2006): 28; Nacira Guénif-Souilamas, "Le balcon fleuri des banlieues embrasées," *ibid.*: 31–5.

8. Christian Bachman and Nicole le Guennec, *Violences urbaines* (Paris: Hachette, 2002).

9. Dominique Vidal, "Casser l'apartheid à la française," *Le Monde Diplomatique*, December (2005): 13–15.

10. Saïd Bouamama, "De la visibilisation à la suspicion: la fabrique républicaine d'une politisation," in *La République mise à nu par son immigration*, ed. N. Guénif-Souilamas (Paris: La Fabrique, 2006), 196–216; Stéphane Beaud and Olivier Masclet, "Des marcheurs de 1983 aux émeutiers de 2005," *Annales* 61, no. 4 (2006): 809–45.

11. Marie-Hélène Bacqué and Sylvie Fol, *Le devenir des banlieues rouge* (Paris: Harmattan, 1997); Alain Bertho, *Banlieue, banlieue, banlieue* (Paris: La Dispute, 1997); Loïc Wacquant, *Les prisons de la misère* (Paris: Raisons d'Agir, 1999); *Ghettos américains, banlieues françaises*, special issue of *Herodote* 122 (2006); Hacèle Belmessous, *Mixité sociale: une imposture* (Nantes: Atalante, 2006); Mustafa Dikeç, "Two Decades of French Urban Policy: From Social Development to the Republican Penal State," *Antipode* 38, no. 1 (2006): 59–81; Robert Castel, "La discrimination négative," *Annales* 61, no. 4 (2006): 777–807; Harari, "Ségrégation territoriale."

12. Olivier Masclet, "Le rendez-vous manqué de la gauche et des cités," *Le Monde Diplomatique*, January (2004), 4; Saïd Bouamama, "La construction des 'petits blancs' et les chemins du politique," *Contretemps* 13 (2005): 39–48.

13. Bertho, "Bienvenue"; Abdellali Hajjat, "Quartiers populaires et désert politique," *Le Monde Diplomatique—Manière de Voir* 89 (2006): 23–8; Hugues Lagrange, "Autopsie

d'une vague d'émeutes," *Emeutes urbaines*, 37–58; Michel Tubiana, "Le silence politique," *Mouvements* 44 (2006): 83–7; Leila Shahid, Michel Warschawki, and Dominique Vidal, *Les banlieues, le Proche-Orient et nous* (Paris: Editions de l'Atelier, 2006), 18, 130–1.

14. Bertho, "Nous," 26–7.

15. Henri Lefebvre, *De l'État, Volume IV* (Paris: Union Générale d'Editions, 1978), 247.

16. Didier Arnaud, "Deux jeunesses se croisent à Saint-Denis," *Libération*, March 28, 2006; Hugues Lagrange and Marco Oberti, "Le Mouvement anti-CPE et L'Unité des Jeunes," in *Emeutes urbaines* (2006): 131–46.

17. Mouvement contre le Racisme et pour l'Amitié entre les Peuples, "CPE-CESEDA: une même logique de précarisation," <http://www.mrap.asso.fr/communiques/cpeceseda>, accessed February 2006.

18. Hajjat, "Quartiers"; Paul A. Silverstein and Chantal Tetreault, "Urban Violence in France," *Middle East Report*, November (2005): 15–20.

19. Shahid *et al.*, *Les banlieues*. These links between geopolitics and neighborhood are made routinely by political formations like Europalestine (which fielded candidates in the 2004 European elections) and the Mouvement pour l'Immigration et la Banlieue (an anti-racist organization).

20. Lefebvre, *De l'État*, IV, 247; Michael Watts, "1968 and All That . . .," *Progress in Human Geography* 25, no. 2 (2001): 157–88.

21. Eleonore Kofman, "Whose City: Gender, Class and Immigrants in Globalizing European Cities," in *Cities of Difference*, ed. R. Fincher and J. M. Jacobs (London: Guildford, 1998), 291–4.

22. Mouvement pour l'Immigration et les Banlieues, "Gestion coloniale de la planète/Gestion coloniale des quartiers" (2003), <http://mib.ouvaton.org/article.php3?id_article=29>.

23. Neil Smith, foreword to Henri Lefebvre, *The Urban Revolution*, trans. R. Bononno (Minneapolis: Minnesota University Press, 2003), xx–xxi.

24. See Christian Schmid, "Raum und Regulation. Henri Lefebvre und der Regulationsansatz," in *Fit für den Postfordismus? Theoretisch-politische Perspektiven des Regulationsansatzes* (Münster: Westfälisches Dampfboot, 2003), 217–42; Kanishka Goonewardena, "The Urban Sensorium: Space, Ideology, and the Aesthetization of Politics," *Antipode* 27, no. 3 (2005): 46–71; Stefan Kipfer, "Why the Urban Question Still Matters: Reflections on Rescaling and the Promise of the Urban," in *Towards a Political Economy of Scale*, ed. R. Mahon and R. Keil (Vancouver: UBC Press, 2008).

25. Henri Lefebvre, *Writings on Cities*, ed. and trans. E. Kofman and E. Lebas (Oxford: Blackwell, 1996), 161.

26. *Ibid.*, 161–2.

27. Henri Lefebvre, *The Production of Space*, trans. D. Nicholson-Smith (Oxford: Blackwell, 1991), 64.

28. On the Zürich and Toronto cases, see Christian Schmid, "The Dialectics of Urbanisation in Zurich: Global-City Formation and Urban Social Movements," in *Possible Urban Worlds—Urban Strategies at the End of the 20th Century*, ed. INURA (Basel: Birkhäuser, 1998); Stefan Kipfer, "Urban Politics in the 1990s: Notes on Toronto," in *ibid.*; Christian Schmid and Daniel Weiss, "The New Metropolitan Mainstream," in *The Contested Metropolis*, ed. INURA (Basel: Birkhäuser, 2003); Kanishka Goonewardena and Stefan Kipfer, "Spaces of Difference," *International Journal of Urban and Regional Research* 29, no. 3 (2005): 670–8.

29. Stefan Kipfer and Christian Schmid, "Right to the City/Bourgeois Urbanism," research agenda prepared for the International Network of Urban Research and Action (March 2004), Toronto.
30. Lefebvre, Urban Revolution, 154.
31. Ibid., 155.
32. The following builds on Stefan Kipfer and Kanishka Goonewardena, "Colonization and the New Imperialism: On the Meaning of Urbicide Today," Theory and Event 30, no. 2 (2007): n.p.; and Kanishka Goonewardena and Stefan Kipfer, "Postcolonial Urbicide: New Imperialism, Global Cities, and the Damned of the Earth," New Formations 59, Fall (2006), 23–33.
33. Henri Lefebvre, Critique of Everyday Life, Volume II, trans. J. Moore (London: Verso, 2002), 315–16.
34. Henri Lefebvre, La pensée marxiste et la ville (Paris: Casterman, 1972), 131.
35. Lefebvre, De l'État, IV, 173–4.
36. Loïc Wacquant, "The Rise of Advanced Marginality: Notes on Its Nature and Implications," in Of States and Cities: The Partitioning of Urban Space, ed. P. Marcuse and R. van Kempen (Oxford: Oxford University Press, 2002), 221–39.
37. Mike Davis, "The Militarization of Urban Space," in Variations on a Theme Park, ed. M. Sorkin (New York: Hill and Wang, 1992), 154–80; Stephen Graham and Simon Marvin, Splintering Urbanism (London: Routledge, 2001); Stephen Graham, "Cities and the 'War on Terror,'" International Journal of Urban and Regional Research 30 (2006): 63–77; Thierry Paquot, "Mauern der Angst," Le Monde Diplomatique, German edition, October (2006): 2.
38. Mike Davis, Planet of Slums (London: Verso, 2006).
39. Stephen Graham, ed., Cities, War, and Terrorism: Towards an Urban Geopolitics (London: Blackwell, 2004).
40. Harry Harootunian, The Empire's New Clothes: Paradigm Lost, and Regained (Chicago: Prickly Paradigm Press, 2004); Colin Mooers, ed., The New Imperialists: Ideologies of Empire (Oxford: Oneworld, 2006).
41. Mike Davis, "The Urbanization of Empire: Megacities and the Laws of Chaos," Social Text 22, no. 4 (2004): 9–15.
42. Michael Hardt and Toni Negri, Empire (Cambridge, MA: Harvard University Press, 2000).
43. David Harvey, The New Imperialism (Oxford: Oxford University Press, 2003); Neil Smith, The Endgame of Globalization (New York: Routledge, 2004).
44. Anthony King, Urbanism, Colonialism, and the World Economy (London: Routledge, 1990); Carl Nightingale, "A Tale of Three Global Ghettos," Journal of Urban History 29 (2003): 257–71; Peter Marcuse and Ronald van Kempen, eds., Globalizing Cities: A New Spatial Order? (London: Blackwell, 2000); Marcuse and van Kempen, Of States and Cities; David Theo Goldberg, "Polluting the Body Politic: Racist Discourse and Urban Location," in Racist Culture (Oxford: Blackwell, 1993).
45. See Mike Davis, "The Predators of New Orleans," Le Monde Diplomatique, English edition, October (2005): 6; Henry Giroux, Stormy Weather: Katrina and the Politics of Disposability (Philadelphia: Temple University Press, 2006); Kristen Lavelle and Joe Feagin, "Hurricane Katrina: The Race and Class Debate," Monthly Review 58, no. 3 (2006): 52–66; Special issue on Katrina in ColorLines, Spring (2006).
46. Lefebvre, De l'État, IV, 237–8.
47. Henri Lefebvre, Une pensée devenue monde (Paris: Fayard, 1980), 160; "Le monde selon Kostas Axelos," Lignes 15 (1992): 131, 135.

48. Henri Lefebvre, *Métaphilosophie* (Paris: Syllepse, 1997), 189.

49. *Ibid.*, 53.

50. "Une Interview d'Henri Lefebvre," *Autogestion et Socialisme* 33/4 (1976): 125.

51. Lefebvre, *De l'État*, IV, 330.

52. *Ibid.*, 331–9.

53. Benita Parry, "Liberation Theory: Variations on Themes of Marxism and Modernity," in *Marxism, Modernity, and Postcolonial Studies*, ed. C. Bartolovich and N. Lazarus (Cambridge: Cambridge University Press, 2002), 126. On the question of Eurocentrism as ideology in marxist debates, see Samir Amin, *Eurocentrism* (London: Zed Books, 1988); Ajaz Ahmad, *In Theory: Classes, Nations, Literatures* (London: Verso, 1992); Pranav Jani, "Karl Marx, Eurocentrism, and the 1857 Revolt in British India," in *Marxism*, ed. Bartolovich *et al.*, 81–100; Neil Lazarus, "Hating Tradition Properly," *New Formations* 38 (1999): 9–30.

54. Kristin Ross, *Fast Cars, Clean Bodies: Decolonization and the Rendering of French Culture* (Cambridge, MA: The MIT Press, 1995); Stefan Kipfer, "Fanon and Space: Colonization, Urbanization and Liberation from the Colonial to the Global City," *Environment and Planning D: Society and Space* 25, no. 4 (2007): 701–26. Gillian Hart, "Denaturalizing Dispossession: Critical Ethnography in the Age of Resurgent Imperialism," *Antipode* 38, no. 5 (2006): 977–1004.

55. Didier Lapeyronnie, "La banlieue comme théâtre colonial, ou la fracture coloniale dans les quartiers," and Nacira Guénif-Souilamas, "La réduction à son corps de l'indigène de la République," in *La fracture coloniale: la société française au prisme de l'héritage coloniale*, ed. P. Blanchard, N. Bancel, and S. Lemaire (Paris: La Découverte, 2005); Sadri Khiari, *Pour une politique de la racaille* (Paris: Textuel, 2006).

56. Crystal Bartolovich, introduction to *Marxism*, ed. Bartolovich *et al.*, 11.

57. *Marxism*, ed. Bartolovich *et al.*; Neil Lazarus, ed., *The Cambridge Companion to Postcolonial Literary Studies* (Cambridge: Cambridge University Press, 2004); Neil Lazarus, *Nationalism and Cultural Practice in the Postcolonial World* (Cambridge: Cambridge University Press); Priyamvada Gopal, *Literary Radicalism in India: Gender, Nation and the Transition to Independence* (London: Routledge, 2005); Timothy Brennan, *At Home in the World: Cosmopolitanism Today* (Cambridge, MA: Harvard University Press, 1997); *Wars of Position* (New York: Columbia University Press, 2006); Laura Chrisman, *Postcolonial Contraventions* (Manchester: Manchester University Press, 2003); Kanishka Goonewardena, "Postcolonialism and Diaspora: A Contribution to the Critique of Nationalist Ideology and Historiography in the Age of Globalization and Neoliberalism," *University of Toronto Quarterly* 73, no. 2 (2004): 657–90.

58. Edward Said, *Culture and Imperialism* (New York: Vintage, 1993); Homi Bhabha, *The Location of Culture* (London: Routledge, 1994); Gayatri Chakravorty Spivak, *A Critique of Postcolonial Reason* (Cambridge, MA: Harvard University Press, 1999); Paul Gilroy *The Black Atlantic: Modernity and Double Consciousness* (London: Verso, 1993); and Robert J. C. Young, *Postcolonialism: An Historical Introduction* (Oxford: Blackwell, 2001).

59. The authors mentioned in note 57 join long-standing debates linking considerations of race, racism, and imperialism to radical Black, marxist, and critical theory. See also Robert Bernasconi with Sybol Cook, ed., *Race and Racism in Continental Philosophy* (Bloomington: University of Indiana Press, 2003); Robert Bernasconi, ed., *Race* (New York: Blackwell, 2001); Denean Sharpley-Whiting, *Negritude Women* (Minneapolis: University of Minnesota Press, 2002); Robin D. G. Kelley, *Freedom Dreams: The Black Radical Imagination* (Boston, MA: Beacon, 2002); Cedric J. Robinson, *Black Marxism:*

The Making of the Black Radical Tradition (Chapel Hill: University of North Carolina Press, 1983).

60. Lefebvre had links to anti-colonial circles during the inter-war period thanks to the surrealists, his *Philosophies* group (which included Paul Nizan, the author of the anti-colonial tract *Aden Arabie*), and, after 1928, the Communist Party. In 1925, for example, Lefebvre was put in military jail upon being conscripted into the army. He was considered "dangerous and subversive" for supporting a call for French troops to fraternize with an uprising of members of the Moroccan Rif; see Bud Burkhard, *French Marxism between the Wars: Henri Lefebvre and the 'Philosophies'* (New York: Humanity, 2000), 49–52, 60. In the mid-1950s, Lefebvre's opposition to the Algerian war was one of the reasons for his final "expulsion" from the PCF. Indeed, the Algerian situation was the obvious context behind the rise to prominence of *colonization* in the vocabulary of Lefebvre and the situationists. See Ross, *Fast Cars*, 162; Remi Hess, *Henri Lefebvre et l'aventure du siècle* (Paris: Métailé, 1988), 156; Kristin Ross, "Lefebvre on the Situationists: An Interview," in *Guy Debord and the Situationist International: Texts and Documents*, ed. Tom McDonough (Cambridge, MA: The MIT Press, 2002), 270; Henri Lefebvre, "Problèmes théoriques de l'autogestion," *Autogestion* 1 (1966): 65; "Address to Revolutionaries of Algeria and of All Countries," and "Class Struggles in Algeria," *Situationist Internationalist Anthology*, ed. and trans. K. Knabb (Berkeley: Bureau of Public Secrets, 1981), 148–52, 160–8.

61. Bartolovich, "Introduction" in *Marxism*, ed. Bartolovich *et al.*, 5–6; Brennan, *At Home*, 36, 106, 240–1.

62. Chandra Talpade Mohanty, *Feminism without Borders: Decolonizing Theory, Practicing Solidarity* (Durham, NC: Duke University Press, 2003); Angela Davis, *Women, Race, and Class* (New York: Vintage, 1983); Dorothy Smith, *The Everyday World as Problematic: A Feminist Sociology* (Toronto: University of Toronto Press, 1987); Himani Bannerji, *Thinking through: Essays on Feminism, Marxism, and Anti-Racism* (Toronto: Women's Press, 1995); Himani Bannerji, Shahrzad Mojab, and Judith Whitehead, eds., *Of Property and Propriety: The Role of Gender and Class in Imperialism and Nationalism* (Toronto: University of Toronto Press, 2001).

63. See Goonewardena and Kipfer, "Spaces"; Kipfer, "Why the Urban Question Still Matters."

64. Lefebvre, *Métaphilosophie*, 292–3.

65. Michael Kelly, *Modern French Marxism* (Oxford: Basil Blackwell, 1982), 192–3; Greil Marcus, *Lipstick Traces: A Secret History of the Twentieth Century* (Cambridge, MA: Harvard University Press, 1989).

66. Lefebvre, *Critique*, II, 326–7.

67. Merrifield, *Henri Lefebvre*, 119.

68. *Ibid.*, 120.

69. Timothy Brennan, "Cosmo-Theory," *South Atlantic Quarterly* 100, no. 3 (2001): 659–91.

70. Our discussion is informed in part by our experiences as members of the International Network of Urban Research and Action (INURA), which has tried to advance five main demands ("disempower global players, make profits unsustainable, no borders for people, autonomy and social justice in everyday life, liberate the urban imagination") with challenging attempts to construct a network which is both transnational in scope *and* built on "organic" links between researchers, social movements and everyday life in particular social spaces.

71. Norbert Guterman and Henri Lefebvre, *La conscience mystifiée*, new edn (Paris: Syllepse, 1999).

INDEX